The New York Times

Guide to

Unforgettable

Weekends

Hungry Minds, Inc.
An International Data Group Company
Cleveland, OH • Indianapolis, IN • New York, NY

Hungry Minds
909 Third Avenue
New York, NY 10022

Find us online at **www.frommers.com**

ISBN 0-7645-6448-X

Editor: Alice Fellows

Design by designLab, Seattle
Digital Cartography by *The New York Times*,
except pages xii–xiii, by John Decamillis and Elizabeth Puhl.

Art on pages 1, 27, 79, 165, 203, 247, 293, and 339 courtesy of the Cousley Collections.

SPECIAL SALES

Bulk purchases (10+ copies) of Frommer's and selected Hungry Minds travel guides are available to corporations, organizations, mail-order catalogs, institutions, and charities at special discounts, and can be customized to suit individual needs. For more information write to Special Sales, Hungry Minds, 909 Third Avenue, New York, NY 10022.

Manufactured in the United States of America.

5   4   3   2   1

CONTENTS

More Getaways in New York State

New Jersey

Pennsylvania

Connecticut

Other Destinations Within Easy Reach of New York City

LIST OF MAPS

More Getaways in New York State

New Jersey

Pennsylvania

Connecticut

Other Regional Maps

TO THE READER

PLEASE BE ADVISED THAT TRAVEL information is subject to change at any time—and this is especially true of open hours and prices. We therefore suggest that you write or call ahead for confirmation when making your travel plans. The authors, editors, and publisher cannot be held responsible for the experiences of readers while traveling. Your safety is important to us, however, so we encourage you to stay alert and be aware of your surroundings. Keep a close eye on cameras, purses, and wallets, all favorite targets of thieves and pickpockets.

ACKNOWLEDGMENTS

THIS GUIDEBOOK REPRESENTS A of hard work by a host of writers and editors at *The New York Times*. Many thanks to all of the writers who gave up their Saturdays to trek up and down the New York region. Also thanks to Wendy Sclight, the deputy Weekend section editor; to Diane Nottle and Jack Schwartz, assistant Weekend section editors; to the map department; to Anne Mancuso, who compiled most of the service information; and to the editors of the Culture copy desk.

A special thanks to the editors at Hungry Minds; to John Darnton, the cultural news editor of *The Times*, for his support of the Weekend staff; and to Mitchel Levitas, who is in charge of book development at *The Times* and who worked to make this book a reality.

—MYRA FORSBERG, EDITOR OF THE WEEKEND SECTION

INTRODUCTION

Nᴇᴡ Yᴏʀᴋ Cɪᴛʏ ɪs ᴛʜᴇ ᴡᴏʀʟᴅ capital of everything except relaxation. But even New Yorkers, and the tourists who flock to the city, need to unwind once in a while, to come down from an emotional state that's equal parts exhilaration, irritation, and suffocation.

As luck would have it, relief is within arm's length. A mythical New Yorker living in a penthouse atop the Times Square tower can take out a compass, a pencil, and a map; draw a circle with a 250-mile radius; and come up with a very nice traveler's pie.

That's the premise behind the essays collected here, most of which appeared on the front page of the Friday Weekend section of *The New York Times*. For several years now, a happy band of correspondents have headed out, notebook in hand, with that rarest of journalistic assignments: to have fun, gather useful information, and write about it enticingly. The geographical rules are simple. The place described must be within an easy day's drive—say, 5 hours, tops. Beyond that, anything goes, and it did.

The writers gathered in these pages have gone whale watching off Long Island, ballooning in Connecticut, and snowboarding in Vermont. They have driven the backroads of the Brandywine Valley in Pennsylvania, explored the Ironbound District of Newark, New Jersey, and sniffed spring flowers in Westchester County, New York. In an inspired act of rebellion, one reporter left Manhattan to rusticate on a Pennsylvania farm. Canny stay-at-homes sought out corners of the city that New Yorkers themselves know little about, like City Island in the Bronx, or cast a fresh eye on familiar landmarks like the Bronx Zoo.

In their heroic pursuit of leisure, the *Times* writers traveled by car and canoe, by balloon and bicycle, while an intrepid few tied on a pair of sneakers and simply walked. No challenge was left unmet. There's a common expression that harried New Yorkers use several times a day: Gimme a break. A cab cuts you off, a cop slaps a ticket on your windshield, the subway doors close in your face, the public telephone takes your quarter without producing a dial tone, the guy in front of you is walking too damn slow. Gimme a break.

Well, here are 46 of them.

—WILLIAM GRIMES

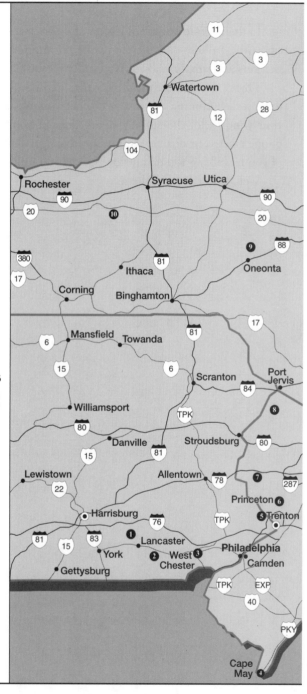

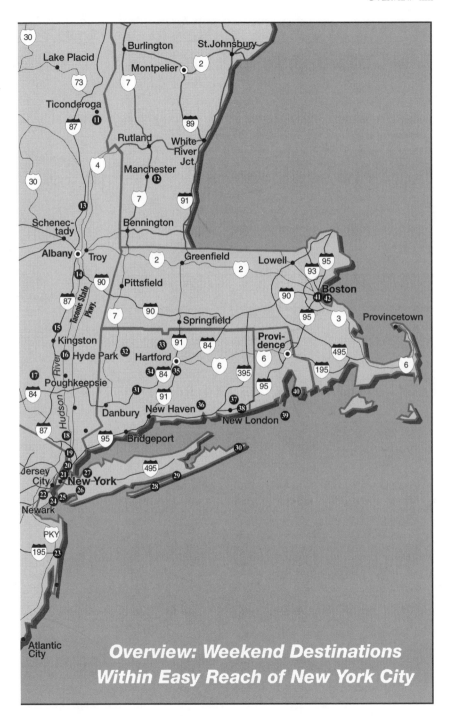

Overview: Weekend Destinations
Within Easy Reach of New York City

Weekending Without Leaving the City

A French Country Inn— on City Island

by Ralph Blumenthal

W E ARE IN A FRENCH COUNTRY inn. We sit on rustic chairs in a mansard room wallpapered in burgundy toile. We sip welcoming glasses of chilled chardonnay from etched goblets. We look out at the water. *En famille,* we inhale the musk of roasting garlic wafting up from the kitchen.

We hear: *vvvvROOOOM!* A motorcycle accelerating to warp speed screams past below the window, followed by a babble of radio from a passing convertible and the pounding rhythms of rap from a next-door neighbor's boom box. The water is not the Loire or the Dordogne. It is Eastchester Bay. We are abroad at home, in the Bronx.

An auberge in the backyard of the Yankees, in a borough that gave its name to a rude cheer and suffered Ogden Nash's cruel put-down, might sound like someone's idea of a joke, but just over the bridge threading Pelham Bay Park to the plump baguette of City Island, voila!: Le Refuge Inn, a 19th-century beige Victorian house that is one of New York City's few genuine inns. If it lacks some of the ambiance and *je ne sais quoi* of its *cousins-cousines* across the Atlantic, this one, at least, is barely 20 minutes from mid-Manhattan (not counting delays on the Bruckner Expressway).

Apart from the eight-room inn on City Island Avenue, City Island itself is well worth a detour, as the *Guide Michelin* might have it. It is a quiet (except in summer) year-round virtual village of some 4,000 permanent residents, with one main drag, many boatyards and marinas, several newish condominium colonies, and some dozen-and-a-half mostly seafood restaurants. A mile and a half long and no more than half a mile wide, the island blends the forlorn mystery of a Hopper dreamscape with a cheerful blue-collar brawn and flashes of intriguing wealth: sports cars behind gated walls; a gleaming black Mercedes convertible outside the bait shop.

A weekend's stay, one overnight, in Le Refuge is enough time to sample the land and sea offerings of City Island as well as the hospitality of the inn, particularly its classic French cuisine, its substantial wine cellar, and a special attraction: regular Sunday-noon chamber music concerts and wine socials (nonguests pay $12 to $15). Small children, who are welcome at the inn but might be disruptive at the recital, can spend the hour swinging and climbing on the backyard playground equipment, which our urban-bred younger daughter found endlessly entertaining.

Le Refuge Inn is the creation of a Normandy-born restaurateur and musician, Pierre Saint-Denis, who for 20 years has been running his highly rated restaurant of the same name, Le Refuge, at 166 East 82nd Street in Manhattan. Less than 5 years ago, en route to Connecticut "in search of a small but accessible hideaway," as he put it, he was driving up I-95 when he saw a sign for City Island, grew intrigued, and turned off to investigate. Just off the bridge, he spotted an old Victorian boardinghouse with a widow's walk and fanciful tower at 620 City Island Avenue. The rest, as they say, is *histoire.*

An athletic figure with short-cropped gray hair and the patient air of a veteran chef and proprietor resigned to the next crisis, Mr. Saint-Denis is not without a sense of humor, volunteering a parallel between his Bronx auberge and "Fawlty Towers."

Having seen a small magazine ad for the inn this spring, we drove up one Saturday to look it over and liked it immediately. We booked two $96-a-night connecting rooms and dinner for a May weekend. (The three-course dinner, prix-fixe at $45 a person, is served to nonguests as well, but only by reservation.) We arrived for our stay before 1pm on Saturday and were greeted by a caretaker who swung open the white gate so we could edge the car, piled with bikes, past pink rhododendron to park in the back instead of searching for a spot on the traffic-clogged avenue.

The parlor–dining room was set with round tables and French country chairs. A grandfather clock (actually, great-grandfather clock, an heirloom that Mr. Saint-Denis's grandfather inherited from his parents) stood silent sentinel, unwound; its tolling is unbearably loud, the innkeeper explained. White lace curtains screened the strong sun that was striping the walls and stout wooden beams. In the corner, a bar was set invitingly with bottles of aperitifs and liquor.

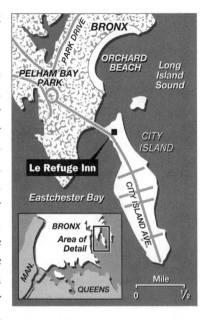

The front door stood open: not just unlocked, but open, testimony to the difference that 13 miles from midtown can make.

Behind the parlor sprawled a large country kitchen with cobalt blue tiles, a well-trafficked part of the inn that leads to a sunporch facing the backyard. Mr. Saint-Denis doesn't just allow walk-throughs, he encourages them.

The third-floor rooms are cozy and charming. Ours—furnished with a comfortable queen-size bed, a small table and chairs, a bureau, a vintage art deco table radio, and a very much up-to-date television—overlooked the bay, with the twin towers of the World Trade Center visible in the far distance. The girls' room had twin beds and a bureau, also an old radio and a new television, and overlooked a neighbor's yard. Ceiling fans in both rooms churned up a soothing breeze.

The first drawback, which I had somehow missed in making the booking, was that the rooms lacked private bathrooms; they shared one with two other occupied rooms on the floor. In fact, we learned, a second-floor suite with private bathroom is $190 a night, but it was already taken that weekend. The floor's black-and-white tile bathroom with its old-fashioned footed tub was sparkling clean, but the shower proved annoyingly fitful, with trickles of hot water and sudden gushes of cold. Between charm and plumbing, I decided, I'll take plumbing.

We spent our first few hours exploring, walking a stretch of City Island Avenue past a small private marine museum that was closed each time we looked in; Burck's Discount Boat Supplies; King Lobster; Artie's of City Island with a big sign, MUSSELLS (yes, spelled "Mussells"); and a small beauty shop, Lina Petite Salon, a funky fossil from the 1950s. As it happened, it was the weekend of the island's third annual arts-and-crafts festival; past the IGA market that is City Island's closest thing to a supermarket, the sidewalks were lined with vendor tables displaying inexpensive jewelry and other doodads. Not to worry: On ordinary days, much of the same merchandise is available in the stores or at tag sales advertised on street poles.

We stopped for lunch in the middle of "town" at the Crab Shanty, a friendly, skylighted family restaurant where for less than $40, including tax, tip, and a beer, we were served more clam chowder, shrimp, baked clams, soft-shell crabs, linguine, salad, and garlic bread than we could ever eat.

When we returned to the room, the second drawback hove into view and earshot. The neighbors next door were setting up outdoor tables, banners, and a suitcase-size radio. Clearly a party was in store. Sure enough, over the next 6 hours or so, into our bedtime, we attended the celebration by proxy, hostage to the revels below.

Before dinner, my wife took our younger daughter into the back-yard while our teenager and I continued our explorations on bike, a mile and a quarter to the far end of City Island Avenue, where two huge eating emporiums with outdoor tables on Long Island Sound vie for visitors' dollars. To the left is Johnny's Reef Restaurant, where patrons line up at fast-food counters for fried seafood platters of shrimp, scallops, squid, clams, and fillet of sole, starting at $8. The scene is similar at the facing Tony's Pier Restaurant, where the menu includes oysters, soft-shell crabs, and a lobster dinner for $16. We also rode down the residential side streets that transect the spine of City Island Avenue like so many little fish bones, finding pretty vistas of bay and sound at the dead ends. By turning right, or north, as we exited the inn, we also discovered a quieter backwater of boatyards and restaurants.

Later, reunited back in the room, we decided to feed our little one in family solitude upstairs rather than inflict her exuberance on our fellow diners. The staff, knowing what was good for them, wisely accommodated us with a room-service platter of steak and veggies. When at last sleep claimed her, despite the ruckus next door, we three felt secure (and hungry) enough to tiptoe downstairs.

We picked our way judiciously and deliciously through an appetizer selection of corn soup, salad, escargots in Chablis, duck pâté, and vegetable terrine, and an entree menu of grilled tuna, soft-shell crab, pepper beef filet, duck à l'orange, pork cutlet with blueberries, and *cervelle de veau*. (We're not much for calf brains and we had sworn off escargots since once adopting a snail as a family pet.) For dessert there were chocolate soufflé, white chocolate mousse, strawberry cheesecake, variously prepared fruit platters, and a cheese tray. The meal was beautifully prepared and served, and it was well accompanied by a 1992 Laboure-Roi Pouilly-Fuisse at $35 and a glass of port from Mr. Saint-Denis's extensive wine cellar, encompassing some 200 varieties, many well priced. He is particularly proud of his collection of 1982 Bordeaux at $40 to $500 a bottle.

The menu changes day to day, week to week, as the whim catches Mr. Saint-Denis. For a while, for example, he was offering to pack picnic hampers for guests who spent the day away sightseeing. But he said he no longer bothered.

The party next door was winding down but still audible when we turned in. Now the night music came chiefly from hot rods and motorcycles roaring off the bridge. When we mentioned it the next morning, Mr. Saint-Denis nodded sympathetically. "Summer drives me nuts," he commiserated. "If you want to know, fall and spring are my best seasons."

Sunday breakfast was a simple but elegant affair of fresh-baked and very buttery croissants with fresh-squeezed orange juice and good strong coffee. Then, leaving my wife to read in solitude, I took the girls on a bike ride to the island's only public school, P.S. 175, three-quarters of the way down City Island Avenue, site of a ball field and two playgrounds, one in the yard behind the school. By the time we returned, the musicians had arrived for the noon concert and were rehearsing, filling the house with resonant strains of Mozart and Haydn.

We took a last look around and packed up. Mr. Saint-Denis had a parting suggestion—nay, command. On the way home, we must, simply must, stop at the Bartow-Pell Mansion Museum and Gardens across the bridge in Pelham Bay Park. I had to admit I had never heard of it but took his careful directions and a brochure.

Within a few minutes' drive, we reached the place, a century-and-a-half–old Greek Revival/Federal–style stone mansion in an exquisite wild setting amid (I have since learned) the largest green space in the city, nearly three times the size of Central Park. We toured the stately rooms, furnished with some especially handsome Empire pieces, and reveled in the tranquillity, blessedly free of traffic din. The Bronx? (Wise up, Ogden Nash.) Yes, thonx!

CITY ISLAND ESSENTIALS

GETTING THERE

By Car To reach City Island from Manhattan by the car, take the Triborough Bridge to the Bruckner Expressway. After I-95 joins the expressway, take I-95 to exit 8B (City Island/Orchard Beach); go to the first traffic light and make a right onto City Island Road.; continue around the traffic circle to the City Island Bridge.

By Public Transportation From Manhattan, take the Uptown no. 6 train to Pelham By Park (the last stop), then take the no. 29 City Island bus.

ACCOMMODATIONS

Le Refuge Inn, 620 City Island Ave. ☎ 718/885-2478). One-bedroom suite with sitting room and private bathroom, $160 weekdays, $190 weekends; room with shared bathroom, $96 (single $74). Rates are based on double occupancy and include breakfast. Children are welcome; a folding bed is available for $15. A cottage at the rear of the inn can accommodate a family of five and includes a living room and private bathroom; it is $160 per weeknight for two ($190 on weekends), $15 for each additional person. Dinner, at $45 per person, is served Wednesday through Sunday starting at 6pm; brunch, Sunday 1 to 3pm, $19.50 per person.

DINING

Crab Shanty, 361 City Island Ave. (☎ **800/640-6522** or 718/885-1810). Open Sunday through Saturday 11am to 1:30am, Friday and Thursday 11am to 2:30am. Reservations necessary on weekend. Lunch entrees $8 to $15; dinner entrees $12 to $33.
Johnny's Reef Restaurant, 2 City Island Ave. (☎ **718/885-2086**). Open March through November, Sunday through Thursday 11am to midnight, Friday and Saturday 11am to 1am.
Tony's Pier Restaurant, 1 City Island Ave. (☎ **718/885-1424**). Open Sunday through Thursday noon to 11:30pm; Friday and Saturday 11:30am to 1am. Lunch and dinner entrees $9 to $16.

ATTRACTIONS

Bartow-Pell Mansion, Pelham Bay Park, 895 Shore Rd. (☎ **718/885-1461**). Self-guided tours offered Wednesday, Saturday, and Sunday noon to 4pm. Admission $2.50 adults, $1.25 students and seniors, free for children under 12.
Focal Point Gallery, 321 City Island Ave. (☎ **718/885-1403**). Open year-round with multimedia exhibitions from October to April, and all-photography shows May through September. Year-round exhibitions feature works by Ron Terner, a photographer and sculptor, owner of the gallery since 1974. Open Tuesday through Thursday noon to 7pm, Friday and Saturday noon to 9pm, Sunday noon to 7pm.
Turtle Cove Golf and Baseball Complex, 1 City Island Rd. (☎ **718/885-2646**). Golf driving range open year-round; miniature golf, March through November; and baseball batting cages, March through October. December through February, daily 8am to 6pm; March through November, daily 7am to 11pm. Miniature golf: $4.50. Driving range: $4 for a bucket of 40 balls, $7 for 80 balls, $9 for 110 balls; from 7 to 11am daily, $9 for 175 balls; $1 for golf-club rental. Batting cages: Baseball tokens $1.75 each (17 balls); 6 tokens for $8.

MORE NEW YORK CITY INNS

Box Tree Hotel and Restaurant, 250 E. 49th St., Manhattan (☎ **212/758-8320**). Room with private bathroom and fireplace $249 Sunday through Thursday, $340 Friday and Saturday; penthouse room $260 Sunday through Thursday, $360 Friday and Saturday. Daily rates are based on double occupancy and include continental breakfast; $100 of the room charge is applied to dinner in the restaurant on Friday and Saturday. Children welcome.
Colonial House Inn, 318 W. 22nd St., Manhattan (☎ **212/243-9669**). Rooms (some with private bathrooms) $80 to $140. Daily rates are based on double occupancy and include continental breakfast.
Inn at Irving Place, 56 Irving Place (at 17th St.), Manhattan (☎ **212/533-4600**). Rooms (all with private bathrooms) $295 to $495, suite with a sitting room $475 to $495. Daily rates are based on double occupancy and include continental breakfast.

No children under 12. A five-course high tea is available Wednesday through Friday at 3pm, Saturday and Sunday at 2 and 4:30pm, at a cost of $30 per person, excluding tax and tip.

There is a restaurant in the building, **Verbena** (☎ **212/260-5454**). Brunch year-round, Sunday 11:30am to 2:30pm; dinner year-round, Sunday, 5:30 to 9:30pm, Monday though Thursday, 5:30 to 10:30pm, Friday and Saturday 5:30 to 11pm.

WILDLIFE IN WINTER AT THE BRONX ZOO

by Bruce Weber

FOR SOME TIME NOW, BECAUSE I have a friend who travels frequently, I have lived in close proximity to animals—hers. They are a dog and a cat, Lucille and Maggie—granted, not exactly critters you find in the wild, but there is a zoolike quality that my apartment has taken on lately, a certain vibrancy and odoriferous spirit. I've been witness to (and occasionally a victim of) a lot of stalking, a participant in a lot of nonverbal communication, a monitor of mood swings. As any pet owner learns quickly, animals make you contemplate them—and yourself.

All this prepared me nicely for my recent couple of days at the International Wildlife Conservation Park, aka the Bronx Zoo, which, like many nonparents, I hadn't visited in decades. The cold-weather season is a particularly good time for adults to visit, I discovered, largely because the great herds of tiny cotton-candy eaters (a populous species of the genus children) are thinned out.

The zoo is open 365 days a year (where are the animals going to go?), but in spring and summer, it has up to 40,000 visitors on Wednesday when admission is free; on a winter Wednesday, the total might be only a few hundred. The local residents feel considerably less overwhelmed, and thus the possibility of encountering them closely is high. You can get near enough for long enough that, like pets, they reveal themselves.

Timmy, for example, the patriarch of the zoo's gorilla clan, doesn't care for hoopla; he tends to seek privacy when there's a crowd. Unlike a number of his show-offy relatives, "he's very, very shy," a keeper in the gorilla house told me.

But there he was sitting in full view when I wandered in, his regal belly protruding, sheltering one of his granddaughters with a protective arm. He was true to form, though, when I was followed by a chattering family of Scandinavian tourists: He stood slowly and lumbered off.

John Behler, the zoo's department of herpetology curator, acknowledged, "It's almost a daunting task to get through the reptile house in midsummer." And Pat Thomas, the curator of mammals, concurred; in particular, he said, the monkey house, a relatively small enclosure (there are 16 species of tamarins, marmosets, and other primates, all from South America), can be maddeningly busy and shrill in high season. "It's not a good educational experience," he said. "You spend more time jockeying for position than watching the animals."

But on the day after Christmas, I was alone there. And I feel as though I left an impression, at least on the white-faced capuchins, many of which paused in their regular antics to regard me. One carried another on his (her?) back; both their faces turned toward me as they negotiated a horizontal vine. Another made a long leap toward the glass, clung to the vertical strip of wood between panes high above me, and, looking down, mocked me with a brief screech before executing a fantastic midair back flip and landing back on a branch.

And a third waited patiently on the floor of the enclosure's foreground until I tentatively reached out my hand and touched my fingers to the glass. A gesture of friendship, I thought. But with a yawp that sounded like "Aha!" he reacted as though I'd fallen into a trap he'd set, leaping immediately to his feet, and pounding on the glass with both hands.

"You fool!" he said, or so I thought.

Like Leaving the City

At 265 acres, the Bronx Zoo is the largest city zoo ("urban wildlife conservation facility" is the preferred phrase) in the country, and 90% of it is viewable in the winter. (There are two closed exhibits: the children's zoo, whose gentle barnyard animals don't do well in the cold, and Wild Asia, which is shut down because one sees it by a monorail train that is treacherous in bad weather. So tigers and rhinos, alas, are out.) With effort, you can walk the zoo in a day, but it is nonetheless sizable enough that it almost feels as though you've left the city.

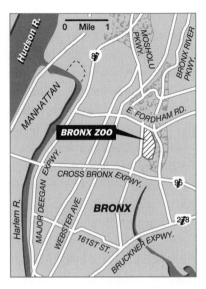

For one thing, the intermittent snorts, whinnies, yips, chortles, squawks, and growls aside, it's quiet, particularly with the attenuated winter crowds. And though the vanished greenery makes the surrounding high rises more apparent, there's an upside to that: The outdoor animals, notably the snow leopards, have considerably less camouflage.

Indeed, the snow leopards (native to the Himalayas—the zoo's 14 examples were born in captivity), with their small, handsome heads, powerful thick tails, and muscular grace, are by themselves worth the trip to the Bronx. I spent the better part of an hour watching a pair of them nimbly roaming their steep, rocky enclosure, wrestling intermittently like the young brothers they turned out to be.

Overall, on a gray day with the wind whipping and the trees shed of leaves, the zoo isn't really a beautiful place. Like a lot of venerable, large institutions, it is in a more or less constant state of rebuilding and renovating, and for some reason in cold weather the construction sites seem a little more glaring.

But there is a kind of peace to be had, a distinct lack of clamor, and walking the footpaths in the cold, among the ponds and grassy meadows, the faux savannahs and mountainsides, you encounter the animals in fanfareless fashion, as though you were meandering the grounds of some elegant if weathered sanitarium and now and then coming across a distracted patient. The animals are just hanging out, doing what they do, and if they're not oblivious, they also aren't rude or dismayed at the gawkery as they sometimes are when the crowds are larger.

"There aren't big behavioral changes in winter," Mr. Thomas said. "Obviously, the animals can't play in the snow in summertime. In summer they seek the shade; in winter they sit in the sun. Both times of year, their movements tend to be governed by the temperature and the availability of the sun." Some animals are particularly active now, unburdened by hot-weather lethargy: The snow leopards and the polar bears, for example, and even the grizzlies, partly because they're all pretty young, are still playful. (They don't hibernate in captivity; hibernation, a slowing down of the metabolism, is a response to a generally diminished availability of food in the winter wild.) "For sheer entertainment, the grizzlies are tough to beat," Mr. Thomas said, watching a couple of them in athletic competition, apparently over the occupation of a rock.

You do, I discovered, bring your own biases, circumstantial and otherwise, to certain exhibits. Some of what I thought about had to do with the nature of captivity, wild creatures out of the wild, that whole bothersome issue. I found myself wondering about that at the cheetah enclosure, where the two lovely animals, capable of running at the speed of a car on a highway, were slinking about sleepily in view of the apartment houses on Bronx Park South. They didn't look cranky or depressed, but still and all. . . .

Not quite as profoundly, how much you enjoy the sea lions slipping in and out of their frigid pool probably depends on how cold you are yourself. Waiting for their daily 3pm feeding, I found them impressive at first, but then I was overcome with sympathetic chills and went inside, leaving them to dine without me.

In or Out, Depending

Much of the zoo is indoors, of course—the reptile house, the gorilla house, and the monkey house are but 3 of the 10 major enclosed exhibits—and in winter even some prime attractions, usually outdoors, are shut-ins.

"In the majority of cases, the outdoor animals stay out," Mr. Thomas said. "The exceptions are gorillas, elephants, giraffes—species not adapted to extreme cold." The keepers decide daily, on the basis of three factors—temperature, windchill, and precipitation—whether to keep the animals inside, and on some days their treatment might vary.

"Elephants can be outside when it's in the 40s," Mr. Thomas said. "Giraffes are a little more sensitive to cold." When the animals are inside, he added, the keepers tend to do more of what he called "behavioral enrichment," hiding treats in their hay, for example, to encourage them to forage, so they'll still be engaged in some semblance of the activity they're accustomed to outdoors.

I've never been a big elephant guy, but watching the giraffes indoors is among the more surreal experiences to be had at the zoo. For one thing, the enclosure is the most pungent place in the zoo. ("Your nose will adjust," a zoo official told me as we walked in.) For another, the giraffe enclosure has a curved wall, painted to suggest an African savannah, and the entire time I was there, a 13-footer was stretching its neck, licking the top of it, perhaps because it was an outside wall and thus cool. In any case, I found myself humming one of the old psychedelic anthems of Jimi Hendrix: "'Scuse me, while I kiss the sky."

Weirdly rangy creatures, of course, the giraffes are startlingly close up, nearly within reach (theirs). Like cows, they stare at you with stupefaction, chewing on hay, their jaws rotating with agonizing steadiness and patience; you just know they'll never finish dinner.

DAY-TRIPPING TO THE ZOO

The **Bronx Zoo** (☎ **718/367-1010**) is at the Bronx River Parkway and Fordham Road in the Fordham section of the Bronx. To get there by subway, take the no. 2 to Pelham Parkway and walk west to the Bronxdale entrance. There is also an express bus run by the Liberty Line (☎ 718/652-8400).

The Aitken Aviary features a South American seabird colony of Magellanic penguins, Inca terns, Guanay cormorants, and other indigenous bird species. Special penguin feedings take place daily at 3:30pm.

The zoo is open November 1 through March 31, daily 10am to 4:30pm; April through October, 10am to 5pm Monday through Friday and until 5:30pm Saturday, Sunday, and holidays; late November to early January during holiday displays there are special hours daily 10am to 9 or 9:30pm. The Holiday Lights display is up from mid-November through early January; additional admission of $7 is required, $4 for children and seniors.

Admission ranges from $5 to $9 for adults, $2 to $4 for children 2 to 12 and seniors, depending on the season; general admission is free for everyone on Wednesday, but there is a charge for rides. Parking $6. The children's zoo is open from the end of March through October, weather permitting. Admission to the children's zoo is $2.

Indeed, the giraffes move with a kind of underwater slowness, which is emphasized by the fact that the adjacent exhibit features a band of tiny, furiously nimble meerkats, the African rodents that are among the zoo's most popular creatures since Nathan Lane's wisecracking characterization of one in *The Lion King*. The contrast made me aware, most poignantly, of what zoos do best: Illustrate by example the variety of creatures in the world. It's an obvious lesson, but for a city dweller like me to be reminded of it was one of the genuine pleasures of my visits. And the indoor exhibits of the zoo, where the animals are generally smaller and more populous, are where this particular pleasure is most intense.

Within a couple of hours, in the ingeniously luminescent World of Darkness exhibit, I found myself in the company of naked mole rats. In Jungle World, I watched an aging black leopard pacing along a branch and a family of gibbons, long-armed vine swingers, athletically making their way through the treetops. In the reptile house, I met Fidel and Maria, two Cuban crocodiles who have been at the zoo since the late 1950s, and Samantha, a 25-foot reticulated python, coiled and torpid-looking in her 3 or 4 weeks between meals, generally a 30- to 40-pound pig. "She's not bored," said Jim McDougal, a zoo herpetologist. "This is basically what she does when she's in the jungle."

Perhaps the variety is best illustrated in the World of Birds, where the names alone of the 100 species—white Bali mynah, carmine bee eater, purple lory, concave casqued hornbill, curassow, tanager, ibis, motmot—are compelling evidence. (While I was in front of his enclosure, the hornbill, a fantastically grotesque creature that suggests a Jimmy Durante caricature, sidled up to the glass and went nose to nose with a 6-year-old crouched there, eliciting an impromptu poem. "Hello, Mr. Birdie," the child intoned. "How come you're so dirty?") There is also a sobering exhibit recalling birds that are now extinct, dozens of them, many of which were still around 50 years ago. One astonishing threat to extant species, according to Donald Bruning, the curator of ornithology, is a proliferation in the wild of animals ordinarily thought of as domestic: dogs and cats. With increasing frequency, Mr. Bruning said, people are simply releasing their pets.

A cat in the wild might kill 300 birds a year, Mr. Bruning said. A recent study in Wisconsin, he said, estimated that there are 1.5 million cats in the wild in that state alone and that they are killing 36 million to 220 million birds annually.

The Lion's Message

I don't know about you. I find this amazing, and once again I found myself thinking about animals in captivity, their instincts on hold. It's a complicated issue, and I'm an amateur at it, but still: Who belongs where? I thought about Maggie and Lucille, their apparent contentment with apartment living, inanimate food, me. What do they think, really? Is this a good life?

And then I encountered the lion. It was the frigid afternoon after Christmas, and I heard him from some distance away. I'd been scrutinizing the gelada baboons, trying to figure out why a young female had apparently been banished from the family cave; she was sitting, unhappily, it seemed, her back to her relatives, shivering a bit, her tufted facial hair blowing in the nippy wind. (I was probably over-psychoanalyzing; the flat rock she was crouching on turned out to be heated.) In any case, the lion's roar, an aching bellow with the piercing resonance of the bass notes from my neighbor's stereo system, beckoned me.

I was not alone; perhaps a dozen other people also gathered round, in interesting, still silence. All, I guessed, felt isolated enough and cowed enough by the furious beastliness to contemplate themselves in awe. Unfenced in, separated from us by a wall and a moat, the lion disappeared behind a rock, then returned to view, maybe 30 feet from where I stood.

He shook his maned head and growled almost silently. Then he turned away; with his back to me, he began bellowing again; they were bleats of a monumental nature, and I noticed that his haunches and the muscles around his ribs clenched with each one. These were literally gut-wrenching cries, not a bellyache or any other specific complaint, but—or so I imagined—a lament of existential proportions.

Maggie and Lucille do not do this, I thought. But it hit me: I do.

WALKING BROOKLYN'S FLATBUSH TRAIL

by Douglas Martin

LET'S BEGIN WITH THE WORST. Danny and I, old sauntering buddies, had decided to try something new, walking in a straight line. Our past perambulations had been around islands, first Manhattan, then Staten Island—attempts to glimpse truths from the outside looking in. Now we were going to walk the length of Flatbush Avenue, more than 10 miles, in search of nothing less than the soul of Brooklyn, the vast borough Thomas Wolfe said nobody could know "t'roo and t'roo."

That, without doubt, includes us, though we both live in the political subdivision taking its name from the Dutch words for broken valley. Douglas Martin, reporter, and Daniel Anthony Perasa, who takes bets over the phone for OTB, somehow turned the wrong way coming out of a diner, not realizing for almost 3 long blocks that we were seeing the same view we had recently passed on the other side of the street.

"If we were going to be honest about it, we'd refer to each other as Dumb and Dumber," Danny says. Then, referring to the avenues identified by letters, Dumb adds, "Before we walk next time, it might not be a bad idea to learn the alphabet."

Our only defense is that we were following a time-honored Brooklyn tradition. Douglas (Wrong Way) Corrigan had taken off from Floyd Bennett Field at the base of Flatbush Avenue on a flight to California in 1938, when this would have been quite an achievement. He misread his compass for 28 hours and ended up in Ireland. His unforgettable first words: "Where am I?" But, hey! In no time at all, the *New York Post* printed a headline celebrating his achievement, backward of course, and in Texas, he was presented with a watch that ran the

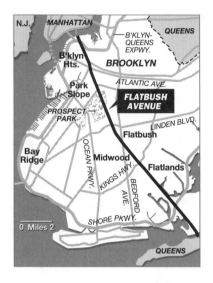

wrong way. He was featured in parades, always in cars going in reverse. And Wrong-Way Corrigan is in our modern-day minds as we begin our stroll virtually where he began his flight.

At the Brooklyn side of Gil Hodges Memorial Bridge, which goes to the Rockaways, in Queens, Danny pronounces it a grand day for walking. "My mother would have said there's just enough blue in the sky for a sailor to make a pair of pants," he says.

Danny is a true Brooklynite, having lived here all his 57 years. By the time he was 12, he figures, his mother must have given him $1 about 100 times so he could spend an afternoon watching the Dodgers at Ebbets Field. (A nickel each way for the subway, 60¢ admission, a nickel for the scorecard, and 25¢ to apportion between hot dogs and sodas, which cost a nickel each.) Blessedly, he does not ooze nostalgia, an incurable Brooklyn disease.

So we've come to Flatbush Avenue, which bisects Brooklyn in the manner that Broadway slices and defines Manhattan. I live in a 12th-floor apartment from which all the windows look out on Flatbush, and have sat mesmerized by the endless procession of tens of thousands of vehicles, while pondering the patterns of our local migrations, the sheer magnitude of the nation's taillights.

Flatbush was first an Indian trail through the woodlands, then the site of a pretty humiliating British victory over forces led by George Washington. Later on, it became the thoroughfare for the parade honoring the one Brooklyn Dodgers World Series victory and, more recently, a favored route of protests by the Rev. Al Sharpton and of regular streams of the Lubavitchers' recreational vehicles noisily heralding the imminent arrival of the Messiah. (The *Brooklyn Eagle* reported in

1946 that the name Flatbush comes from the Dutch words *vlachte bos,* which mean "plain woods.")

The meanings of the avenue, from huge to tiny, were superbly evoked in a book by Alan Abel, now a Canadian, who grew up in the neighborhood of Flatbush in central Brooklyn, and went on to practice journalism around the world. His book, *Flatbush Odyssey: A Journey Through the Heart of Brooklyn* (McClelland & Stewart, 1995), describes his wanderings and the lovely, evolving relationship between him and his Brooklyn mother, united again during a 3-month visit. My favorite part was Mr. Abel's discovery while researching his book that what he thought were the autographs of every Dodger player in his long-cherished team yearbook from the mid-1950s were almost surely the work of a graphologically gifted batboy known as "Charley the Brow."

Gulls & Crows

But this article is about our walk, and we're now between the bridge and Floyd Bennett Field. It is a landscape so bleak it reminds Danny of the Midwest, at least *The Wizard of Oz* part. There are towering swamp grass, scrub trees, every so often parts of cars—enough components, Danny guesses, "to build a car that wouldn't work." Gulls squawk, crows caw, and planes descend on Kennedy Airport. It does not seem like the city, though there is a small homeless encampment with enough borrowed shopping carts to start a Pathmark, and we suspect snakes lurk in the grass.

We come to the Marina at Barren Island, a parking lot for yachts. What would you name a boat, Danny? *"Never Sink II,"* he snaps. Then Highway Patrol Precinct No. 2, a not-unhandsome brick building. The Department of Transportation's Flatbush Yard. Then the Marine Park Golf Course, where plaid people are waiting to tee off on a course designed by Robert Trent Jones. A short way down, we come to some very large fishing boats of the sort that prowl the great ocean banks. Then Toys "R" Us and, in a little bit, Kings Plaza Shopping Center, looking as if it had just arrived from Nowhere, USA. Is this Brooklyn, root land of George Gershwin and Woody Allen?

Danny fills the emptiness with some advice to walkers: Never stop. "If you stop walking, bad things are going to happen to you," he says ominously. He is singing what I think is an old Guy Lombardo song, which was also favored by the Ebbets Field organist Gladys Goodding: "Give me the moon over Brooklyn, down Flatbush Avenue."

Just past Avenue S, we spot the New Floridian Diner and know its call is for us. We enter a palace of chrome, mirrors, and phones. Waitresses wear pink bow ties and frilly aprons. Tom Jones is on the jukebox. The cakes all have at least three layers, are a foot high, and are displayed like artworks. The menu is 14 pages. There are cocktails (the kamikaze, for $4.95), sandwiches (open-faced Romanian steak, $13.50), and acres of freshly baked muffins. They don't have pineapple knishes like the ones Danny remembers from a long time ago at Coney Island, but I think this just might be as good as it gets.

The Wrong Turn

It was here we made the wrong turn on a one-way journey. Perhaps it was the directionally challenging intersection of more than two streets. Maybe it was our genuine fascination with the menu of the Lucky Star Finest Chinese and Italian Food to Take Out. It could have been our preoccupation with the woman crossing the street against the light while reading a book. "A true New Yorker," Danny mumbles approvingly. "The lady doesn't know the meaning of fear."

Soon we are back on course, trodding back toward Manhattan with hope in our hearts and sheepish grins on our faces. At Baughman Place, we see an old-fashioned pizzeria, Lenny & John's, and bite. The excellent cheese ball is 65¢, and on Tuesday, you can buy a whole pie for $5. The photographs on the wall take you back to an older Flatbush Avenue. One was taken in 1956 and shows the view north from Flatlands Avenue. Alan Ladd was starring in Santiago at the old Marine Theater. A 1946 picture, showing the intersection of Flatbush and Flatlands, records the once-ubiquitous trolley cars that Brooklynites used to have to dodge between (hence, the ball club's name).

Most intriguing is a 1922 photo of a house built in 1800 that is said to be still standing. The address is 1587 East 53rd Street, between avenues M and N. We ask a counterman for directions. "Too far to walk," he answers.

Maybe for him. But we are now determinedly unidirectional. As the neighborhood of Flatlands oozes into that of Flatbush, we pass Four Aces Pawnbrokers, with a menagerie of stuffed game in the window, including a toothy beaver. At a bakery, we have reason to suspect we are overcharged when it becomes apparent we are both ignorant and from outside the neighborhood. "Pretty smooth," says Danny. "A good old-fashioned New York hustle."

Flatbush, once a Jewish and Irish neighborhood, now teems with people from all over the world, and they race about on errands. Radios blare, and in-line skaters, walkers' worst enemies, start to appear. A teenager passes with a carton from the ASPCA; it meows.

A woman who bumped Danny as she raced past comes back when she sees him stopping to tie his shoe. "You should have told me," she says. "I would have tied it for you." Danny, who thinks his baldness is the punishment of an unjust God, does not appreciate this kindness. "I'm an athlete," he growls. "I'm a long-distance walker."

Sampling Soul Food

Knowing that lunch heals all, we find ourselves in a soul food restaurant between Cortelyou Road and Dorchester Road. The barbecued chicken wings with fresh corn bread had beguiled us, and does not disappoint. A long, long counter with 22 stools. Lazy ceiling fans. Free jazz on Saturday night, a gospel choir on Sunday night. "If this place were in Manhattan, the prices would be twice as much, the crowd would be three times the size, and it would be half as enjoyable," Danny summarizes.

Walking is slow, which is fine. We wander into African grocery stores, stop to appreciate the tinkling concerto of an ice-cream truck, and notice that the produce markets carry chunks of Jamaican pumpkin. A botanica offers holy water in two varieties, 99¢ and $1.59. Why? Street music changes from soca to calypso to hip-hop every few feet.

We worship at those awesome monuments to money, the corner banks. A Republic Bank branch at Caton Avenue has elegant chandeliers and words of wisdom chiseled in the walls: "THE HABIT OF SAVING IS ITSELF AN EDUCATION. IT ENCOURAGES EVERY VIRTUE. IT TEACHES SELF-CONTROL." Danny shakes his head, and is walking again in no time. "That sounded like something Scrooge might have said at the beginning of the book," he puffs. "But that's all right."

We almost miss Erasmus Hall Academy, founded by Alexander Hamilton and the man who later shot him to death in a duel, Aaron Burr. Situated between Church and Snyder avenues, it grew into the adjacent high school attended by Barbra Streisand, Bobby Fischer, and Beverly Sills. Inside the gate stands the original 1786 academy building, a Georgian Federal gem.

But we don't stop, being a bit put off by the gate. "It looks like it could be part of a penitentiary," Danny growls. We also skip the original Flatbush Town Hall, seat of Flatbush's government until it became part of Brooklyn in 1894, 4 years before Brooklyn itself became part of New York City. It is a half block off Flatbush, on Snyder Avenue, and we, understandably enough, have sworn off detours.

Where we linger is the Reformed Protestant Dutch Church, with its towering steeple. It is so beautiful, we Brooklynites half forgive the fact that it is made of Manhattan schist. And we find the graveyard surrounding the church a strangely peaceful retreat from the cacophonous street. The Dutch inscriptions on limestone have pretty much worn away, but some of the ones etched on brownstone remain legible: *Hier Lyt Het Lighaam.*

Near the cemetery are other shells. One is Loews King Theater, once one of the most exuberant of the great movie palaces. Both Danny and Mr. Abel in his book recall fabulous ice-cream places. But the way today's Flatbush Avenue pulsates with life makes it hard to dwell on mythic yesterdays. Across the street from the dignified old church, a street preacher is just shifting into high gear, dancing as if there might be no tomorrow. "Hallelujah, Jesus, sweeter than a honeycomb!" he shouts.

Step by step, we approach the empty corner of Brooklyn's heart. Ebbets Field Houses, a housing development, loom just 2 blocks off Flatbush. Danny's mood turns dark. He tells of a friend who had bought an original seat from the stadium and chained it to a flagpole in his Brooklyn front yard. It was stolen in no time. He muses about the ultimate fate of the villains who stole the beloved "Bums" from their native land.

The closest we can get to a visible memory is the McDonald's on Empire Boulevard, which has taken the trouble to assemble autographed Brooklyn Dodgers pictures for its walls. Danny discusses each. Babe Ruth is a surprise to me, but he did once wear a Dodgers uniform as a coach in the late 1930s.

Danny approvingly notes that the pitcher Don Drysdale was the meanest man, definitely the meanest pitcher, ever to play. He recalls someone asking Drysdale if he would knock down his own mother. "Certainly not," he supposedly answered. "She's not that good a hitter."

We amble on, with the Brooklyn Botanic Garden on one side of Flatbush Avenue and Prospect Park on the other. You can't see into either very well, but some days you can hear the music of the exquisite Prospect Park carousel. The park's zoo has replaced its larger animals with smaller ones, more tastefully displayed. So the roars of lions that once would have accompanied our walk are no more. On the other hand, a Dutch home built in 1783, Lefferts Homestead, pulsates with new life, as it has become a focus for children's programs.

We walk through the elegant Grand Army Plaza, an expansive and tasteful urban space that is also my front yard. We walk down a long hill and come to the Brooklyn Academy of Music, a boxlike building that Caruso inaugurated in 1908 by singing the title role in Faust. Across the street is the Williamsburgh Savings Bank Building, Brooklyn's tallest building. Its lobby is an awesome space with pillars rising like trees. "If there were red hats hanging from the ceiling, I'd swear I was in St. Patrick's Cathedral," Danny says.

Incense & Cabs

We trudge on, somehow gaining energy as we get closer to "the City," as Brooklynites persist in calling Manhattan. The smell of peddlers' incense permeates the air, and we occasionally see yellow cabs, a sight unknown in the borough's interior. After Fulton Street, we are walking on Flatbush Avenue Extension, built as an access to the Manhattan Bridge, which opened in 1905. We pass another Toys "R" Us, reminding us that this is pretty much what we began with. We see a man wearing a Yankee cap. Good grief.

At the famous Junior's restaurant, we only window-shop the huge cheesecakes. We cross Flatbush Avenue to the former Paramount Theater—where Frankie Lymon and the Teen-Agers, Chuck Berry, and others got rock and roll going 4 decades ago—hoping to see the great Wurlitzer organ, which remains. A security guard kindly leads us to what has become a gym for Long Island University, but an archery class prevents us from entering.

Traffic is everywhere. Suddenly, we are at the end: the blue Manhattan Bridge with its dainty four knobs on top. Garbage surrounds us. A man slowly harvests bottles from the weeds. Clouds cover the sun.

It is 3:40pm, about 7 hours after we started. We have passed seven Irish bars, six McDonald's, and more than 100 nail parlors. We look at each other and break out laughing.

"It certainly doesn't end with a glorious hurrah, does it?" Danny says.

Long Island

A DAY AT THE RACES:
BETTING AT BELMONT

by William Grimes

THE FIRST RACE AT BELMONT ON A sizzling hot day turned out to be almost too much for one bettor. Standing near the finish line against the chain-link fence that runs along the home stretch, he stamped his right foot furiously, punched the air with one hand, and, as five closely bunched horses pounded toward the wire, screamed nonstop, a study in the more brutish emotions. "Come on, move it! Get the lead out and move it! Do it!" This ridiculous figure was none other than myself.

I had never been to a racetrack before. Except for the Triple Crown, thoroughbred racing had seemed pointless, a small footnote to the day's sports results on the local television news, marginally more interesting than curling or caber tossing.

What a difference a day makes! I walked into Belmont Park in Elmont, Long Island, a duffer, a lamb waiting to be fleeced, a low roller with a stake of $100 and a dream: to play the ponies and win. I left Belmont . . . well, to get the official result, read on.

Knowledge is power. I was determined to do research before placing my first bet, enough to make the afternoon something more than an exercise in picking horses with funny names. Two books seemed essential. The first was Tom Ainslie's *Complete Guide to Thoroughbred Racing*. Written in a lively style, it is a sober, informed tutorial on how to handicap a race, with an in-depth discussion of "the jockey factor," "the distance factor," "the speed factor," and other fundamentals, as well as simple explanations of various types of bets and betting systems.

The second book on my self-education program was a collection of Damon Runyon stories. It seemed desirable to steep myself in the argot of the racing world, and to make the acquaintance of characters like Hot Horse Herbie and Little Alfie, the guys in yellow-checked suits whom I would undoubtedly encounter at the track.

There are few things more pleasing to the eye than Belmont Park on a fine day. The track encloses an ovoid Eden, a lush, landscaped park with two sizable ponds and topiary bushes that are cultivated in the racetrack's own greenhouse. High-pressure spigots spray water across the grass, swathing the infield in a romantic, shimmering mist. An intricately sculptured chamaecyparis bush stands to the left of the grave of Ruffian, a valiant filly that perished in the line of duty. Specifically, she broke a leg during a match race with Foolish Pleasure on July 6, 1975, and had to be destroyed, ending a brilliant career.

The four-story track building, which parallels the home stretch, is divided into grandstand and clubhouse areas. To enter, visitors pay $2 and walk through turnstiles to what looks like the approach to an amusement park or zoo. An additional $2 gets you into the clubhouse. At several stands, vendors sell *The Racing Form* ($3) and tip sheets compiled by handicapping experts. Also on sale is *Post Parade* ($1.50), the track program. Like *The Racing Form,* it offers past-performance stats on each horse running that day, as well as the morning line, a track expert's estimate of how the public will bet each horse.

Off to the right, just beyond the first newsstands, is the paddock, where, before each race, the horses are paraded around a small track, called the walking ring.

An Early Look

Keen-eyed bettors use the paddock parade to look for disturbing signs in their favorite horse. If you see a horse trying to kick his handler to death, for example, it might be wise to alter the betting strategy for that race. I found it immensely reassuring whenever my picks turned out to be lean, slightly high-strung animals with good posture and what seemed like a can-do attitude.

It's a short walk from the paddock to the ground-level grandstand and the real business of the park, betting. The atmosphere and the architecture are a little like a baseball stadium, with hot dog and beer stands scattered throughout. There are restaurants too, but it's safe to say that most people do not come to the track with a fine meal uppermost on their minds. No, the 450 overhead television monitors tell the real tale of the place, flashing a constant stream of information on the changing odds, as the minutes to post time tick away.

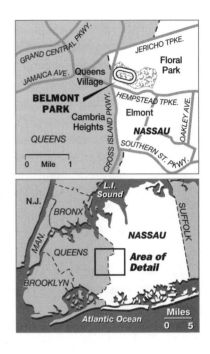

For the first time since leaving high school, I felt keen regret at not having tried harder in math. If only they had presented word problems in horse-racing terms, with actual money on the line, rather than those bland farmers plowing fields into complicated fractions, or freight trains carrying wheat. The subject takes on real urgency when you're trying to choose between two horses and can't quite figure out whether 7–2 odds are better or worse than 4–1 and by how much. My plight was even worse. Only late in the day did I discover that a $2 bet on a horse at even odds pays $4. I thought the bettor simply broke even. All around me, people who did not look like college material seemed to have no trouble performing nine-digit calculations in their heads as the odds on the board changed.

The mathematically challenged might want to request a helpful pamphlet called *Thoroughbred Racing Made Easy,* which the New York Racing Association gives away at information booths on the ground floor and second floor.

Nine Little Adventures

I studied *The Racing Form,* and evolved a simple strategy. I read the capsule descriptions of each horse in the "Closer Look" section of the paper, examined the horse's recent track record and career stats, checked out the jockey's winning percentage, narrowed the field to a plausible few, and studied the odds on the board to see which way the money was flowing. For the purposes of this article, I bet every one of the day's nine races, something no real handicapper would do.

The procedure for placing a bet is simple. Walk up to a window and state, in the following order, the amount of the bet, the type of bet (for example, win, place, or show), and the number of the horse (not the name), which is indicated on all the printed guides.

There's an automated version of this procedure. At specially marked windows, bettors can buy vouchers, which they then insert into screen-activated machines (called "SAMs") that present betting options. By touching the screen, the bettor can choose the amount and type of bet.

With one exception, I stuck to win, place, and show bets, meaning that I bet that my horse would come in first (win), first or second (place), or among the top three (show).

Danger in Winning

Four great truths seemed to emerge. First, as Tom Ainslie succinctly puts it, "It is more fun to win than to lose." Too much fun, perhaps. A well-trained thoroughbred running all out is the second-most beautiful sight in nature, surpassed only by the sight of the same horse coming on strong in the home stretch and finishing in the money. In the excitement, it's all too easy to bet foolishly.

Second, it's best to study *The Racing Form* the night before the race. There's simply too much information to digest at the track, with less than 30 minutes between races.

Third, long shots are long shots for a simple reason. They are highly unlikely to win. On my race day, only one horse came in at odds much longer than 5–1, and seven of the nine races were won by favorites.

Fourth, the trickier variations on win, place, and show betting—the exactas, trifectas, pick threes, and pick sixes, intended to spice things up for the betting public—should not be tried by the novice bettor. Most bettors at the track put their money on exactas, in which they predict the first two horses to cross the finish line, in exact order, thereby getting a much larger payoff on their bet. A trifecta, as the name suggests, requires the bettor to predict the top three finishers in order. The daily double, pick three, and pick six bets require the bettor to select the winners of two, three, or six consecutive races. As Ainslie points out, it's hard enough to pick one winner in one race. The wise handicapper focuses his energies accordingly.

My first race was an emotional tune-up: $5 to win on Color Me Speed, which I thought showed potential (for reasons that are obscure in retrospect), and, as a hedge, $5 to show on Here's Noah, the odds-on favorite.

After placing my bet, I sat down on one of the green wooden benches at track level, near the finish line, by far the most exciting vantage point, I later decided. Those who wish may pay the surcharge and enter the clubhouse areas on the second, third, and fourth floors, where you get a better view of the first half of the race. But even with binoculars (rentable for $3.50), the action seems a little remote. At track level, you get the rawer emotions, and the unbeatable close-up view of the final drive to the finish line.

From Murmur to Roar

As the race begins, a tense quiet reigns. Most of the bettors remain seated on the benches, with scattered enthusiasts yelling out a few choice words of encouragement. "Stay up with the rat pack there, buddy boy," I heard one bettor yell. Across the infield, the horses look like mechanical models.

As the horses round the final turn, the murmur of the crowd becomes a roar. The people in the seats rise, as though gripped by a supernatural power, and advance like zombies toward the fence, eyes fixed on the race. The final flat-out stretch run unleashes pandemonium.

It's fun. I now have a better understanding of why the crowds turn out in downtown Teheran for a rousing "Death to America" rally.

Color Me Speed nearly pulled it off but was nosed out at the finish by Here's Noah, who returned a profit of $3.50. So I was down $1.50 after one race.

In each of the next two races, I played it safe and bet one horse to place. Both finished in the top two, and I collected a profit of $31 on $20 in bets.

Over the next several races, I increased the amount of each bet but stuck to the basic, admittedly wimpish strategy of trying to bet on one or two horses to finish in the money. I was turning a profit. Dribs and drabs, true, but while other bettors were tearing up their slips, I was returning to the windows to cash in.

The Damon Runyon color was not particularly evident, although after Julie Krone rode Great Triumph to a closely run second-place finish, one elderly fellow with no teeth repeated, "She got the old schnozzola in there, Julie, she got the old schnozzola in there!"

Off by One Place

In the eighth race, I got greedy. Ignoring Ainslie, I bet a $30 exacta. That is, I bet $30 that Splendid Buck, one of the top horses that day, and Apprentice would finish first and second, respectively. That was not a dumb bet, but it wasn't smart either. The dumb part was that I thought I was betting a quinella: that is, predicting the first two horses, but not in any particular order. It turned out to be moot, since my horses finished one-three rather than one-two.

This was a blow. My hard-won confidence was shaken. With only one race to go, I was looking at a loser of a day. Returning to basics, I applied my mind to *The Racing Form* and located two good-lookers, Out of the Realm and Incredible. A third horse, Scudbuster, looked strong on paper, but I rejected him because the name was nearly as irritating as the No. 4 horse, Homey Don't Play. I put $25 each on Out of the Realm and Incredible to place.

It was a great race, run on turf. Both horses started out at the back of the field. Out of the Realm, in fact, ran dead last through the first half of the race and for a brief moment looked as though he might stop to nibble flowers. At the three-quarter mark, he was still running eighth in a 10-horse field.

The Argot to Start With

Here is a glossary of words commonly used at the race track:

Win: Horse bet must finish first.

Place: Horse bet must finish first or second.

Show: Horse bet must finish first, second, or third.

Daily Double: Horses bet must finish first in respective races. Available in first and second races of the day, and also in last two races.

Exacta: Horses bet must finish first and second in exact order. Available for all races.

Quinella: Horses bet must finish first or second in any order. Available for race nos. 2 and 4.

Instant Double: Winners picked in two consecutive races. Happens when an exacta or quinella wager is canceled because of late scratches.

Trifecta: Horses bet must finish first, second, and third in exact order. Available for race nos. 5, 7, and 9 and all stakes races.

Pick Three: Horses bet must finish first in race nos. 2, 3, and 4, or 6, 7, and 8.

Pick Six: Pick the winners of race nos. 3 through 8 and you win or share in 75% of the day's pool. The consolation payoff, 25% of each day's pool (not including carry-over), is returned to bettors who have picked five winners of the six designated races. On any day that no bettor selects all six winners, 75% of the pool is held over and added to the next day's Pick Six pool, and 25% of the pool (not including carry-over) is returned to a bettor or bettors who pick the highest number of winners of the six designated races.

Parlay Wager: A way to roll over winnings from one race into a bet on subsequent races. This is a convenience only because the payoff is the same as if the bets were placed individually. Using a parlay betting slip, combine at least two races, to a maximum of six races. The slip can contain any combination of win, place, or show wagers.

Incredible, meanwhile, was up with the leaders, in third position, just behind the detestable Scudbuster. Then, the miracle. Out of the Realm poured it on. With no more apparent effort than a driver shifting gears, he passed the field and won by a length and a half.

And the second horse? It was Incredible over Scudbuster in a photo finish.

I headed to the betting window and pushed across my slip. The man behind the window pushed back a crisp $100 bill.

Memo to the boss: I'm giving three weeks' notice.

Belmont Essentials

Belmont Park Race Track is located in Elmont, Long Island (☎ **718/641-4700; www.nyra.com).** The season runs from May 7 until July 22, shuts down until September 7, and then runs through October 28.

Getting to the Track By car, take the Cross Island Expressway to exit 26D. The **Long Island Rail Road** (☎ **718/217-5477**) offers a round-trip rail package from Penn Station that includes $1 off the price of admission to the racetrack.

Track Hours and Admission The track is open every day except Monday and Tuesday (on holiday weekends there is racing Monday, and Tuesday and Wednesday are dark). Doors open at 11am and the races begin at 1pm, with the last race at approximately 5pm. Admission is $4 for the clubhouse, $2 for the grandstand.

MANSIONS OF LONG ISLAND'S GOLD COAST

by Peter Marks

Peering out the car window at palaces protected by ornate, wrought-iron gates, pointing out homes hidden in manicured forests of linden and copper beech trees, Paul Mateyunas was in his glory. Here he was, doing what he loved best, leading a spur-of-the-moment safari into the heart of mansion country, a legendary land from the era when Long Island was still the private preserve of the very rich.

As the car crisscrossed the country lanes, the names of the wealthy families that once dominated the landscape rolled off Mr. Mateyunas's tongue: Here lived the Whitneys and Phippses; there the Vanderbilts and Du Ponts. His anecdotes were about vast fortunes and unfathomable expenses, about famous houseguests and lavish parties, and eccentric millionaires who built closets as big as duplexes and lay down each night on what once had been Napoléon's bed.

Mr. Mateyunas could not be described as to the manner born; his family estate is a split-level in Northport, Long Island. But he adores the great houses of Long Island's Gold Coast as if he had grown up in one, a passion stirred in him at the age of 8, when his parents took him to a concert in an amphitheater amid the ruins of a mansion in Lloyd Harbor, where he realized for the first time that not everyone on the island grew up on a quarter-acre lot.

"It wasn't like from a purely materialistic view," said Mr. Mateyunas, a college student, who during high school worked part-time as a guide in the Vanderbilt mansion in Centerport, an elegant,

Spanish-style house on Long Island Sound that is now a museum run by Suffolk County. "It became an appreciation of the time period, the etiquette, the manners. It isn't the money; it's the beauty of what the money did."

During the first 40 years of this century, Long Island was not America's quintessential suburb. It was America's Monte Carlo, a place where the rich came to see, be seen, and spend exorbitant amounts of money. Mostly what they spent it on were their sprawling estates, mansions they built to impress each other and to resemble the houses of the European nobility they sought to emulate. Hundreds of captains of industry and commerce, and even some from the world of entertainment, kept estates here at one time or another, from J. P. Morgan to F. W. Woolworth, from Lewis C. Tiffany to Henri Bendel. Eddie Cantor, for a short time, maintained a small mansion in Great Neck. William Randolph Hearst had a huge one in Sands Point, but not as huge as the even grander palace, San Simeon, he built in northern California.

At its height, there were some 600 to 700 mansions on Long Island's Gold Coast, a roughly 30-mile-long stretch of the North Shore, from Great Neck to Eatons Neck. Many of them are gone, destroyed in fires, demolished by families unable to afford their upkeep, or sold off and subdivided by housing developers. Today, of the 200 to 300 still standing, about half are privately owned, and most of the others have been converted for use as schools, college buildings, religious retreat houses, and country clubs.

And then there are a handful of estates that are open to the public, a few extraordinary homes that give the ordinary wage earner of today the chance to gawk at the excesses the rich enjoyed in the years before income taxes and the Depression made such splendor less fashionable—and less affordable. Filled with original artwork and furnishings, the treasures their owners collected on European jaunts or commissioned from the world's leading artists and artisans, the estates are vestiges of a Long Island that has been crowded out by parkways and subdivisions. They are remnants of that Lost Island, the moneyed haven immortalized by F. Scott Fitzgerald in *The Great Gatsby*.

Robert MacKay, director of the Society for the Preservation of Long Island Antiquities, said Long Island truly was mansion central, the place where the rich indulged their passion for play. "There is little question that though the Hudson Valley was important earlier, and Newport has had more visibility, more country houses were built on Long Island, and in greater concentration, than in any other part of the country," he explained. "It was clearly their national resort."

Despite the efforts by Mr. MacKay's organization and other preservation groups, many of the old houses have not been saved, an indication, perhaps, of Long Islanders' ambivalence toward the Island's haughty roots. But even so, a few of the families managed to ensure the survival of their houses by leaving them to local governments, or endowing nonprofit boards to run them. Several others that remain in private hands are accessible only by special arrangement, like Oheka, the Cold Spring Harbor castle built by Otto Kahn, the German-born financier. The house, the second-largest private residence in the nation, is no longer inhabited, but it has been rented for weddings or as a movie location.

Some of the houses open to the public, like Falaise, the former estate of Harry Guggenheim, a philanthropist whose uncle Solomon built the Guggenheim Museum in Manhattan, are so meticulously preserved that they look as if the family might return in a couple of hours. In the carport of the house, which is perched on a cliff overlooking Long Island Sound, Guggenheim's purple Cadillac is parked next to a station wagon once owned by his great friend and frequent guest Charles A. Lindbergh. Meanwhile, the table in the dining room remains set with the dinner service Guggenheim used when he served as ambassador to Cuba, and the cabinets in the trophy room remain filled with loving cups, including one from the 1953 Kentucky Derby, which was won by his thoroughbred Dark Star.

"He had an affinity for Normandy," Adele Wall said, as she escorted a visitor around the house where she has been a volunteer tour guide for more than 20 years. It was an affinity he could afford to explore, for the Norman-style mansion appears to have been spirited whole from the French countryside. Set into the walls of the lower foyer are medieval friezes taken from the wall of a municipal building, somewhere in France.

Mrs. Wall, who brought up a family just off the grounds of the estate, in Sands Point, says that when Guggenheim left the house to Nassau County upon his death in 1971, he also left precise details about how his house should be shown, right down to the placement of his favorite photographs on a table in the living room, the direction through the house that tour guides should take, and the seasonal sequence of plantings around the swimming pool: blue and white lilies in the spring, followed by orange enchantment lilies, white and yellow chrysanthemums, and, in the fall, bronze and yellow chrysanthemums.

It is this kind of obsession with detail that can make the exploration of the homes so enthralling. There is always something more to see, whether it is a camouflaged doorway in the library or a stuffed Indian tiger in the foyer.

"I just couldn't believe people lived like that," said Ruth Katz, a mortgage broker from Manhattan who grew up in Great Neck. Several years ago, she started visiting the homes that were open and got so hooked that she began to compose maps of the Gold Coast, trying to identify the precise whereabouts of houses she had read about but could not get into. Even the ruins of old homes long gone have become a source of mystery and detective work.

"We used to drive by this one place in Sands Point when we were little, and my father would say, 'A convent was here,'" Ms. Katz recalled, laughing. "He didn't know! No, a convent wasn't here; William Randolph Hearst was here!"

The wealthy came to Long Island in the early part of the century because it was convenient to New York City, where many maintained their primary homes. "For reasons of business and social discourse, America's wealth had to be in New York," said Mr. MacKay. "But it was also wound up with a new lifestyle. Whereas the Victorian wealthy stayed in the city year-round, venturing out only to stay in hotels, by the turn of the century, you had the great explosion in American recreation. It is here on Long Island that we see the development of golf, with the first country club in the country."

Once they arrived, the families, spending anywhere from several hundred thousand dollars to $5 million—fortunes at the time—created the castles of their fantasies. They hired renowned architects like Stanford White and the New York firm of Delano & Aldrich to build in the style of French châteaus and Italian villas and English country houses. They erected stables and polo fields, rose gardens and golf courses. They mounted priceless European sculptures on outside walls, and priceless Flemish tapestries in the interior. They experimented with crude forms of air-conditioning: In the home of William K. Vanderbilt, electric fans blew cool air off blocks of ice in the basement that circulated through indoor pipes.

The displays of wealth and pedigree were so ostentatious they sometimes bordered on self-parody. In 1924, for instance, the *New York Times* reported that a party for the Prince of Wales at Harbor Hill, a Roslyn Harbor estate, was attended by 1,200 guests, including people with such fanciful titles as the Duke and Duchess of Penaranda and the Marquis de Coquille.

And as if his 127-room château, Oheka, would not stand out enough, Kahn employed an army of laborers for 2 years to build a mountain on his estate: He wanted the castle to sit upon the highest point on Long Island. (Despite the Herculean effort, it doesn't.)

Many of the estates became the families' retreats during the spring and fall, part of an annual cycle of migration from one palatial abode to another. In the former home of John S. Phipps that is now called Old Westbury Gardens, visitors are provided as authentic a look at an English country house as the Guggenheims provided for the French. Phipps built the house after the turn of the century for his English wife, Margarita Grace, of the famous shipping family.

The house is grand and the gardens are grander. It is nearly impossible to believe that just beyond the walled garden of tulips and the trellises draped with wisteria and the tiny thatched English cottage—a gift from Phipps to his daughter, Peggy, on her 10th birthday—lies the Long Island Expressway. The houses, in fact, remain so peripheral to daily life on Long Island that many of its inhabitants barely know they are there. Orin Z. Finkle, an accountant who has long had an amateur's interest in architecture, has lived within a few miles of the estates since the 1950s. But it was not until the 1980s, when he was given a book, *The Mansions of Long Island's Gold Coast* (Rizzoli International Publications, 1987), that he realized the scope of the legacy that had been left.

"For three months, I kept that book on my night table and looked at it every night before I went to bed," he said. The book set Mr. Finkle on a mission to catalog the houses, and to collect old magazines and postcards from the early 1900s that mentioned the estates. Over the years, he, like Mr. Mateyunas, elevated house hunting to an art, befriending owners of many of the remaining estates, and even taking others on private tours of some of them.

"What struck me was their beauty; it was like looking at a painting or a work of art," Mr. Finkle said. "It was so different from what I knew. I had grown up in a typical development house in Carle Place. Every time I would go to one of the houses, I would feel so in awe."

It is that feeling that keeps Mr. Finkle going, the same feeling that has consumed Mr. Mateyunas. Most visitors may be able to leave the houses at the end of a tour, but these two never really do.

Mr. Mateyunas, in fact, even took a piece of one home with him: He bought a chandelier that once hung in the Mill Neck home of Alice Tully at an antiques store.

It now sits, in a box, in his den.

GOLD COAST ESSENTIALS

GETTING THERE

All of the mansions listed below are accessible by car from the Long Island Expressway, or by the **Long Island Rail Road** (☎ **718/217-5477**); taxis are available at the train station. During the summer, the Long Island Rail Road offers special package tours of the mansions that include all transportation and admission fees, as well as lunch. Tours are available July and August. Call for details.

VISITING THE MANSIONS

Here is a listing of mansions open to the public on the Gold Coast of Long Island that are mentioned above.

Chelsea Center, Rte. 25A, East Norwich (☎ **516/571-8550**). Open Wednesday through Friday noon to 4pm; closed Saturday, Sunday, major holidays, and for special events. Admission by donation.

Coe Hall (part of Planting Fields Arboretum State Historic Park), Planting Fields Rd. (at Chicken Valley Rd.), Oyster Bay (☎ **516/922-0479**). Open April through September, daily noon to 3:30pm; closed on major holidays. Admission and house tour $5, $3.50 for seniors, $1 for children 7 to 12, free for children under 7. Parking $5.

Coindre Hall, 101 Brown's Rd., Huntington (☎ **516/423-4369** or **516/423-7448**). Closed to the public; in use as a catering facility.

Falaise (the former Guggenheim estate), Sands Point Preserve, 95 Middleneck Rd., Sands Point (☎ **516/571-7900**). Call for hours and admission prices.

Frick Estate, Nassau County Museum of Art, Rte. 25A (west of Northern Blvd.), Roslyn Harbor (☎ **516/484-9337** or 516/484-9338). Open Tuesday through Sunday 11am to 5pm; closed major holidays. Admission $4, $3 for seniors, $2 for students, free for children 12 and under.

Old Westbury Gardens (the former Phipps Estate), 71 Old Westbury Rd., Old Westbury (☎ **516/333-0048**). Open from the last weekend in April to mid-December, Wednesday through Monday 10am to 5pm; closed Tuesday and Thanksgiving Day. For the gardens alone, admission is $8, $6 for seniors, $3 for children 6 to 12; admission to the house and gardens is $10, $8 for seniors, $6 for children 6 to 12; admission is free for children under 6 and members of Old Westbury Gardens.

Vanderbilt Mansion and Museum, 180 Little Neck Rd., Centerport (☎ **631/ 854-5579**). Open early May to early November, Tuesday through Sunday noon to 5pm; early November to early May, Tuesday through Friday noon to 4pm, Saturday and Sunday noon to 5pm.

Admission (including grounds, house tour, and exhibits) $8, $6 for students and seniors, $4 for children under 12; add $3 for sky show in the planetarium.

Wiley Hall (United States Merchant Marine Academy; former summer home of Walter P. Chrysler), at the foot of Steamboat Rd., Kings Point (☎ **516/773-5527**). Open daily 9am to 5pm; closed July and federal holidays. Admission is free.

FIRE ISLAND: FOR FAMILIES, TOO

by Ralph Blumenthal

IT'S A BAREFOOT SOCIETY, CAR-FREE and carefree, but as long as anyone can remember, Fire Island, the skinny sand spit stretched along the underside of Long Island, has had its distinctive hierarchy. At the top are the natives, flinty souls who live year-round on the 32-mile-long barrier island between the end of Robert Moses State Park and Moriches Inlet, where the Hamptons begin. The natives, it is said, look down on the home owners and other summer folk who seasonally throng the roughly two dozen communities. The home owners turn up their noses at the renters. The renters disdain the groupers who chip in for housing shares. And all feel superior to the day-trippers who sail in on the morning ferries and sail out again in the evening.

Which left us somewhere near the bottom—hotel guests on Fire Island. Yes, there are hotels on Fire Island. No, you wouldn't generally pick them over a house. But between a hotel and nothing, the choice was clear. For 5 days, my wife and I and our two girls sampled the many delights of New York's quasi–Key West with its own rich social and cultural history. We breathed the same fresh salt air and patronized the same restaurants and shops as any third-generation islander. We splashed in the same roiling surf, hunted for the same horseshoe crabs and shells on long stretches of deserted beach, strolled and bicycled the same few blocks between the bay and beach, and took the same water taxis to the same outlying communities. And we felt entirely welcome. Indeed, there is probably only one restrictive community, Point O'Woods, where outsiders, whether natives or off-islanders, might get the cold shoulder; but even here we carried out a beach-based incursion without incident.

Yet a word of caution. To book a hotel on Fire Island on a summer weekend is to cast one's fate not to the winds but the singles. A commune of wildly celebrating youth in a Fire Island group house can be noisy, but when the party is compressed into a thin-walled hotel room, the disruption can be truly hellish, as we found out on our last night in Ocean Bay Park. Still, some hotel managements are more lax than others. And Friday and Saturday nights are definitely wilder; weekdays can be positively idyllic.

The first thing many new visitors want to know is where the name Fire Island comes from. The truth is, nobody knows. Some have linked it to the signal fires of whalers or wreckers who tried to lure ships ashore for plunder, or to the one-time fiery stands of poison ivy. Others say it grew out of a misreading on early Dutch maps of *vier*, or four, islands. Either way, the name, accurately enough, evokes blissful summer vistas of burning sands and blazing sun, as well as the constant peril of fire.

Resort development began in the 1890s with the establishment of a Chautauqua Assembly, a movement for Christian betterment through learning and the arts, in what became Point O'Woods. In the early 1900s, just to the west, developers bought up tracts and began selling vacation lots to Brooklynites and other confined city folk for what became the village of Ocean Beach, Fire Island's de facto capital. Served by growing ferry links across Great South Bay, birds of a feather flocked to like-minded communities: boat owners to Saltaire, fishery workers to Seaview, casino lovers to Ocean Bay Park, families to Kismet. Homosexuals driven from other communities found a welcome in Cherry Grove, creating one of the earliest centers of gay life in the nation.

Stars of the Broadway stage, stalwarts of the Algonquin Round Table, artists, bohemians, and assorted hangers-on soon found their way to the quirky seasonal salons of Fire Island, where the politics were often decidedly leftist, and a Stalinist group house might well blackball an applicant rumored to be a Trotskyite. Irving Berlin, Fanny Brice, Clifford Odets, Truman Capote, Tennessee Williams, Jimmy Durante,

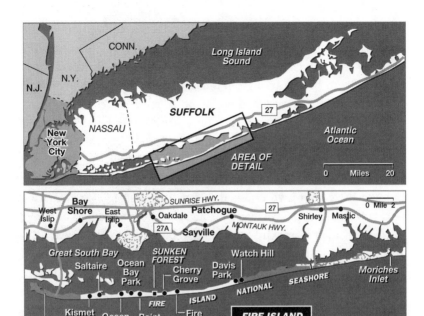

Woody Allen, Lee Strasberg, and Marilyn Monroe all made their way
there, as did Mel Brooks and Carl Reiner, who honed their "2,000-
Year-Old Man" routine on dinner audiences. And everyone mobilized
in the early 1960s to thwart Robert Moses's plan to build an access road
through Fire Island. (*Smile, You're on Fire Island,* a history of the island
with photographs by Arthur Hawkins, published by Photo News Long
Island of Bethpage, Long Island, is available for $19.95 at the Ocean
Beach Historical Society on Bayview Walk.)

My own memories of Fire Island go back to the 1940s when, as a
child, I stayed with friends in an Ocean Beach cottage lighted by
kerosene lamps. The icebox was indeed cooled by a block of ice, hauled
from the market in a red wagon. And the ferry passed a house still sunk
in the water from the devastating 1938 hurricane.

Amazingly, as I found again on our most recent trip, Fire Island has
changed little from those days except perhaps for the now-ubiquitous
deer that calmly feast on bushes and overturned trash bins as you pass.

The concrete walks (rustically wooden in some communities) are still lined with old, whimsically named cedar-shingled cottages hemmed in by pines and bayberry. The shops and restaurants prettily arrayed around Ocean Beach's minigreen might have changed names but little else. Feet, wagon, bicycle, and boat (golf carts and trucks for contractors and provisioners) are still the only means of transportation.

Reaching Fire Island from Manhattan is a kind of three- or four-corner shot requiring connections to and from the Long Island Rail Road or a jitney to the ferries at Bay Shore, Sayville, or Patchogue. You can also drive your own car, at the cost of daily charges in a parking field at the ferry dock. We reserved four seats at $17 each on a Tommy's Taxi van that left from 53rd Street and Second Avenue and delivered us an hour later to the Bay Shore ferry terminal, where $40 purchased round-trip ferry tickets (half price for our 5-year-old) to and from Ocean Beach.

I had reserved two kitchenette units for 2 weekday nights at a randomly selected hotel called Clegg's, which turned out to be directly across from the ferry dock (not that anything in Ocean Beach is more than a few steps from anything else). As we lugged our bags up a narrow staircase, I thought the place resembled an old sailor's rooming house. Indeed, we learned, it was built in the 1920s by the grandfather of the current proprietor.

Our units each came with two beds, private bathroom with shower, and a stove, sink, and refrigerator. The furnishings of table, captain chairs, chest of drawers, and makeshift closet were more Salvation Army than the Ritz, but clean if not immaculate. Apartment C faced the bay and overlooked tennis and basketball courts. A cool sea breeze from two exposures sent the blinds slapping, rendering the air conditioner superfluous. One of the bed blankets bore a cigarette burn hole (the owner, horrified, promptly threw it out). Apartment A, which our daughters shared, was even larger, but with one exposure. There were four other apartments with bathrooms, and 13 smaller rooms that shared four skylit bath and shower rooms.

Our youngish hosts, Tyler Clegg Sterck and his wife, Jeanne, threw in use of beach chairs and a sun umbrella and even two balloon-tire bicycles that could be ridden only outside Ocean Beach. (Bike riding within the village is banned in the summer season, one of many prohibitions that have earned the community a reputation as "The Land of No.") What the hotel did not provide at the time, however, was daily room cleaning. (The owner says he has since remedied this.)

Still, comparing our quarters later with other accommodations in Ocean Beach, we did not do badly. The Houser Hotel, another 1920s fixture on the bay, over a popular bar and Chinese restaurant, has a dozen small rooms with sinks and toilets but shared shower rooms in the hall. The Ocean Beach Inn on Bay Walk, its name notwithstanding, has 20 motel-style rooms with private bathrooms, also over a busy bar and restaurant.

We were taken with one little gem: the Four Seasons Bed and Breakfast on Dehnhoff Walk, a health-food–oriented lodge of eight rooms with gleaming polyurethaned wood floors, bright curtains, and plump inviting quilts on the beds. Here, too, however, the rooms are without private bathrooms, and there are no provisions for children. Otherwise, hospitality reigns: Rooms come with breakfast and a sumptuous afternoon tea, cold juice drinks for the taking, a patio stocked with magazines, and use of bicycles, fishing tackle, and a backyard gas barbecue.

Another darling guest house, Place in the Sun, on Surfview Walk halfway between bay and beach, also caught our eye. Open to non-smokers only, it has a large skylit living room paneled in knotty pine and five rooms with two shared bathrooms plus an outdoor shower and sauna.

Otherwise, it seemed, the pickings in Ocean Beach were slim: isolated rooms or the occasional rooming house with barracks-like accommodations and little privacy or little sanitation or neither.

When it comes to dining, Ocean Beach offers the widest selection on Fire Island. We had a pleasant alfresco lunch at Maguires on the bay, where the time waiting for your food can be whiled away with your children at the adjacent community playground and sandpit. Our younger daughter, Sophie, made the swings and climbing apparatus her favorite Fire Island destination.

We had another fine waterside seafood dinner at Matthew's on the bay, and a pleasant dinner celebrating the 17th birthday of our elder daughter, Anna, at the Island Mermaid by the ferry dock, where the setting sun, reflecting blindingly in the restaurant mirrors, kept us rearranging our seats like musical chairs.

We also enjoyed the Albatross, with its patio tables affording a lovely view of the passing scene in the village center, and the funky Sun and Moon Cafe across the mall. For breakfast, we favored Rachel's, a few steps away, a clean, well-lighted place of knotty pine hung with photographs of Fire Island in the snow. One morning, Sophie stared toward the back and proudly read aloud, "Birthday room, parties only." I did a double take. What the sign said was BATHROOM, PATRONS ONLY.

What you don't want to do in Ocean Beach is eat takeout with a knife and fork on the walks, another no-no, along with drinking anything at all on the walks. Because of the strict ban on consuming alcoholic beverages outside homes, bars, and restaurants, drinking from open containers, even a soda can or pop bottle, is suspect, a ticketable offense likely to land you in village court in front of a decidedly unsympathetic judge.

A sign of the times hangs at the bay bathing beach adjoining the playground: NO FACILITIES PROVIDED. NO SWIMMING BEYOND FLOATS. NO FOOD OR DRINKS. NO DOGS ALLOWED. NO DISROBING. NO RADIOS WITHOUT EARPHONES. NO BALL PLAYING OR FRISBEES. Actually, veterans like Ildiko Trien, executive editor of *The Fire Island News,* the scrappy local paper, say that things have relaxed significantly from the days when Ocean Beach was notorious for ticketing visitors so bold as to eat a chocolate-chip cookie in public.

For a change of scene one afternoon, we left the girls behind and telephoned South Bay Water Taxi for a 20-minute wave-tossed ride east to Fire Island Pines, a chic community where straight and gay society intersect and Elizabeth Taylor and Richard Burton, Hedy Lamarr, Barbra Streisand, Montgomery Clift, Marlene Dietrich, and Rock Hudson have been among the many celebrity visitors. A sign by the dock advised: GROUP THERAPY 5PM. EVERYONE MUST ATTEND.

The blue-and-turquoise–balconied Botel overlooks the Italianate harbor, but except for top-floor suites that sleep four, rooms share bathrooms and offer little in the way of amenities. We meandered the wooden walkways, ogling some extraordinary mansions, and sipped banana daiquiris on the terrace of the Botel's Blue Whale, where the menu lists a "Hedda Cheddar Burger," a "Le Fifi Burger," and a "Midnight Blue Burger." Next door, the Pines Pantry is amazingly well provisioned, stocking necessities from margarita salt to live or fresh-cooked lobsters.

We had hoped to stop at another Fire Island landmark on the way back, the Belvedere in Cherry Grove, but the water taxi was over-booked and it became too late. As it turned out, we probably would have been denied entry anyway. The "clothing optional" resort for gay men says it does not admit sightseers. I had to content myself with a description from *The Fire Island News:* a cross between "a Venetian villa overlooking the Grand Canal and the faux decoration of a Disneyland castle." Inspired by the Miami mansion Viscaya, the Belvedere is owned by John Eberhardt of the pencil dynasty, and is far and away the most luxurious hostelry on Fire Island. Clearly, though, it is not for everyone.

After several days in Ocean Beach, we were ready for the 5-minute water-taxi trip two communities east to Ocean Bay Park. We had booked rooms for 2 nights at the Fire Island Hotel and Resort, which includes time-sharing units and boasts an island rarity, a good-size pool.

Unfortunately, our room faced it, along with loudspeakers blaring oldies. The place was also a little run-down. After a refreshing swim (and to get away from the music), we walked a block to the bay to lunch at the cavernous Flynn's, another Fire Island fixture, which becomes a raucous singles rendezvous at night. We found a place to rent bicycles for $14 each a day at the nearby Schooner Inn, another bayfront restaurant and bar next to a small pizza parlor. Debbie, my wife, settled on a three-wheeler with a rear basket that served as rumble seat for Sophie, and we rode off to explore adjacent Seaview to the west, a community of handsome homes, playgrounds, groceries, and liquor shops.

Later, on foot we headed the other way toward Point O'Woods. A fence restricts access, but we circumvented the ban by entering on foot from the beach. Despite the vaunted exclusivity, it didn't look much different from other communities, perhaps just a little more overgrown and defiantly natural. No one challenged us, and we strolled back to the beach. We walked most of the 2 miles or so east along the surf to the Sunken Forest, a national park of wind-pruned 200-year-old holly and sassafras trees, but before we could make it to the raised wooden walkway into the canopied forest, Sophie's legs wore out and we turned back.

Back in Ocean Bay Park, we had some good meals at the Inn Between, an informal restaurant on the bay walk between Flynn's and the Schooner Inn. And for future reference, we scouted the nearby Sea Shore Motel with 20 simple rooms, including six efficiency units that might appeal, if not to the luxury-minded, to singles, young couples, or families bent on a few economical days on Fire Island.

Our first night in the Fire Island Hotel and Resort passed quietly, at least after we prevailed on the management to turn off the loud-speakers, but on the second night the weekend brought an end to our idyll. At 2am that Saturday, we were jolted awake by a fearful shrieking from across the hall. Our neighbors, four young women, were evidently home from Flynn's with some male company. Slamming doors, hyster-ical laughter, and curses filled the night. Sure that the row would wake our daughters, I rapped on the opposite door and appealed for quiet, to no avail. Finally, two other roused guests and I went to find the manager.

The office was locked. A handwritten sign on the door read: FOR AFTER-HOURS HELP, COME TO SECOND HOUSE ON RIGHT (BRIGHT BULB ON TOP OF ENTRANCE STEPS). KNOCK LOUDLY OR ENTER AND CALL FOR HELP. We sleepless caucused. There was no clear second house on the right with or without a bright bulb. At 3am, I went to the phone booth outside the hotel and dialed 911.

Twenty minutes later, two Suffolk County foot patrolmen and a jeep unit arrived. I led the officers to the din and went back to our room. From behind the closed door, we could hear arguing, a girl shouting for an officer to get his foot out of the door, and someone screaming that the police had no warrant. I put the pillow over my head. Slowly the fracas subsided.

Sophie and Anna, of course, slept through it. In the morning, Sophie's enthusiasm was undimmed. "After eight more grades," she asked, "can we move to Fire Island?"

FIRE ISLAND ESSENTIALS

GETTING THERE

GETTING TO THE FERRIES

By Car   To reach the Fire Island ferries in Bay Shore, Sayville, and Patchogue, Long Island, by car from Manhattan, take the Long Island Expressway to exit 53 (Bay Shore), exit 59 (Sayville), or exit 63 (Patchogue).

By Train   The **Long Island Rail Road** (☎ **718/217-5477** or 516/822-5477) provides daily service from Penn Station to the three towns; one-way fares range from $6.50 to $7.25 on off-peak trains, $9.50 to $10.75 for peak-hour trains; children 5 to 11 pay 50¢ during off-peak hours, half of the adult fare during peak hours; children under 5 ride free at all times. The ferry terminal at Patchogue is within walking distance of the railroad station, and the ferries at Bay Shore and Sayville are a short taxi ride away.

In summer, the railroad also offers excursions to the Sunken Forest and Watch Hill beaches and to Robert Moses State Park on Fire Island; these include a round-trip train ride and the ferry (or bus ride to Robert Moses State Park). The excursions are offered weekends from Memorial Day through the end of June and then daily through Labor Day.

FERRIES

Fire Island Ferries, off Montauk Hwy., Main St., Bay Shore (☎ **631/666-3600** or 631/665-3600). Operates year-round to Ocean Beach, Fair Harbor, Dunewood, Atlantique, Kismet, Saltaire, Ocean Bay Park, and Seaview. From late June to early September, ferries leave every 60 to 90 minutes for the 25-minute ride daily for a total of 18 to 19 trips; Monday through Thursday and Sunday from 7am to 11pm (until midnight Friday and 1am Saturday); from early September to mid-October, a reduced schedule begins at 7am, with 9 trips Monday through Thursday and 13 to 14 trips Sunday; from mid-October to late December, 2 to 4 trips a day begin running at 7:30am; from December 24 to February 28, weather permitting, there are 2 trips Monday through Friday and Sunday, and 3 on Saturday. From March 1 to mid-May, 3 to 8 trips daily (with the greater number in late spring) from 7am; from mid-May through late June, there are 7 trips Monday through Thursday and 15 to 16 Friday through Sunday, beginning 7am Friday and Saturday and 8am Sunday and running until 9pm. Monday through Thursday, 11:30pm Friday, 1am Saturday and 10pm Sunday. The fare is $11.50 round-trip, $6 one-way; $5.50 round-trip for children 2 to 12 and for dogs. Reservations not necessary. Parking $10 per day Friday through Sunday, $6 per day Monday through Thursday, or $45 weekly; free parking in winter.

Patchogue Ferries (☎ 631/475-1665). Operates ferries to Davis Park and Watch Hill in the National Seashore park from two ferry terminals in Patchogue: at County Road 19 for Watch Hill (from May through Nov), and Brightwood Street for Davis Park (from Mar through Nov). Ferries leave Patchogue Monday through Thursday 6:20am to 10:30pm, Friday 6:20am to 12:30am, Saturday 7:30am to 1am, Sunday 7:30am to 9:15pm. Fares $5.50 one-way, $10 same-day round-trip; $3.25 one-way for children 2 to 11, $5.50 same-day round-trip; $3.25 round-trip for dogs. Ferries leave every 60 to 90 minutes for the 20- to 25-minute ride. Free parking at Watch Hill ferry for all; parking at the Davis Park Ferry is free for residents of Brookhaven and $15 per day for nonresidents.

Sayville Ferry Service, 41 River Rd. (☎ 631/589-0810). Operates ferries to Cherry Grove and Fire Island Pines year-round, and to Sunken Forest and Water Island from May through October. Mid-May through early September, ferries leave every hour on the half hour for the 20- to 25-minute ride, beginning Tuesday through Friday at 7am, Saturday and Sunday at 8am, Monday at 5:30am. Early-September to October, Monday to Thursday, five boats daily; Friday to Sunday, eight boats daily. October through mid-December, three to six boats run daily; mid-December through mid-March, service on weekends only; daily service starts again in mid-March, with two to four boats beginning at 9am. The fare is $11 round-trip, $6 one-way; $5 round-trip or $2.75 one-way for children under 12; $3 round-trip or $1.75 one-way for dogs. Fare to Sunken Forest $9, $5 for children under 11. Parking $7 daily.

VIA LAND & WATER TAXI

David's Taxi (☎ 516/665-4384 or 516/665-0191). Operates from May through November, weather permitting, between the Bay Shore Ferries (see "Ferries," above) and 68th St. and Third Ave. in Manhattan. Taxis depart Monday through Thursday every 2 hours 9am to 8:30pm, Friday hourly 9:15am to 10:15pm, Saturday hourly 8:15am to 9:30pm, Sunday hourly 8:15am to 7pm. One-way fare is $17 Monday through Saturday, $20 Sunday.

South Bay Water Taxi (☎ 631/665-8885). Operates cross-bay year-round, weather permitting; also between Fire Island communities. Call for rates.

Tommy's Taxi, 88 Park Ave., Bay Shore (☎ 516/665-4800). Operates from April through the end of October between Manhattan and the Bay Shore Ferry. In season departures from Second Ave. and 14th St., Second Ave. and 53rd St., Third Ave. and 81st St., in Manhattan daily 8am to 10pm. One-way fare is $17 Monday through Saturday, $20 Sunday and holidays.

ACCOMMODATIONS

The Belvedere, Bayview Walk, Cherry Grove (☎ 631/597-6448). Open May to October 1. Weekdays $80 to $150; weekends $150 to $250, weekend 2-night packages $300 to $500.

Clegg's Hotel, 478 Bayberry Walk, Ocean Beach (☎ **631/583-5399**). Open May through October 1. Daily rates based on double occupancy, with shared bathroom: Sunday $105, Monday through Thursday $85. There is a $270 weekend package for a Friday- and Saturday-night stay. Children welcome; those under 10 stay free. Studio apartments also available for $160 to $185 Sunday; $145 to $165 Monday through Thursday; and $380 to $420 for a 2-night stay on Friday and Saturday. Two-night minimum on weekends; 3-night stay on holidays. Weekly rates also available. No smoking allowed.

Fire Island Hotel and Resort, 25 Cayuga Walk, Ocean Bay Park (☎ **631/583-8000**). Open end of May to early October. Sunday through Thursday $109 to $205, Friday and Saturday $160 to $650.

Fire Island Pines Botel, Harbor Walk, Fire Island Pines (☎ **631/597-6500**). Call for rates.

Houser Hotel, Great South Bay on East Bay Walk, Ocean Beach (☎ **631/583-8900**). Open May through September. Weekends $75 per person, weekdays $50 per person.

Place in the Sun, 987 Surfview Walk, Ocean Beach (☎ **631/583-5716**). Open May through mid-September. Call for rates.

Sea Shore Motel, Bayview Walk, Ocean Bay Park (☎ **631/583-5860**). Open April to mid-September. Call for rates.

The Seasons Bed and Breakfast, 468 Dehnhoff Walk, Ocean Beach (☎ **631/583-8295**). Open April through October. Call for rates.

DINING

Albatross, 320 Bay Walk, Ocean Beach (☎ **631/583-5697**). Open mid-March to early October.

Flynn's, 1 Cayuga Walk, Ocean Bay Park (☎ **631/583-5000**). Open mid-May to mid-September.

The Inn Between, at Oneida St. and Bay View Ave., Ocean Bay Park (☎ **631/583-0111**). Open May 15 to early October.

Island Mermaid, Bay Walk, Ocean Beach (☎ **631/583-8088**). Open April 15 to early October.

Maguires, Bay Walk and Bungalow Walk, Ocean Beach (☎ **631/583-8800**). Open late April to mid-October.

Matthew's Seafood House, on the bay, Ocean Beach (☎ **631/583-8016**). Open mid-May to mid-September.

Rachel's, 325 Bay Walk, Ocean Beach (☎ **631/583-5953**). Open April through September.

Schooner Inn, 57 Bay Walk, Ocean Bay Park (☎ **631/583-9561**). Open mid-May to mid-September.

Sun and Moon Cafe, 310 Bay Walk, Ocean Beach (☎ **631/583-8300**). Open March through October.

ATTRACTIONS

FIRE ISLAND NATIONAL SEASHORE

Sunken Forest, Sailors Haven (☎ **631/597-6183** for park information, 631/589-8980 for ferry information). A National Park Service site with beach, picnicking, nature walks, and a marina. Open mid-May through mid-October. Grounds are open daily around the clock for boaters. Admission is free.

Watch Hill (☎ **631/597-6455** for park information, 631/475-1636 for ferry information). A National Park Service site, with camping, a restaurant, and a general store open mid-May through mid-October.

Grounds are open daily around the clock for campers and boaters. Admission is free. Call for camping fees.

HISTORICAL SOCIETY

Ocean Beach Historical Society, Bayview and Cottage walks, Ocean Beach (☎ **631/583-8972**). Changing exhibitions every season. Call for hours.

THE HAMPTONS (AFTER THE CROWDS HAVE GONE HOME)

by George Vecsey

IT'S SAFE NOW. IT'S SAFE TO GO BACK to eastern Long Island.

I am not referring to the dangerous fire that swept through 5,500 acres of pine barrens near Westhampton in the late summer of 1995, casting a smoky pall over the very name "Long Island." When I say it's "safe," I am referring to the peace and quiet that falls over the land after Labor Day. The Hollywood biggies and politicians and doctors and writers and lawyers and junk-bond specialists who clog the narrow highways with their sports cars and four-wheel drives have now returned to the city to make more mischief and earn more money.

That means you can hear the ocean again. Not only that, but at this time of year you can also catch a glimpse of a few surviving acres of cornfields, pumpkin patches, vineyards, and rolling dunes. You can pick apples, take a walk on the beach, or sail or play golf or tennis. You can go fishing at the peak of the striped-bass season without running into somebody you recognize or overhearing any New York gossip. Or you can go indoors to the museums and art galleries and occasional movies and live entertainment of the fall season.

Oh, weekends are still a bit frenzied in a few corners—most New Yorkers wouldn't want it any other way—but in general, eastern Long Island could almost be called bucolic.

"This is really the best time of the year out here," said George R. Eldi, the manager of the Seafood Barge in Southold, on the North (or non-Hampton) Fork of Long Island. "The weather is great for fishing and sailing right through October, and really through Christmas. Then people go to Florida or stay in Manhattan in their winter homes." The wonderful secret of eastern Long Island is that because it is surrounded by saltwater, it is often a few degrees warmer than the city, with less snowfall.

You can even avoid the stereotypical Hamptons visit because there are two forks to Long Island. I was traumatized by the South Fork years ago when I was a correspondent on Long Island. The low point of that hitch might have been getting stuck in a hideous summer weekend traffic jam to cover a Hamptons fund-raiser for a presidential campaign by Lloyd Bentsen.

Ever since, I have avoided eastern Long Island from Memorial Day to Labor Day. I have this recurring nightmare of being hungry and having headwaiters turn me away with the chilling words, "Sorry, pal, the Spielberg party needs the table." In the fall, however, I always love to return to the diners and the farm stands and the IGA grocery stores. It's almost real country.

Recently, my wife and I needed a few hours of peace and quiet, and we braved the Long Island Expressway, with its tailgating trucks and careening vans, but somewhere around Yaphank (love that name) it all calmed down. We headed east along Sunrise Highway, noticing the burned-out acres in Westhampton, merely a blotch on the landscape now thanks to the brave people who put out the fire. We crossed the bridge over the Shinnecock Canal, a modest waterway that always gives me a tiny shiver of adventure, like crossing a frontier from France into Spain.

We took a glance at the civilized pleasures of Southampton village, near the Parrish Art Museum, and we made a detour through the old mansions behind thick hedges. (When I was in college in 1959, I once found myself wading next to Sen. John F. Kennedy of Massachusetts in the surf at Southampton Town Beach. I always think of that when I drive through: a lanky young man in sunglasses, in saltwater up to his hips, the whole world in front of him.) There are plenty of trendy restaurants in Southampton, but I gravitated to the Southampton

Princess Diner on Montauk Highway for bluefish, moist and plump and not at all oily, a few hours out of the waters off Montauk. Bill Paul said his co-owner and chef, Steve Kalagoras, cooks with a dash of *koutourou*, which is Greek for "a little of this, a little of that."

Well fortified, I now needed closer contact with the ocean that had contributed that lovely bluefish. We took a leisurely drive through the main drags of Water Mill and Bridgehampton. (I once had the pleasure of visiting a military man named Powell who was staying at a summer house near here. I often wonder what became of him.) After admiring the harvested fields of Sagaponack, we kept going east past the movie theater, upscale bookshops, ice-cream emporiums, and art galleries of East Hampton, which were gearing up for the annual Hamptons International Film Festival.

But we were not looking for Columbus Avenue East. We wanted a beach. We kept driving until we reached Hither Hills State Park, jammed during the season with campers and day-trippers, but on a lovely fall afternoon it was deserted. Not even a parking fee.

We parked a few feet from the beach, spotting one couple a few hundred feet away. I took off my shoes (a regular J. Alfred Prufrock) and dared to walk along the beach barefooted. There was a man with an NYFD ball cap sitting by his surf-casting pole, smoking a Viceroy, drinking a Budweiser. He had caught a striper the night before, he said, but now the waters were roiling because of a hurricane far out at sea.

"Best time of the year for fishing," he said. He swigged his Bud. He was ahead of the game.

My wife and I found a deserted corner—in fact, a deserted mile—of beach. We lay down in the sun and fell asleep. For an hour. Worth the drive. If it gets nippy later in the fall, you'll just have to walk briskly.

Refreshed, we drove all the way to the tip of Long Island, past rolling hills and guest cottages and neat little hotels. Judging from the VACANCY signs, there is room at the inn. At Montauk Point, tourists were traipsing into the lighthouse for a $4 fee, but we made the necessary U-turn—otherwise, you get very wet—and headed for Montauk Harbor. There we saw sailboats and commercial fishing boats and ferries and cruise boats. Back on Montauk Highway, we stopped on the hill in Napeague where you can pull off on a scenic overlook and gaze down at the ocean and Napeague Bay. In a heated car, it's probably gorgeous all winter long.

From there we drove west and cut north along Route 114, through backwoods that still look like backwoods, toward Sag Harbor, the old whaling village. We strolled along the dock, noticing signs that cultural life goes on all winter. We walked down the main street, which was sweet and quiet at the end of a working day. We half expected to see John Steinbeck and his dog, Charley. Or maybe Steve Martin and Daryl Hannah in the movie *Roxanne*. At dusk, we took an end table on the porch at the American Hotel, which would be totally impossible during the 3 summer months. The waiters had time to give us personal attention. We were already feeling like locals.

"It's a madhouse during the season," one waiter cautioned us. "And you still need reservations on weekends in the fall." That was the end of our South Fork day trip. We didn't have time to take a ferry over to Shelter Island, pretty but mostly private, also reachable by ferry from Greenport on the North Fork.

A few days later we returned to eastern Long Island. Our second day trip was to the North Fork, straight out to Southold, where we had a pleasant lunch by the window of the Seafood Barge, with a great view of Peconic Bay. We did not order from the handsome wine list, but Mr. Eldi, the manager, told us: "The dry summer was good for the grapes out here. If it's too rainy, they are too watery." We would inspect those grapes firsthand. After lunch, we meandered back west a few miles, toward the dozens of wineries that have been developed in the past generation. The operators of the Pellegrini Vineyards in Cutchogue brag of their 30 acres of grapevines that "with climate and annual rainfall paralleling that of Bordeaux, we are graced with a 220-day growing season." We were attracted by the wooden cloister-style building with a tower above the salesroom. After a dozen samples, graciously offered, we bought a number of bottles.

Next we headed to the wide-open farmland north of Riverhead, great just for light and space. We happened to drive past Briermere Farms at 4414 Sound Ave., whose bakery sells flaky, buttery, fruity homemade pies (not inexpensively, either).

We could have gone apple and pumpkin picking at half a dozen farms on the North Fork, but I had another beach in mind: Wildwood State Park, between Wading River and Baiting Hollow. My family used to camp there in the late 1950s. It looks exactly the same today: wooded sites in the hills, one rustic "roundhouse" (I hope they still don't have hot water in the showers; I wouldn't want to have suffered in vain), and a narrow path leading down to the beach on Long Island Sound.

The day we went, the peaceful waters were still warm enough for swimming in the 70° sun. I counted four people on the beach. We sat on the boardwalk and ate an apple turnover from Briermere Farms. The Spielberg party never showed.

Hamptons Essentials

GETTING THERE

By Car Take the Long Island Expressway (I-495) to exit 70 (Rte.111 South), then follow Rte. 27 East into the Hamptons.

By Train The **Long Island Rail Road** (☎ 718/217-5477 or 516/822-5477) provides daily service from Penn Station to the Hamptons; call for timetable and for information.

By Bus The **Hampton Jitney** (☎ 800/936-0440) provides service to the Hamptons year-round. The 2- to 3-hour trip costs $24 one-way or $43 round-trip. All of the pickups are along the east side of Manhattan, with drop-offs on both the east and west sides. Discounts for students and seniors. Reservations necessary.

ACCOMMODATIONS

American Hotel, Main St., Sag Harbor (☎ **631/725-3535**). May to Columbus Day. Weekdays $195, weekends $285, all with continental breakfast. Two-night minimum on weekends (3 nights in July and Aug). Dining room open for lunch Saturday and Sunday noon to 4pm, for dinner daily 5 to 10pm, until 11 Friday and Saturday.

Montauk Motel, 76 S. Edison St., Montauk (☎ **631/668-2704**). Most units are efficiencies with kitchenettes. September 15 through November 15, $85 weekdays, $95 weekends. Mid-November through mid-May, $75 weekdays, $85 weekends. Memorial Day through mid-September, $100 weekdays, $125 weekends. Also cottages, $175 weekdays, $200 weekends; off-season, $125. Two-night minimum in August and on holiday weekends.

DINING

Also see the American Hotel under "Accommodations," above.

Seafood Barge, 150 Old Main Rd., Southold (☎ **631/765-3010**). Open June through Labor Day, Sunday through Thursday noon to 9pm, and Friday and Saturday noon to 10pm; mid-September through Memorial Day, Monday through Thursday noon to 2:30pm and 5 to 8pm, Friday noon to 2:30pm and 5 to 9pm, Saturday noon to 10pm, Sunday noon to 8pm; November through mid-May, weekends only.

Southampton Princess Diner, 32 Montauk Hwy. (☎ **631/283-4255**). Open Sunday through Thursday 6am to midnight, Friday and Saturday 6am to 1am. Complete dinners $12.95 to $15.95.

ART MUSEUMS & GALLERIES

Arlene Bujese Gallery, 66 Newtown Lane, East Hampton (☎ **631/324-2823**). Open year-round; November through March, weekends only.

Guild Hall, 158 Main St., East Hampton (☎ **631/324-0806**). A museum and cultural center with art exhibitions and festivals, educational programs, theatrical productions, discussions with writers, and special events offered year-round. Open Memorial Day through Labor Day, Monday through Saturday 11am to 5pm, Sunday noon to 5pm; Labor Day through Memorial Day, Wednesday through Saturday 11am to 5pm and Sunday noon to 5pm. Suggested admission $3 (free for members). Theater tickets $8 to $40.

Lizan–Tops Gallery, 66 Newtown Lane, East Hampton (☎ **631/324-3424**). Open year-round, Thursday through Monday 11am to 5pm.

Parrish Art Museum, 25 Jobs Lane, Southampton (☎ **631/283-2118**). The museum has a year-round program with exhibitions, concerts, lectures, and children's programs. Open Monday, Thursday, Friday, and Saturday 11am to 5pm, and Sunday 1 to 5pm. After Labor Day through Memorial Day, closed Tuesday and Wednesday. Suggested admission $3, $1 for seniors, free for children and students.

Vered Gallery, 68 Park Place Passage, East Hampton (☎ **631/324-3303**). Call for hours.

WINERIES

Open hours at wineries change with the season; call before you go.

Bedell Cellars, Rte. 25, Cutchogue (☎ 631/734-7537).

Hargrave Vineyard, Rte. 48, Cutchogue (☎ 631/734-5158).

Lenz Winery. Rte. 25, Peconic (☎ 631/734-6010).

Palmer Vineyards, 108 Sound Ave., Aquebogue (☎ 631/722-9463).

Pellegrini Vineyards, Rte. 25, Cutchogue (☎ 631/734-4111).

Pindar Vineyards, Rte. 25, Peconic (☎ 631/734-6200).

Wolff Estate, 139 Sagg Rd., Sagaponack (☎ 631/537-5106).

OTHER ATTRACTIONS

Bay Street Theater, Bay and Main sts., Sag Harbor (☎ 631/725-9500). Offers a weekend series of play readings, concerts, and cabaret performances in the spring and fall, and a daily summer season of four plays from May 21 through Labor Day. There are also annual benefits and other events. Tickets range from $28 to $42. Call for current schedule.

Briermere Farms, 4414 Sound Ave., Riverhead (☎ 631/722-3931). Open May through September, daily 8am to 6pm (to 5pm rest of year). Pies $11 to $21.

East Hampton Marine Museum, Bluff Rd., Amagansett (☎ 631/324-6850). One of six sites operated by the East Hampton Historical Society. The museum has an ongoing exhibition, "350 Years of In-Shore Fishing." Open spring and fall, weekends 10am to 5pm; summer, daily 10am to 5pm; and by appointment. Admission $4 adults, $2 seniors, $2 for children under 16.

Hither Hills State Park, Old Montauk Hwy., Montauk (☎ 631/668-2554; 800/456-2267 for camping reservations). Open year-round, daily from sunrise to sunset; camping allowed mid-April through mid-November. Memorial Day through Labor Day, daily parking fee $5, camping fee $16.

Montauk Point Lighthouse Museum, Montauk State Park, 2000 Montauk Hwy., Montauk Point (☎ 631/668-2544). Closed early December to early May except for special weekends and daily during school breaks. Hours for museum and tower: May 14 to June 17, daily 10:30am to 5pm; Memorial Day weekend, Saturday and Sunday 10:30am to 7:30pm, Monday 10:30am to 5pm; June 18 to July 1, daily 10:30am to 6pm; July 2 to August 31, daily 10:30am to 6pm (until 7:30pm Sat); Labor Day weekend, Saturday and Sunday 10:30am to 7:30pm, Monday 10:30am to 6pm; September 4 through October 8, weekdays 10:30am to 4:30pm, weekends 10:30am to 5pm; October 12 through October 29, weekdays 10:30am to 4:30pm, weekends 10:30am to 5pm; November 3 through 25, weekends, and special holidays 10:30am to 4:30pm; Thanksgiving weekend 10:30am to 4:30pm; and by appointment. Admission $4 adults, $3.50 seniors, $2.50 children 6 to 12, free for children from 41 inches to 12 years old. To climb the tower, you must be at least 41 inches tall.

Riverhead Foundation for Marine Research and Preservation and Atlantis Marine World, 431 E. Main St., Riverhead

(☎ **631/369-9840** or 631-208-9200). Featuring a rescue Center where viewers can observe the rehabilitation of seals, sea turtles, and other sea creatures, and an aquarium that opened in June 2000. Open spring through Labor Day, daily 9am to 8pm; rest of year until 6pm. Admission $11.50, $10 for seniors, $9 for children 3 to 11.

Suffolk County Farm and Education Center, part of Cornell Cooperative Extension, Yaphank Ave., Yaphank (☎ **631/ 852-4607**). A working farm with work-shops and seasonal festivals. Open April through December, daily 9am to 3pm. Pumpkin festival in October. Donations accepted.

Wildwood State Park, Hulse Landing Rd. (off Sound Ave.), Rte. 25A, Wading River (☎ **631/929-4314;** 800/456-2267 for camping reservations). Open year-round, daily from dawn to dusk; camping allowed from the first weekend in April until Columbus Day. No parking fees mid-September through mid-May; parking $5 to $7 from Memorial Day through Labor Day; $5 for weekends from Labor Day through Columbus Day.

BICYCLING FROM MANHATTAN TO MONTAUK

by Bruce Weber

A ROUTINE PLEASURE OF BICYCLING is possession of the land; you ride a mile, you feel you own it. So why would anyone want to pedal from Manhattan to Montauk? There is, after all, more accommodating and cheery real estate available to the acquisitive cyclist than Long Island, at least that portion of it between the East River and the South Fork, a stretch that many New Yorkers are familiar with only through strategy sessions aimed at devising the quickest, most painless traverses—via motorized transport, of course—on Friday and Sunday evenings.

However, as a cyclist who has made big chunks of the trip a dozen times in the last few years of renting a summer house near the beach—and now the whole thing—I can report that the journey is a worthwhile enterprise. The route has its pitfalls, yes. Long Island isn't exactly Paumonok anymore, the Indians' beach-rimmed woodland in the shape of a fish, and I don't think residents of Nassau County or even western Suffolk should be surprised or offended to learn that for the cyclist, their home terrain is no velodrome.

At more than a century (cycle-ese for a 100-mile ride), it's not a wise endeavor for the physically unprepared. But in many ways, the length of Long Island is the perfect bike ride. The path between skyline and lighthouse is a day's journey, grueling but doable, its end points compelling, even romantic demarcations, symbolically worthy as destinations. The landscape is various enough, defining a historical regression of sorts, from industry to agriculture. (Or a progression, if you're

65

going east to west.) There are plenty of places along the way to refuel the body or repair the bike, and there are hardly any hills. As for the traffic, the malls, the unpleasant un-bucolicism of much of the trip, well, cyclists have been known to be attracted to the challenge of conquering territory as well as to the reward of possessing it.

Everyone more or less knows how to get to Montauk from Manhattan. You take the Long Island Rail Road or the Long Island Expressway. The distance, as the crow flies, is about 125 miles, according to a Rand McNally road map, 3 hours or so by car or rail. And, indeed, it is a function of how provincial New Yorkers are that over the years, in maybe 20 different conversations, otherwise intelligent people, learning that I'd made this trip, have said to me something like: "I didn't know they allowed bikes on the Long Island Expressway," as if it were impossible to actually get anywhere on other roads that might exist. Or else unthinkable that anyone might want to take them.

For my latest two-wheeled journey, I began in Greenwich Village and followed a not-so-straight-as-a-string route: along the northern perimeter of the island and then, instead of crossing diagonally through Riverhead, at the island's east-end crotch, to reach the South Fork, angling slightly out of the way to trace the North Fork, veering south and across Shelter Island before taking on the final eastward leg. The total distance was 137 miles, according to my odometer, and that seems about right—though truth be told it was a new one and I never did quite trust it. I left my apartment shortly after 5am (there is no better biking in America than on Third Avenue at dawn); some friends met me at the Montauk Lighthouse (thank goodness) just before 8pm. That's slow, I grant you. But I won't apologize. I believe that when tired, you should rest.

Over the 59th Street Bridge

You probably don't think of the 59th Street Bridge as a particularly romantic spot, but as a place to experience the sun coming up, it's pretty great. Pedaling over the open-grated pedestrian path on the lower level, you get a real sense of urbanity meeting nature. There's a good view south, the East River proceeding at its stately pace, dividing

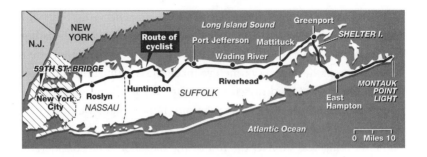

Manhattan from Brooklyn and Queens almost haughtily, as if it were actually still running through the wilderness. And ahead of you, from somewhere beyond the city, the sun is coming up, setting the dense air alight and glinting off the cinders in it.

The bridge spills you into what is ordinarily one of the most traffic-congested road nests in the city. But at this hour you actually have it to yourself, more or less, and negotiating your way onto Northern Boulevard for the first lengthy leg of the ride is easy, even pleasant.

Are city streets cleaner at dawn? Probably not, but the shardlike threats to bicycle tires are not so seemingly everywhere, perhaps because everything seems a little more spread out. There's space on the street, a feeling of vacancy, room to move. The sensation is as close as I've ever had to replicating the great daydream about a New York City emptied of people. And Northern Boulevard, which at midday is as undistinguished a main thoroughfare as any in the city, seems capacious.

It's 7 miles or so before you make a jog around Shea Stadium and through College Point, but after you join Northern Boulevard again you could stay on it, if you wanted to, for 100 miles (it turns into State Route 25A), all the way to Greenport. Of course, you wouldn't want to, mainly because all the way out there's the threat of congestion. It's peculiar that the most populous stretch of the boulevard's length is also the only one pleasant enough to ride, for an hour or two anyway.

Thirteen or so miles out, there's a brief but steep upward pitch, which heralds the Nassau County line. That's the good news. The bad news is that then you're in Nassau County. And by that time it's just about rush hour.

The passage through Great Neck and Roslyn is nerve-racking, with the worst stretch over the Roslyn Viaduct crossing Hempstead Harbor. There's a way to get on the pedestrian path, I assume, because there is a pedestrian path, but every time I've made the trip, hurtling downhill, I've missed it and found myself pedaling madly to get beyond the 200 or so yards of narrow roadway that has no shoulder at all but does have four lanes of rushing traffic.

Presuming you survive, the rest of the day should be considerably more relaxing.

For many New York City residents (most, I suspect), the geography of Long Island is a complete puzzle. The names of the towns are familiar from local news reports; there's even a weird music to them, like the words to a rhythmic, regional folk song: Syosset and Speonk . . . Yaphank and Wyandanch . . . Patchogue . . . Setauket . . . Ronkonkoma . . . Quogue. But who really knows what these places are like or even where they are? Oyster Bay. North shore or south? How about Lindenhurst? See what I mean?

Bicycling solves this problem.

I now know, for example, that beyond Roslyn, Northern Boulevard becomes the Hempstead Turnpike, which divides Syosset from its northern neighbor (answer to quiz), Oyster Bay, before crossing the Suffolk County line and entering Huntington. I also know that Brookville, between Roslyn and Syosset (but judging from the road signs and map notations it isn't so much an actual town as it is an area), is the place to veer off the main road. Muttontown Road would be worth it just for the chance to see the road sign and pronounce it out loud, but it's pleasant riding as well, shady and meandering through the woods and past a country club.

From Syosset, head for Woodbury (the road to look for is called, helpfully, Syosset-Woodbury Road) and then Huntington, where you want to get on Pulaski Road, which will take you straight through into Smithtown. Pulaski is kind of a suburban Belt Parkway, not Main Street but not the expressway; it takes you into neighborhoods, over railroad tracks, past parks, and through intermittently spaced traffic lights. It's pleasant enough, though not exactly the Natchez Trace.

Negotiating Smithtown, which on this trip is really the gateway to a better life, is a little tricky. The key is turning onto Edgewood Avenue at the top of the Main Street hill; you're suddenly away from a commercial strip and onto a more promising kind of thoroughfare, the well-traveled country road, where bikes have to coexist with cars but do so amiably. Edgewood runs into North Country Road (Route 25A again, but kind of sweet at that point), which takes you through Stony Brook.

You can follow 25A toward Long Island Sound and into the town of Port Jefferson, but you'll have to climb a nasty hill to get out of Port Jeff and back on track. You'll also miss perhaps the niftiest shortcut of the journey. A hundred yards or so beyond the Stony Brook train station, there's a right onto a semihighway that takes you under the train tracks and past the State University campus. Just before the campus entrance, however, there's a left onto what looks like a tiny enough road to be an affluent person's driveway. Take it, and then an immediate right.

This is Lower Sheep Pasture Road, and a more agreeable, rolling ride the suburbs of New York do not offer. It ends with your being spilled across Main Street in Port Jeff, at the top of the hill you didn't have to climb, and back onto North Country Road, which has, by now, given up its designation as a state highway. Follow North Country through Miller Place (that's a town, not a street) and it will take you back to 25A. From there, through Rocky Point (where there's a Friendly's for a milkshake or, just beyond it, a pretty decent diner for lunch; I got there a little past noon), Shoreham (home of the famously ill-fated Lilco nuclear plant), and Wading River, the ride is an undistinguished but not unpleasant straight shot along a modestly traveled road with a smoothly paved, reasonably commodious shoulder. At this point, you have a decision to make.

Just east of Wading River, the road forks. Route 25A turns south, joins up with Route 25, and crosses through Riverhead on its way around Peconic Bay to the South Fork. It's not a bad journey, particularly once you hit the neck between the bay and the Atlantic Ocean. By then you're in the Hamptons. But I prefer staying north, which means turning off 25A onto Sound Avenue.

The Quest for a Second Wind

By now you're 75 miles or so into the trip and, if you're human, beginning to feel that enough might be enough. Encountering at this point the best bicycling of the day is thus either a good thing or a bad thing, depending on whether you feel that a jolt of rural beauty is just what you need or that you really should be fresher to appreciate it.

Sound Avenue stretches about 17 miles to Mattituck, on the North Fork, and if you look on a map you'll see there's nothing there. It's not spectacular, just nice. It's fields and tangled woods and the kind of quaint housing with wraparound porches and big yards you associate with, say, Wisconsin. (The first time I made this trip, I sat down for a breather on somebody's front lawn, fell asleep, and was awakened when the children who lived there got off a school bus.) There are sod farms stretching to forever, like God's golf course. And as you go farther east, the vineyards and wineries begin.

There are no bike services, just a farm stand or two and maybe a gift shop and an antiques store along the way, but make sure your water bottle is full and your blood sugar plentiful: There is nowhere to get a Snapple or a Gatorade or a packet of Oreos. The little mall where the road forks toward Mattituck is welcome. It's 13 more miles to Greenport, tough miles psychologically with still about 40 to go, but the late-afternoon light is consoling (something about how the descending sun hits a spine of land with water on either side) and there's respite (albeit brief) at the Shelter Island ferry.

The Day Is Done

Shelter Island is, of course, one of the great bicycling day trips on the East Coast. There's little auto traffic; the terrain is hilly enough for a good workout but not so grueling as to discourage you from having fun. There are huge old houses along the beaches, the incredibly well-groomed community of Dering Harbor, a wildly overgrown swampy shoreline dotted with osprey nests—maybe the most civilized bicycle sightseeing available anywhere.

PRACTICAL ADVICE ON PEDALING TO MONTAUK

It makes sense, if you are making the trip the way I did it this time, from west to east, to take the northern route. It's a little longer, but you get Queens and Nassau out of the way early, before the traffic problems become onerous. If you are going the other way, toward Manhattan, a route along southern Long Island is better.

From the Hamptons to Patchogue, it's more or less a straight shot along Route 27A (not the Sunrise Highway), with occasional ventures off the beaten path. Once into Nassau, if you take Merrick Road—a passable, if busy, suburban main drag—through Massapequa, Seaford, Freeport, and Valley Stream, there's reasonably easy access to the subway at Jamaica Station, where I recommend you hop on the train instead of negotiating, in the late afternoon, an increasingly difficult web of streets the rest of the way.

Those who want to modify their trip by shortening it might consider going partway on the **Long Island Rail Road** (☎ **718/217-5477** for schedule and fare information). Along the north shore, you can skip Queens and Nassau County entirely, for instance, and take a train from Penn Station to Cold Spring Harbor or Huntington, skipping over about 35 rather unscenic miles. Or, along the south shore, you can go to Patchogue, about halfway out.

The Long Island Rail Road requires a permit, for children as well as adults, to take a bike on board. Available by mail and at the ticket office at Penn Station, the permit costs $5; by mail, it takes about 10 days to process. Once you've got it, it's good until you lose it (I'm on my third). Applications are available at most train-station ticket offices. There are some restrictions: bikes aren't allowed on most rush-hour trains, for instance. Also, bicycle permits for Metro North can be used on the Long Island Rail Road, and Long Island Rail Road bicycle permits can be used on Metro North. For bike permit information, call ☎ **718/558-8228.**

Another option is to take your bike part of the way on the Hampton Jitney, a bus line serving the South Fork of Long Island, with stops from Westhampton to Montauk. It costs an additional $10 to board the **Hampton Jitney** (☎ **800/ 936-0440** for information and reservations) with a bicycle, and reservations are suggested; there are no restrictions on time or day of travel.

On this trip I was interested in none of this; it was after 4 o'clock when I got off the first ferry, and I bolted straight through along Route 114, 4 miles to the other side of the island (not a bad ride, just expedient where you'd rather not have to be) and onto the south ferry, which dropped me in Sag Harbor.

If it sounds as if I'm rushing to a conclusion, well, that's realistic representation for you. Truthfully, I didn't much want to go on (I like

Sag Harbor), but for the sake of completeness, I did, crossing the South Fork into East Hampton and then bolting straight east along Route 27, aka the Montauk Highway, through picturesque Amagansett and out onto the long, windswept flats. (Don't do this trip on a Friday; by this time of the evening, the highway can be bumper-to-bumper with week-enders.) At dinnertime, I passed Lunch, the diner, then climbed the cruel hills that for some reason exist out at the land's very extreme, as if Manhattan, sitting on one end, has tipped the island up like a fat man on a seesaw. Truly, the steepest climbs on the journey finish it, and as you approach the lighthouse you rise to the level of its foundation.

It was nearly dark when I finally arrived, and the lighthouse light was on. As I loaded my bike into the back of my friends' station wagon, it started to rain.

"How do you feel?" they asked me. "Thrilled?"

"Pooped," I said. "Hungry. I'll figure it out later."

I put Long Island in my back pocket and took it home with me.

On the Lookout for Whales

by Michael T. Kaufman

CALL ME A SCHLEMIEL.

But there I was, some dollars in my purse and not much to interest me on shore as summer was wearing down on the island of the Manhattoes. I felt the call of the sea and thought I would sail about a little in search of whales and adventure.

I could have signed on with any of a number of companies offering whale-watching expeditions from ports stretching up the coast from Mystic, Connecticut, to Bar Harbor, Maine, but the closest was one offered out of Montauk Harbor on Long Island.

In response to a call, I was told that whale-watching excursions departed every weekend until the end of September, when both whales and watchers petered out. The voyages, the voice on the telephone explained, take 4 to 7 hours. There are no guarantees of seeing whales or anything interesting. It could be cold, so passengers should bring layers of clothing. It could be very choppy, so they should dose themselves with Dramamine. The sun might be very strong, so they should bring sunblock.

Listening to this remarkably soft sell, I envisioned myself spending the full 7 hours queasy with *mal de mer,* skin scorched yet chilled to the bone, and nary a whale in sight. But if humankind allowed its will to bend and break under such premonitions, Columbus would have hugged European shores and the world would still be flat. Boldly, I reserved two places for a Sunday voyage for myself and my wife, committing $38 a seat.

Following instructions, we were at the pier next to the Block Island ferry slip by 10am. Along with 212 other prospective watchers, we boarded the *Viking Starship*, a sturdy vessel of 140 feet. There are hard metal seats running the length of the ship on both port side and starboard. Inside there are upholstered seats, but these offer poor views of the water. There is a canteen selling candy, potato chips, hot dogs, hats, sunblock, and whale-watch T-shirts. As the motor turned over, the woman behind the counter was talking with a volunteer crew member about a recent voyage. "It was really a great trip," she said. "Nobody threw up."

At that moment the water was calm, the sky was blue and cloudless, and a strong sun was made more tolerable by pleasant breezes. The only tension involved the prospect of whales. Would there be any whales? How many whales? What would we have to see for the outing to be successful? What was the minimum basic experience we should expect for our $38? A whale's back arching as it disappeared? A spewing whale and excited cries of "thar she blows"? A breaching whale flying out of the water? Or maybe even a spectacular literary metaphor?

Soon we left Peconic Bay for the swells of the ocean. Montauk Lighthouse lay off to port, and straightaway in the distance was the silhouette of Block Island. Suddenly the captain cut the engines. The watchers stopped chattering. Could we have whales already?

All the whale-watching outings are accompanied by a naturalist. On our trip, the naturalist was Annie Gorgone. "One o'clock, right next to the ship," she called out over a loudspeaker. The passengers all rushed to the starboard side to look. "It's not a whale, but it's pretty weird," said Ms. Gorgone, describing what she identified as an ocean sunfish.

About 5 feet from the ship and about a foot below the surface was a 4-foot-long fish that looked as if whoever designed it had stopped in the middle of the job, leaving its torso to end abruptly without a tail. It kept flipping its dorsal fin through the air from one side to the other, but it stayed stationary, looking at the people who were looking at it. "These fish can move pretty fast," Ms. Gorgone said. "But this one doesn't seem to be in any hurry. They eat jellyfish."

Whale Bonding

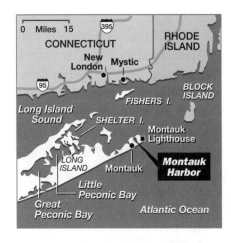

In the stare-down between fish and passengers, the fish won and we were again under way. It was good to see the sunfish, but what of whales? Would there be whales? It was easy to see how someone might obsess over whales.

Then, after a little more than an hour at sea, there was a whale. "Eleven o'clock," Ms. Gorgone shouted as the captain slowed the ship. Now people ran to port, watching as the whale broke the surface some 150 feet ahead of the *Viking Star,* only to dive down with a wave of its splendid 8-foot-wide flukes.

"That's a humpback whale," the naturalist explained. "He is not fully grown yet. He seems to be 2 or 3 years old, and he measures about 35 or 40 feet long. Actually, we don't know if he's a he or a she, but I've been calling him a he. If that bothers anyone, I apologize." Ms. Gorgone went on to explain that this same whale had been spotted in this patch of ocean on every voyage for the previous 4 weeks. In fact, she said, the whale was the only whale spotted in that time. The ship maintains regular contact with fishing boats in the region seeking information about whale sightings, but for some time no one had reported seeing anything more than the adolescent humpback that was submerged somewhere around us.

"Nine o'clock, right next to the boat," Ms. Gorgone shouted, and sure enough up came the whale about 10 feet from the middle of the ship, close enough so that some passengers could feel the spray of its spout and smell its breath, which by human standards was foul. "What it blows out through the blowhole is not water," Ms. Gorgone said. "It is mucus, similar to what happens when we sneeze." I was not lucky enough to get sneezed on, but I was pretty close. I definitely felt that, however briefly, the whale and I shared private if not intimate space. I can't speak for the whale, of course, but from my vantage point, something like bonding had taken place. It had become my whale.

Ms. Gorgone explained that the whale had moved away from its pod to graze on its own on large quantities of bait. On each deep dive it descended to a depth of 40 feet and stayed down for about 3 minutes before coming up for breath. As she spoke, the captain steered the ship, positioning it in anticipation of where my whale would next surface.

And so for the next hour and a half, passengers with cameras at the ready rushed from 9 o'clock to 3 o'clock and back again to catch glimpses of the whale—my whale—coming up and going down. Sometimes the creature would be off our side by a city block, sometimes much closer, though never again just a spit and a sneeze away.

In all I counted 37 deep dives, a number confirmed by the volunteers from the Riverhead Foundation for Marine Research and Preservation who were keeping records on how long it stayed down, how far it went, and what the sonar revealed about fish stocks below. The nonprofit foundation, which runs a telephone hotline service to spot and rescue beached whales, also studies whale behavior and movements.

At one point, my whale vigorously slapped its tail as it descended. "He does that sometimes, but we don't know what that maneuver means," said Ms. Gorgone. She said that a week earlier the whale kept breaching, hurling his entire body out of the water. "He did it 36 times," she said. "We don't really know why they do that either."

As the whale kept diving, not all the passengers kept watching. A bearded man approached Ms. Gorgone and asked, "Are we going to try to find other whales or are we going to stay around here?" You could see he wanted to move. Patiently, she explained that if we left, we would probably not find any other whales, and if we were lucky enough to spot some minke whales, they would quickly descend and vanish. "This guy here is pretty wonderful, and he keeps coming back," she said.

Another passenger approached to ask if the whale would do any "other tricks." With even more patience, Ms. Gorgone explained that it was a wild animal and that no one could tell what it would do.

Each new surfacing now brought fewer oohs and aahs, and no longer did quite so many people rush from one side of the ship to the other. Aware of ripples of antsiness among the passengers, Ms. Gorgone and the captain decided to head back for Montauk after less than 4 hours at sea.

For one last time I watched my whale break through the plane where water and air met and then arc down. I imagined it was singing.

WHAR SHE BLOWS: WHALE-WATCHING ESSENTIALS

Here is a sampling of whale-watching trips departing from harbors in the Northeast: **A. C. Cruise Line,** 290 Northern Ave., Boston, MA 02210 (☎ **800/422-8419** or 617/261-6633). Trips lasting about 6½ hours mid-April to Labor Day, Tuesday through Sunday at 10:30am; weekends only from Labor Day to mid-October. Tickets $22; $16 for and children 12 and younger.

Bar Harbor Whale Watch Company, 1 West St., near Town Pier, Bar Harbor, ME (☎ **800/508-1499** or 207/288-3322). Daily trips of 2½ to 3 hours from early June through mid-October (depending on weather). From June 11 to July 1, and August 26 to October 15, 9am and 1pm; July 2 to August 25, 8:30am and 1 and 4:30pm. Tickets $39, $25 for children 6 to 14, $8 for those 5 and younger. Also, sightseeing and fishing excursions.

Cape Ann Whale Watch, P.O. Box 345, 415 Main St., Rose's Wharf, Gloucester, MA (☎ **800/877-5110** or 508/283-5110). Four-hour trips April through mid-October. Call for schedule. Tickets $26, $21 for seniors, $16 for children under 16.

Cape May Whale Watch and Research Center, 1286 Wilson Dr., Cape May, NJ (☎ **609/898-0055**). Call for schedule and prices.

Captain John Boats, 117 Standish Ave., Plymouth, MA 02360 (☎ **508/746-2643**). Call for schedule and prices.

Dolphin Fleet Whale Watch, MacMillan Wharf, off Commercial St., Provincetown, MA (☎ **800/826-9300** or 508/349-1900). Daily trips, lasting 3 to 3½ hours, from mid-April to the end of October. The number of daily trips depends on the season, with six in the early spring and late fall and as many as nine during the summer; departure times are at 9am in the spring and fall and 8:30am in the summer. Tickets, in spring and fall, $19, $17 for seniors, $16 for children 7 to 12, free for those 6 and younger. In the summer, each fare is an additional $1. Reservations recommended.

Fisherman's Wharf, off Rte. 1 (at the drawbridge), Lewes, DE (☎ **302/645-8862**). Three-hour dolphin and nature cruises depart Saturday and Sunday at 2pm from Memorial Day through mid-June, and daily at 2pm from mid-June through Labor Day. Tickets $23, $11 for children under 13.

Hyannis Whale Watcher Cruises, 269 Mill Way Barnstable Harbor, Barnstable, MA 02630 (☎ **800/287-0374** or 508/362-6088). Daily trips of 3½ to 4 hours April through October at 8am, noon, and

5pm. Tickets $26, $21 for seniors, $16 for children 4 to 12, free for those 3 and under. Reservations suggested.

New England Aquarium Whale Watch, Central Wharf, off Atlantic Ave. and Milk St., Boston, MA (☎ **617/973-5281**). Three-and-one-half to 5-hour trips, from early April through early November: Early May through June, weekdays at 10am and weekends at 9:30am and 3:30pm; July through Labor Day, daily at 9:30am and 12:30 and 2:30pm; Labor Day to mid-October, weekdays at 1pm and weekends at 9:30am and 2:30 and 3pm; April and the last 2 weeks in October and early November, weekends at 10am. Tickets $26.50, $21 for seniors, $19 for children 12 to 18, $16.50 for children 3 to 11. Reservations recommended.

Portuguese Princess, 70 Shankpainter Rd., Provincetown, MA (☎ **800/442-3188** or 508/487-2651). Fisherman's Wharf. Season runs mid-April through late October. Call for schedule and prices.

Riverhead Foundation for Marine Research and Preservation, 431 E. Main St., Riverhead, NY (☎ **631/369-9840**). Call for schedule.

Viking Fishing Fleet, Edgemere Rd., off Rte. 27 East, Montauk, NY (☎ **631/668-5700**). June, whale-watching weekends only; July 4 through Labor Day, daily. Boarding at 10am and sailing at 10:30am; the boat returns between 4:30 and 5pm. Tickets $38, $35 for seniors, $20 for children 5 to 12, free for those under 5.

The Hudson Valley

GARDEN-HOPPING IN WESTCHESTER

by William Grimes

IN THE REST OF THE WORLD, SPRING arrives in a riot of color and a burst of warmth. Birds chirp and hearts gladden. In New York, the schedule is a little different. After winter slams down on the city like a frozen, cast-iron lid, imposing a color regime of gray and black, spring works a cruel hoax. It lingers just off-stage in the seasonal drama and, with the audience primed for an appearance, it lingers some more.

The calendar pages flip from mid-April to mid-May. The city is lashed by a cold, stinging rain; the ground is held captive in a binding frost. Then, it happens. The long-awaited star steps out onto center stage, executes some frantic dance steps, sings three songs, and then races off. If you blink, you miss it. That was spring. Now it's summer.

For the color-deprived, mid-May is the time. Throughout the region, gardens come into their glory, working double time to make up for a punishing winter. In Manhattan, of course, the grand seasonal shift is purely a matter of temperature and foot-level visibility. (In winter, you can't see the sidewalk; in spring, you can.) Farther afield, though, nature puts on a show.

Here's the drill. Take a map, trace a circle with a radius of about 100 miles, and divide the circle into bite-size sectors. The belt that begins about 40 miles out from Times Square includes prime horticultural territory and therefore is the ideal destination for a quick day trip to take in a handful of public and private gardens.

The Garden Conservancy, a nonprofit group that helps preserve fine gardens, has made life easier for anyone who wants to smell the roses in New York and Connecticut. The group, which was founded in 1989 and has its headquarters in Cold Spring, New York, took its lead from a highly popular British program run by the National Gardens Scheme, in which gifted amateurs open their gardens to the public for browsing.

The Conservancy put together in its *Open Days Directory* a list of 372 private gardens in the New York area that the public could visit on certain days. The admission fee for each garden was $5, with the proceeds going to the conservancy's preservation programs. The directory, initially sold for $8, included public gardens in the areas, making it a one-stop-shopping guide for the garden-happy. The first year's print run was 5,000 copies, which sold out almost immediately.

The gardens are open on selected Saturdays and Sundays from late April to late September.

Showoffs & Foliage

Pick a weekend, a nice destination, and some gardens. My wife and I settled on a doable chunk of northern Westchester that included Bedford and Katonah, rich and rolling country with imposing Colonial houses and some very serious gardens.

Stop no. 1 was the Katonah home of Roxana Robinson, a gardener better known as the author of *Georgia O'Keeffe: A Life* and the short-story collection *Asking for Love*. The *Open Days Directory* gives precise driving directions to each garden, and participants put out a helpful sign with the conservancy's symbol, a blazing sun with a human face. Ms. Robinson's husband, Tony, collected admission fees at the garage, and visitors simply walked into the family's backyard through a white wood gate flanked by two enormous hostas.

The Robinson garden lies somewhere in the middle range of gardens in the conservancy's list. It's not too big, not too small; it's not too structured, but not haphazard either. It provokes envy, but it's possible to believe that two hardworking enthusiasts created it, rather than a team of specialists.

When the Robinsons bought their house in 1978, the garden consisted of foolproof plants like hostas, peonies, and daylilies. Ms.

Robinson went to work. "I began making beds, and gradually it took me over," Ms. Robinson said. "It's the reason my novel isn't finished."

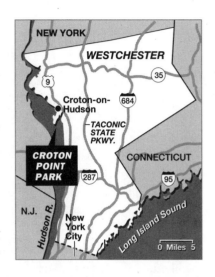

Her method was simple. "It was trial and error and survival of the fittest," she said. Antique roses did not make it. Rugosas did. Other survivors, deployed in modest-size beds, include bleeding hearts, their bunched, cup-shaped petals dangling like cluster earrings, and brunnera, an almost absurdly tiny flower with a blue so deep it pierces. Intermingled with the show-off flowers are foliage plants, like lamb's ears (named for their droopy, fuzzy leaves), which serve as foils. Clusters of phlox spill over a stone wall, and extensive, neat beds of lavender-colored veronica lead to a large dogwood tree.

There was trouble in paradise on the fine May day we visited. In broad daylight, unembarrassed at being perceived as a total cliché, a large king snake slithered across a path and into a tight cluster of lamb's ears, whose trembling marked the fiend's progress. Ms. Robinson was nonchalant. "They're good for the garden," she said. Not good for birds, however. Ms. Robinson, investigating cries of distress from a nearby tree, found out that the snake had snatched a baby cardinal from its nest.

Garden stop no. 2 was a bust, a rather feeble string of borders that looked anemic against a Colonial house of grand proportions set on multiple hilltop acres. Garden nos. 3 and 4, however, were showstoppers.

In Bedford Hills, Phillis Warden has planted perennial beds punctuated by weird, desert-type shrubs that move along the perimeter of the backyard, leading to a water garden and a carp-filled pool. Outside the backyard fence, the plantings follow shelflike outcroppings of rock in a waterfall that leads to a woodland area.

Planting Xanadu

Not far away, in Bedford, Penelope and John Maynard have created a kind of Xanadu around their house, on a commanding height overlooking Indian Hill in Bedford. A winding stone walkway leads from one pocket-size garden to the next, each with its own color scheme and subtle variations on major themes.

In a formal garden, surrounded by a stone wall, dramatic purple-black Queen of Night tulips dominated the central bed. Nearby, taxicab-yellow lily tulips with racily pointed petals played into a color scheme of burgundy, white, and yellow. Ms. Maynard, a garden designer who helped create the open-days program, makes the most of foliage plants like a variegated euonymus, which droops over the stone wall near the lily tulips in a pompadour of green-and-gold leaves. "Flowers come and go, fleetingly, but the leaves remain," said Ms. Maynard. "Variegation is very important," she added. "It draws a plant forward."

Another bed contains *actinidia kolomitka,* the male kiwi plant, whose leaf ends look as if they have been dipped in white paint. As the season progresses, the tips turn pink, producing a tricolor effect—again, variegation. Stalking the grounds are two caramel-colored ocicats. A short-haired breed with brown dots, ocicats are a cross between a Siamese and an Abyssinian.

The John Jay Homestead, in Katonah, has four gardens that are tended by three volunteer groups, and the site is worth a flying visit, especially if you are packing a picnic lunch. Roam the Federal-style house and its immediate grounds, by all means, and admire the rose arch that protects the grave of one of the family horses. The standouts, though, can be found well below the house, near the drive.

The sunken formal garden, shaded by enormous red cedars, strikes a romantic note, and lilacs perfume the air in late spring. At the center of the garden is a sundial, surrounded by beds of lady's mantle, bleeding hearts, ferns, and thistle. Next to the formal garden is an extensive herb garden maintained by the Herb Society of America. Its brick-lined beds enclose the usual suspects, like chives, sage, and tarragon, along with more exotic citizens like hyssop, rue, and tansy.

Music & Color

The extensive and varied gardens at the Caramoor Center for Music and the Arts, also in Katonah, demand a long, leisurely look. Caramoor, a Mediterranean-style estate built in 1912 by a very rich lawyer, is best known for its summer music festival, but the horticultural program is outstanding. In 1989, the Caramoor Garden Guild took on the responsibility of restoring the gardens, which had languished.

"The gardens had fallen into disrepair, if you can use the word to describe a garden," said Eileen Burton, then Caramoor's horticultural director. "There was poison ivy in the beds." There's no poison ivy now. The formal sunken garden was replanted in roses, lilies, and daisies, in a color scheme of pink, white, and silver, the better to be seen at night during the music festival. In the center of each of the four main beds stands a huge terra-cotta amphora, and at the corners, there are urns filled with heliotrope, giving off a seductive licorice-vanilla perfume. (Ms. Burton is no longer at Caramoor.)

Near the Italian pavilion, a roofed picnic area with an antique tile floor, the Garden Guild recently created a butterfly garden. As luck would have it, butterflies are attracted to violet, gold, and orange, the colors in the tiles, so the color scheme dovetailed perfectly with the existing decor.

Another innovation was the Sense Circle, a garden and moatlike fountain surrounding an old dovecote. The garden, with trees, hedges, grass, and flowers arranged in concentric circles, has been designed to appeal to those with visual impairments or disabilities, with bright colors, strong perfumes, and the pleasing sounds of splashing water and rustling trees.

The entire estate is a kind of folly, and maybe even a little foolish. What sense does it make to create an Italo-Spanish estate in suburban New York? None at all. At Caramoor, Venice meets Tuscany by way of Byzantium, yet in an American melting-pot kind of way, this seemingly preposterous mix works. For the city-bound, it offers space, light, color, and fragrance, all the things that spring is supposed to be about.

ESSENTIALS FOR GARDEN-HOPPING IN THE TRI-STATE AREA

The Garden Conservancy publishes a tour guide of private and public gardens in New York, Connecticut, New Jersey, and 14 other states. The 2001 *Open Days Directory,* which costs $15.95 ($10.95 for Conservancy members), plus $4.50 shipping and handling, can be ordered by telephone (☎ **888/842-2442**) or by mail from the Garden Conservancy, P.O. Box 219, Cold Spring, NY 10516. MasterCard and Visa are accepted.

Admission is $5 to each private garden in the directory, or $25 for six tours ($20 for Conservancy members). Reservations are not necessary. A sampling of public gardens in the metropolitan region follows. Days, hours, and admission prices vary, so you should call ahead to the specific gardens before you visit.

NEW YORK CITY

Brooklyn Botanic Garden, 1000 Washington Ave. (at Prospect Park; ☎ **718/ 622-4433**). A 52-acre site that includes a rose garden featuring 5,000 bushes and 1,200 to 1,500 varieties, as well as a Japanese garden and a children's discovery garden. Open Tuesday through Friday 8am to 4:30pm; Saturday, Sunday, and holidays 10am to 4:30pm. Admission is $3 for adults, $1.50 for students and seniors, and free for children 15 and younger.

New York Botanical Garden, Southern Blvd. and 200th St., Bedford Park, the Bronx (☎ **718/817-8700**). A 250-acre site where more than 250 varieties of roses bloom. Open Tuesday through Sunday 10am to 4pm. Admission is $6.50 for adults, $4 for students and seniors, $2 for children 2 to 12.

Queens Botanical Garden, 43–50 Main St., Flushing (☎ **718/886-3800**). Thirty-nine acres with a Victorian wedding garden, a demonstration garden, a rose garden with 20 varieties, an herb garden, a pinetum, a woodland garden, and workshops. Open Tuesday through Sunday 8:30am to 4:30pm. There is no admission.

Wave Hill, Independence Ave. and 249th St., Riverdale, the Bronx (☎ **718/ 549-3200**). A 28-acre site with several gardens, greenhouses, historic buildings, woodlands, and lawns. Hours and admission prices are seasonal. October 15 to April 14, open Tuesday through Sunday 9am to 4:30pm; April 15 to October 9, open Tuesday through Sunday 9am to 5:30pm (open until sunset Wed in June and July). General admission March 15 to November 14, $4 general admission, $2 seniors and students, free for members and children under 6; free admission for all visitors all day Tuesday and 9am to noon Saturday. Admission free for all visitors November 15 to March 14.

Family Art Projects, a series of free workshops, is offered year-round on Saturday and Sunday 1 to 4pm. There are free dance performances most Wednesdays and Sundays in July. October through April, the park stages classical and jazz concerts; $15 general admission, $12 for seniors, $10 for students and members.

HUDSON VALLEY

Caramoor Gardens, Girdle Ridge Rd. (off Rte. 22), Katonah (☎ **914/232-1253; www.caramoor.com**). One hundred acres with woodlands, meadows, perennial, medieval, and butterfly gardens; art exhibitions, workshops, and a performance series. Admission $6, includes house and gardens; gardens open year-round, daily 10am to 5pm; guided tours, May through October, Wednesday through Friday and Sunday, 1 to 4pm, Saturday 1 to 5pm, and by appointment.

Hammond Museum and Japanese Stroll Garden, off June Rd. (Exit 7, Rte. 684 North), North Salem (☎ **914/669-5033**). A 3-acre Japanese garden. Spring through fall, Wednesday through Saturday noon to 4pm; closed late October through March. Admission is $4 for adults, $3 students and seniors; children under 12 are free.

John Jay Homestead State Historic Site, 400 Rte. 22 at Jay St., Katonah Bedford (☎ **914/232-5651**). Local garden clubs maintain three garden areas, including an herb garden and planting designs from 1800 through the 1930s; there is also a garden that is handicapped accessible. Nature activities for children, walking tours every Sunday at 2:30pm April through October. Self-guided grounds tours available year-round 8am to sunset. Free admission.

Kykuit, Pocantico Hills (☎ **914/631-9491**). The Rockefeller estate, with woodlands, a rose garden, and sculpture. Guided tours of the estate are offered from late April through early November. The tours, which begin at Philipsburg Manor in Sleepy Hollow (formerly North Tarrytown), take 2 hours. Reservations are not required. Each tour is $20, $19 for seniors, $17 for students. Not recommended for children.

Montgomery Place, River Rd., Annandale-on-Hudson (☎ **914/758-5461**). A 434-acre, 200-year-old estate with a 19th-century picturesque landscape, including thematic gardens, perennial rose borders, a lily pond, an herb garden, orchards, forests, and waterfalls. Open April through October, Wednesday through Monday 10am to 5pm (closed Tues); November and the first 2 weeks of December, Saturday and Sunday 10am to 5pm. Admission $6, $5 for seniors, $3 for children 5 to 17, free for children under 5.

LONG ISLAND

Longhouse Reserve, 133 Hands Creek Rd., East Hampton (☎ **631/329-3568**). Sixteen acres divided into areas of hedges, grasses, and flowering plants. Daffodils bloom in late April. Open late April through mid-September. Contribution $10.

Madoo Conservancy, 618 Sagg Main St., Sagaponack (☎ **631/537-8200**). Two acres with a hooped rose walk, an Oriental bridge, sculptures, fountains, and a gazebo.

Among the varieties are roses, poppies, rhododendron, pines, and topiary. Open May through September, Wednesday and Saturday, 1 to 5pm. Admission $10, free for children under 6.

Old Westbury Gardens, 71 Old Westbury Rd. (☎ **516/333-0048**). About 150 acres of gardens, with a walled perennial garden, formal rose garden, cottage garden, vegetable gardens, meadow, nature walks, and cafe. Concerts held every Wednesday July through mid-August. Open last weekend in May through November, Wednesday through Monday 10am to 5pm; early December, Wednesday through Monday 11 to 4pm (call for exact dates). Admission $6, $5 for seniors, $3 for children 6 to 12.

NEW JERSEY

Cross Estate Garden, Morristown National Historic Park, Ledell Rd. (off Rte. 287), near Mendham (☎ **973/539-2016**). A 6-acre site with a walled formal garden, pergola, rhododendron and woodland garden, shrubbery, walks and lectures. Call for hours and admission.

Frelinghuysen Arboretum, 3 E. Hanover Ave., Morristown (☎ **973/326-7600**). Two hundred acres with a rose garden, antique rose collection, fern garden, 11 demonstration gardens, and shade gardens. Open daily 9am to 4:30pm. Free admission.

Leonard J. Buck Gardens, part of the Somerset County Park Commission, 11 Layton Rd., Far Hills (☎ **908/234-2677**). Thirty-three acres with woodlands, forests, wildflowers, lake and stream, azalea meadow, fern collection, and rhododendrons. There is also the Rudolf van Dergoot Rose Garden in East Millstone with a perennial garden, arboretum, and shrubs. Open year-round, Monday through Friday, 10am to 4pm; mid-March through November, also open Saturday 10am to 5pm, and Sunday noon to 5pm. Donation $1.

New Jersey State Botanical Garden at Skylands, Morris Rd. (Rte. 511, Sloatsburg Rd. exit), Ringwood (☎ **973/962-9534** or 973/962-7527). Ninety-six acres with gardens of lilacs, azaleas, peonies, evergreens, wildflowers, and woodlands; lectures, workshops, and other activities. Open daily 8am to 8pm. Parking fee $3 Memorial Day through Labor Day; free parking other times.

CONNECTICUT

Gertrude Jekyll Garden at the Glebe House Museum, Hollow Rd., Woodbury (☎ **203/263-2855**). Half-acre English-style mixed border and foundation planting, stone terrace, and rose allée. Open daily from dawn until dusk. Donation $2.

Hillside Gardens, 515 Litchfield Rd., Norfolk (☎ **860/542-5345**). Five acres with blooming peonies, irises, azaleas, honeysuckles, geraniums, and woodlands. Open May to September 15, weekends only 9am to 5pm. Free admission.

University of Connecticut Bartlett Arboretum, 151 Brookdale Rd., Stamford (☎ **203/322-6971**). A 63-acre garden with woodlands, annual and wildflower gardens, a perennial border, workshops, and a greenhouse. Open daily 8:30am to sunset. Free admission.

A Rockefeller's Aerie:
Kykuit

by Paul Goldberger

Forget Bill Gates and never-mind Leslie Wexner; no name in American history connotes money like Rockefeller. Public enough to have a consistently high profile, private enough to have an aura of mystery that never entirely disappears, this family has symbolized American wealth for most of the 20th century.

So it should not be at all surprising that the public opening of Kykuit, the Rockefeller family estate at Pocantico Hills, New York, was greeted with an interest more or less akin to that surrounding the start of public tours of Buckingham Palace. Historic Hudson Valley, the nonprofit organization (and Rockefeller creation) that is managing the tours of Kykuit (rhymes with "high cut"), reports that the first few months of tours in 1994 were virtually sold out, and that demand remains high, 5 years after the first tour group passed through Kykuit's iron gates.

The Rockefeller property is like nothing else in the United States. Kykuit (the name comes from a Dutch word meaning "lookout") is not by any means the largest villa built by an American fortune, and it is far from the most distinguished one architecturally. As a house, it is, in fact, oddly restrained, almost hesitant, and rather tight in its proportions. But it stands at the crown of a hill overlooking the Hudson River, commanding a stunning 300-acre site in the midst of several thousand more acres of Rockefeller land, all in the middle of the Westchester suburbs. Barely over 20 miles from Manhattan, and within view of the

Tappan Zee Bridge, the site contains the expanse of a vast estate in the Adirondacks, and confers upon the visitor every bit as much a sense of distance from the city.

This is the true test of great wealth: not the mere possession of land, but the possession of a huge expanse of land close to the city, where others are content with half an acre. Is it an accident that John Hay Whitney and William S. Paley had huge estates in Nassau County just a few miles east of the Queens line? Huge private holdings have all but disappeared within 50 miles of New York City, and the Rockefeller property today is larger than almost any of them ever were, even in the heyday of American fortunes. It's notable that when John D. Rockefeller began acquiring land in the Tarrytown area in 1893, the first 400-acre parcel he purchased had already been earmarked for a real-estate subdivision. He bought all the lots and took it off the market, then kept expanding.

Some years ago, 800 of the Rockefeller acres were given to the State of New York as a park preserve. The heart of the Rockefeller holdings, however, is not the public park but a 300-acre fenced site including Kykuit, not to mention a nine-hole golf course, numerous formal gardens, a huge stone garage structure called the Coach House, an indoor athletic building called the Play House, and a greenhouse pavilion called the Orangerie. (The last two are not part of the public tour, but the Coach House, which holds the family's collection of antique coaches and automobiles, is.)

Eighty-seven of these 300 acres are now owned by the National Trust for Historic Preservation, which acquired them under Nelson Rockefeller's will. Rockefeller, the former vice president and governor of New York who died in 1979, was the most public and flamboyant Rockefeller, and he envisioned the estate—which he owned jointly with his brothers, Laurence and David—less as a private retreat than as a monument to the family. Several family members were more than a little surprised when, after Nelson's death, it turned out that he had left his one-third interest in the property entirely to the National Trust.

Nelson Rockefeller's gesture set in motion the process that led ultimately to the opening of the estate to the public. It took 15 years, however; in part because his brothers, preferring not to share ownership of the whole property with the National Trust, made a deal to swap their interest in Kykuit and its immediate surroundings for the trust's share of the whole property. The trust ended up owning 87 acres and the house outright; the family kept the rest and, since the trust has no funds of its own, agreed to maintain the property through the Rockefeller Brothers Fund. The fund assigned Historic Hudson Valley, operators of Westchester County properties like Sunnyside and Philipsburg Manor, to run the public tours.

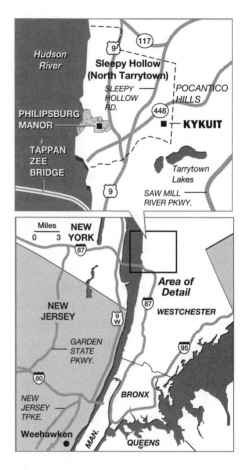

Cartesian Order on Top

Visitors drive not to the Rockefeller property but to the visitor center of Philipsburg Manor, a mile or so away on Route 9 in the village of Sleepy Hollow (formerly North Tarrytown). Vans carry each tour group of 18 to the estate, through the main gate and up a winding road to the forecourt of Kykuit at the hilltop.

The landscaping is relaxed and easy in the lower reaches of the hillside, with wide expanses of rolling lawn, carefully tended trees, and pieces from Nelson Rockefeller's impressive collection of 20th-century sculpture placed with precision by Rockefeller himself. But the mood changes at the hilltop, where the beaux-arts sensibility of William Welles Bosworth, the architect who more than any other gave Kykuit its form, takes over. Suddenly the natural lushness gives way to formal geometries, and the rural ease to a rigid Cartesian order.

Is Kykuit a French château sitting atop an English landscape, then a kind of Versailles in the sky? It's actually even more of a hybrid than that, both as a building and as a total work of architecture and landscape. The history of Kykuit's design, not unlike the negotiations over its ownership that consumed much of the 1980s, is a complex tale. Suffice it to say that the original house on the property was relatively modest, fitting the preferences of the senior John D. Rockefeller. When it burned in 1902, Rockefeller first asked Dunham A. Wheeler to design a simple house to go at the highest point of the site, but eventually gave in to the views of his son, John D. Rockefeller, Jr., who had more ambitious notions of what sort of country seat the Rockefeller family should have. The Rockefellers hired Delano & Aldrich, who later became one of the most celebrated purveyors of traditional architecture to the rich, to produce a Georgian house, but the senior Rockefeller insisted that the design follow the outline of the relatively modest T-shaped floor plan of Wheeler's unbuilt design.

Eventually John D. Rockefeller, Jr., managed to bring in two other players: Ogden Codman, to design the interiors and furnishings, and Bosworth, to lay out the gardens, which soon became grander and more elaborate than the house itself. When the senior Rockefellers decided they were less than happy with the house, which was completed in 1908, the younger Rockefeller had it almost completely reconstructed, expanding it from three to four stories and giving it a new classical facade of rough stone by Bosworth.

Five Different Visions

Kykuit as it stands today, then, is a collaboration of three architects and two clients, none of whom had precisely the same vision of what it should be. (There is actually even a fourth architect: Herbert Newman, who was brought in by the Rockefeller Brothers Fund to make some behind-the-scenes improvements to ready the house for public visitation.

Mr. Newman also renovated the basement of the old carriage barn into a handsome private conference center for the fund.) Considering the complexity of its authorship, the place is not nearly as much of an architectural camel as it could have been; there is a certain graciousness to Bosworth's classical facade, and the house's mix of idiosyncrasy and restraint stands in welcome contrast to the self-important hauteur of the average pile of stone in Newport.

And it turned out, perhaps in spite of itself, to be a perfect expression of the Rockefeller ethos. This is not a modest house, because the Rockefellers were not modest, but neither is it a house that seems designed to project any sense of extravagance. A great deal of money was spent here, but every stone proclaims money spent out of a sense of duty, not out of a sense of hedonism. There is nothing vulgar here, and that alone separates Kykuit from almost every great house produced in the golden age of American wealth.

You might say that Kykuit is what you get when you merge John D. Rockefeller's Baptist restraint with American extravagance: something slightly at odds with itself, a house that seems to want to be grand and to disappear at the same time. The shape of the house is itself tight, almost urban, disproportionately tall and narrow in the manner of a great town house. It is a country house in a corset.

An Urban Feel Inside

It feels even more urban when you enter the narrow, vaulted vestibule that seems like the ground-floor entrance to a town house. A small paneled sitting room, once John D. Rockefeller's office, is to the left; another small sitting room, with delicate, Adamesque detailing, is to the right. It is only the view straight ahead through the house to the extraordinary vista of the Hudson beyond that reminds you where you are.

The main tour takes visitors through the main rooms of the first floor, moving in and out of the building to encompass portions of the surrounding gardens. (A separate tour, the Garden and Sculpture Tour, offers a more in-depth view of the gardens.) It is the gardens, mostly laid out by Bosworth, that are the truly spectacular thing here. In many ways, the land has it all over the architecture, since the site is so full of grand gestures, and the house, whatever its virtues, is so empty of them. The one room that tries to do something spectacular, the so-called music room at the heart of the structure, which has an elliptical opening to the floor above, sums up the problem of this house: It is too tall, too tight, too unwilling to let itself go.

Yet how like the generation of Rockefellers who built Kykuit! John D. Rockefeller disapproved of drinking, dancing, and other pleasures; the music room was designed to hold a pipe organ, and Sunday-afternoon organ music was the elder Rockefeller's favored entertainment. His son, John D. Rockefeller, Jr., was more comfortable with grand architectural gestures, but even for him, a sense of duty always came first. He envisioned Kykuit not as a palace of pleasure but as the serious expression of the stature of a great family. If this freed Kykuit from the vulgar excesses of Newport and Fifth Avenue, it also gave the estate more than a whiff of dry formality.

It's no accident, then, that Kykuit lacks such showy symbols as a grand staircase; the second floor (which is not included in the public tour) is reached by a stair that is not much larger than the one you would find in a suburban house, tucked behind the partition that once contained the pipe organ. The main public rooms are hardly small, but neither do they approach the institutional scale of the ballrooms and reception rooms of so many American palaces of this period; indeed, these rooms always feel domestic, which was presumably the intention. They are furnished conservatively, with a mix of antiques and plain upholstered pieces, and have a number of paintings of note, including a Gilbert Stuart portrait of George Washington in the library and John Singer Sargent's portrait of the senior Rockefeller in the dining room, as well as numerous examples of Chinese ceramics.

Paintings & Sculpture

The real energy in both the house and grounds, however, comes from those portions of Nelson Rockefeller's collection of 20th-century painting and sculpture that remain here. Rockefeller, who occupied the house from 1960 on, removed the old pipe organ and put a large Miró in its place (the original has since gone to the Museum of Modern Art in Manhattan, with a copy now hanging in the Kykuit music room). He put Giacometti lamps in the alcove overlooking the river, and Picasso etchings in the stairwell, starting a dialogue between the generations that enlivens the house considerably.

Rockefeller also converted portions of the basement and underground tunnel system into contemporary art galleries, which remain more or less as he left them, period ensembles from the early 1960s. The first two rooms, jammed tight with smaller works by Fritz Glarner, Larry Bell, Robert Motherwell, Ernest Trova, Ibram Lassaw, and Mary Callery—not to mention Picasso, Braque, and Calder—provide splendid insight into the catholicity of Rockefeller's modernist taste. These rooms were a marvelous, highly personal indulgence, not just in the quantity of art they contain—there are more than 100 works—but also in the way in which Rockefeller intended them to make up a complete and discrete modernist world within the historical fabric of Kykuit.

Visitors walk through most of the galleries, passing some larger portraits of Nelson and Happy Rockefeller by Andy Warhol, as well as two George Segals and two Leger rugs, with glimpses of several Picasso tapestries, before moving outdoors again to the gardens. The tour includes most, but not all, of Bosworth's formal gardens, which is where the architect's beaux-arts instincts took full reign: There are planted terraces, reflecting pools, an allée of linden trees, a semicircular rose garden, and numerous distinct gardens, each a kind of outdoor room in itself. (A Japanese garden, a stone grotto, and a putting green can all be viewed from a distance but are not included on the tour.)

The landscape has a clear order to it: rigid and formal at the hilltop close to the house, gradually opening up to wide, rolling vistas as the space tumbles down toward the river. The high site creates the marvelous illusion that the property runs all the way to the Hudson River (in fact, the whole village of Sleepy Hollow exists between Kykuit and the river, utterly invisible from the house); and with the Palisades largely protected from development on the river's west side, the sense of being in a distant wilderness is nearly total.

Most spectacular, however, is Nelson Rockefeller's sculpture, which was placed sensitively, and at times brilliantly, around the property.

Some pieces, like Max Bill's granite *Triangular Surface in Space,* at the end of a formal pergola, are on a formal axis, very much part of Bosworth's beaux-arts organization. Others, like Calder's metal stabile, *Large Spiny,* and Maillol's *Night,* are set more in nature; some pieces, like an unusually strong Henry Moore, *Knife Edge—Two Piece,* have been sited both to tie into the axis of the house and to be out on the open landscape. Rockefeller is said to have moved his favorite pieces frequently, and to have chosen many of the sculpture sites by hovering over the property in a helicopter.

The 20th-century sculpture remaining at Kykuit is, on balance, the best art at the estate, and its relationship to the architecture, the gardens, and the natural landscape is the most powerful aesthetic experience to be had here—at least, the most powerful man-made one. Few things can equal the drama of Kykuit's site, a drama enhanced by the sense that it is almost illicit to have a piece of landscape like this in the midst of suburbia. Rockefeller's sculpture, placed with precision and with total respect for the order of the house, nonetheless manages to break the place wide open, celebrating Kykuit's natural glories and at the same time filling the property with a sense of fresh air.

KYKUIT ESSENTIALS

Kykuit, the Rockefeller family estate in Pocantico Hills, New York, can be visited only on a 2-hour escorted tour. Visits to the 300-acre estate leave every day except Tuesday from the visitor center at nearby Philipsburg Manor, on Rte. 9 in Sleepy Hollow (formerly North Tarrytown).

GETTING THERE

By Car Philipsburg Manor can be reached by the Gov. Thomas E. Dewey Thruway to Tarrytown (exit 9); take Rte. 119 to Rte. 9. Or take the Sawmill River Parkway to Rte. 287, then follow Rte. 119 to Rte. 9.

By Train There is also a Tarrytown stop on the Hudson line of Metro-North (☎ **212/532-4900**); weekend round-trip fare from Grand Central Terminal is $11.

Taxis are available at the train station for the short ride to Philipsburg Manor; one-way fare is about $4.

By Bus The no. 13 Beeline Bus (☎ **914/ 682-2020**) makes a stop at the Tarrytown train station and runs north along Rte. 9; the southbound bus is the no. 138; one-way fare is $1.40.

TOURING THE ESTATE

From late April to early November, there are two separate tours, both of which take approximately the same length of time: the House and Garden Tour and the Garden and Sculpture Tour. The first tour, held weekends only, includes time in the gardens and is recommended as a basic introduction to Kykuit. The Garden and Sculpture Tour is held weekdays at 3pm. Both tours, administered by Historic Hudson Valley, begin at Philipsburg Manor with a short film about Kykuit and the Rockefeller family; visitors are then taken by shuttle van to the estate.

Tickets for either tour are $20, $19 for seniors, $17 for students; the tours are not recommended for children under 12. Tours, which are first come, first served, begin daily at 10am and run every 20 minutes; the last tour departs Philipsburg Manor at 4pm on Saturday and Sunday and 3pm on weekdays. Reservations are necessary for groups of 10 or more; call ☎ **914/631-9491.**

CRUISING TO KYKUIT

In addition, there is a special 7-hour Hudson River cruise and guided Kykuit estate tour offered by New York Waterway (☎ **800/533-3779**). Boats leave Saturday and Sunday from the Manhattan terminal at 12th Ave. and 38th St. for a 1½-hour cruise up the Hudson River to Tarrytown; buses then transport passengers to Philipsburg Manor. Round-trip cruise and tour tickets are $60; $55 for seniors. Reservations are necessary.

HAPPY TRAILS ALONG
THE RIVER

by William Grimes

FOR MOST OF THIS CENTURY, THE
Hudson has been the John Barrymore of rivers, noble in profile but a
sorry wreck. Decades of bingeing on toxic chemicals gradually took its
toll, and although the river's grandeur could not be denied, most people, looking at the Hudson, could only shake their heads in sorrow. The
mighty river, once home to porpoises and even one reported whale, had
entered the final stages of decline, fit habitat only for a few funky fish.

Then, the impossible happened. In an awesome display of
willpower, the Hudson took the pledge. Thanks to the good efforts of
environmental and education groups like Scenic Hudson, the Open
Space Institute, and the Hudson River Valley Greenway, along with
large infusions of cash from the Lila Acheson and DeWitt Wallace
Fund for the Hudson Highlands and the political push behind the
Federal Clean Water Acts and other environmental laws, the river came
back from the brink and is on the way to sound health, with two pleasing results.

First, a cleaner river has meant a return of fish and other wildlife.
Second, heightened river consciousness has led many riverside towns
and counties, as well as the above-mentioned organizations, to reclaim
land along the riverfront and open it up to hikers, bikers, and picnick-
ers. In the past few years, acres of land that had been languishing in
government hands, as well as new parcels acquired by environmental
groups, have reconfigured the Hudson's banks.

For day-trippers, fishermen, history buffs, boaters, hikers, bikers,
and, yes, even swimmers, the Hudson River Valley has taken on a new

allure. A decade ago, travelers had to search long and hard for a decent bed and a good meal. In recent years, dozens of new restaurants, inns, and bed-and-breakfasts have filled the gap.

The grand estates along the banks of the Hudson have always drawn a big audience, but these box-office stars now have a strong supporting cast. Visitors can round out a trip to the Vanderbilt Mansion, for example, by hiking downriver along a new trail to the Franklin D. Roosevelt estate. Up and down the river, parks and boat launches have been opened and new hiking trails have been marked. Beginning in the summer of 1996, swimmers were able to bathe in the Hudson for the first time in nearly a decade, when the river beach at Croton Point Park reopened.

"In the last 10 years, the area has really come together in a way it never had," said Tim Mulligan, the author of *The Traveler's Guide to the Hudson River Valley.* "In the next edition of my book, I'm going to have to redo the whole thing."

In June 1996, Scenic Hudson, a nonprofit preservation group that has acquired many sites along the river, opened Poets' Walk, a 120-acre park in Red Hook, New York, just north of the Kingston-Rhinecliff Bridge in Dutchess County. In an area dominated by grand robber-baron estates, Poets' Walk competes by appealing to the more lofty human faculties. Billing itself as a "romantic landscape park," it offers a seductive blend of meadow, glade, and woodland, with sinuous trails descending to the banks of the Hudson.

Meadows & Flowers

The only man-made real estate comes in the form of rough-hewn bridges that cross streamlets, a gazebo-like viewing pavilion overlooking the river from a commanding height, and a shelter with benches at the end of a woodland trail.

But who needs real estate? Visitors follow a mowed path across bright meadows scattered with wildflowers: bachelor's buttons, Queen Anne's lace, black-eyed Susans, and daisies. The silence is thick enough to slice. The viewing pavilion makes a convenient halfway stop. A half mile downhill, the Hudson rolls along between shapely hills, its placid surface lightly supporting small sailboats and enduring with mild patience the torment of type-A jet skiers.

The prospect is indeed romantic, with the Catskills floating bluely to the northwest. More pleasure lies ahead, as the path turns rightward and winds through a cool forest downward to the "summer house" shelter overlooking a small pond, railroad tracks, and the river. After a poetic, romantic pause, visitors can pick up the trail and follow it as it loops back toward meadowland with views of the river and back uphill to the starting point.

Anyone with a hankering to see a house can follow River Road north to Montgomery Place, in Annandale-on-Hudson, a 19th-century country estate set on more than 400 acres of rolling woodland, lawns, gardens, and waterfalls. The house itself is a gem. The original house, a somewhat austere Federal-style structure built in 1802, was transformed by the architect Alexander Jackson Davis and the landscape architect Andrew Jackson Downing into an elegant country estate, with porticos, pavilions, verandas, and a spacious north portico with a stunning view of the river.

Poets' Walk created a park where none existed. In other projects along the river, parcels of land have been stitched together by trails, a less dramatic approach that has opened up long stretches of riverfront. Visitors to the Mills Mansion in Staatsburg can now walk down to the riverside, turn just below an old logging trail, and follow a challenging trail along the river as far as Norrie Point Park. In its first couple of hundred yards, the trail takes you up and over miniprecipices with rather fearsome sheer drops to the river below. Immediately, the trail heads downhill, and hikers can gaze across the glassy waters of a broad inlet, a scene straight out of a Fitz Hugh Lane painting.

"This is all owned by the state and all cohesively managed," said Dave Sampson, the executive director of the Hudson River Greenway Communities Council, a branch of the Greenway. "You couldn't put that together now for all the money in the Environmental Trust Fund."

Similarly, the Vanderbilt Mansion in Hyde Park has been linked by a trail system to the Franklin D. Roosevelt Home and Val-Kill cottage, the Eleanor Roosevelt National Historic Site. The river path, separated from the riverbank by railroad tracks, affords only intermittent glimpses of the Hudson; but the path is cool and soft underfoot, and at Bard Rock, hikers can turn left, cross the tracks, and arrive at a breezy outcropping with picnic tables.

For years, conservation groups have reached into their arsenal for a sobering statistic: More than 70% of the population that lives along the Hudson does not have access to the river. "I grew up on the river, and you didn't have a problem with access," said Rene Van Schaack, the executive director of the Greene County Soil and Water Conservation District. "As time passed, it became tougher and tougher to get access, as parcels were bought up, especially with the boom in second-home

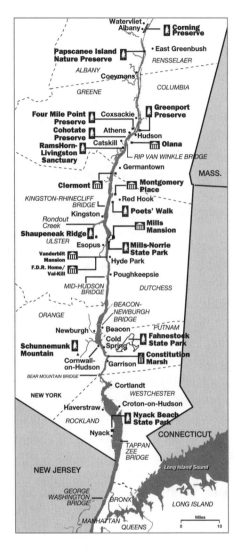

ownership during the eighties. As the river has gotten cleaner, though, more people want to get to it." Esopus, which has more shoreline along the river than any town between New York City and Albany, had no public access to the river until 1990, when Scenic Hudson acquired land and created a pocket-size park of about three-quarters of an acre, which it has added to more recently.

A Different Landscape

There's a finite amount of riverfront. Rather than sit still as more and more of it fell into private hands, state and local officials, along with environmental groups, have moved quickly in recent years to acquire land and open it up. The landscape along the river looks quite different now than it did even 5 years ago.

"In a way, it all has to do with the decline of IBM, which dominated the valley for so long," said Mr. Mulligan. "People were thrown back on their own resources. Local papers now talk about their communities as tourist destinations, and towns up and down the river, which used to be highly competitive and jealous of each other, are now working with each other." In East Greenbush, near Albany, the Open Space Institute opened Papscanee Island Nature Preserve, a string of three parcels of land near the fringe of an industrial area. The 150 acres include woodland, wetlands, and a small farm.

In Greenport, the Columbia Land Conservancy now runs a 450-acre park called the Greenport Preserve, with hiking trails that lead to bluffs overlooking an extensive wetland complex along the Hudson. New York State has added 2,000 acres to Fahnestock State Park in Cold Spring that include ridge trails with breathtaking views of Storm King Mountain. At the same time, the New York–New Jersey Trail Conference cleared and marked 22 miles of trails in the park.

On Schunnemunk Mountain, in Cornwall-on-Hudson, the Open Space Institute has acquired a 2,100-acre tract, with ridge trails maintained by the New York–New Jersey Trail Conference, that permits hikers to look out over 50 miles of the Hudson Valley and long stretches of the river. Since May 1996, hikers have been able to walk the Shaupeneak Ridge, west of Kingston, for a commanding view of the river.

In Greene County, the Soil and Water Conservation District manages a 52-acre parcel just south of Athens. Called the Cohotate Preserve, it includes 3,500 feet of river frontage. The preserve has self-guided interpretive trails. The county has also created, with Scenic Hudson, a 7-acre preserve at Four Mile Point, near Coxsackie.

Paddling in the Marshes

For years, the Audubon Society has offered guided canoe trips through Constitution Marsh, midway between Garrison and Cold Spring, in the Hudson Highlands. In cooperation with Scenic Hudson, it added another expanse of wetlands to its portfolio, the RamsHorn-Livingston Sanctuary, situated along RamsHorn Creek, south of Catskill and across the river from Olana, the estate of Frederic Edwin Church. At nearly 800 acres, RamsHorn is the largest tidal swamp forest on the Hudson, a kind of northern bayou that visitors can explore by foot or canoe (bring your own), paddling along the creek to its confluence with the Hudson. The preserve encompasses nearly 500 acres.

Several towns along the river, including Cortlandt, Coeymans, Beacon, and Haverstraw, have cleaned up existing river parks or opened new ones. Kingston, in particular, has energetically restored its historic waterfront area, Rondout Landing, and visitors can take ferries and cruise ships from the old port.

For bicycle riders as well, the picture is becoming brighter. "The Palisades Interstate Park Commission and the Taconic Region are getting more biker-friendly," said Peter Kick, the author of *Twenty-Five Mountain Bike Tours in the Hudson Valley.* "At Norrie Point, for example, they opened their trails to mountain bikers." Mr. Kick singled out the 14-mile stretch of the Mohawk-Hudson Bikeway between Watervliet and Albany for special praise, as well as the bike trail at Nyack Beach State Park, a 10-mile round-trip between the park and Haverstraw.

Whales and porpoises have not yet returned. Modern-day Americans can only wonder at Walt Whitman's description of the bald eagle he saw soaring over the river as he rode a northbound train. But the river itself flows on, cleaner than it has been in living memory, imposing and lovely, what one 19th-century guidebook called "a noble threshold to a great Continent."

Essentials for Hudson-Hopping

GETTING THERE

By Car There are so many destinations that there are no one-size-fits-all travel directions. In general, to reach the towns along the eastern Hudson by car, take the Saw Mill River Parkway or the Thomas E. Dewey Thruway to Tarrytown; pick up Rte. 9 and follow it north along the river. For towns on the west side of the river, cross the Tappan Zee Bridge and take the Palisades Parkway north to Rte. 9W.

By Train The Hudson line of Metro-North (☎ **212/532-4900;** 800/638-7646 outside New York City) provides train service as far north as Poughkeepsie, originating at Grand Central Terminal. Metro-North also offers seasonal travel and tour packages to Hyde Park and the Hudson River estates operated by Historic Hudson Valley; special day trips are also offered to various fairs throughout the area, including the Croton Point Park River Fair in early August. Call Metro-North at the number above for train schedules and other information.

HUDSON RIVER CRUISES

Great Hudson Sailing Center (☎ **800/ 237-1557** or 845/429-1557) operates 43-foot sailing vessels from the Rondout Waterfront in Kingston, and from the Haverstraw Marina, Beach Rd., Haverstraw, from May through October. Call for sailing schedule and rates.

North River Cruises, Rondout Waterfront, Kingston (☎ **845/679-8205**). You can take a 90-minute trip on the Hudson River aboard the motor yacht Teal. May through October, cruises Saturday and Sunday at 1 and 3pm; July 4 through Labor Day, sunset trips Friday, Saturday, and Sunday at 7:30pm. Tickets $13, $12 for seniors, $10 for children under 12. Call a week in advance to check schedule since the boat is not available if chartered.

The Rip Van Winkle, Rondout Waterfront, Rondout Creed (at the foot of Broadway), Kingston (exit 19 of the Gov. Thomas E. Dewey Thruway; ☎ **845/255-6515**), offers 2-hour cruises south to just above Hyde Park, past lighthouses and mansions, and back to Kingston. May through October, weekends at 2pm; July 4 through Labor Day, Tuesday through Sunday at 11:30am and 2pm. Tickets (available 1 hr. before cruise time) are $13, $12 for seniors, $6 for children 4 to 11, free for children under 4.

A MUSEUM

Hudson River Maritime Museum, Rondout Waterfront (at the foot of Broadway), Kingston (☎ **845/338-0071**). Open May through October, daily 11am to 5pm. Admission $4, $5 for seniors and children 5 to 12, free for children 5 and under and museum members.

Boat trips to the lighthouse are offered daily in July and August, and weekends May through June and September through October. Boat trips depart from the museum at 11:30am, and 1:30, 2:30, and 3:30pm. Tickets, which include admission to the museum, are $9, $8 for seniors and children 6 to 12, free for children under 5.

HISTORIC HOUSES

Clermont State Historic Site, off Rte. 9G, 15 miles south of Hudson in Clermont (☎ 518/537-4240). A 500-acre estate with the mansion of Robert R. Livingston, a signer of the Declaration of Independence; there are also formal gardens, hiking trails, and a visitor center. Open April through October, Tuesday through Sunday and Monday holidays 11am to 5pm; November through December 15, weekends 11am to 4pm; closed mid-December through March. Admission $3, $2 seniors, $1 children 5 to 12, free for children under 5.

Mills Mansion, Mills-Norrie State Park, off Rte. 9, between Hyde Park and Rhinebeck in Staatsburg (☎ 845/889-8851). The 190-acre beaux-arts estate of Ogden and Ruth Livingston Mills is part of the 900-acre New York State Historic Site with hiking trails, river views, and guided tours. Open early April through Labor Day, Wednesday through Saturday 10am to 4:30pm, Sunday noon to 4:30pm; September after Labor Day through October, Wednesday through Sunday noon to 4:30pm; closed November through March. Admission and house tour $3, $2 for seniors, $1 for children 5 to 12, free for those under 5. Free admission to grounds.

Montgomery Place, River Rd., Annandale-on-Hudson (☎ 914/758-5461). The early 19th-century, 434-acre estate of Janet Livingston Montgomery, widow of Gen. Richard Montgomery, who was killed during the Revolutionary War. The estate features gardens, hiking trails, picnicking, and a waterfall. Open April through October, Wednesday through Monday 10am to 5pm; November, weekends 10am to 5pm; first 2 weekends in December, noon to 5pm. Closed the rest of December through the end of March. Guided tours begin every 45 minutes. Admission to house and tour $6, $5 for seniors, $3 for students and children over 6, free for children 5 and under. Admission to the grounds is $3, free for children under 5.

Olana, Rte. 9G (1 mile south of the Rip Van Winkle Bridge), Hudson (☎ 518/828-0135). The 250-acre estate of the 19th-century artist Frederic Edwin Church is now operated by the New York State Office of Parks, Recreation, and Historic Preservation. Open April through May, Wednesday through Sunday 10am to 4pm; June through mid-October, Wednesday through Sunday 10am to 5pm; mid-October through October 31, Wednesday through Sunday 10am to 4pm. Guided 50-minute tours begin every 20 to 30 minutes; tours limited to 12 people, so reservations are recommended. Admission $3, $2 for seniors, $1 for children 5 to 12, free for children 4 and under.

Roosevelt-Vanderbilt National Historic Site, Hyde Park. Includes the Vanderbilt Mansion (☎ 845/229-7770), a 211-acre estate with a formal Italian garden, and the 300-acre estate composed of the Franklin D. Roosevelt Home (☎ 845/229-8114 or 845/229-2500) and Val-Kill (☎ 845/229-9422), the Eleanor Roosevelt cottage.

All of the sites, which are operated by the National Park Service (☎ 845/229-9115), have walking trails and are part of the Hyde Park Trail. Open May through October, daily 9am to 5pm; November and December, weekends 9am to 5pm; Val-Kill is open November through April, weekends only 9am to 5pm. Admission to all three sites $18, $9 for seniors with a national parks golden pass. Admission to Val-Kill $5.

PARKS & PRESERVES

Clarence Fahnestock State Park, Rte. 301 (off Taconic State Parkway), Cold Spring (☎ 845/225-7207). Twenty-two miles of trails newly added. Open daily, dawn to dusk. Free admission. Beach parking for Canopus Lake $5.

Cohatate Preserve, Greene County Environmental Education Center, Rte. 385 (north of the Rip Van Winkle Bridge), near Athens (☎ 518/622-3620). Open daily, dawn to dusk. Free admission.

Croton Point Park, Croton Point Ave. (off Rte. 9), Croton-on-Hudson (☎ 914/271-3293). Open daily, dawn to dusk. Free admission.

Four Mile Point Preserve, Four Mile Point Rd. (Rte. 385), near Coxsackie (☎ 518/622-3620). Open daily, dawn to dusk. Free admission.

Greenport Preserve, off Rte. 9, north of Hudson (☎ 212/505-7480). A 450-acre park with trails and extensive views across the river to the Catskill Mountains. Open daily, dawn to dusk. Free admission.

Nyack Beach State Park, Rte. 9W at Broadway, Nyack (☎ 845/358-1316, 845/268-3020, or 914/786-2701). Hiking, biking, fishing, picnic tables. Open year-round, dawn to dusk. Parking $5 May through Columbus Day.

Papscanee Island Nature Preserve, State Rte. 9J, East Greenbush, Albany (☎ 212/505-7480). About 150 acres with woodland, wetlands. Open daily, dawn to dusk. Free admission.

Poets' Walk, County Rd. 103 (River Rd.), north of the Kingston-Rhinecliff Bridge, Red Hook (☎ 845/473-4440). A 120-acre park with trails for hiking and benches for contemplation. Open daily, 9am to dusk. Free admission.

RamsHorn-Livingston Sanctuary, Grandview Ave. (off Rte. 9W), Catskill (☎ 518/943-6895 or 845/473-4440). A tidal swamp forest with 480 acres operated by Scenic Hudson and the Northern Catskills Audubon Society. Open daily, dawn to dusk. Free admission.

Schunnemunk Mountain, Otterkill Rd. (off Rte. 32), Cornwall-on-Hudson (☎ 212/505-7480). A preserve of several miles along a mountain ridge, with hiking trails. Open daily, dawn to dusk. Free admission.

FURTHER READING

Fifty Hikes in the Hudson Valley, by Barbara McMartin and Peter Kick (Backcountry Publications, Woodstock, Vt.; $15).

The Traveler's Guide to the Hudson River Valley, 4th edition, by Tim Mulligan (Random House; $14).

Walks and Rambles in the Western Hudson Valley, by Peggy Turco (Backcountry Publications, Woodstock, Vt., $15).

WEST POINT: PITCHING CAMP WHERE THE OLD SOLDIERS LIVE ON

by Ralph Blumenthal

HERE TOWERED PATTON, BINOCU-
lars in hand, vigilant against an unseen enemy. Or perhaps, as West
Point lore has it, looking for the library. There stood bronzed
MacArthur, defiant, campaign jacket flung over an arm. And the five-
star Ike, businesslike, hands on his hips, gazing over the Plain.

We had come to the granite Army citadel some 60 miles up the
Hudson from Manhattan to rub shoulders with history and perhaps a
future president, and set up base to reconnoiter the mid–Hudson
Valley. Our contingent numbered four: two generals and two recruits,
gender female.

We found no shortage of attractions, martial or pacific. Perched on
a bluff on the west bank of the Hudson estuary where plunging hills
squeeze the water into placid pools, the United States Military
Academy occupies one of the more spectacular pieces of real estate in
the East, as George Washington recognized when he ordered its fortifi-
cation during the Revolution as "the Gibraltar of America." All around
lie reminders of the republic's embattled past: statues to heroes and
martyrs, captured trophies of war, and in the bristling museum,
weapons of every murderous variety, from caveman spears and medieval
maces to models of a tactical atomic cannon and the "Fat Man" nuclear
bomb dropped on Nagasaki, Japan.

Beyond, the Hudson Valley beckoned with more side trips than we could ever hope to make in a weekend: manor houses and historic mansions and restorations, antique villages, Colonial churchyards, old inns, and waterfront restaurants. Although West Point can be reached from midtown Manhattan in 1½ hours, for historical interest I mapped a midway stop at the Old Dutch Church on Route 9 in Sleepy Hollow (formerly North Tarrytown). Over the years, I had driven past it countless times, always vowing someday to, well, tarry, just as I promised that someday I would stop to read all historic markers I whiz by. Alas, the little stone church built in 1697 was locked. I learned later that it was closed to public tours until June.

But the graveyard yawned open, ancient tombstones pitched at grotesque angles. We picked our way among them as I told the girls the story of Ichabod Crane and the Headless Horseman, who in Washington Irving's picaresque tale carried his severed head in his hands and began his nightly ride in the burying ground.

It got my younger daughter's attention. "Headless Horseman?" Sophie repeated.

"It's just a story, honey," my wife said reassuringly.

"I smelled the gravy," Sophie said.

We looked at each other. Gravy? "From the graves," Sophie said.

At Peekskill, Routes 6 and 202 veer west, hugging the cliffs over the Hudson for a roller-coaster ride to the Bear Mountain Bridge. (Stop at the scenic overlook before the bridge for a panoramic view.) From the bridge, it was only a few minutes' ride north on 9W to Highland Falls, the one-street village of small restaurants and souvenir shops that abuts the academy. At Thayer Gate, one of the three access points to the reservation, an M.P. sized us up and waved us through to the Hotel Thayer, its Neo-Gothic turrets and crenellated roofline looming just above us on the right.

The 194-room hotel, built in 1926 and named for Superintendent Sylvanus Thayer, who arrived in 1817 to set the academy's rigorous standards, exuded baronial grandeur. The lobby of pitted black-and-white marble and unit escutcheons featured a large stone fireplace, rustic chandeliers, and massive beams hung with flags.

At dusk, while the rest of the squad bivouacked in the room, I drove down Thayer Road marveling at the granite-hewn administration buildings and barracks. Continuing on foot to the main parade field, called "the Plain," I stopped at the stations of American military piety: the larger-than-life statues of Washington, who had first laid out the site and now sat stiffly on horseback outside his eponymous dining hall; Eisenhower (class of 1915); Gen. Douglas MacArthur (1903), whose mother moved into the since-demolished West Point Hotel while he was a cadet; and Gen. George S. Patton, Jr. (1909), whose borderline grades

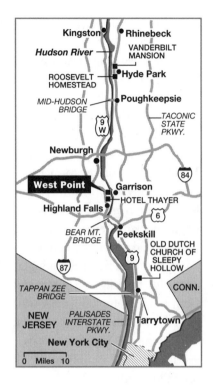

were only later traced to undiagnosed dyslexia. Far from needing binoculars to find the library, authorities now say, Patton in fact might have been one of West Point's brightest graduates.

I was crossing the Plain when a distant bugler sounded "Retreat" and the Stars and Stripes at Trophy Point began to inch down the pole. Two cadets heading home for the weekend stopped midfield, hand over heart, and so, reflexively, did I. Then came a puff of smoke and, a beat later, a thunderous report from a blank charge in a cannon by the flagpole.

At Trophy Point, where a soaring granite cylinder memorializes the Regular Army dead in the "War of the Rebellion" and a ring of 150-pound links recalls the immense chain the Colonists stretched across the river to stymie the British navy, I watched a pink sunset glow settle over the fjordlike vista of snaking river and mirrored mountains.

In case we didn't realize that the buffet dinner in the mullion-windowed dining room was a good deal at $19 a person, our waitress was glad to tell us, poking my shoulder for emphasis. "You can"—poke—"go back as many times"—poke—"as you like," she said cheerily. And so we did, repeatedly filling our plates with salad and shrimp, raw vegetables, seafood salad, chicken breast in cream sauce, carved roast beef, lamb chops, and breaded fish. Across the candlelit chamber, several couples slow-danced to a pianist's repertoire of Chopin and Tchaikovsky.

We began the next day at the visitor center and museum in Highland Falls on the former site of Ladycliff College, which the military academy absorbed in 1984. The museum has a grisly enough collection of armaments to satisfy the bloodthirstiest little Power Ranger. Of particular interest are the early firearms and this quote, which I thought had a lot to say about the direction of civilization: "A man with a gun was capable of defeating a mounted knight who had spent his whole life training for combat and whose weapons had cost a fortune." Both the museum and the visitor center have gift shops well stocked with Army sweatshirts, caps, books, tchotchkes, and the like.

A commercial tour bus leaves from the visitor center for an hour's excellent tour of the military academy, at a cost of $6 for adults and $3 for children under 12.

We learned, for example, that women, first admitted to the academy in 1976, now account for 10% of the enrollment. That 13,000 applicants compete for the 1,100 plebe openings. That West Point boasts five presidents: Eisenhower; Ulysses S. Grant; Jefferson Davis of the Confederacy; Fidel V. Ramos of the Philippines; and Gen. Anastasio Somoza Debayle, who graduated in 1946 and became the dictator of Nicaragua (he was assassinated in Paraguay in 1980). That all 4,000 cadets dine together and that if they perform their jobs properly they can all be served in 3 minutes and finish eating in 20. That it's considered unlucky to catch your own hat after you fling it into the air at graduation. And that if a cadet escorts his date to Kissing Rock overlooking the Hudson, said date must kiss said cadet or said rock will crash into the water, killing all of West Point.

We didn't do much mingling with the cadets we saw walking around in their traditional gray tunics. Most were off for the weekend and others went about their business in areas of the academy off-limits to visitors.

To explore more of the Hudson Valley, we drove through the reservation, north on 9W, over the Mid-Hudson Bridge and north on Route 9 to the village of Rhinebeck, a nascent Hampton on the Hudson. I had made reservations for restaurateur Larry Forgione's storied Sunday brunch at the 1766 Tavern, the Beekman Arms, which calls itself the oldest continuously operated inn in America.

Although the drive took well over an hour and we arrived after the ostensible 1:30pm buffet cutoff, we were nonetheless graciously seated and loosed on the tables groaning with Belgian waffles, cheese blintzes, salmon, pâté, bagels, bacon, sausages, salads, eggs of all kinds including omelets to order, fruit, and fancy desserts, all for $19.95 each for the grown-ups, $10.95 each for the kids. "Look," said Sophie, spearing melon on a swizzle stick, "fruit-fa-bob."

Waddling out 2 hours later, we explored the stores and boutiques set along the village's crossroads. Summer Moon had an ecological special: 20% off jeans made with hemp. At the Antique Market and Gallery I bought a flaking issue of the *New-York Times* (then hyphenated) from 1868 for $7.

We were hoping to see some of the mansions we had passed south along Route 9, so we pushed off. At Hyde Park, we drove into the Vanderbilt estate, just missing the last tour, which had filled up at 3:30pm. But we were rewarded by views of the colossal 1890s mansion, rearing up through the trees like Manderley. The visitor center afforded some exhibits of the yachts and other accoutrements of the family called the richest in America in their time.

Next we tried the Franklin Delano Roosevelt homestead just to the south and here we were in luck. There was still time to visit the house, grounds, and museum. After the palace of the Vanderbilts, the little 35-room granite house with green shutters seemed almost quaint, but, as at West Point, history supplied the drama.

We gazed at the simple bed where the future president first greeted the world on January 30, 1882; his wheelchair made of a kitchen chair with the legs sawed off; the leash and blanket of his beloved Scottie,

Fala; the encoded black phone for wartime calls to the White House; the strange sequence of bedrooms: Eleanor's sandwiched between her husband's and her mother-in-law's.

Crossing the grounds past the garden where he and Eleanor now lie together under a simple block of marble, we entered the museum, exclaiming at the girlish frocks young Franklin wore, the accomplished letter he wrote his mother at the age of 5, the drama of his 1932 acceptance speech: "I pledge you, I pledge myself, to a new deal for the American people." My favorite exhibit was Roosevelt's 1936 Ford Phaeton, a blue-green convertible with brown leather seats and hand controls and an ingenious metal box on the steering column that dispensed lighted cigarettes.

On the way home the next day we crossed the Bear Mountain Bridge and detoured north to Garrison's Landing for a last view of West Point, perched on the ramparts, glinting like gunpowder in the morning light.

WEST POINT ESSENTIALS

GETTING THERE

By Car To drive to the United States Military Academy, near Highland Falls, New York, use the George Washington Bridge or the Tappan Zee Bridge to reach the Palisades Parkway. Continue to the end of the parkway, and there, at the Bear Mountain traffic circle, take Rte. 9W north to Rte. 218, and continue to West Point.

By Bus Bus service to West Point is provided by Short Line (☎ 212/736-4700) from the Port Authority Bus Terminal, Eighth Ave. and 41st St., Manhattan. Weekend buses run twice daily, at 8:45 and 11:15am. One-way fare $12.70, round-trip $24.15; half fare for children 5 to 11.

VISITING WEST POINT

Visitors Center at West Point and West Point Museum (☎ 845/938-2638). The center operates daily 9am to 4:45pm (closed Thanksgiving, Christmas, and New Year's). Academy grounds are open daily 9:30am to dusk, and the museum is open daily 10:30am to 4:15pm. Admission is free.

Daily 1-hour bus tours of the Academy are offered by **West Point Tours** (☎ 845/446-4724). November to March, tours leave from the visitor center daily at 11:30am and 1:30pm. April to October, tours leave Monday through Saturday every half hour 10am to 3:30pm, and

Sunday 11am to 3:30pm. The fare is $6, $3 for children 11 and under, and free for those under 2. May to October, daily 2-hour tours that include more walking are also offered at 11:15am and 1:15pm; the fare is $8, $5 for children, free for children under 2.

ACCOMMODATIONS & DINING

Beekman 1766 Tavern, Beekman Arms, Rte. 9, Rhinebeck (☎ **845/871-1766**). Sunday brunch 10am to 2pm (last seating at 1:30pm), $19.95 per person, $10.95 for children 10 and under. Monday through Thursday 11:30am to 3pm and 5:30 to 9pm; Friday and Saturday 11:30am to 3pm and 5:30 to 9:30pm; Sunday 3:30 to 8:30pm. Lunch entrees $8.50 to $11.95; dinner entrees $17.95 to $25.95. Reservations suggested.

Hotel Thayer, on the grounds of the Academy (☎ **800/247-5047** or 845/446-4731). Weekend rates $150 to $200 double or single, $400 to $600 for suites accommodating two to eight; children 17 and under stay free with accompanying adult. Sunday brunch 9:30am to 2:30pm is $25.95 per person, half price for children under 12.

OTHER AREA ATTRACTIONS

Franklin Delano Roosevelt Home, Library, and Museum, Rte. 9, Hyde Park (☎ **845/229-2501;** library 845/229-8114). The home and museum are open daily 9am to 5pm. Admission $10, $5 for seniors with national parks golden pass, free for children under 17.

Old Dutch Church of Sleepy Hollow, Rte. 9, Sleepy Hollow (☎ **914/631-1123**). The church, a branch of the Reformed Church in America, is open for tours Memorial Day weekend through Labor Day, Monday, Wednesday, and Thursday 1 to 5pm and by appointment. The graveyard is open all the time; graveyard tours Memorial Day weekend through October, Sunday at 2pm. Donations accepted.

Vanderbilt Mansion, Rte. 9, Hyde Park (☎ **845/229-7770**). Daily 9am to 5pm. Admission $8 adults, $4 for seniors with national parks golden pass, free for children under 17.

WOODSTOCK'S OLD-TIME NEW AGE KARMA

by Jon Pareles

BACK IN THE 1980s, I WAS WALKING down a street in Woodstock when a Volkswagen microbus pulled over and the scraggly-haired driver asked, "Can you tell me where the rock festival was?"

At the time, I was in Woodstock, England.

The Woodstock festival of 1969, and its 25th anniversary sequel in 1994, didn't happen in Woodstock, New York, either. The first one was in White Lake, New York, 60 miles away in Sullivan County; the second one was closer to Woodstock, in the neighboring Ulster County town of Saugerties. Yet a hippie mythos still clings to Woodstock itself, where my wife and I recently spent a long weekend.

Tucked among bucolic and sometimes-spectacular Catskill scenery, with a full-time population of 6,290 (as of the 1990 census), Woodstock is the counterculture's country retreat, where the upstate woodlands meet the New Age. It's a haven of hearth-baked bread, folk-rock on the local radio station (WDST, at 100.1 and 96.9 FM), art galleries, artisans, and spiritual seekers. Under "houses of worship," a Chamber of Commerce brochure lists not only the Dutch Reformed Church but also a Tibetan Buddhist monastery. Among the various "Welcome to Woodstock" stickers at local stores, one reads, IF YOU LIVED HERE, YOU'D BE OM NOW.

Yet despite its legendary name and a century of experience as a tourist magnet, Woodstock remains a friendly, close-knit small town. There is no traffic light at Woodstock's main intersection, where Tinker

Street meets Rock City Road, and the cluster of stores stretches just a few blocks.

On a recent Friday afternoon, before the weekend influx from New York City, Tinker Street was populated by women without makeup and men with ponytails. People in their 20s and people in their 50s all wore the ponchos and fringed buckskin, patched jeans, and embroidered shirts of the international peasant-wear economy. Running shoes were the only sign of the 1990s. Still, the shoe store in the center of town featured Birkenstocks.

Woodstock drew utopian free thinkers long before the 1960s. During the 19th century,

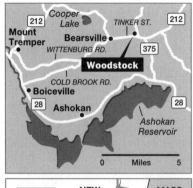

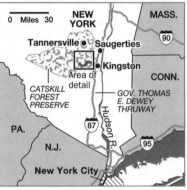

according to Alf Evers's comprehensive *Woodstock: History of an American Town* (Overlook Press, 1987; $39.50), it was an industrious (and none too environmentally conscious) hamlet, logging hemlock trees from the Catskill mountainsides and using the bark to tan leather.

In 1902, a wealthy Englishman, Ralph Radcliffe Whitehead, started an arts colony, Byrdcliffe. To realize the ideals of the Arts and Crafts movement, it would produce old-fashioned handmade goods and run a summer arts school. Handicrafts couldn't support Byrdcliffe, but painters, potters, musicians, weavers, and actors had discovered Woodstock.

The Art Students League, based in Manhattan, opened a Woodstock summer school in 1906, and other groups of artists soon followed. The Maverick colony, just across the town line, drew social reformers, visual artists, and performers, and presented summer festivals from 1915 to 1931, the real Woodstock festivals. In 1921, factions of the Communist Party convened at the Overlook Mountain House hotel and united as the Communist Party of America. Through the 1920s, artists, theater people, and the tourists who arrived to gawk at them kept Woodstock thriving.

Rockers arrived later, when Bob Dylan and the Band settled upstate in the late 1960s and recorded *Music from Big Pink* (a big pink house in West Saugerties) and *The Basement Tapes*. Other musicians, including a jazz contingent, are still in the hills, descending to play rock at Joyous Lake, the town's rock club, or jazz at the intimate auditorium of the Kleinert/James Arts Center. Well-known bands like Phish record albums in the wooded privacy of Bearsville Studios.

We visited the Woodstock Historical Society, which displayed a newspaper clipping from 1929, headlined "Nude Bathing Parties Offend"; the town was divided over whether to restrict such shenanigans at risk of losing tourists. An exhibition of paintings by Woodstock artists included a striking self-portrait from the early 1930s by Petra Cabot: a young woman with a modish black hat and a confident gaze. A woman with long white hair walked in and told the caretaker, "I must have that painting so I can photograph it." It was Ms. Cabot, who smiled as she looked at her self-assured 21-year-old self. "Oh, we had some great times," she said. Woodstock, we kept realizing, is a place unto itself. It is a town where the biggest, pushiest crowd we saw was the one that mobbed the biweekly Saturday-morning used-book sale at the library. The proprietor of Readers' Quarry, a small, well-organized used bookstore told us about it. "If I see you there," she said, "I won't be able to talk. I'll be too busy."

Peace & Apples

One attraction during our weekend visit was the town's "harvest festival." Like other town fairs, it had a local apple farmer demonstrating an antique cider press. But being Woodstock, it also started with a "peace ceremony," a parade of schoolchildren with assorted national flags. A man walked by wearing a crystal the size of a dill pickle around his neck; a teenager had a saucepan for a hat. On the outdoor stage, the group Women Who Drum followed a Hebrew blessing with a Seneca peace prayer.

We picked up *The Woodstock Journal,* a weekly paper run by Ed Sanders that prints the local police blotter (with regular marijuana-possession arrests) and poetry along with muckraking. Mr. Sanders, now an author and historian, was a prime mover in the zoning laws that keep Woodstock green; in the 1960s, he founded the folk-rock provocateurs the Fugs, whose song title "Refuse to Be Burnt Out" provides the paper's watchwords.

The paper announced that it would celebrate a move to new offices with an exhibition of paintings by Alf Evers, whose book we had been consulting. The paintings were Depression-era scenes of a rural Woodstock and of Mr. Evers's travels; a label on a Bermuda landscape read, "Notice the pink sand." Mr. Evers, now in his 90s, and Mr. Sanders were surrounded by well-wishers at the opening. On the doorstep a woman was exclaiming: "He's not just a writer! Everyone has multiple personalities!"

At Bread Alone, the Woodstock outlet for a bakery in nearby Boiceville, we could easily distinguish unhurried Woodstockers from the jostling weekenders who mobbed the place on Saturday morning. We tried the organic breakfast tea and substantial currant scones; on a return visit, we picked up a flourless chocolate torte, rich but not overly sweet. A sign in the bathroom read: THIS NOTE IS SINCERELY ADDRESSED TO THE PERSON STEALING THE POSTERS OFF THE BATHROOM WALLS. PLEASE STOP! IF YOU HAVE ANY REGRETS, YOU'RE FORGIVEN. ENJOY THE ART AND PLEASE DON'T TAKE ANY MORE POSTERS.

Down the block is Pieces of Mine, which sells stones and crystals; its advertisement promised consultations. "What are you drawn to?" asked the woman at the counter. "What you are drawn to is what you need." We picked red tiger eye, jade, amethyst, and turquoise. The woman smiled. "You've covered almost all seven chakras," she said. "You just need something yellow."

"I was just looking at the amber," my wife said.

"It looks like a higher power has directed you," the woman said. Quickly, she added: "I don't mean to say that you're not responsible for your decision. It's your own higher power from within that has guided you."

All for the Spirit

Mirabai Books, one of the bookstores in town, concentrates on spiritual and holistic health books. One bookcase covers a full cycle: *Death and Dying, Reincarnation,* and *Channeling.* We looked into Dharmaware, which sells Buddhist items. An employee with his dreadlocks looped into a topknot was busy moving merchandise between storefronts. "We're in a state of transformation," he said. Nearby was the Tibetan Emporium; as we walked in, the proprietor was chanting along with a CD of Buddhist monks. The emporium is run by the director of Karma Triyana Dharmachakra monastery, a traditional Tibetan Buddhist temple built in the 1980s. We drove up Meads Mountain Road to see the impressive white-and-red temple, with its multicolored floral ornaments, and happened onto the daily tour.

"Nothing here is for decorative purposes," the guide said, taking us through the main temple, with its golden statues, bright banners, and embroidered pictures of saints, all of them sewn by the temple's abbot. "Everything here has a spiritual meaning behind it."

We wished we had worn thick socks; we took off our shoes before entering the temple, and the floors grew cold during the tour. The guide invited people to come back for the regular prayers at 5am and 5 and 7pm. Foregoing materialism, she didn't mention the center's bookstore and gift shop.

Across the street was the path up Overlook Mountain, renowned for the view from 3,140 feet. The trail ascends about 2 miles on a steady upward grade to the hulk of the Overlook Mountain House, the third hotel on the same site. Affixed to the concrete walls, eroding photographs and documents (all biodegradable, a sign said) describe the three attempts to maintain a luxury hotel on the slope, all commercial failures; all three burned down.

Past the hotel site, the main trail leads to a former fire observatory tower. The stairway to the second story has been removed, but intrepid types still climb the scaffolding for the view above the trees. A narrower path, to the right after the hotel ruins, heads along a ridge and offers a less perilous unobstructed view, with a silvery ribbon of the Hudson River, forested hillsides, and the gleaming Ashokan Reservoir below. James Fenimore Cooper, writing before the reservoir was created, declared, "It is a spot to make a man solemnize."

Up Meads Mountain Road from the monastery is the Magic Meadow, a Woodstock landmark that was mired in small-town controversy. Some Woodstockers had made a ritual of going to the meadow to greet the full moon. But the meadow is on private property, and to discourage moonstruck trespassers, the town put up no-parking signs. Claiming an infringement of religious freedom, people who received parking tickets took the case to court, where it was pending during our visit. We looked at the meadow by daylight; it is a neatly mowed clearing with a peaceful pond.

There was more mountain scenery to explore. Cold Brook Road, from Woodstock to Boiceville, snaked through a valley with fields and mountains on one side. And when we picked up *Hiking the Catskills* (New York–New Jersey Trail Conference, 1989; $14.95) at the Bookmart, the thoughtful owner was ready to suggest her favorite walks. After we admitted we were tired from our Overlook climb, she suggested a spectacular drive, climbing Platte Clove Road through Saugerties to Tannersville, and back via Main Street in Tannersville and Route 214 to Route 28. The road's hairpin curves keep it closed November to April.

We spent nights at two different bed-and-breakfasts. The Woodstock Country Inn—on a secluded road in Bearsville, part of Woodstock Township—is in a house built by an artist, Jo Cantine, whose luminous portraits and tropical landscapes still decorate the walls. Our room was whitewashed and uncluttered, with wicker furniture and a firm, comfortable bed; it had a view of the surrounding hills.

The innkeeper, Carol Wandrey, has lived in Woodstock for 30 years, and she was a fount of information on everything from visiting rockers to good places to stroll. She also introduced us to the web of small-town connections. Jo Cantine's grandson owns the Bear Cafe, generally considered the best restaurant in town.

Like so much else in Woodstock, the Bear mingles the homegrown and the internationalist. It's a high-ceilinged place with one windowed wall looking out over the Sawkill Brook. Its bread, baked by someone named Heather, is like that of a model grandmother: crusty on the outside, tender within. The mixed green salad was organic and very fresh, and we followed it with noodle dishes from disparate cultures: udon noodles with shredded vegetables in a complex, spicy broth, and penne with grilled vegetables in a portobello broth. Dinner for two was about $76. The Bear eclipsed the other local restaurants we visited.

For our last night in Ulster County, we moved to the Onteora Mountain House in Boiceville. Richard Hellmann, the mayonnaise mogul, retired to the mountainside lodge at the age of 50 on a doctor's advice and lived for 44 more years. Built on Mount Ticetonyk, it faces a spectacular panorama of mountains stretching into the distance, with the sunset framed by distant hills.

Its owners have filled its high-ceilinged Arts and Crafts interior with Korean antiques, making it more formal than the Woodstock Country Inn; at the head of our bed was a painting of the Buddha and his disciples. The lodge's original pool table, with Mission-style legs, is in a downstairs game room. Breakfast was eggs Hellmann, a high-cholesterol construction of an English muffin, spinach, poached eggs, and, of course, mayonnaise. "Our founder," the innkeeper said.

For dinner, we tried a place where it seemed as if the 1960s had never happened. La Duchesse Anne, a French restaurant in the former Mount Tremper Inn, has a player piano by the bar, stocked with James P. Johnson and Fats Waller classics. For dinner, we enjoyed a *cotriade,* a Breton fish soup with tomato and a hint of cream, and a grilled tuna in sorrel sauce, neither in the least multicultural and both satisfying. We declined the foot-high napoleons on the pastry cart. Dinner for two was about $60.

On the way home we made two stops. One was the Sunfrost Farms in Woodstock for local apples (at $3.99 for a half peck) and Bosc pears (99¢ a pound). It also runs a juice bar and stocks foods like olive spread (black and green) and the rare *maitake* (hen of the woods) mushrooms.

Sampling Ice Cream

And in Kingston, we visited the headquarters of Jane's Homemade Ice Cream and concluded that her Killer Chocolate surpassed any other chocolate ice cream in our experience. At the main store, we asked if it was sold anywhere in New York City; we were told, at the restaurant at Saks Fifth Avenue and the Carlyle Hotel, among other places.

At $2.80 for two hefty scoops, we chose pralines and cream and pumpkin, both worthwhile, and the remarkable cappuccino Kahlúa calypso, with deep espresso flavor and a crunch. The ice cream would speed us back to Manhattan, while the apples and pears, over the days to come, would continue to remind us of pastoral surroundings and small-town hospitality.

WOODSTOCK ESSENTIALS

GETTING THERE

By Car From Manhattan, take Thomas E. Dewey Thruway to the Kingston exit (exit 19) and pick up Rte. 28 West; follow Rte. 28 West to Rte. 375 North and take Rte. 375 North to Rte. 212 West; continue on Rte. 212 West, which turns into Tinker St., the main street in Woodstock.

By Bus Adirondack Trailways (**☎ 800/225-6815** or 212/967-2900) provides daily bus service to Woodstock from the Port Authority Bus Terminal, Eighth Ave. and 42nd St., Manhattan. Buses depart for the 2½-hour ride daily at 10am and 12:30, 3:30, and 5pm. Fare $20 one-way, $38 round-trip ($10 and $19 for children 3 to 11, free for those 2 and under who sit on a parent's lap).

ACCOMMODATIONS

Onteora, the Mountain House, 96 Piney Point Rd., Bolceville (**☎ 845/657-6233**). Daily room rate, with private bathroom, $200 to $270; rates are based on double occupancy and include full breakfast; 2-night minimum stay on weekends. Children over 12 welcome.

Woodstock Country Inn, Bearsville (**☎ 845/679-9380**). Mid-May through November 1 and holidays, daily room rates range $165 to $250; after November 1, they range $125 to $200; all have private bathrooms. Rates are based on double occupancy and include breakfast; 2-night minimum stay on weekends. No smoking; not recommended for children.

DINING

Bear Cafe, Bearsville Theater Complex, Rte. 212, Bearsville (☎ 845/679-5555). Open Wednesday through Monday 5 to 10pm. Entrees range $13.95 to $23.

Jane's Homemade Ice Cream and Restaurant, 305 Wall St., Kingston (☎ 845/338-8315). Open Sunday through Friday 9am to 6pm, and Saturday 9am to 5pm. Prices range $4 to $7.

La Duchesse Anne, Rte. 212 and Wittenberg Rd., Mount Tremper (☎ 845/688-5260). Open Thursday through Monday 5:30pm and Sunday 11:30am. There is no set closing time. Entrees average $16 to $22.

Woodstock Bread Alone, 22 Mill Hill Rd., Woodstock (☎ 845/679-2108). Open Sunday through Thursday 7:30am to 5pm (6pm during summer), and Friday and Saturday 7:30am to 6pm (5pm during summer.) Soups, salads, and sandwiches average $4.50 to $7.

LOCAL LANDMARKS

Karma Triyana Dharmachakra, 352 Meads, Mountain Rd., Woodstock (☎ 845/679-5906). Open daily 5am to 8pm. No fee.

Woodstock Historical Society Museum, Comeau Rd. (off Tinker St.), Woodstock (☎ 845/679-2256).

The Woodstock Journal, Wittenberg Rd., Woodstock (☎ 845/679-2969).

Woodstock Reformed Church, 18 Tinker St., Woodstock (☎ 845/679-6610). Open Tuesday to Friday, 9am to noon or by appointment. No fee.

HIKING

Overlook Mountain, off Meads Mountain Rd., Woodstock (☎ 914/256-3000). Open daily, dawn to dusk.

SHOPPING

BOOKSTORES

Mirabai Books/Sacred Space, 23 Mill Hill Rd., Woodstock (☎ 845/679-2100).

Reader's Quarry, 70 Tinker St., Woodstock (☎ 845/679-9572).

Woodstock Library, 5 Library Lane (at Tinker St.; ☎ 845/679-2213).

A FARMERS' MARKET

Sunfrost Farms, 217 Tinker St., Woodstock (☎ 845/679-6690).

OTHER SHOPPING

Dharmaware, 54 N.E. Tinker St., Woodstock (☎ 845/679-3270).

Pieces of Mine: A Metaphysical Gateway, 7 Maple Lane, Woodstock (☎ 845/679-4289).

Tibetan Emporium, 5 Rock City Rd., Woodstock (☎ 845/679-3808).

LIVE MUSIC

ROCK

Joyous Lake, 42 Mill Hill Rd., Woodstock 9 (☎ 845/679-0367).

JAZZ

Kleinert/James Art Center, 34 Tinker St., Woodstock (☎ 845/679-2079).

WHERE HISTORY
MEETS NATURE

by Lisa W. Foderaro

Cold Spring, New York

THIS HUDSON RIVER VILLAGE, ITS Main Street lined with antiques stores under ornate cornices, appears caught in a time warp, a faded Victorian postcard sprung to life.

In recent years, people have streamed in from all over just to admire the architecture or browse in Salmagundi Books or sup at the Vintage Cafe. Most end up at the river's edge, awed by the ancient Hudson Highlands, which loom from the opposite bank: enormous mounds of granite and dense green forest.

There is, in fact, not a whole lot to do right in the village, except soak up the atmosphere. But that seems to be exactly the point.

Fifty miles north of Manhattan on the river's eastern shore, Cold Spring is too far away to be a suburb and yet too close to be a farm community. It has thus escaped the bland shopping-center culture of the one and the hardworking pragmatism of the other. Instead, it seems to have found its calling by tapping into an odd but distinct pastime: the search for small-town America.

People want intimacy, charm, a whiff of history. Cold Spring seems to be the answer, if at times self-consciously so: Under a shingled gazebo, a quartet in red-and-white–striped vests can be found on weekends belting out songs by Duke Ellington and Hoagy Carmichael.

Modern facts of life like the dry cleaners and the supermarket moved, conveniently, from the heart of the village to a retail strip out on Route 9D years ago. That left the Main Street, which slopes toward the river, poised to become a National Historic District in 1982. And that, in turn, led to the germination of antiques stores, boutiques, restaurants, and inns.

What makes Cold Spring a weekend retreat rather than merely a stopover during a Sunday drive is its proximity to some of the historic and natural highlights of the region. There is, for instance, Boscobel, a lavishly restored Federal mansion, and Constitution Marsh, a small private wildlife sanctuary managed by the National Audubon Society whose watery labyrinth is home to many species of birds and fish.

Cold Spring's 19th-century streetscape isn't entirely museum quality. There are some forgettable dwellings from the 1950s and 1960s included in the mix of antique two- and three-story houses and buildings. But there are enough of the latter to make up for the former. Two that stand out are 73 Main Street, a faded brick building dating from 1820 that houses the Pig Hill Inn, and 49 Main Street, an 1898 ecru structure whose facade is decorated with cast-iron Corinthian columns. It is occupied by the Irish Imports gift shop.

Guided walking tours, led by the Putnam County Historical Society, depart from the building at 72 Main Street on Sunday May through mid-November. The tour provides a satisfactory overview of Cold Spring's beginnings, but be prepared for the possibility of a long-winded narration of sometimes-dubious veracity. One guide punctuated several accounts by saying, "Again, I'm taking liberty, but I think I might be right on that." A more focused examination of the region's past can be found in Frances F. Dunwell's *Hudson River Highlands* (Columbia University Press, 1991). The book, available at Salmagundi, at 66 Main Street, includes a chapter on Cold Spring and is generously illustrated with maps, color plates, and photographs.

Cold Spring grew up almost overnight with the creation of a federally subsidized iron foundry in 1817. From then until the end of the Civil War, it cranked out cannonballs and artillery, as well as cotton presses, steam engines, and other cogs in the accelerating Industrial Revolution. At the same time, the Hudson Highlands were gaining international attention for their staggering beauty: 15 miles where the river narrows and deepens, slicing through the Appalachian Mountain range. The founding of the popular new military academy at West

Point across the river in 1802, and the invention of the steamboat 5 years later, drew travelers from the United States and Europe. Gliding up the river in style, they took in the voluptuous mountains on either side and learned of America's military heroism during the Revolutionary War.

In the early 1830s, Fanny Kemble, a visiting British actress, overcome by the scenery, wailed in her diary: "Where are the poets of this land! Have these glorious scenes poured no inspiration into hearts worthy to behold and praise their beauty?" Actually, painters like Thomas Cole, Asher B. Durand, and Frederic E. Church had already arrived, and an art movement, the Hudson River School, was born.

Today, the best place in Cold Spring for viewing the Highlands is from a plaza with Victorian-style benches that juts into the

river at the foot of Main Street. (To get there, you must cross under the Metro-North train tracks.) Directly opposite is Crows Nest Mountain, whose timeworn, rounded peaks rise to 1,400 feet. To the north is Storm King Mountain; to the south, the fortress-like campus of West Point.

The Hudson Highlands and surrounding countryside also offer dramatic views of fall foliage. Two especially scenic drives are along the Taconic Parkway from Putnam County through Columbia County, and on Route 9D between the Bear Mountain Bridge and the city of Beacon.

Pig Hill Inn

Right at the river's edge in Cold Spring is Hudson House, an 1832 inn with two tiers of verandas offering water and mountain views that keep guests happily anchored. Its rooms are comfortable and, as the inn's brochure attests, "quaintly decorated." But the Pig Hill Inn's nine rooms, each filled with antiques and each done in a different style, are notable in the village for charm and originality.

One bizarre twist: All of the furniture and accessories at the Pig Hill Inn are for sale, from four-poster beds to hatboxes. The prices are tucked discreetly under chair cushions or inside armoire doors. At times, amid the cherry wood and chintz, you feel as if you're staying overnight in an antiques store, but it can be educational.

Comforts are sprinkled throughout the inn. All rooms with private bathrooms come with queen-size beds and air-conditioning, and most have wood stoves. The bathrooms are equipped with fluffy white towels, and bars of Neutrogena in addition to bath soap. And newspapers are left outside guests' doors in the morning. Televisions and telephones are nowhere to be found, or heard, adding to the inn's serenity.

Breakfast is served until the civilized hour of 10am, either in the dining room or out back in a quiet garden. An egg soufflé roll stuffed with spinach, mushrooms, and cream cheese was as light as a cloud. It was sufficiently weighed down, however, by a basket of buttery biscuits and a parfait dish of berries and heavy cream. In the afternoons, a plate of homemade chocolate-chip cookies is put out for guests in the lobby.

If you are still in the market for old furniture and collectibles, there are several stores to choose from just outside the inn's door. At Ann Stromberg, at 167 Main Street, where the hushed drawing-room atmosphere seems to purr, "You can't afford it," you might find a coin silver tea set made in New York City in 1825 ($3,600) or a massive mahogany sideboard from 1820 Philadelphia ($6,500).

Boscobel

In neighboring Garrison, Boscobel, which loosely translated from the Italian means "beautiful woods," offers a window onto the tastes and manners of the aristocracy during the region's infancy. Begun in 1804 by States Morris Dyckman, a Loyalist in the American Revolution, and completed by his widow, Elizabeth, the mansion is a striking example of New York Federal domestic architecture. Its exterior, painted a muted gold, is festooned with cream-colored, carved wood swags linking columns that support a unifying pediment. Its interior, filled with the works of 19th-century New York cabinetmaker Duncan Phyfe, is accented with needlepoint rugs, crystal chandeliers, clocks, and spyglasses.

The house was originally situated 15 miles to the south. But threatened with demolition in the 1950s (to make way for new construction), the structure was saved by the philanthropist Lila Acheson Wallace, who had it dismantled and moved, piece by piece, to its current site on a bluff overlooking the Hudson.

When the house first opened in 1961, it had been restored with all things English. But then the inventory lists were found. Mrs. Dyckman, it turned out, was a patriot after all, at least in terms of design. All her furniture had been American, and the interiors had to be completely redone by the private group, Boscobel Restoration Inc., which owns and operates the site.

The tours are packed with interesting facts about the challenges of a life of luxury predating electricity and plumbing. The grounds, with their formal gardens and river views, are as special as the house itself, which is set back from Route 9D.

Xaviar's

After you've experienced such refinement, dinner anywhere other than Xaviar's would seem an anticlimax. The *2000 Zagat Southern New York State Survey* gives the two Xaviar's restaurants—one on Route 9D in Garrison and the other farther south, in Piermont, New York—top ratings for food, decor, and service in the three-state region.

But it's not the intoxicating flavors of the cannelloni of quail or the salmon with coriander and caviar that linger longest. It is the grandeur of the setting: the ballroom of the Highlands Country Club, where 20-foot ceilings and oceans of space between tables create a palatial atmosphere.

The decor is elegant but spare. The walls, painted a Wedgwood blue, are lined with portraits. At either end of the room are fireplaces whose mantels hold great sprays of fresh flowers, illuminated by recessed spotlights. The tables are awash in linen, crystal, candles, and flowers, and in one corner of the room, a harpist performs.

Through the arched windows, the golf course appears as a throbbing emerald sea in the fading light. As the Tahitian vanilla bean soufflé with chocolate sorbet arrives, you realize you're having one of Spalding Gray's perfect moments.

The Xaviar's in Garrison serves dinner Friday and Saturday nights only. Diners choose between two tasting menus, each with six courses and six different wines. There is also a Sunday brunch. The dinner prix-fixe is $80 per person, but the blow is softened when the check comes on a bed of rose petals, inside a silver-plated chest.

Constitution Marsh Sanctuary

The Hudson River has a way of making you want to get closer to its rhythms, and Constitution Marsh Sanctuary, off Indian Brook Road in Garrison, puts you right on its surface. The small number of visitors that can be accommodated will find a 270-acre tidal marsh that is a rich environment for all kinds of birds, as well as freshwater and saltwater fish, from brown trout to needlefish.

The trail from the eight-car parking lot passes by the visitor center and reaches a short boardwalk leading into the marsh's pale green forest of narrow-leaf cattails and pickerelweed, waving in the breeze. The visitor center focuses more on the river's ecology than on bird watching. But the sanctuary is still a birder's paradise. Recently, an osprey hunting for fish flew directly overhead, its gigantic wings flapping as if in slow motion.

From the sanctuary, colors turn electric as the sun deepens the blue of the river and brightens the green of the marsh. Dimensions expand, too. Without trees or buildings for scale, the Hudson, Highlands, and sky seem to merge, rising and widening before your eyes. Back toward Cold Spring, Mount Taurus—or Bull Hill, as locals prefer—reveals itself for the first time, hovering over the village like a giant protector.

TOURING, EATING, SLEEPING: COLD SPRING ESSENTIALS

GETTING THERE

By Car To drive to Cold Spring from New York City, take the Henry Hudson Parkway to the Saw Mill River Parkway; continue on the Saw Mill to the Taconic State Parkway; take the Taconic to Rte. 301, which becomes Main St. in Cold Spring.

By Train Cold Spring can also be reached by train on the Hudson Line of Metro-North (☎ 212/532-4900). Trains from Grand Central Terminal run about every hour, beginning at 8am on weekends, and the ride takes about 1 hour and 15 minutes. Round-trip fare on Saturday and Sunday is $15.50, $1 for children 5 to 12, free for children under 5. Some taxi service is available from the train station in Cold Spring.

ACCOMMODATIONS

Hudson House, 2 Main St., Cold Spring (☎ 845/265-9355). Year-round, Monday through Thursday $140 to $185; Friday through Sunday $150 to $225. Rates are based on double occupancy and include full breakfast on weekends. Children are welcome.

Pig Hill Inn, 73 Main St., Cold Spring (☎ 845/265-9247). With private bathroom, $145 weekdays; $170 Friday through Sunday. Shared bathroom, $120 weekdays, $150 Friday through Sunday. Rates are based on double occupancy and include full breakfast. Children are welcome; an additional cot in the room is $25 per day, and the breakfast is an additional $11 to $13. A tea room at the inn, serving breakfast and lunch, is open Wednesday through Sunday, 8am to 5pm.

DINING

Xaviar's, Rte. 9D, Garrison (☎ 845/424-4228). Open for dinner Friday and Saturday 6 to 9pm and for Sunday brunch (sittings at 11:30am and 2:30pm). Prix-fixe six-course dinner $80; prix-fixe brunch $38. No credit cards accepted.

ATTRACTIONS

Boscobel, Rte. 9D, Garrison (☎ 845/265-3638). Call for hours and admission prices.

Constitution Marsh Sanctuary, Indian Brook Rd. (off Rte. 9D), Garrison (no phone). The visitor center is open May through October, Tuesday through Sunday 9am to 5pm. Trails are open year-round. Donations accepted. Access is limited; when the parking area is full, visitors are asked to return at another time.

PADDLING DOWNSTREAM, SLOWLY

by Bruce Weber

W E LAUNCHED AT CATSKILL, NEW York, from a public park just below the Rip Van Winkle Bridge, in the dense, warm air of a fog lifting at dawn. There, about 30 miles south of Albany, the Hudson River, its sleepy girth about 1,000 yards across, moved lazily southward, and we were grateful for its laziness, neither of us (I had solicited the aid of a friend for the occasion) having been in a canoe in some years. The water was bath warm, and we were grateful for that too.

Our first few strokes were awkward, and the nose of our borrowed canoe wandered back and forth across the longitudinal center for a while as I, in the stern, steered us uncertainly around the mouth of Catskill Creek and into the main current, toward New York City.

How did this happen to a couple of landlubbers like us?

It was my fault.

When a river runs by the house, I want to hitch a ride on it. I can't help it. All that movement, from somewhere, to somewhere: It's piquing.

So what is it about the Hudson, the huge beckoning thing that most New Yorkers ignore? Like the purloined letter hidden in plain sight, it has been flowing within view of my windows (well, some of my windows; I've moved a lot) for 20 years now, but until I decided to solve the situation recently, I'd never been out in it. Not on my own steam, anyway; the Circle Line ferry doesn't count.

Besides, the imagery in my head was irresistible: me in a tiny canoe, paddling home from the far north, finally riding the lethargic current under the George Washington Bridge and down the west side of Manhattan; to the west, the Palisades, with the late-afternoon shadows being cast over the water by the sun fading over New Jersey; to the east, the rush-hour traffic heading up along the West Side Highway toward the Bronx. As I pull ashore at Battery Park, the Statue of Liberty waves at my back. In this fantasy, I'm wearing fringed buckskin, a primitive discovering the city.

It is possible to do this, I learned, buckskin or no, but for me it didn't work out quite that way, there being problems in reconciling the imagery with my ambition of a mere weekend's worth of paddling and the logistics of undertaking such a journey with rusty skills and, crucially, no canoe.

It was John Cronin, the executive director of the Hudson Riverkeeper Fund, an environmental watchdog group, who pointed out that though the Hudson is a fine and underused venue for paddlers, the closer you get to the city the less accommodating the riverbanks become. Places to dock safely are few; leaving the canoe becomes a problem, and motels aren't particularly easy to find or get to. (As it turns out, I'm not much of a primitive when it comes to sleeping out at night.) "It's adventurous, but in lower Westchester and New York City, you've kind of stranded yourself," Mr. Cronin said.

Nowhere, in fact, Mr. Cronin added, does the Hudson have a terribly booming

riverside culture that would encourage precisely the kind of endeavor I'd proposed. In the end, he recommended the Catskill region, where the river is peaceful and wide and scenic, generally crossable in a canoe without overt danger from wind-whipped whitecaps or ships churning up a threatening wake, and with reasonably accessible amenities on shore.

The lower Hudson, Mr. Cronin reiterated, is great for canoeing, but canoeists don't use it much. Perhaps, he said, this is because it is dominated by motor craft, from jet skis to pleasure yachts to the occasional tour boat and barge. He didn't, in any case, know where I could rent a canoe, and neither did anyone else I spoke with.

You can rent canoes on the upper Hudson, way to the northwest above Albany in the Adirondacks, where white-water enthusiasts are challenged by a 14-mile sluice between the Indian and Boreas rivers known as the Hudson Gorge. You can rent canoes on the Delaware, to the southwest; but none of the outfitters I called was willing to cart a canoe several hours to the Catskills for me, and I didn't even ask if they'd let me do it myself. The tourist board for Greene County, where Catskill is, couldn't help me, either.

"Why don't you come up here and go golfing?" the woman at the tourist board suggested on the phone. "We have plenty of that." A marine yard in Catskill was willing to sell me a new aluminum canoe for $700 and then buy it back from me after the trip for $500. But for a trip such as mine, I was advised, an aluminum boat would be about as comfortable and sleek as a bathtub. (As it happens, I missed a place, Loric Sports in Staatsburg, near Rhinebeck, that rents canoes and kayaks for use on the Hudson.)

In the end, happily, I was able to borrow a canoe, and it was a beauty. Made by We-no-nah, it was a two-seat, 17-foot boat made of lightweight Kevlar. And it was painted a nifty, woodsy color I came to think of as Hiawatha green.

We outfitted ourselves—life jackets, paddles, waterproof baggage toters, and map covers—at Cold Brook Canoes, a garage-based business in Boiceville, New York, some 16 miles off the Thruway, where the proprietor, Ernie Gardner, wouldn't let us go without being assured we knew what we were doing (we lied a little), and without suggesting that we pay $25 to join the Hudson River Waterway Association, a group of boaters and environmentalists who promote the river as a recreational site. It wasn't the association Mr. Gardner was touting; with the membership comes the *Hudson River Waterway Guide,* a mile-by-mile description of sights on the river between Troy and the Battery, along with suggestions of places to rest, swim, camp, or store your canoe for the night while you're off in search of a motel. It was invaluable.

Waters in Motion

In 1990, an adventurer named Peter Lourie canoed the entire 315-mile source-to-mouth length of the Hudson, from Lake Tear of the Clouds on the slope of Mount Marcy in the Adirondacks to the Battery, and wrote a book about it, *River of Mountains* (Syracuse University Press, 1995).

"The northern half is a true river with a strong current," Mr. Lourie wrote of the Hudson, "but the lower half is tidal, a leviathan's arm of the sea, an estuary, a sunken river from the days of the glaciers, not a normal river at all. In the first 165 miles from Lake Tear to Albany, the Hudson drops nearly 4,300 feet. But from Albany to Manhattan, for another 150 miles, the Hudson drops a mere one foot." This explains why Mr. Lourie had a guide with him in the northern waters and why he was able to paddle the lower Hudson alone. The water is wide, essentially calm, imminently negotiable. Still and all, it must have been quite a haul, mainly because of the tides from the Atlantic Ocean, which run all the way upriver beyond Albany. These fight the generally slow-moving current to the degree, Craig Poole, president of the waterway association, wrote in the guide, that "a log dropped in the water at Troy would take months to reach Manhattan." For every 8 miles the log was carried downriver on the current and the ebb tide, he continued, "the flood tide might shove it back up as much as 7½ miles."

The Indian name for the river—Muhheakunnuk—is translated by Mr. Poole as "great waters constantly in motion." Mr. Lourie's translation is "water that flows both ways." Either way, for canoeists the message is clear: You're better off traveling with the ebb tide.

It is the shifting tides, by the way, stirring up the river-bottom sediment that are responsible for the river's characteristic mud brown color. In fact, the river is reasonably clean these days, especially compared with the way it was before the Federal Clean Water Act of 1972.

The tides shift in cycles lasting about 6 hours, so each day there are two optimal canoeing intervals, though one of them is in the middle of the night. (A tide table, available at most marinas, as well as in the waterway guide, is essential.) Our first day, high tide at Catskill was about 6am, and by my amateurish calculations that meant the tides would shift and be moving in the proper direction about an hour later. We pushed off about 7:30am, and I must have been more or less correct; the water was slow, but we didn't seem to be fighting it. There was no wind, the surface of the river was glassy, and the sense of steady movement was encouraging if not exhilarating. We were moving; it was apparent we could get somewhere.

For a time, I stayed close to the reedy western shore, working on my J-stroke, trying to stay in sync with my partner, who was working out a rhythm of her own, paddling first on one side of the canoe, then the other, flexing her shoulder muscles. The river was ours at that hour, and it was marvelously quiet, the boat almost imperceptibly shushing through the water. There were wooden duck blinds like gaping faces waiting empty in the marshes, but no ducks. The only wildlife were gulls preening on the river buoys.

An inlet to the west—Inbocht Bay, the map called it—left us in open water for the first time, and it was emboldening, a look-ma-no-hands sensation. We began to wonder how fast we were traveling, how to read the map and the river for distance (no odometer on the canoe, after all), how far we could get in a day. We didn't have a plan, really, for our 2-day journey, or a solid destination. Figuring this was New York State and not the wilderness, we just trusted we'd be somewhere we could stop comfortably when we needed to, and we'd see where we were when we got there.

We passed a few small villages on the banks—Cementon on the west (with its gargoyle-ish cement factory), the more benign-looking Germantown on the east, a more benign and bucolic shore in general—and by midmorning we'd gone 10 miles or so and reached

Esopus Creek, the entrance marked by an old and creakily elegant lighthouse. Up the creek is the pleasant town of Saugerties, reviving as a weekend retreat after a bout of hard times, where we had thought we might stop for lunch after the tide shifted, but we were ahead of our estimated schedule and so we pushed on. We snacked in the boat, doffed our sweatshirts, and paddled in earnest, sweating.

I suspect, in our enthusiasm to get someplace, to put some distance behind us, we missed some things—silent, overgrown, and twisty creeks; wildlife in the marshes; the exploration of some islands (the waterway guide says Magdalen Island, just below Saugerties, contains Indian ruins and middens)—but by midday the trip had become travel, the pleasure of it the pleasure of traveling on one's own power, not unlike that of hiking or bicycling. The river was a road.

Battling the Flood Tide

We took a break about noon, hauling the canoe up on a gravelly beach just north of the Kingston-Rhinecliff Bridge, where we promptly fell asleep and were wakened, I would say an hour later, by some rough-house waves lapping the beach as the tide shifted. The water climbed the shore and nearly carried the canoe away; our towels got soaked.

For the rest of the day we battled the flood tide, which was a weird sensation because it doesn't feel as though the river is backing up on you. What it feels like is that your paddling has become ineffectual; you're working harder for less reward. In addition, other boats were now in evidence, and avoiding the larger ones, the yachts, so as not to wobble in their wakes, became part of the strategy.

Many people had told me before the trip that the river would be so crowded on a weekend, particularly on Labor Day weekend (which was when we traveled), that it could get dangerous for a canoe. But it never became so, though there was ample river traffic, and the sheer size of the two barges that passed us was intimidating. I was surprised at the general courtesy of the yacht captains, who frequently would slow to a crawl as they passed us. (A notable exception to this were the police boats, which blew by us without a look, so quickly we could barely read the word "sheriff" emblazoned on their hulls.)

For all of those reasons, it was late afternoon by the time we pulled onto the sand at Kingston Beach; a local man advised us not to stay there. It was a hangout for teenagers at night—"a bad element," he said—and the canoe would be gone by morning. He directed us around the point (another lighthouse) and into Rondout Creek, where we'd find restaurants, a marina to leave our boat, and easy access to town. I missed the turn, though, and we ended up a little bit south, in Port Ewen.

There we paddled into the Hidden Harbor Yacht Club, a private marina, and had to do some fast talking before the commodore, Spencer Rohrlick, allowed us to be the first canoeists ever to leave a canoe there. He lightened up after a bit, though, and even offered to let us sleep on his boat, the Edelweiss. We declined. Instead, another club member drove us to a motel in town. Nice folks.

"I have an affinity for people who like the water," the club member explained.

At the motel, where the accompanying restaurant had a wedding room, we had the option of taking the honeymoon suite. We declined that too.

On Esopus Island

The next morning, we called a cab for the ride back to the yacht club, and the cabbie, who bragged he'd been on the job for 15 years, promptly got lost and drove us into Kingston before we managed to correct him. On the water, things immediately went better, the morning once again tranquil and the river, for a while, beatifically serene.

We had the boon of a following breeze and the confidence brought by a day's experience, and we traveled briskly around a river bend marked by the Esopus Lighthouse, which, built in 1837, rebuilt in 1872, is now being restored (a sign on the side makes a plaintive request for donations). A man in the nearby marsh was readying a duck blind for duck season, which begins in October, and before the sun rose above the trees on the eastern shore, it felt like autumn.

By late morning, however, it was hot, and we pulled to shore on Esopus Island, at the top of another bend in the river, known as Crum

Elbow. We swam in a cove in the island lee, the water warm and shallow, and the river bottom so mucky that I lost a boat shoe in it. It is a lovely spot (marred only by the graffiti on the island rocks), the moored boats of the Poughkeepsie Yacht Club visible, swaying like cradles in the water on the eastern shore.

The rest of the morning was a bit more exciting, as the wind gained momentum and the first real waves arose in the river. Happily, for an hour they pushed us along, a mild surf that angled toward the east and downstream. Just north of Poughkeepsie, however, where two bridges span the water, the tide began to shift and the waves that had been working in our favor began to rollick in place. We had to fight through them. We stuck close to shore; the wind was strong and we bobbed with increasing ferociousness.

The bridges stayed in front of us, it seemed, forever, a sort of mockery of our lack of progress. We crawled past the boathouses for Marist and Vassar colleges and finally crossed under the first of the bridges, a disused railroad trestle, and docked for a rest in a town park where the jet-ski rental concession was doing a great business. It was noisy, the first city feeling I'd had on the trip. And so we didn't rest as long as we wished, plunging off again into the flood tide and an afternoon of hard paddling.

Below Poughkeepsie, the eastern shore of the Hudson gets rather unscenic—a highway runs along it part of the way, and several industrial sites also mar the view—so, with a hubristic push, we crossed the river and sought the opposite shore, which was indeed more pleasant. By late in the afternoon, with the sun on the downward slope and heading behind the trees on the small hills, we were able to trail through the shade on the western bank. By that time, my legs were good and sunburned, and my partner had need to soak a T-shirt in the water and wrap it around her head to fend off a swoon.

By 5 o'clock, we were ready to quit for the day, but there was nowhere to quit; the shore was green but uninhabited. A freight railroad track followed the riverbank, and above it was nothing but woods. The waterway guide suggested that a town called Milton might provide a stop—there's a winery on the shore, it said—but the winery was closed down and the only things there were a dilapidated dock and some propane tanks. It took us another hour to find welcoming civilization, another private club, alas—the Marlboro Yacht Club, just north of Newburgh—but the same sense of welcome. Another invitation to leave our canoe. Another ride to a motel.

And so we were back on land for good.

Roots in the Watery Soil

Perhaps this sounds like an anticlimactic or even melancholy finish, but in fact weariness at the end of a journey is a good thing, begetting reflection and satisfying sleep. Besides, our shoulders were well exercised and our sea legs sturdy.

The next morning my partner had a business appointment in Manhattan and took the train from Beacon, and it was left to me to reclaim the car in Catskill, drive back down Route 9W to pick up the canoe, and return it. This is a whole other story, involving some fruitless hitchhiking and eventually a long cab ride with, coincidentally, the same hapless cab driver in Kingston who had lost himself on his own home turf. Once he drove me to my car, he insisted on following me back. In the future, I'll plan better, borrow a second car, plant it downriver, and aim for it as a destination.

Or maybe I'll just stay on the river.

It took a whole day of riding in one car or another to get the canoe back to its rightful owner and to get myself back to the city, long enough for me to begin missing my brief life on the Hudson, which no longer seemed like such an evanescent thing. I'd been in it, grown to know it, left my modest mark: a wake that in a way felt a little like roots in soil.

And if I'd been a little more patient it would have brought me all the way home.

CANOEING ESSENTIALS

CANOE RENTALS & GUIDED CANOE TRIPS

Appalachian Mountain Club, New York–North Jersey Chapter, 5 Tudor City Place, Manhattan (☎ **212/986-1430; www.amc/ny.org**). Offers guided day canoe trips on the lower Hudson River that circumnavigate Manhattan and New York Harbor, and weekend trips on the northern Hudson, above Warrensburg. Call for schedule and prices.

Beaver Brook Outfitters, Rtes. 8 and 28, Wevertown (☎ **(888/454-8433** or 518/ 251-3394; www.beaverbrook.net). Canoe rentals $30 a day, $25 for each additional day; rates include life vests (child-size vests available), paddles, and padding for transporting canoes. A credit card is necessary for rentals. Open Memorial Day through Labor Day, Monday through Thursday 8am to 6pm, Friday and Saturday 8am to 7pm, Sunday 9am to 5pm. Labor Day through November, Monday through Saturday 8am to 6pm and Sunday 9am to 5pm. December through Memorial Day, daily 8am to 6pm. Single- and multiple-day canoe trips on the Hudson River are offered; $40 to $150 per person for day trips, $180 to $300 for multiple days, depending on the number of participants.

Boat House, 2855 Aqueduct Rd., Schenectady (☎ **518/393-5711**). Canoes to be used on the nearby Mohawk River are rented hourly, with all necessary equipment; $10 per person for up to 2 hours, $5 an hour thereafter. The daily rate is $30 if you want to take a canoe to another destination; $35 for the second day, $25 for the third day, and $10 for each additional day. A credit card is required. Open April through Labor Day, Monday through Friday 10am to 8pm, Saturday 10am to 4pm; closed Sunday. Labor Day through October and March, Tuesday through Friday 10am to 6pm, Saturday 10am to 4pm; closed Sunday and Monday. November and December, Tuesday through Friday noon to 6pm; closed January and February.

Cold Brook Canoes, Rte. 28, Boiceville (☎ **914/657-2189**). Canoes, kayaks, and related water equipment are for sale, along with books and videotapes. Open March through mid-October, Thursday through Monday 10am to 5pm; mid-October through February, Friday and Saturday 10am to 5pm and by appointment.

Mountainaire Adventures, Rte. 28, Wevertown (☎ **800/950-2194** or 518/251-2194). About 4 hours from Manhattan. Guided canoe trips on the Hudson River, from Warrensburg to Lake Luzerne. Day trips $80 per person, $60 each additional person (includes all equipment and lunch). Overnight trips $100 per person, $80 each additional person (includes equipment and meals).

Northern Pathfinders, Lake Clear (☎ **800/882-7284**). Daily canoe rental $25, including life jackets, equipment, and padding for transporting canoe on car. Credit card or $300 deposit is necessary. Guided daily and overnight canoe trips on the Hudson River are also offered. Day trips $125 per person, $90 each for two people, $75 each for three, and $65 each for four or more. Open year-round.

ORGANIZATIONS

American Canoe Association, 7432 Alban Station Blvd., Suite B-232, Springfield, VA 22150 (☎ **703/451-0141**). **American Red Cross,** Westchester County chapter, 106 N. Broadway, White Plains, NY (☎ **914/946-6500,** ext. 250).

Offers pamphlets, films, and videotapes on water safety. Classes are held depending upon enrollment.

Professional Paddlesports Association, P.O. Box 248, Butler, KY 41006 (☎ **859/ 472-2205**).

FURTHER READING

Quiet Water Canoe Guide: New York State, by John Hayes and Alex Wilson (Appalachian Mountain Club Books; $15.95). Can be ordered by calling ☎ **800/ 243-0495.**

River of Mountains: A Canoe Journey Down the Hudson, by Peter Lourie (Syracuse University Press, 1995; $29.95).

HORSE RACING & MORE AT SARATOGA SPRINGS

by William Grimes

THE WORLD OF HORSE RACING CAN be harsh, even seamy sometimes. An aqueduct on a freezing winter day, for example, is not a sight to gladden the heart, and the sound of grown men banging on trash cans and cursing when their long shot falters does not please the ear. The horses still look noble, but there's not much else to prop up the image of thoroughbred racing as the sport of kings. When the wind off Jamaica Bay howls down the back stretch, there's only one thing to do: Dream of Saratoga.

The annual summer meeting at Saratoga Springs, New York, now more than a century and a quarter old, is horse racing's Garden of Eden: 5 weeks of top-quality racing presented in ideal surroundings, and wrapped in the festive atmosphere of a county fair. Money is wagered, of course. But for a brief, idyllic interlude, finer feelings come to the fore.

Love would not be too strong a word to introduce here. Horseplayers really do love their sport, and the horses that compete in it. It says everything about Saratoga that one year a fan organized Fourstardave Day, in honor of the old-timer who trotted out onto the main track and won a turf race 8 years in a row. For his special day, Fourstardave was walked over to Siro's restaurant, a Saratoga institution situated just through the trees near the clubhouse entrance. There he was presented with the keys to Saratoga Springs.

Come on, now, admit it. That's nice.

If racing fans go a little crazy at Saratoga, it's not their fault. The atmosphere intoxicates them. The racetrack itself, laid out in 1863 and remodeled in 1902, has the charm of Fenway Park multiplied by Wrigley Field. In the all-wooden grandstand (a Victorian masterpiece with cupolas), old-fashioned ceiling fans stimulate the air. To signal the scratches for the next race, a worker hoists wooden plaques up a pole. It's one of the few racecourses anywhere in the world with a gazebo in the infield.

Most unusually, the track is of a piece with the town, a genteel mineral-springs spa with gambling and racing tacked on. It was a Victorian Las Vegas, a town for high rollers, swells, and nabobs riding the big-money wave of the Gilded Age. Henry James found the place disgusting. But time has worked a transformation. A bit of the raffish feeling lives on. There is excitement in the air. But the summer homes that James dismissed as vulgar eyesores now count as masterpieces, high-Victorian jewels set in spacious lawns, radiating a sense of amplitude and the platinum-plated confidence that comes with multiple millions of dollars.

A century ago, big-money people lived more publicly, on a broader stage. The noble obligation to make a spectacle of oneself lives on in the fabled theme parties given by Marylou Whitney, now well on in years but still game. One summer, Mrs. Whitney, dressed as the Good Witch Glenda, set out arm in arm with the Cowardly Lion, the Tin Man, the Scarecrow, and Dorothy, skipping her way to Canfield Casino for the Over the Rainbow Ball as a crowd of 300 commoners gaped. Score one for the good old days.

Somewhat more seriously, Saratoga Springs attracts thousands of visitors who have no intention of placing so much as a $2 show bet. Throughout the summer the Saratoga Performing Arts Center offers a schedule of rock concerts, concerts by the Philadelphia Orchestra, and performances by the New York City Ballet. The town is also the site of the National Museum of Dance. There is more to the place than horses. But no horses, no Saratoga.

For the horseplayer, Saratoga is summer camp, a place to watch horses, think horses, and talk horses from dawn to dusk. For some time now, my wife and I have nourished the theory that we could be winning horseplayers if only we had the time to focus on the game full-time, undistracted by the annoying intrusion of things like jobs. We gave it a good try one year, using Saratoga as our proving ground. For 4 days, we watched the early-morning workouts at the main track and the nearby Oklahoma training track (the origin of the name is a mystery). We attended handicapping seminars. We paid homage to the great names of racing, past and present, human and equine, at the National Museum of Racing. We watched the 2-year-old horse auctions. To get in the spirit, my wife read *Saratoga Backtalk,* the latest in

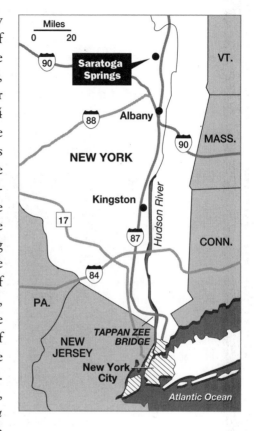

Stephen Dobyns's excellent series of Saratoga mysteries, and we both consulted a volume on the secret language of horse behavior. We studied *The Daily Racing Form* with the devotion of yeshiva students, bet our way through the day's card, and, on leaving the track at the end of the day, picked up the next day's Racing Form and prepared to do it all over again. It was heaven on earth.

Morning's Clarity

The morning workouts, and breakfast at the main track, are a Saratoga institution. Check out both tracks. Workouts at the Oklahoma training track are quieter and less public. Trainers use the track as a stamina-builder, because its deep surface (it looks like chocolate cake mix)

makes the horses work harder. In the morning, you can hear the sounds that get obliterated by the crowd: the snorting and snuffling as the horses shift into high gear, the back and forth between riders, the one-way conversation between rider and horse.

At the main track, breakfast is served in the Clubhouse Porch 7 to 9:30am on race days. As trainers, jockeys, and big-name horses turn up, Mary Ryan delivers running commentary, more or less in the manner of a Hollywood reporter covering the entrance of the stars on Oscar night. For the benefit of the crowds, she will coerce trainers and jockeys into raising their hands for easier identification. This is all highly entertaining.

"Now, here's a trainer we don't see that often on the track, Christophe Clement," said Ms. Ryan one bright morning. "Bon-*jour*, Christophe." Mr. Clement, a Frenchman who specializes in turf runners, smiled indulgently. Ms. Ryan followed up with a bit of expert commentary, pointing out that Mr. Christophe likes to have his horses begin their workout by standing stock still for several minutes, observing the action but not moving.

The horses, of course, get the star buildup. Who's this? Why, it's Fourstardave himself, out for a morning constitutional. He gets a nice hand from the crowd.

Tips from Insiders

Several times a week, The Daily Racing Form presents hourlong free seminars at Siro's, which begin at 10:30am. This is the best deal in town. Racing Forms in hand, my wife and I sat down under a tent next to the restaurant, ordered coffee and coffee cake, and settled in for a highly educational session. Each seminar starts off with a guest, usually a jockey or a trainer. Then a Racing Form editor and a handicapper go over the day's card, debating the pros and cons of various horses.

Tony Heyes, at that time a handicapper for the *Daily News,* talked about his approach to analyzing races and betting. Mr. Heyes, who is British, also offered some useful tips on how to size up European horses and recalled, wistfully, the day that he managed to collect five win bets on the same race, thanks to the peculiarities of the British betting system.

At another seminar, Mike Luzzi, a New York jockey, carefully avoided giving any inside tips, but he did reminisce on his early days racing horses at the Timonium Fair in Maryland, whose tiny racetrack presents unusual challenges. For one thing, horses that can't negotiate the tight turn into the home stretch often crash right through the rail and wind up next to the Ferris wheel.

As one day blended into the next, the world of the racetrack seemed to unfurl slowly, revealing itself in brief flashes: an insight here, a choice bit of language there, a pungent anecdote. Hanging over the rail one morning, I struck up a conversation with a part-time horse owner from Virginia who gave his theory as to why horses shipping in from Laurel and Pimlico in Maryland do well at Saratoga. He affectionately referred to his own steeds as "a bunch of bums."

This sort of trackside talk is as old as the sport, whose history in America is the subject of the National Museum of Racing, situated directly across from the track. Its permanent exhibition describes the earliest days of racing in Colonial America, when horses sped along irregular paths through the woods. Visitors can read about Sir Archy and Diomed, the fathers of all-American racehorses, and about the rise of New York in the 19th century as the power center of American racing. In the Hall of Fame room, visitors can call up pictures of the great horses and jockeys on computer terminals. In many cases, the computer file includes scenes of winning stretch drives, so you can see the likes of Ruffian and Secretariat in action.

Go with a Plan

Watching the races at Saratoga requires a game plan. Weekends, especially, can be an unholy crush, and even the weekday crowds are no joke. A reserved seat is a must, and repeat visitors often order theirs as early as January every year. The sections run from B to Y (excluding I), with B halfway between the finish line and the 16th pole and Y overlooking the turn into the stretch. Each day, tickets for that day's grandstand sections W, X, and Y go on sale at 8am at a booth near the grandstand entrance. A limited number of clubhouse seats (sections B through L) are available as well, except on the days of the three biggest stakes races, the Travers, Alabama, and Whitney. The price is $4. About 500 clubhouse seats for the next day's races go on sale in the evening at the Holiday Inn downtown. Starting at 10am, the booth also sells advance tickets for sections R through V at $4. Advance ticket holders often have extras that they need to unload, usually at face value. Look for a cluster of people holding tickets aloft.

Learn to use the screen-activated machines, known as SAMs, which allow you to place a bet using a voucher. This beats standing at the end of a long line with a sure thing and only 2 minutes left before the race starts. Go to any window, ask for a voucher in the amount of money you intend to spend that day, and use the slip as cash. After the voucher is inserted into the machine, the screen presents a menu of options that are easily deciphered. Simply press the option you want. Bet as little or as much as you like, up to the amount of the voucher. After placing your bets, don't forget to remove not just the betting slips, but also the voucher with your remaining cash on it.

If you want to check out the horses in the paddock parade, get out there early. Places along the rail fill up quickly. Also, remember that it is a long, long walk back to the grandstand seats.

My wife and I did not become winning horseplayers, but we did become more scientific losers. There is some satisfaction in knowing that your losing bet was not a stupid bet. There's a difference.

Besides, we collected other, richer dividends. One afternoon, on the way back to the Six Sisters bed-and-breakfast, a Victorian guest house just up the street from the racetrack, we saw a strangely familiar figure on the porch of the house next door. It was Mike Smith, one of the nation's top jockeys and the rider of Sovereign Kitty, a disappointing second in that day's seventh race. We went up to our room, sat down on the balcony, and discreetly listened in as Mr. Smith replayed the race. It was the next-best thing to riding the horse ourselves. Sure, we had a win bet on the horse. But we didn't hold a grudge. We didn't even want to bang a trash can and curse.

AT & AROUND THE TRACK: SARATOGA ESSENTIALS

GETTING THERE

By Car If you are driving, take the Gov. Thomas E. Dewey Thruway to exit 24 and pick up the Northway (Rte. 87 North) and take it to exit 14 (Union); the entrance to Saratoga Raceway is on Union Ave.

By Train Amtrak (☎ 800/872-7245) offers a special round-trip package every Saturday and Sunday during racing season. Trains leave Manhattan's Penn Station early in the morning, arrive in Saratoga Springs in time for the first race, and return in the early evening. The round-trip fare includes a free beverage each way, free bus transportation to and from the racetrack, grandstand admission, and a racing program.

ACCOMMODATIONS

Saratoga Springs positively bristles with bed-and-breakfast establishments in eye-catching Victorian houses. The four cited below represent a small sampling; the rates quoted are for double occupancy. Rooms are extremely difficult to reserve and cost much more in August, as well as during Skidmore College's parents' weekend (first week in Oct) and graduation weekend (last week in May) and the Newport Jazz Festival (late June or early July).

The Saratoga Springs Chamber of Commerce (☎ 518/584-3255) offers help in finding a room, but in racing season it can give only one or two listings to each caller.

Adelphi Hotel, 365 Broadway (☎ 518/587-4688). Built in 1877, the Adelphi offers old-time Saratoga atmosphere in spades. The hotel shows its age, but the public rooms reflect the Victorian era in full flower. Open third week of May to third week of October. Rooms are $105 to $400. Café Adelphi, with garden tables in the back, serves cocktails and desserts Wednesday through Sunday 5:30 to 11pm; open daily during racing season.

Batcheller Mansion Inn, 20 Circular St. (☎ 518/584-7012). Racing season, $260 to $400; May 1 until racing season and September and October, $175 to $295; November to April, $125 to $250.

Chestnut Tree Inn, 9 Whitney Place (☎ 518/587-8681). Racing season, $185 to $275; off-season, $85 to $135 (higher on special event weekends).

Six Sisters, 149 Union Ave. (☎ 518/583-1173; www.sixsistersbandb.com). Racing season, $275 to $320; September, October, and April through mid-July, $100 to $130; November through March, $75 to $140. November through April, the Six Sisters offers a 2-night spa package with Crystal Spa for $280 to $360. All with breakfast. No smoking allowed.

Union Gables, 55 Union Ave. (☎ 800/398-1558 or 518/584-1558). Racing season, $260 to $300; November through Memorial Day, $110 to $145; Memorial Day through late July and September and October, $135 to $180. Rates are per room, single or double occupancy.

DINING

Eartha's Kitchen, 60 Court St. (☎ 518/583-0602). Nouvelle American. Open Wednesday through Sunday 5 to 10pm. Entrees $18 to $24.

43 Phila Bistro, 43 Phila St. (☎ 518/584-2720). Eclectic American. Open Monday through Saturday 6 to 10pm. Entrees $18 to $27 (in season, $18 to $30).

Hattie's, 45 Phila St. (☎ 518/584-4790; www.hattiesrestaurant.com). Old standby serving Southern home cooking. Open Wednesday through Sunday 5 to 10pm.

July 15 through Labor Day, daily 8am to midnight. Entrees $12.95 to $16.95.

Siro's, 168 Lincoln Ave. (☎ 518/584-4030). Contemporary continental. Open mid-July to early September, daily 6pm to 4am. Entrees $24 to $44.

Wheat Fields, 440 Broadway (☎ 518/587-0534). Pasta. Open Monday through Thursday and Sunday 11:30am to 9pm, Friday and Saturday 11:30am to 10pm. Entrees $7.95 to $16.95, specials $11.95 to $17.95.

SARATOGA RACEWAY

Schedule and Tickets Starting in late July and ending around Labor Day, there is racing every day except Tuesday, beginning at 1pm. Tickets are $2 for general admission and $4 for the clubhouse; admission is free for children 12 and under. Parking gates open at 7am; $2 for general parking, $5 for preferred parking. For

information, call ☎ 518/584-6200, ext. 4306.

Racing Seminars Free hourlong seminars on the day's races are sponsored by *The Daily Racing Form* at 10:30am Wednesday through Sunday at Siro's restaurant, 168 Lincoln Ave. (☎ 518/584-4030).

MUSEUMS

National Museum of Dance, just down the road from the Saratoga Performing Arts Center on Rte. 9 (☎ 518/584-2225). Photographs and video displays about George Balanchine and Bronislava Nijinska, sister of Vaslav Nijinsky, can be seen at this museum. Open year-round, by appointment. Admission $4, $3 for students and seniors, $1 for children 12 and under.

National Museum of Racing, 191 Union Ave. (☎ 518/584-0400). Paintings, historical photographs, videos, and life-size

re-creations of paddock areas and jockey rooms are included in the exhibitions here. During the racing season, the museum is open daily 9am to 5pm; at other times of the year, it is open Monday through Saturday 10am to 4:30pm and Sunday noon to 4:30pm. Admission $7, $5 for students and seniors, free for children 5 and under.

The museum also offers walking tours of Saratoga Raceway during racing season; see "Walking Tours," below.

WALKING TOURS

Congress Park Walks In July and August, the Urban Heritage Area (☎ 518/587-3241) offers 1-hour walking tours of Congress Park that focus on Saratoga's mineral springs and its social history. The tour leaves from the Saratoga Springs Urban Heritage Area Visitors Center across from Congress Park, Tuesday through Thursday at 10:30am and by appointment. The cost is $2 per person.

Self-Guided House Tours The Saratoga Springs Preservation Foundation's brochure *A Stroll Up North Broadway* ($1) allows visitors to take a self-guided tour of the North Broadway neighborhood, featuring houses from the 1880s to a contemporary solar home. Brochures can be obtained from the Saratoga Springs Preservation Foundation, 117 Grand Ave. (☎ 518/587-5030), open Monday to Friday 9am to 5pm.

Track Tours The National Museum of Racing (☎ 518/584-0400) offers a 2-hour walking tour of the training track during the racing season at the Saratoga Raceway that focuses on the early history of racing at Saratoga. Tours leave, rain or shine, from the museum, 191 Union Ave., June through October, daily at 8:30am. The cost is $10 for nonmembers, $5 for members.

PERFORMING ARTS

Saratoga Performing Arts Center, off Rte. 9 (☎ 518/587-3330; www.spac.org). The center holds an annual arts festival that begins in June and continues through Labor Day. The New York City Ballet performs here for 3 weeks in July, Tuesday through Saturday. The Philadelphia Orchestra performs for 3 weeks in August, Wednesday through Saturday. the center also has a six-series chamber music festival that complements the orchestra's season, and it offers about 30 special-event concerts featuring leading pop, country, folk, and rock artists. In late June or early July, it hosts the 2-day Freihofer Jazz Festival. Call for this year's schedule.

To reach the center, take the Thomas E. Dewey Thruway to exit 24 (the Northway) and continue to exit 13N to Rte. 9; the entrance to the center is on Rte. 9.

RAMBLING THROUGH ULSTER COUNTY

by William Grimes

LONG BEFORE ULSTER COUNTY, New York, came into being, Indians of the Mingua nation planted maize in the fields around present-day Kingston. They fished and hunted. They lived the good life. They called their domain "the pleasant land."

Well, fair enough. The no-frills appellation suggests that the Mingua (the Mingos of James Fenimore Cooper's Leatherstocking Tales) were a judicious people, not inclined to boosterism, ill-adapted to practice the dark arts of public relations and advertising. In short, reliable.

The pleasant land of Ulster County lies along the west bank of the Hudson River, about 100 miles north of Manhattan. It is neither spectacular nor chic. If its principal towns—Kingston, Woodstock, Saugerties, and New Paltz—could qualify as jewels, they would be small carat. The scenery delights and soothes rather than overwhelms. It is a land of small pleasures.

Ulster County has a little of this, a little of that. It has vineyards and rolling hills. It has large forests, lakes, and reservoirs. It has ice caves. It has not one but two mountain ranges, the Shawangunks and the Catskills, and two splendid parks. It has decent restaurants, a microbrewery, and its very own wine trail. It has an annual garlic festival. It is, in the words of a turn-of-the-century guidebook, "a land flowing with milk and honey, a land of corn and wine." Thumbs up to all of the above.

Manhattan's Dutch heritage survives only in the city's place-names. But in Ulster County, the Dutch influence pops up at every turn in the form of stone houses, many of them built in the late 17th and early 18th centuries. Built of Shawangunk (that's pronounced shon-gum, locally) grit, with sloping, high-pitched wooden roofs, the houses have distinctive jambless fireplaces that date back to medieval Flanders.

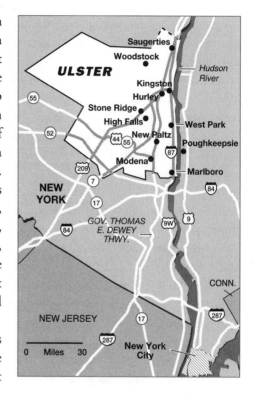

Ulster County takes great pride in these little houses. Huguenot Street in New Paltz has six, making it the oldest street in the United States with its original houses. One, the Jean Hasbrouck Memorial House, was named by the Architectural Record of March 1926, a monthly trade publication, as the finest example of medieval Flemish stone architecture in North America—a rather arcane honorific, but the house is indeed eye-catching. The local Huguenot Society operates tours of the houses on Huguenot Street and of Locust Lawn, a nearby 1814 Federal mansion once occupied by Josiah Hasbrouck, the local grandee. The little town of Hurley has 10 stone houses and 15 others are nearby.

Many of the stone houses carry on as private homes and inns. One is Baker's Bed and Breakfast, outside Stone Ridge, a farmhouse built in 1780. Baker's sits on high ground overlooking a few nearby farms, a gaggle of geese, and, off in the distance, the tower at Mohonk Mountain House, the county's most renowned resort. The farmhouse is a gem, a tight-knit package of stone, thick beams, and foot-wide floor planks. Upstairs, it still has the original wall paint, made with buttermilk and blueberries. The smell of wood smoke permeates the place, and in cool weather, a cast-iron stove in the communal living room radiates warmth, slowly sending the resident cat, curled underneath, into a narcotic daze.

My wife and I took a room with private bathroom for $98 a night (a third-floor loft with sitting room and fireplace is $128). It had a solid old four-poster bed, a rusticated armoire, and a dresser. They built solid in the old days, but they didn't build big. The bathroom and the closet occupied mere niches. Nevertheless, the room was cozy and pleasing to the eye.

There's something important to know about geese. They rise early, and they celebrate the morn with a "Hallelujah" chorus of honks that continues for a very long time. You'd think that a toot or two would do it, but no. Geese go at it with the gusto of a barroom drunk into the third verse of "My Way."

There was no problem, therefore, in rising for breakfast, which is huge. One morning it was smoked trout, eggs Benedict with sautéed Jerusalem artichokes, and scones with raspberry jam. The next it was homemade granola and yogurt, ham, and something called a Dutch baby, sort of a glorified popover with a thick, almost custardy base. It comes out of the oven in a crock; it's eaten with maple syrup and it is very, very good.

The inn owner later informed me that the geese were in the midst of mating season, hence the high volume, but that nevertheless, as a concession to guests, he had slimmed down the flock to just a few geese.

Heading Out

Stone Ridge turned out to be a good base of operations. It is attractive but not twee, little more than a few stone houses strung along a state road, along with the imposing Inn at Stone Ridge (known locally as Hasbrouck House). The inn, a Dutch Colonial mansion, has a highly inviting little tavern just inside the entryway with seasonal beers on tap from the Woodstock Brewery in Kingston. The inn's restaurant, Milliways, specializes in regional American cuisine. The extensive wine list is all-American.

Another advantage to Stone Ridge is its proximity to High Falls, a tiny hamlet with much historical interest. Like many other towns in Ulster County, High Falls is witness to an economy that came and went. It flourished in the heyday of the Delaware & Hudson Canal, built in 1828 to carry household coal from northeastern Pennsylvania to Kingston, where it was transferred to large barges that floated downriver to New York City. High Falls had the highest concentration of locks on the canal, five of them, which raised or lowered barges 70 feet. The railroad made the canal obsolete by the late 19th century, and High Falls settled into a doze. The Delaware & Hudson Canal Museum in High Falls tells the tale, and it offers self-guided walking tours to the canal, the locks, an old icehouse, a telegraph office, and the remains of sawmills that predate the canal.

A Tavern from 1797

High Falls is also home to the county's most celebrated restaurant, the Depuy Canal House, a comfortable tavern from 1797 that serves dinner Thursday through Sunday and lunch on Sunday. The bill of fare is ambitious and, if you take advantage of the set menus, a bargain. The restaurant offers a four-course menu for $50 and a seven-course menu for $65. À la carte prices are $8 to $11 for soups and appetizers and $20 to $44 for entrees.

We started with a half bottle of Veuve Clicquot and nibbled on free hors d'oeuvres: chickpea puree on endive and a mock black caviar in a phyllo pastry cup. The caviar was made of amaranth, a grain, which had been soaked in brine and then cooked in squid ink and a little Vietnamese fish sauce. Although it didn't taste all that much like caviar, it was at least cruising in the neighborhood.

All-American Main Street

Ulster County has no mandatory tourist destination. Therefore, it is perfectly okay to browse, guilt-free. An hour here, a couple of hours there should do it. Saugerties gets my vote as having the main street most likely to restore faith in traditional American values. Around one corner lies the heartwarming sight of a real, live small-town movie theater, the kind that has to be described as "the local bijou." At the same time, Saugerties has more than its share of spiffy restaurants, including Cafe Tamayo (nouvelle-ish) and Featherstone's (English).

Woodstock no doubt has abundant charms, but for purely personal reasons, I made a wide detour around it. Any town boasting of its artists' colony earns my instant suspicion. The term conjures up images of bad, overpriced jewelry and unspeakable objects labeled "sculptures." I prefer to visit a good reptile farm, and Woodstock doesn't have one.

Although Kingston shows every sign of having fallen on irreversible hard times circa 1920, it should have historical interest for New Yorkers. It was once the state's third-leading metropolis, after New York City and Albany, and for a time was the state's capital. The river made it. The fortunate confluence of Rondout Creek and the Hudson transformed a small Dutch settlement into a thriving center for the warehousing and distribution of flagstones, bluestone, cement, gravel, coal, and agricultural produce. After the Revolution, New Yorkers voted to make Kingston the capital of the United States.

A whiff of the glory days can be felt at Rondout Landing, on the river, and along the West Strand, a block of 19th-century Italianate commercial buildings that have been restored. The chief feature of the waterfront is the Rondout II Lighthouse, built in 1913.

Along the Wine Trail

Enough history. On to the wine trail, Ulster's highway of pleasure. Actually, there are two trails. The Shawangunk Wine Trail, marked by signs decorated with a cluster of grapes, starts south of New Paltz at Modena. Follow Route 44/55 west to Route 7. Turn south, then west again on Route 52. The white-streaked Shawangunks loom off to the west. A second string of wineries is off Route 9W between West Park and Marlboro. Most wineries offer tastings and sell their wares. (Some impose a small tasting fee, which is deducted from the price of the bottle if you buy.)

The Hudson Valley is not the Côte d'Or, but there are some decent chardonnays to be found. West Park Wine Cellars is probably the best known. The bold few might wish to sample a Hudson Valley red. The standout wine on my visit was a grape variety new to me, a weirdo French hybrid called Ravat, after its inventor. It's a fairly hefty, fruity white that makes a terrific aperitif. It's a good souvenir and a good symbol for Ulster County. It's not a great wine, but a good wine, a little off the beaten track and worth the search. It's the wine you'd expect from a pleasant land.

Touring, Eating, Sleeping: Ulster County Essentials

GETTING THERE

To reach Ulster County from the metropolitan area, take the George Washington Bridge to the Palisades Interstate Parkway North to the Gov. Thomas E. Dewey Thruway.

ACCOMMODATIONS & DINING

Baker's Bed and Breakfast, 24 Old Kings Hwy., Stone Ridge 9 (☎ 845/687-9795).
Cafe Tamayo, 89 Parition St., Saugerties (☎ 845/246-9371). Open Wednesday through Saturday 5 to 9:30pm (until 10pm Fridays and Saturdays); Sunday 11:30am to 9:30pm. Brunch entrees $6.75 to $12; dinner entrees $12 to $20.
Depuy Canal House, Rte. 213, High Falls (☎ 845/687-7700). Open Thursday through Saturday 5:30 to 10pm, Sunday 11:30am to 2pm and 4 to 9pm. Closed January to February 14. Menu changes daily; dinner entrees $20 to $44.
 Inn at Stone Ridge (Hasbrouck House), Rte. 209, Stone Ridge (☎ 845/687-0736). Closed Monday and Tuesday. Five suites, with breakfast, $195 to $425.

ATTRACTIONS

Delaware and Hudson Canal Museum, Mohonk Rd., High Falls (☎ 845/687-9311). Open Memorial Day to Labor Day, Thursday through Monday 11am to 5pm and Sunday 1 to 5pm; May, September, and October, Saturday 11am to 5pm and Sunday 1 to 5pm. Suggested admission $3, $1 for children, $7 for families.

Hudson River Maritime Museum and Rondout Lighthouse, 1 Rondout Landing, Kingston (☎ 845/338-0071). Open May through October, daily 11am to 5pm. Admission $3, $2 for seniors and children 6 to 12, free for children 5 and under and museum members.

 Boat trips to the lighthouse are offered weekends in May and June, daily in

July and August, and weekends in September and October. Boat trips depart from the museum beginning at 12:30pm. Tickets, which include admission to the museum, are $8, $7 for seniors and children 5 to 11, free for children under 5.

Hudson Valley Garlic Festival, Cantine Field (exit 20 off the Gov. Thomas E. Dewey Thruway), Saugerties. Food, lectures, cooking demonstrations, crafts, and entertainment sponsored by the Kiwanis Club of Saugerties. Held on the last weekend in September. 10am to 5pm. Admission (good for both days) $3 in advance, $5 at the door. For information, send a stamped, self-addressed envelope to the Garlic Festival Committee, P.O. Box 443, Saugerties, NY 12477, or call ☎ **845/ 246-3090** for a recorded message.

Huguenot Street Stone Houses, New Paltz. The Jean Hasbrouck, Abraham Hasbrouck, Bevier-Elting, Lefevre, Deyo, and Freer-Lowe houses, as well as the French Church and the Grimm Gallery and Museum line Huguenot Street. From the Thomas E. Dewey Thruway, take exit 18 and turn left onto Main St. (Rte. 299); continue to Huguenot St. and turn right. The interiors of the houses may be seen only on guided tours (see Huguenot Historical Society, below).

Huguenot Historical Society, New Paltz (☎ **845/255-1660** or 845/255-1889). The group sponsors tours of the stone houses along Huguenot St. Tours are offered May though October, Tuesday through Sunday 9am to 4pm; they can also be arranged by appointment during the winter. The

2½-hour Huguenot St. tour includes stops at most of the stone structures; the fee is $10, $9 for seniors and students, $5 for children 6 to 12, free for children under 5. the 1½-hour tour includes two houses and the stone French Church; the fee is $6, $5 for seniors and students, $3 for children 6 to 12, free for children under 5. A tour of one house is $3 per person.

A tour of the Terwilliger House and Locust Lawn in Gardiner is available by appointment through the Huguenot Historical Society for $7, $6 for seniors, $4 for children under 12.

Old Dutch Church, 272 Wall St., Kingston (☎ **845/338-6759**). Self-guided tours Monday through Friday 9am to 4pm; guided tours by appointment. Admission and tours free.

Senate House State Historic Site, 296 Fair St., Kingston (☎ **845/338-2786**). Open mid-April through October, Wednesday through Saturday 10am to 5pm and Sunday 1 to 5pm; open to groups by appointment in winter. Admission $3, $2 for seniors, $1 for children 5 to 12, free for children under 5.

Trolley Museum of New York, 89 E. Strand, Kingston (☎ **845/331-3399**). Call for hours and admission prices.

Volunteer Firemen's Hall and Museum of Kingston, 265 Fair St., Kingston (☎ **845/331-0866** or 845/331-4065). April and May, Friday 11am to 3pm and Saturday 10am to 4pm; June through August, Wednesday through Friday 11am to 3pm, Saturday 10am to 4pm. Admission by donation.

VINEYARDS

Here is a sampling of vineyards in the Shawangunk region and along Rte. 9W. Many of them close or cut back their hours December to June.

Adair Vineyards, 52 Allhusen Rd., New Paltz (☎ **845/255-1377**). Closed January and February.

Baldwin Vineyards, 176 Hardenburgh Rd., Pine Bush (☎ **845/744-2226**).

Benmarl Winery, Highland Ave. (off Rte. 9W), Marlboro (☎ **845/236-4265;** www.benmarl.com). A music and art festival with concerts, art displays, and crafts demonstrations runs in early July. Admission for tours and tasting $5 adults, children free; special admission price for entertainment.

Brimstone Hill Vineyards, 61 Brimstone Hill Rd., Pine Bush (☎ **845/744-2231**).

Royal Kedem Wineries, Rte. 9W, Marlboro (☎ **845/236-4281**).

West Park Wine Cellars, Rte. 9W, Burroughs Drive, West Park (☎ **845/ 384-6709**).

THE ROOSEVELTS' HUDSON OASES

by Laurence Zuckerman

"You WOULD BE UNBEATABLE AND you would help greatly to defeat Governor Dewey," Harold Ickes wrote to Eleanor Roosevelt on May 21, 1945, urging her to run for the United States Senate from New York. It was only a month after her husband, the president, had died. Mrs. Roosevelt, despite decades of political activism, demurred. But more than half a century later, Ickes's son, also called Harold, urged another first lady to run for the Senate from New York. And as everyone now knows, Hillary Rodham Clinton accepted the challenge.

Comparisons between the two women began even before the Clintons moved into the White House in 1993. They were encouraged by the new first lady herself, who conspicuously placed a portrait of Mrs. Roosevelt in her White House office. They continued when she solicited advice from Roosevelt scholars and later, in 1996, admitted to having imaginary conversations with Eleanor at the urging of an outside adviser. (Many news organizations called the sessions "séances.") To people of a certain age, Eleanor Roosevelt is still as beloved, and hated, as she was when she died in 1962 at the age of 78—one of the most outspoken and controversial women of the century.

But when the comparisons cropped up again last fall, I had to admit that I knew very little about Mrs. Roosevelt. So it was in the spirit of putting both first ladies in perspective—and treating ourselves to a gourmet meal in the process—that my wife and I headed north along the Hudson River toward Hyde Park, home of the Roosevelts and the Culinary Institute of America, alma mater of many of the country's most celebrated chefs. My parents had taken me to Hyde Park as a boy to visit Springwood, the Roosevelt ancestral home, and the nearby Vanderbilt Mansion. The only things I recalled from that visit were Franklin D. Roosevelt's car, which was specially outfitted so that the president could drive it without having to depend on his paralyzed legs, and the long, steep meadow stretching down to the Hudson behind the Roosevelt mansion that seemed to demand exploration.

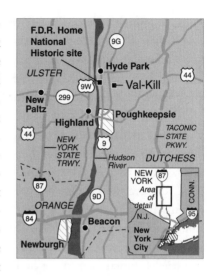

I was happy to discover that the hill with the view of the river is still as precipitous as I had remembered. There are several miles of walking trails around the property, including one that leads to the river and connects to the Vanderbilt Mansion, another historic site 3 miles to the north, making a visit worth a trip if only to hike.

Had I been more interested in Mrs. Roosevelt the last time I was in Hyde Park, there would not have been much to see. But in 1972, the Franklin Delano Roosevelt Library, which was built adjacent to Springwood while the president was still alive, added an Eleanor Roosevelt wing. In addition, in 1984, the cottage 2 miles away that Eleanor Roosevelt lived in after the president's death was opened to the public after being saved from the wrecking ball of a developer. It can be reached from the main house by car or along a pleasant walking trail. Mrs. Roosevelt said that the cottage, which is called Val-Kill after the stream nearby, was the only home that was ever truly hers. Her mother and her father, who was the younger brother of Theodore Roosevelt, died by the time she was 10. She was reared by her maternal grandmother and passed between boarding school and the homes of relatives before she married her distant cousin Franklin Delano Roosevelt in 1905.

After that, she was under the thumb of her imperious mother-in-law, Sara Delano Roosevelt, who installed the newlyweds in a town house adjoining hers on East 65th Street in Manhattan—with open doors on each floor connecting the two buildings. In the sitting room at Springwood, where the clan spent summers and holidays, there was a special easy chair for F. D. R. and one for S. D. R. but neither apparently thought of making a place for E. R.

During the first decade of her marriage, Mrs. Roosevelt bore six children and tried hard to be the dutiful wife and daughter-in-law. Then in 1918, she discovered her husband's affair with her social secretary, Lucy Mercer. The wound never fully healed, but it liberated Mrs. Roosevelt to develop her passion for social activism. Ken Ringle recently wrote in the *Washington Post* that the Roosevelts "were so dysfunctional a married couple that they make the Clintons look like June and Ward Cleaver." But in fact, despite many painful episodes, the Roosevelts functioned quite well together. Though both pursued amorous relationships with others after 1918, they continued to work well together and never lost their affection for each other.

A small illustration of how the Roosevelt household ran is in the E. R. wing at the Roosevelt library. It is a typewritten note from Mrs. Roosevelt to her husband's secretary, Missy LeHand, whom many Roosevelt intimates considered to be a surrogate wife. Passing on a doctor's bill for one of the Roosevelt boys, Mrs. Roosevelt, who had a warm relationship with Miss LeHand despite her affair with the president, wrote that she feared her husband would "have a fit" when he saw how expensive the charge was. At the bottom, the president had scrawled instructions to Miss LeHand: "Pay it. Have had fit."

Val-Kill itself can also be seen as a symbol of the unique relationship between the Roosevelts. In 1924, Franklin provided the land and built a fieldstone Dutch colonial cottage for Eleanor and two political friends, giving her a refuge from Springwood. The two friends, Nancy Cook and Marion Dickerman, lived in the cottage. Mrs. Roosevelt was a regular visitor when she was in Hyde Park. Her husband would come over to join in the fun and to swim in the pool that was fed by the stream.

Soon after the cottage was built, Mrs. Roosevelt put up the money to start a small factory next door, run by Miss Cook, that made reproductions of early American furniture. When the business folded in 1936, Mrs. Roosevelt converted the factory building into a residence for herself alone. That became her home after she left the White House and is now a shrine maintained by the National Park Service. (The stone cottage is used as an office by a private group devoted to perpetuating her ideals.) Visitors to Val-Kill start at the Playhouse, an annex used for parties and gatherings during Mrs. Roosevelt's days, now a theater featuring a documentary on her life. Next door is her stucco cottage, which is most notable for its modesty and simplicity. There is a study where Mrs. Roosevelt and her loyal secretary, Malvina Thompson, known as Tommy, responded to sacks of mail, and where Mrs. Roosevelt wrote "My Day," her 6-day-a-week syndicated newspaper column that began in 1936 and continued until her death.

Adjoining the study is a little apartment where Miss Thompson lived. The bedrooms upstairs are small and plain. Mrs. Roosevelt's, decorated with photographs of friends and family, is connected to a screened-in, wood-paneled sleeping porch where she preferred to spend her nights in the summer. The living room is filled with books and more photographs of family and friends. There are several comfortable chairs pulled close together. Throughout her life, Mrs. Roosevelt loved reading poetry aloud and having it read to her.

In the small dining room, where dozens of friends and family regularly were squeezed around the table, meals were served family style. Large silver candelabras that belonged to Mrs. Roosevelt's mother stand next to restaurant-supply drinking glasses. It is as if Mrs. Roosevelt was rebelling against the formal tradition she was forced to adhere to for most of her life, first as a debutante, then as a governor's wife, and finally as first lady.

After Mrs. Roosevelt died, the property was sold and the house was divided into private apartments. But the archivists from the Roosevelt library took extensive photographs of the house, which were used to restore it after a preservationist group bought the property in 1977. Many of the original objects, such as a Chinese sandalwood chest with carved dragons, have found their way back to the house as gifts from collectors. Others, like a painting over the mantel in the study, have not been recovered and so the space is left blank.

In retrospect, what is most striking about Mrs. Roosevelt is how much more radical she was in the middle of the 20th century than

Mrs. Clinton has been at the end. Mrs. Roosevelt was much more out-spoken about race, poverty, foreign policy, and dozens of other topics than Mrs. Clinton has been. And like Mrs. Clinton, Mrs. Roosevelt was strongly criticized for her stands, often cruelly. But as her biographer Blanche Wiesen Cook has pointed out, there was more support for an activist first lady in the 1930s, when a prominent network of social reformers existed, than there is today.

Mrs. Roosevelt also seemed to have had more freedom in her personal life. Her closest friends and political allies, beginning in the 1920s, were two lesbian couples. She lived with one—Cook and Dickerman—when she was in Hyde Park, and rented a small apartment in the Greenwich Village town house of another couple, Esther Lape and Elizabeth Read. After Roosevelt was elected governor of New York in 1928, Mrs. Roosevelt became involved with Earl Miller, the state trooper who was assigned as her bodyguard. Later, she had what might have been a love affair with an Associated Press reporter, Lorena Hickok, and then began a close friendship with Joseph P. Lash. He would become a journalist and her future biographer, but was then a left-leaning student leader half her age whom she had met on a train.

While these relationships were the subject of rumors at the time, one can only imagine what today's press would have done with any one of them. Walking the beautiful grounds around Val-Kill, it is fun to imagine the many picnics with family and friends at the outdoor barbecue, or Earl Miller, who was an Olympic-grade athlete and circus performer, teaching his "Lady," as he referred to Mrs. Roosevelt, how to dive into the pool. (It took her about 10 years to perfect her technique.)

Then there were the many notables who passed through, including Nikita S. Khrushchev, the Soviet leader; Emperor Haile Selassie of Ethiopia; and Shirley Temple. John F. Kennedy visited in August 1960 to try to win Mrs. Roosevelt's backing for his presidential campaign. She was a strong supporter of Adlai E. Stevenson and was not fond of Joseph Kennedy, John's father, who had been ambassador to Britain in the 1930s. But after Kennedy and Mrs. Roosevelt lunched at Val-Kill, she agreed to back the young senator, provided he worked closely with Stevenson and his allies.

Having steeped ourselves in Mrs. Roosevelt's rich life, we headed to the Culinary Institute of America, known as the C.I.A., for lunch. (Its Food and Beverages Institute is known as the F.B.I.) Housed in an old Jesuit seminary on a cliff overlooking the Hudson, the institute operates four restaurants and one cafe staffed by its students. Our lunch at the American Bounty restaurant was sublime, and reasonably priced by New York City standards. Over deep-fried squid with baby arugula, avocado and lemon-cilantro vinaigrette, pan-roasted fillet of striped bass, and wine, we talked about the Roosevelts, among other things.

Back in 1945, Mrs. Roosevelt told Harold Ickes she would not run for the Senate because "it was not the way in which I can be most useful." Instead, President Harry S Truman appointed her a delegate to the fledgling United Nations, where she accomplished what she said was her proudest achievement: passage of the Universal Declaration of Human Rights.

Perhaps Mrs. Roosevelt realized that holding elected office is a mixed bag. It can raise the moral authority of some, like her husband, but it can also demean the stature of others.

SIGHTS & FEASTS: HYDE PARK ESSENTIALS

The Eleanor Roosevelt home at Val-Kill, the Franklin Delano Roosevelt Library, and the Culinary Institute of America are all in Hyde Park, New York, about 90 miles north of Manhattan. Both Val-Kill and the Roosevelt home known as Springwood are administered by the National Park Service. For information call ☎ 845/229-9115.

GETTING THERE

By Car   From New York City, take the Sawmill River Parkway to the Taconic State Parkway north. Exit at Rte. 55 west (Poughkeepsie). Follow Rte. 55 west to Rte. 9 north. Follow Rte. 9 to the library. To Val-Kill, follow Rte. 9 to St. Andrews Rd. Take a right to Rte. 9G. Turn left. The park entrance will be a half mile on the right.

By Train   The Hudson Line of Metro-North (☎ 212/532-4900) offers regular service from Grand Central Terminal to Poughkeepsie, which is a short taxi ride from Hyde Park. Tickets cost $9.50 to $13 one-way; 50¢ for children ages 5 to 11, free for children under 5.

ACCOMMODATIONS

Beekman Arms, 6387 Mill St., Rhinebeck (☎ 845/876-7077, www.beekmanarms. com). There is a 2-night minimum stay on weekends May through October.

June through October, rooms range from $95 to $145; November through May, $85 to $145. Rates include continental breakfast. The Beekman 1766 Tavern serves dinner Monday through Thursday 5:30 to 9pm, Friday and Saturday 5:30 to 9:30pm. **Belvedere Mansion,** 10 Old Rte. 9, Staatsburg (☎ 845/889-8000; www. belvederemansion.com). Each room in this mansion overlooking the Hudson, built in 1900, has a private bathroom. Rates range from $95 to $275 and include full country breakfast at 9 and 10am. **The Saltbox Bed and Breakfast,** 277 Ruskey Lane, Hyde Park (☎ 845/266-3196). Situated just outside Hyde Park in a rural area surrounded by horse farms. Call for rates.

DINING

The Culinary Institute of America, on Rte. 9 in Hyde Park, has four restaurants and one cafe open to the public. All reservations can be made at ☎ 845/471-6608, or online at www.ciachef.edu. Reservations, especially for weekend days, fill up quickly and should be made several weeks in advance. The **American Bounty Restaurant** is open Tuesday through Saturday 11:30am to 1pm and 6:30 to 8pm; lunch entrees cost $11.95 to $16, dinner entrees $15 to $22. The **Escoffier Restaurant** is open Tuesday through Saturday 11:30am to 1pm and 6:30 to 8pm; lunch entrees $12.50 to $17.50, dinner entrees $22.50 to $20.25. The **Caterina de Medici Restaurant** is open Monday through Friday 11:30am to 1pm and 6:30 to 8pm; fixed-price lunch $24.50, fixed-price dinner $30.95. **St. Andrew's Café** is open Monday through Friday 11:30am to 1pm and 6:30 to 8pm; lunch entrees $10 to $18, dinner entrees $12 to $20. **Apple Pie Bakery Cafe** is open Monday through Friday 8am to 6:30pm; salads, sandwiches, and pizza $1.75 to $5.75; no reservations required.

The Brass Anchor, 31 River Point Rd., Poughkeepsie (☎ 845/452-3232), just down the road from the Culinary Institute and overlooking the Hudson River, specializes in seafood. Open daily 11:30am to 3pm and 5 to 10pm; lunch entrees $7 to $15, dinner entrees $14 to $35, fixed-price brunch on Sunday.

ATTRACTIONS

Val-Kill is open May through October, daily 9am to 5pm; November through April, Saturday and Sunday 9am to 5pm. The grounds are open daily year-round until sunset. There is a $5 admission charge.

Springwood is open daily 9am to 5pm. The grounds are open daily 7am to sunset, and access is free. Admission to Springwood is $10 for adults, which includes entry to the Franklin Delano Roosevelt Library and Museum; free for children under 17. Guided tours are conducted every half hour. The library is administered by the National Archives. For information call ☎ 800/337-8474. Open daily 9am to 5pm. All three sites are closed on Thanksgiving, Christmas, and New Year's Day.

More Getaways in
New York State

A *BELLA* WEEKEND AT
MOHONK MOUNTAIN HOUSE

by Michael T. Kaufman

L'ALBERGO DI MONTE MOHONK È
bello e romantico—molto bello, molto romantico.

I probably could not have said that before I recently spent a Tower of Babble Weekend learning Italian at Mohonk Mountain House, a remarkable hotel magnificently situated within a 7,000-acre wilderness in the Shawangunk Mountains, just 90 miles from New York City. But the resort, which has been a moderately well-kept secret since it was founded in 1869, does encourage flights of rhapsody, in whatever language.

Still owned and managed by the descendants of Alfred and Albert Smiley, the Quaker twin brothers who first stumbled on the site and set about developing it, Mohonk Mountain House has acquired its very own atmosphere, a blend of splendor and comfort with a bracing touch of ennobling asceticism.

The awesome views of glacial lakes, mountain crests, and sloping valleys are all the more impressive for lying so close to the city. There are 85 miles of private paths that can be used for walking, cross-country skiing, or carriage rides. There are cliffs to climb and well-tended gardens to look at and sniff, and more than 100 gazebos in which to rest, read, or scan the horizon in solitude. There is a golf course. There is a library. And many of the 261 rooms have working fireplaces.

Not one of them, however, has a television set. Nor is there a bar in the hotel, though liquor is available with meals, a departure from tradition. Of the many public rooms in the sprawling main building, there are only two where smoking is permitted. And despite the many sports and activities available, there is no indoor swimming pool. No stars entertain in the evening, though there are often talks by naturalists and it is not uncommon for guests to organize their own concerts around the piano. Pets are forbidden. Children, on the other hand, are very much welcome and much in evidence. There is an old-fashioned soda shop, and, in what seems to be a concession to those who think croquet too tame an after-dinner activity, there is a small room of pinball machines and electronic games.

"All of this has been thought out over decades," said Helen Dorsey, the hotel's promotion manager, in a conversation that took place after I had checked out. "Mohonk is not for everyone. It is not and never has been restrictive, but the kind of people who find their way here do not need to be entertained. From the beginning, our greatest attraction has been this setting." Indeed, for the first century of its existence, Mohonk never needed to advertise. Friends of the Smileys were the first guests and they carried the word, first, through Quaker communities, and then to the well-to-do of all religions who were fascinated by nature and interested in its conservation.

By the late 1960s, when a portion of the old, largely patrician clientele was flying to more distant holidays, Mohonk, which was designated a National Historic Landmark in 1986, began to change a little. Liquor was made available. Cars were admitted onto the grounds instead of being confined to lots a mile or so away, from which guests and baggage had been transferred to the hotel by horse-drawn carriages. Special day programs were established so that visitors could book ahead to eat a single meal and visit the grounds, or just hike or ski. And programs organized around different themes were expanded, particularly for the off-season months.

It was just such a program—the Tower of Babble Weekend—that drew my wife and me to the hotel on an early April weekend. We had reserved our places a month earlier, sending off tuition checks of $250 each to the Language Immersion Institute at the State University College at New Paltz, which had developed this particular program and which conducts similar workshops at a number of different locations. I picked beginning Italian; my wife registered for intermediate Spanish. We could have picked almost anything, from Arabic to Yiddish, provided that a minimum of four others did the same.

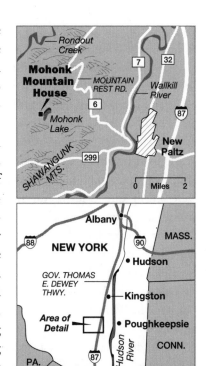

We drove from the city on Friday evening, arriving within 2 hours at the hotel's lower gate off Mountain Rest Road, some 4 miles past New Paltz. After checking for our names, a staff member waved us through to start up the magic mountain. We emerged from heavy forest to a plateau and lake, over which the hotel loomed, a massive stone and wood building that is an eighth of a mile long with towers standing six stories high. Built in sections over the years, it stands as an integral whole, combining the outdoorsy utility of Adirondack camps with an imposing, castle-like grandeur.

Valets, part of the year-round staff of 250, parked our car and we were led to our fifth-floor room in the tower, overlooking the frozen lake and the labyrinth, a jumble of rock formations on the far shore. The room, about 30 feet square with large windows, had a balcony with three rocking chairs, but the freezing temperatures made the fireplace much more appealing. The wood was already stacked, and with the help of a packet of some kind of incendiary gel that was provided, it took only a single match to start a happy fire.

On the Arts and Crafts–style desk, which coexisted nicely with Victorian and Adirondack pieces of furniture, a booklet of guest information included a greeting from the Smiley family that said in part: "We invite you to follow in the footsteps of our predecessors; waken to the sounds of nature; view a panorama virtually unchanged for generations; explore our House, a building of immense architectural interest. Please allow time to sit quietly in a comfortable nook to read or reflect." It sounded very appealing but there was no time. My wife and I had arrived there to learn, and the instruction started with Friday dinner. My table had eight students of beginning Italian. There were 12 at the intermediate Spanish table. There were also tables for German and French, and one for five teachers from Tenafly, New Jersey, who were setting out to learn Korean because there were many pupils of Korean ancestry in their school.

Our teacher introduced himself as Francisco Bonavito from Isla Staten. He kept speaking to us in Italian, explaining one Italian word or phrase with another Italian word or phrase. Remarkably, things were sinking in. The food, by the way, was varied; hearty and plentiful if not superb. We tended to talk about it a lot, but mostly to acquire vocabulary.

After dinner there were two more hours of Italian, these involving skits, songs, and questions and answers. The theory seemed to be to break down our inhibitions and our fear of making mistakes or sounding stupid. Signor Bonavito kept telling us that speaking was most important, and that grammar and structure would come later.

At 10:30pm, tired but excited, I joined my wife for some tea in a lounge. "Cara mia," I said. "Mi corazón," she answered.

Since Saturday's schedule called for virtually uninterrupted instruction until 11 at night, I decided to get up at dawn and scout the grounds. It was snowing and the footing was icy as I started out around the lake. At the far side there were trails leading up through the rocks and boulders that looked enticing, but signs barred the way because of ice. A broader path led up toward Paltz Point, rising above the hotel to a height of 1,500 feet. On clearer days, the tower at the top offers views stretching up the Rondout Valley of the Catskills and down the Hudson River toward New York City.

Braced by the jaunt, I was ready for breakfast and Italian at 8 o'clock. I am not bad at languages but I am terrible at school: I have trouble sitting. And yet I not only endured the proceedings, I thoroughly enjoyed them, all through Saturday and half of Sunday. (It might have been worse if the weather had been better.) Among the things I learned from Signor Bonavito was what to say when I visit a farm in Umbria, how to argue for a hotel room in Rome, and how to chat with an old high-school instructor when I meet him at a bus stop in Bologna.

Thanks to the teacher and his energetic, enthusiastic approach, my classmates and I were able to play charades, sing "Old MacDonald," read magazines, and argue politics, albeit primitively, all in Italian. I also learned the etymology of the Italian word *ciao,* which derives from the word *schiavo,* meaning "slave." People would greet each other by saying, "Sono vostro schiavo" ("I am your slave"), and after a while that was shortened to the now cheery and democratic "ciao."

As for the efficacy of the method, my wife and other students seemed very pleased. Some spoke of returning for more when the next Tower of Babble Weekend was held.

As for me, all I can say is that 37 years ago as a Columbia University graduate student, I spent a full academic year learning Finnish. Now, after just one weekend at Mohonk, there is absolutely no question that my Italian is much, much better than my Finnish.

MOHONK MOUNTAIN HOUSE

Mohonk Mountain House is on Mohonk Lake near New Paltz, New York (☎ **800/772-6646** or 845/255-1000), and can be reached via exit 18 of the Gov. Thomas E. Dewey Thruway. The hotel's 261 rooms range from $177 to $180 (after Apr 1, 2001) for the least expensive single to $512 to $535 for the most expensive double. Suites range from $467 to $650. Rates are based on double occupancy and include three meals and afternoon tea daily.

The resort offers a variety of special programs, among them Holistic Way: Embodying Yoga; A Walkers and Runners Rally; Birding and Spring Nature; A Festival of the Arts; Hiker's Holiday; Garden Holiday; and Music Week. All involve prior registration; some require a fee in addition to the hotel's charges for room and board. Call for the current schedule and further information.

IN PURSUIT OF THE NATIONAL PASTIME: COOPERSTOWN

by Bruce Weber

THIS MAY NOT BE YOUR RECRE-
ational fantasy, but it is mine: You wake up in a small village on a pristine morning, a midnight storm having cleared the air and left it clean
and aromatic. You climb on a bicycle and cruise around the corner and
down Main Street, around the traffic circle, past the National Baseball
Hall of Fame and Museum, and before you know it, you are out of town,
on the quiet, gently sloping road heading north along Lake Otsego.

The east side of the lake, which James Fenimore Cooper called
Glimmerglass, remains almost entirely, and remarkably, undeveloped.
The sensation is of passing through an underused wooded park, the still
water (almost no boats) on your left, a hill rising to the right on which
a semigroomed cemetery is cut into the trees.

About 10 miles out of town, the woods give way to fields, a farmhouse here and there. And then, the first commercial establishment: a
batting range! It's 10am, and the proprietor is just opening for the day.
Nothing like swatting a few majestic home runs against the backdrop
of a blue mountain. A Sunday dream.

This actually occurred (okay, except for the home runs), the highlight of the recent weekend I spent in Cooperstown, New York, wor-
shiping at the shrine of the national pastime and marveling at the
authentic aura of small-town America the place gives off in spite of
the tourists who are drawn there like runners being waved home by the
third-base coach.

It's not an ersatz thing; this is an old-timey-feeling place, maybe the
most nostalgia-inducing locale in America. And though there's more to

Cooperstown than baseball, baseball is in the air, and if not right in front of you, then around every curve.

Baseball, in fact, serves Cooperstown like a talisman, fending off the cheapening effects of commerce even as it attracts them. Historically, this is baseball's established trick; it has itself, after all, survived artificial turf, the designated hitter, domed stadiums, expansion, and players' strikes with its fundamental integrity, if not entirely intact, then having sustained only superficial injury. It says something, I think, that though the outskirts of town are getting crowded with motels, in the village itself the bed-and-breakfast rules, often in 19th-century homes.

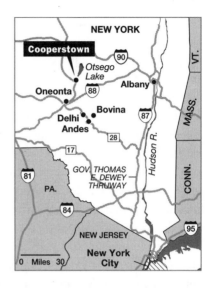

"Ninety-five percent of our guests are here for the Hall of Fame," said Pam Miller. In 1988, she and her husband, John, turned their home into the Chestnut Street Guest House, the pleasant bed-and-breakfast where I stayed. "Baseball fans are interesting, nice people," she said. "We might not feel as comfortable if it was the Wrestling Hall of Fame."

Built on a Fiction

There is something to be said for Cooperstown as a place that feels genuine but isn't, entirely, and that is lent its sheen of bucolic Americana by baseball. Spawned by the American spirit of enterprise in the wake of the Revolution, Cooperstown, after all, was founded by a man who was something of a pretender.

William Cooper, who established the village on the south shore of Otsego in 1786, grew up poor but married above his station and tried his whole life to achieve a gentleman's bearing and reputation. As portrayed by Alan Taylor in his book *William Cooper's Town,* which won the Pulitzer prize for history, Cooper was a Quaker-born, badly educated wheelwright who parlayed a highfalutin' ambition and a gift for real-estate speculation into a judgeship and a stint as a United States congressman.

His youngest son, James Fenimore, became a novelist, according to Professor Taylor, only when his inheritance began to dwindle under the burden of his father's bad debts. In *The Pioneers,* the son's third novel, set in the fictional village of Templeton (read Cooperstown), he drew on his father for the character of Judge Marmaduke Temple, "a man of good intentions but loose scruples, of expansive vision but flawed manners," Professor Taylor writes, "of benevolent paternalism but blundering execution."

It was in June 1816, 7 years after the founder's death, that the town trustees, led by Isaac Cooper, James's older brother, enacted a fine of $1 for anyone playing "at ball" in village streets; the ordinance was directed at town ball, a game played with a ball and bat that did not originate in Cooperstown and that would later evolve into baseball.

By now, historians have discredited the legend that Abner Doubleday invented baseball in Cooperstown in 1839. (Its development is more rightly associated with Alexander Cartwright, whose Knickerbocker Baseball Club played in and around New York City in the 1840s.) But as Professor Taylor writes, "Because of its 1816 ban on ballplaying in the village center, Cooperstown can better claim to have tried to prevent the invention of baseball."

Still, for a fan, a trip to Cooperstown feels like traveling to the beating heart of something. But it's not just the famous shrine. It's also that baseball is a pastoral game, transplanted to our urban centers; part of its nostalgic appeal for the urban population has undoubtedly to do with its being played on greenswards in the middle of cities. So even if the Abner Doubleday story is a fiction, the surroundings nonetheless honor the nature of the game.

Verdant Territory

For a city dweller, particularly a New York City dweller, the sense of visiting the idyllic womb of baseball begins before you get there. The whole area—Delaware and Otsego counties, which lie underpublicized north and west of the Catskills and east of the Finger Lakes—is surprisingly and consistently verdant and charming. It is characterized by the kind of landscape—rolling farmland, wildernessy foothills, lush valleys—that is featured in "I Love New York" ads, but that I always envision as having been borrowed from the state tourist bureau of Virginia or somewhere. The two-lane roads, winding and bucolic, that separate the well-spaced towns—Andes, Delhi, Bovina—bespeak the kind of territory that is just out of convenient reach of the city; from Manhattan, it's about a 4-hour drive to Cooperstown.

Okay, in a baseball mood, maybe I had an inclination to romanticize it all. From my downtown perspective, this was real country, though I said as much out loud to a local hitchhiker I picked up— "Real country here, huh?"—and he rolled his eyes. In Andes, attracted by a thickly crusted and juicy-looking blueberry pie in the window of a cafe, I stopped for a lunch that promised to be countrified.

As it turned out, though, the real find in town was the import shop next door, Paisley's Country Gallery, whose owner, John Gregg, said he transplanted himself there 9 years ago from New York City after driving through town, just as I was doing, and falling in love with the two-story building in which he now has his shop. His place smelled of wood chips and pine needles, and most of the merchandise was good country stuff offered inexpensively (I bought wind chimes and woven baskets to hold flowerpots), even though it turned out that most of the inventory was from places like the Philippines and Sierra Leone.

Far less exotic and not even authentic, unfortunately, was the blueberry pie, which had a canned filling that I might have bought at my neighborhood Sloan's.

Replete with History

In the village itself, baseball sits like Kellogg's in Battle Creek, the proud raison d'être but an ordinary part of things. Most days, Doubleday Field, the bandbox semipro ballpark that witnesses a major-league exhibition game once every summer, is quiet. The Hall of Fame is at the end of the block, looking more like a small, noble high school than a Mecca for nostalgia buffs and hero worshipers.

"Full of baseball vacationers, Main Street has the soullessly equable, bustly air of a better-than-average small college town the week the kids come back for fall," wrote Richard Ford in his novel *Independence Day*, whose climactic scenes take place in Cooperstown. (Nineteen ninety-six was a good literary year for Cooperstown: *Independence Day* also won a Pulitzer.) "Shops on both sides are selling baseball everything: uniforms, cards, posters, bumper stickers, no doubt hubcaps and condoms; and these share the street with just ordinary villagey business entities—a drugstore, a dad 'n lad, two flower shops, a tavern, a German bakery, and several realty offices."

On my Cooperstown weekend, there was a baseball day and there was a non-baseball day, which inevitably had some baseball in it. (That batting cage out at the other end of the lake, for one thing.) It isn't the Metropolitan Museum of Art or anything, but you could—and I did—spend hours at the National Baseball Hall of Fame.

It was founded by Stephen C. Clark, whose grandfather was the business partner of Isaac Merritt Singer, the man who popularized the sewing machine; the ensuing fortune made the Clark family a dominant influence in Cooperstown for generations. Sometime in the 1930s, Clark acquired a weathered ball reputed to have been owned by Abner Doubleday, and recognizing a marketing opportunity when he saw one, he used it to establish a museum, which he opened in 1939, exactly a century after Doubleday was supposed to have had the brainstorm that spawned the game.

Today, the National Baseball Hall of Fame and Museum is replete with stuff that, if you are the kind of person who watches the "Baseball Tonight" recaps of the day's major-league action on ESPN (I am such a person), will make you gasp with a child's pleasure. There's the Babe Ruth room, with his bat and his locker, and the Hank Aaron room, ditto. There are Rickey Henderson's shoes from the season he set the stolen-base record. And there's the newer, techno stuff: the interactive video screen where you can choose which presentations to watch, film clips of Clemente or Koufax.

Even if you are just along for the ride with someone whose obsession is as thorough as mine, there is interesting history to be witnessed.

The evolution of the catcher's mask and the first baseman's mitt. A collection of original scores of popular songs about baseball. A room devoted to baseball movies, from *The Pride of the Yankees* (a goofy, sentimental biography of Lou Gehrig, starring Gary Cooper, which I loved) to *A League of Their Own* (Penny Marshall's much more artful look at the women's professional teams of the 1940s, which bored me).

I'd actually been here before, but it pleased me that the place holds up after multiple viewings. I felt validated in my interest; baseball has depth. The museum proves it. (It was also satisfying to me that discount admissions are available to the Hall of Fame and the nearby Farmers' Museum and Fenimore House, if you buy tickets to all three at once.)

One thing that is a little strange is the Hall of Fame itself, the paneled vestibule in which the plaques honoring the greats of the game are somberly displayed. The plaques are boring, with little information beyond dry statistics. The room is uninspiring. And the faces of the enshrined, beaming gold and in relief from each of the plaques, look nothing like the men themselves actually did (or do). I don't get why this has to be; it isn't comforting.

A Cap for Every Head

There are better likenesses up the street in a delightfully weird commercial establishment called the American Baseball Experience, which, among other things, features a wax museum in which Casey Stengel sits grumpily in a corner hunched over a crystal ball and Pete Rose is depicted in a head-first slide, though he's suspended overhead, as if Superman were wearing a Cincinnati Reds uniform instead of his blue pajamas.

The rest of the day I spent happily consuming—books, a key chain, T-shirts, postcards, and, nearly, a Thurman Munson rookie card. (I decided against it; I'm not a collector of any kind. It's just cheap souvenirs that appeal to me.) Cooperstown is not just the baseball capital of America, it's the capital of baseball stuff. Main Street, for its three-block length (this is a remarkably small town), is lined with memorabilia shops of particularly inelegant design.

And though the real antiques are far too expensive, the browsing is fun, and there is no place in the world where there is a better selection of high-quality baseball caps. Many are the good wool kind, with an actual size that doesn't depend on an adjustable plastic strap on the back, and nowhere did they cost more than $20, which helps explain why everyone walking on Main Street is wearing at least one. (It's not unusual to see a boy with a couple of them stacked on his head.) Having not been paying attention a couple of years ago when Spike Lee's *Malcolm X* inspired the wearing of caps with Xs, I managed to fill a gap in my alphabet collection, with a white cap emblazoned with an orange X, for the 1936 Cuban X Giants, a Negro League team.

As it turns out, Cooperstown is not a great eating town. They say the Otesaga Resort Hotel, a gigantic place on the lake that is far too grandiose for its surroundings, serves equally grandiose fare, but I didn't go there. Too formidable. I had a nice bowl of chowder and a Caesar salad at T. J.'s Place, which also displayed and sold memorabilia, and, more pertinently, had a big-screen television. The Yanks were on.

Cultured Neighborhood

In season, I probably would have gone to the opera. That's no joke. The Glimmerglass Opera opened its season recently with Jack Beeson's 1965 opus, *Lizzie Borden,* and Donizetti's *Don Pasquale.* I stopped there on my bicycle circumscription of the lake after my pause at the batting cage—the whole bike route is about 27 miles, a truly exemplary recreational ride—and found the place well groomed, bordering on elegant. The grounds of the 900-seat Alice Busch Opera Theater, on the west shore of the lake, are, in the manner of Tanglewood, a place for picnicking on the lawn and strolling in the summer sunset before the music begins.

The whole southwestern corner of the lake turned out to be what I ended up thinking of as the cultured neighborhood, though it had elements of the upper-caste pretension I imagine was in the character of William Cooper. The Otesaga is here, with the Leatherstocking Golf Course and its prerequisite men in plaid pants, pastel sweaters, and tam-o'-shanters.

Just a half mile or so north of the village, on opposite sides of the shore road, are two fine museums, both run under the auspices of the New York State Historical Association. One, the spacious and pristine Fenimore Art Museum, built on the site of the novelist's home, has a superb collection of American Indian art and craft—clothing, pottery, beadwork, utensils made by artisans—as well as examples of American folk art, local paintings, and historical artifacts (including the desk at which DeWitt Clinton, once governor of New York, was sitting when he died).

Perhaps the most striking exhibit features the life masks done by the 19th-century sculptor John H. I. Browere: 22 bronze heads of American statesmen and celebrities made between 1823 and 1833. Men like John Quincy Adams, Martin Van Buren, and Thomas Jefferson are arranged in an eerie circle, their lines of vision crossing, their visages far more persuasively real than any of the more recent stars totemized at the Baseball Hall of Fame. Then, too, the Fenimore House sits on a great lawn above the lake, and the view over it from the back terrace garden is more regal and deliciously high-handed than most baseball fans are used to.

If the Fenimore House has a delicacy to it, an intellectual bent, the Farmers' Museum across the road celebrates more earthy qualities. Once a working farm owned by James Fenimore Cooper, the site replicates an entire 19th-century village; original buildings, from as early as 1795—including a tavern, a schoolhouse, and a blacksmith shop—have been moved to Cooperstown from as far as 100 miles away. It's quaint, impressive in an almost-but-not-quite European sort of way. (Americans don't often get a chance to appreciate many such home-grown collections of century-old structures.) And on a warm morning, with Historical Association employees demonstrating broom- and cabinetmaking, or reenacting a game of town ball on the lawn, you can almost regret progress.

The Farmers' Museum was my last stop, and just before I left, I ducked into one of the transplanted buildings, the general store (ca. 1828), for a last bout of shopping. There, among the rock candy, beeswax candles, freshly made brooms, and cast-iron candleholders, was a hand-sewn baseball. Wound yarn wrapped in graying leather, it was soft, a little misshapen, more on the order of what a cat, rather than a Little Leaguer, would play with today. I picked it up, had a catch with myself, then put it back, solid in the knowledge that some things do, in fact, improve with age.

COOPERSTOWN ESSENTIALS

GETTING THERE

By Car   From New York City, the quickest, if least amusing, route to Cooperstown is north on the Thomas E. Dewey Thruway (Interstate 87) to Albany; then west on Interstate 88 to Rte. 20, continuing west on Rte. 20 to Rte. 80 South; continue on Rte. 80 South along the west shore of Otsego Lake of Cooperstown.

Alternatively, there are several scenic roads through the Catskills that are accessible from I-87. For example, at Kingston, take New York State Rte. 28 West, which winds through the mountains and turns north at Oneonta. At Colliersville, take Rte. 28 North to Cooperstown. Drive time is about 4 hours, a little less perhaps by the first route, a little more by the second.

By Bus   Adirondack/Trailways operates buses daily from the Port Authority Bus Terminal in Manhattan to Cooperstown. Round-trip fare for the 5½-hour ride is $81.90; half-price for children 2 to 11; free for children under 2. For information call ☎ **800/225-6815.**

ACCOMMODATIONS & DINING

Chestnut Street Guest House, 79 Chestnut St. (☎ **607/547-5624**). Open May through October. Rooms (all with private bathrooms) $100 to $135; $160 suite. Rates are based on double occupancy and include continental breakfast. Two-night minimum.

Otesaga Resort Hotel, Rte. 80 (Lake Rd.; ☎ **800/348-6222** or 607/547-9931). Open late April through mid-November. Rooms range from $305 double to $445 suite. (From Memorial Day through Labor Day, $325 to $465.) Rates are based on double occupancy and include breakfast and dinner. Children 6 and younger staying with parents are charged only for meals; children 7 to 18 years pay $45 per day.

T. J.'s Place/The Home Plate, 124 Main St. (☎ **607/547-4040**). Open year-round, daily 8am to 8pm. Dinner entrees $8 to $15.

BASEBALL HALL OF FAME & OTHER ATTRACTIONS

Combination Tickets   Combination tickets are available for admission to the Baseball Hall of Fame, the Farmers' Museum, and the Fenimore House Museum for $22; $15 for children 7 to 12.

Farmers' Museum, Rte. 80 (Lake Rd.; ☎ **888/547-1450** or 607/547-1500). Twenty-seven historic buildings, including a tavern and a general store, re-create an 1840s village. Also, the Lippitt Farmstead, a working farm that features demonstrations of crafts of the period, with exhibitions of tools, stoneware, and folk art. Open April through May and October through November, Tuesday through Sunday 10am to 4pm; June through September, daily 10am to 5pm; closed December through March. Admission $9, $4 for children 7 to 12, free for children 6 and under.

Fenimore Art Museum, Rte. 80 (Lake Rd; ☎ **607/547-1400**). The house, which dates from 1932, has exhibitions of North American Indian art, paintings, photographs, and other items. Open April through May, Tuesday through Sunday 10am to 4pm; June through December, daily 10am to 5pm. Admission $9, $4 for children 7 to 12, free for children under 7.

Glimmerglass Opera, Rte. 80 (☎ **607/ 547-2255;** www.cooperstown.net/ glimmerglass). Call for schedule and prices.

National Baseball Hall of Fame & Museum, 25 Main St. (☎ **607/547-7200**). Open May through September, daily 9am to 9pm; October through April, daily 9am to 5pm; April and October through December, the museum remains open until 8pm. on Fridays and Saturdays. Admission $9.50, $8 seniors, $4 for children 7 to 12, free for children 6 and under.

Paisley's Country Gallery, Main St. (Rte. 28), Andes (☎ **845/676-3533**). Open Thursday through Sunday 10am to 5pm.

A 150-MILE VOYAGE BY CANAL

by Elisabeth Bumiller

"*L*ock 25, Lock 25, Lock 25. This *is the vessel* Onondaga *requesting westbound passage. Over.*"

I felt silly, but what fun it was. Anyone traveling on the Erie Canal in upstate New York must call ahead by two-way radio to the laconic men and women operating the locks. Lock-tenders, as they're unofficially called, report that canal amateurs tend to get overexcited by the radio, as if reliving a childhood fantasy about navigating a battleship. "It's new to them," said Joe Pidgeon, the lock-tender of bucolic Lock 25 near Savannah, New York. "You can tell when they pull up to the lock, because they keep chirping."

Two weeks ago, my family and I piloted our own rented boat—the 10-ton, 34-foot, very personable *Onondaga*—for nearly 150 miles on the Erie and Cayuga-Seneca canals. Over 5 days we went from just north of Syracuse to Seneca Falls to the edge of Rochester and back. (Different kinds of boats are available for weekends.)

We traveled at 6 miles an hour, ate and slept on the *Onondaga*, and saw wilderness, sleepy courthouses, and one wastewater treatment plant. Not every sight was exquisite. But the clock slowed down, and distances seemed much farther, just as they had in an earlier century. Although we've lived in India and Japan, and have trekked in Nepal, this turned out to be one of the most exotic things we have ever done.

The magic of the canal is not so much its remote stretches of beauty, but the sensation it offers of traveling along an artery of history. To float down the Erie Canal is to have an intimate connection with the way it was built to be used. Many of the small towns we passed had remnants of the 19th-century mills that drove the industrial revolution

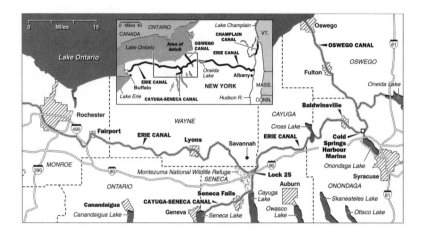

and used the canal to ship their goods. We were right down in the water, where the power was.

To arrive at Seneca Falls, site of the first women's rights convention, by water—to tie up our boat just below Wesleyan Chapel, where in 1848 Elizabeth Cady Stanton read the "Declaration of Sentiments," demanding that women be given the vote—made the journey more personal and gave the town a lost-in-time feel (at least until a group of 20th-century teenagers turned up to drink in the park right outside our boat).

The 340-mile-long Erie, finished in 1825, was America's greatest canal. Before the railroads and highways, it connected the Great Lakes to the Atlantic Ocean as the crucial route for shipping the crops and products of the Western states to the East. It did nothing less than transform New York City into a commercial superpower. Philadelphia had been the nation's chief seaport, but 2 decades after the canal was finished New York was supreme.

DeWitt Clinton, the New York City mayor and then New York governor who spent a political career promoting the canal's creation—his dream was at first derided as "Clinton's Ditch"—is today considered a visionary for what he imagined the canal would do for New York. "The city will, in the course of time, become the granary of the world," he once wrote, "the emporium of commerce, the seat of manufactures, the focus of great moneyed operations."

Our adventure began at 7am on Saturday. The four of us—my husband, me, and our two children, ages 8 and 4—drove the 5 hours from our home in Westchester County to Cold Springs Harbour Marina near the northern edge of Onondaga Lake, just above Syracuse. After loading up with groceries, we boarded our boat for an orientation by Carl Peterson, 17, of Mid-Lakes Navigation, the largest and oldest boat-rental company on the Erie.

Mr. Peterson showed us around the barge, from the diesel engine to the head and shower, then told us it was time to cast off. I put the children in life jackets and undid the lines while my husband, Steve Weisman, took the tiller under Mr. Peterson's eye.

Steve has had some experience with boats, but not with a 10-ton barge; the *Onondaga*, though easy to handle, took practice. Amazingly, Mid-Lakes rents to complete novices, but it also heartily recommends that you take out $1 million in liability insurance. We did that, through Mid-Lakes, for $75.

While Steve practiced his turns in the canal, I unpacked and looked over our new home. The boat was a marvel. A decade ago, Mid-Lakes began building what it calls "Lockmasters," modeled on 19th-century European canal boats, for recreational use on the Erie. The *Onondaga*, one of the newest Lockmasters, had a steel hull, with a metal exterior painted a pleasing red, gold, and forest green.

Inside, it looked like a floating Adirondack cabin with light-pine paneled walls and braided rugs. There was a double bed, a sofa that turned into bunk beds for the children at night, and a small dining table with cushioned benches up in the bow. In the kitchen was a two-burner stove, an oven, a sink, and a small refrigerator and freezer.

Elizabeth Wiles Wing manages the nine Mid-Lakes Lockmasters, and she is a woman after my own heart. The *Onondaga* was not only immaculate but also obsessively well equipped, from a portable propane grill to a potato peeler to a corkscrew to salt and pepper shakers. There were even two bicycles strapped to the top deck.

Mr. Peterson helped us through the first lock, No. 24, in Baldwinsville. It wasn't that easy. While Steve steered the boat through the gates and along the cement wall, I stood in the bow and grabbed for one of the lines hanging from the top of the lock. (The lines were covered with the most fantastic green slime I have ever seen. Ms. Wing thoughtfully supplied rubber gloves.)

Steve, in the stern, grabbed for a line, too. We held the *Onondaga* parallel to the wall as the gates closed and millions of gallons of water filled the lock. In minutes we were lifted up 11 feet. Then the gates in front of us opened, and out we glided. The locks, 36 in all, are necessary because of the 568-foot rise in the canal as it stretches west from the Hudson River to Lake Erie.

We tied up alongside a cemetery in Baldwinsville, said goodbye to Mr. Peterson, grilled some salmon for dinner, then went to bed and slapped miserably at mosquitoes all night. We bought a can of Raid the next day, and it saved us for the rest of the trip.

We cast off on Sunday at 10am, marveling at the blue herons, the red-tipped maple leaves, and the labor of the 19th-century workers, many of them Irish immigrants, who fought malarial mosquitoes as they dug the canal through the Montezuma Marsh, now the Montezuma National Wildlife Refuge. We were not in the original Erie Canal, but the enlarged Erie built after 1905, parallel to the first, which made use of existing rivers and lakes. Even at that time, railroads had cut heavily into the canal's traffic, and by the 1950s, the opening of the St. Lawrence Seaway and the New York State Thruway made it obsolete.

Today the focus is on tourism. In a 5-year plan, millions of dollars in federal and state money are being spent to improve the canal's locks, moorings, and bike paths. In 1992, the legislature created the Canal Recreationway Commission and renamed all four interconnected canals in the state—the Erie, the Cayuga-Seneca, the Champlain, and the Oswego—as the New York State Canal System.

We arrived in Seneca Falls by 6pm, and on Monday morning toured Wesleyan Chapel and Elizabeth Cady Stanton's home, where a park ranger, Richard Pardee, told us that Stanton considered Seneca Falls an "awful, mud-rutted town." I thought it was better than that, but no doubt things have improved. By 2pm, we were back on the water, headed west.

The days fell into a nice pattern. We would cast off around 8am, eat breakfast and lunch while under way, then anchor on a quiet stretch in the hot afternoons for a swim. The water was murky, a little creepy, but cold. I never saw anybody else swim in the canal, except for a teenage boy who jumped 60 feet from the top of a railroad bridge, screaming at the top of his lungs. (It was a stunt, and he survived.)

My husband was happy because he discovered he could read while he drove the boat, although only half a page at a time; I navigated from the detailed charts supplied by Mid-Lakes. I also became an avid reader of the *Onondaga's* logbooks, which Mid-Lakes encourages boaters to keep. Most log entries were about restaurants and birds spotted along the way, but a few were soulful reflections from boaters who suddenly had found time to think.

"Met lovely old man in Clyde," wrote a woman from Skaneateles, New York. "Must have been 85 plus—working his 5 by 10 store after 63 years!! He's lonesome & wants to talk but I can tell he doesn't want to be inappropriate. We buy some stuff and linger—it's hard to pull away. Hope we see him again—he's a really lovely human being. Working to stay alive, psychologically—more power to him. . . . Testimony to the human spirit, like the canal."

We stayed Monday night in Lyons, and by Tuesday reached Fairport, an affluent suburb of Rochester. We looked over the Fairport Historical Museum, went on a walking tour of some 19th-century Greek revival and Italianate homes, had dinner at the Green Tavern, and went to bed in a thunderstorm.

Fairport has revitalized its canal front, and it's spiffy; but it also felt like an upscale mall. It would be awful if every canal waterfront looked the same way.

On Wednesday morning we turned back toward home, reaching Lock No. 25, and Mr. Pidgeon, its lock-tender, by dinner time. It was 6 more hours to Cold Springs Harbour Marina, so we decided to stay overnight. The lock was pretty, and surrounded by woods.

"You can tie up anywhere you want," said Mr. Pidgeon, who was cutting the grass. He also plants flowers at the lock, and polishes to a burnished gleam the lock's brass and copper switches and contacts, circa 1915.

Mr. Pidgeon, who lives nearby, said he loved meeting boaters, and once offered his office for the night to a 70-ish man who was navigating the canal by canoe in a driving rain. Mr. Pidgeon's 13-year-old son sometimes goes fishing near the lock for trout and bass.

A former electrician who brings an eloquence to his job, Mr. Pidgeon said he considered himself less an employee of the state and more a "guardian" of a fine museum. "How's that saying go?" he said. "Once you find a job you love, you never work another day in your life."

Early the next morning, a beautiful mist rose up from the canal. We were sad to head home.

"Lock 25, Lock 25, Lock 25. This is the vessel Onondaga *requesting eastbound passage. Over."*

CANAL ESSENTIALS

RENTING A BOAT

Canal Princess Charters, Box 421, Tonawanda, NY 14151 (☎ **716/693-2752**). Drive-your-own houseboats, sleeping a family of six or two couples, are available from mid-May to the end of October on the western Erie Canal, starting at $500 for 2 days (in early spring or late fall only); $700 for 3 days; $800 for 4 days; $1,200 for a week.

Collar City Charters, Troy Town Dock and Marina, 427 River St., Troy, NY 12180 (☎ **800/830-5341**). Drive-your-own canal boats, available May through October on the Champlain Canal. Weekly rate, $1,700 to $2,000, includes fuel, linens, locking fee, and lessons.

Erie Canal Cruise Lines, 714 Union St., Suite 907, Manchester, NH 03104 (☎ **800/962-1771;** www.canalcruises.com). Drive-your-own canal boats, sleeping up to six, are available on the Erie Canal May through October. Boats range from 34 to 42 feet; rates range from $1,200 to $1,800 for a half week to $1,700 to $2,700 for a full week.

Mid-Lakes Navigation Company, Box 61, 11 Jordan St., Skaneateles, NY 13152 (☎ **800/545-4318**). Drive-your-own canal boats, from 33 to 42 feet, sleeping two to six people. They are available from mid-May to mid-October at $1,800 to $2,300 a week. Mid-Lakes will not rent boats for weekends, but offers 2- and 3-day canal cruises on the *Emita II,* a passenger boat with a captain and crew. Guests stay in hotels at night but are served meals on the boat. Rates start at $311 per person double occupancy, including lodging, for a 2-day cruise ($529 for 3 days).

DINING

Bridge Tavern, 72 Geneva St., Lyons (☎ 315/946-6542). Old family restaurant since the turn of the century. Boaters recommend the Alaskan King crab.
Green Tavern, 1 Walter St., Fairport (☎ 716/377-9888). Casual.

Lock 24, 33 Water St., Baldwinsville (☎ 315/635-2794). Casual, very friendly.
Richardson's Canal House, 1474 Marsh Rd., Pittsford (☎ 716/248-500). No jeans or children. Prix-fixe three-course dinner $40 per person; à la carte entrees $14.95 to $45.

ATTRACTIONS

Fairport Historical Museum, 18 Perrin St., Fairport (☎ 716/223-3989). Open Sunday and Tuesday 2 to 4pm, and Thursday 7 to 9pm. Has Fairport walking tour map. Free admission.
Women's Rights National Historical Park, 136 Fall St., Seneca Falls ☎ 315/ 568-2291). Includes the visitor center, Wesleyan Chapel, Declaration Park, and the Elizabeth Cady Stanton home. Open daily 9am to 5pm. Admission $2, free for children under 17; tours $1.

SUFFRAGISTS SLEPT HERE & ROUSED A NATION

by Elisabeth Bumiller

"I AM AT THE BOILING POINT!" Elizabeth Cady Stanton wrote to Susan B. Anthony about the fledging women's rights movement in the spring of 1852. "If I do not find some day the use of my tongue on this question, I shall die of an intellectual repression, a woman's rights convulsion! Oh, Susan! Susan! Susan! You must manage to spend a week with me before the Rochester convention, for I am afraid that I cannot attend it. . . . How much I do long to be free from housekeeping and children, so as to have some time to read and think and write."

Stanton's cry of frustration was sent from Seneca Falls, New York, her unhappy home on the outskirts of what was then a depressing 19th-century mill town. Anthony, who would be her friend and collaborator in the fight for suffrage over the next half century, was in Rochester in a prosperous neighborhood of merchants and bankers, an enormous psychic distance, but only 50 miles on the map. Jane Hunt, who was the host of the 1848 tea party that gave birth to the first women's rights convention, was only 3 miles from Seneca Falls, in Waterloo, New York. Mary Ann M'Clintock, whose home was the site for the drafting of the Declaration of Sentiments read by Stanton at the Seneca Falls convention, was in Waterloo, too.

Only 12 miles west of Seneca Falls, in Geneva, New York, Elizabeth Blackwell received the first medical degree conferred on a woman, in 1849. That same year, in Seneca Falls, Amelia Bloomer started *The Lily,* her women's rights publication. Eight years later, just 25 miles east of

Geneva, Harriet Tubman settled in Auburn, New York, after helping hundreds of slaves reach freedom on the Underground Railroad.

The geography is striking: So many women seeking reform rose to prominence in such a short time span in such a small space in western New York! Not long ago, my husband and I and our two children, ages 9 and 5, spent a long, glorious weekend exploring the area.

Since there were a lot of musty 19th-century houses to be seen, we interspersed the antiques and display cases with parks, beaches, vineyards, and some of the most elaborate hotels of the Finger Lakes. As a result, the children were kept from mutiny—in fact, our 9-year-old daughter enjoyed much of the Women's Rights National Historical Park—while the adults found the weekend a revelation. Trips are so often geared to one huge (male) historical figure, like Jefferson at Monticello. But we found it a more intimate experience to pick out a series of less monumental homes that serve as a record of women connected by time, place, and passion.

We started out late on a Friday night from our home in Westchester County, drove 2 hours to Albany, then collapsed at a motel. This gave us a good start on Saturday for the Anthony house in Rochester, 4 hours away. We arrived in time for an afternoon tour of the well-tended, three-story red-brick house with wisteria growing alongside the front porch. Anthony lived here for the last 40 years of her life, her most politically active period, when she traveled extensively for suffrage. Inside is a proper Victorian home, now a dark and sleepy museum, but with touching mementos: Anthony's satchel and alligator purse, walls of pictures of suffrage leaders, the simple bed in which Anthony died.

Our well-informed and talkative guide, Betty Allinger, related one of the most famous stories associated with Anthony and the house: how in 1872 Anthony tested the laws and voted, only to be arrested at home 2 weeks later by a United States deputy marshal and then taken away in a streetcar. When the conductor asked Anthony for her fare, Anthony retorted, "I'm traveling at the expense of the Government."

The next morning, Sunday, we went to tour the home of Stanton, which I had seen on a previous trip, only to learn that one guide was off and the other out sick. As a result the house would be closed until

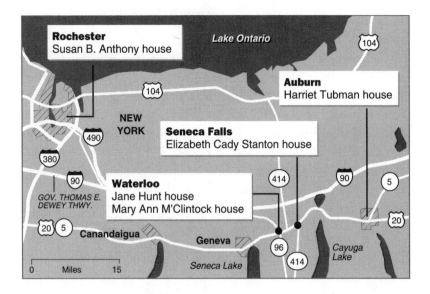

Thursday. (I recommend calling ahead to all the houses when planning a trip; despite what guidebooks say about hours, many are open at odd times.) Grumpily wondering if this would ever happen at Monticello, I was still able to tour the visitor center of the Women's Rights National Historical Park as well as the restored Wesleyan Chapel where the first women's rights convention was held. The park, part of the National Park Service, is scattered across urban parcels in Seneca Falls and Waterloo, and includes the Stanton house on the edge of town.

When I returned home, I called Jack E. Shay, the park-service ranger who had led my extensive tour of the Stanton house on the earlier trip, and who is also the co-author of *Arcane America,* which he called a "thinking person's travelogue" about 101 of the best places you've never heard of. Mr. Shay can tell you all about Stanton's wallpaper (mostly a white-and-green floral, one of the brighter patterns of the day) and her piano (a Gilbert from Boston).

Stanton's house is a light and relatively airy white clapboard farmhouse, with elements of modified Greek Revival style, decorated with Stanton's original mahogany fold-open desk. "She had good taste," Mr. Shay said. "She was used to living in rather expensive digs." The house is missing two wings, but it still has a feeling associated with its most famous owner: clean, strong, confident lines, no nonsense, no gewgaws.

Stanton, who supplied the speeches that Anthony delivered ("I forged the thunderbolts and Susan fired them"), had moved from Boston, where she had been part of a progressive, liberal circle that included William Lloyd Garrison, Bronson Alcott, Ralph Waldo Emerson, and Nathaniel Hawthorne. The switch to Seneca Falls seems to have been made for her husband's political career in the legislature in Albany and also because her father, an influential judge and former congressman, owned the house and gave it to the couple. Although Stanton despised the drudgery of Seneca Falls, she also admitted in a letter to Anthony that "it may be well for me to understand all the trials of woman's lot, that I may more eloquently proclaim them when the time comes."

On Sunday we also took a look at the big, four-columned, red-brick Jane Hunt house on East Main Street in Waterloo, from the out-side only. The house is privately owned, but there was a FOR SALE sign out front. The real-estate agent, Greg Peet, will tell you that the asking price is $139,900 for three bedrooms, three bathrooms, and history. The park service said it was interested in buying the house, and Mr. Peet said the owners were concerned about its preservation; but he also said they wanted to sell to the highest bidder. Not far away is the M'Clintock house, a red-brick Federal-style building owned by the park service, and under extensive restoration. We peeked briefly inside; it is a shell at the moment.

In Geneva we looked for the site of the Geneva Medical College, long burned down, which Elizabeth Blackwell attended. On Main Street we found all that's left: a plaque, and also Joan Braun, who came out of her house when she saw us looking confused. Mrs. Braun, the immediate past president of the Geneva Chamber of Commerce, showed us where the college had been, then invited us in to see her house and its view of Seneca Lake. I asked if people came by often on the trail of Dr. Blackwell. "All the time," she said. "I love it."

Then she pointed us to an Elizabeth Blackwell statue a short walk away on the campus of Hobart and William Smith Colleges, a tribute to a woman who was rejected by at least 15 medical schools before her admission to Geneva. On the statue is part of an 1847 letter that Blackwell sent from Geneva: "I cannot but congratulate myself on having found at last the right place for my beginning."

Our last stop was the Harriet Tubman home, where the Rev. Paul G. Carter and his wife, Christine, showed the children an evocative cartoon of Tubman's life, then gave us a tour of the simple two-story white-frame house with a big front porch. Most of the furnishings are not original, but Tubman's bed and Bible are here, and the tour was somber and moving.

We spent one night at Belhurst Castle in Geneva, an expensive old ivy-covered Romanesque pile that looks out dramatically over Seneca Lake, and another at Geneva-on-the-Lake, a small resort just up the road that has less personality and higher prices than Belhurst Castle. We had a basic tour and wine tasting at the Wagner Winery in Lodi and a good dinner at Pasta Only's Cobblestone Restaurant in Geneva. One of the highlights for the children was a hike up through the amazing gorge at Watkins Glen State Park at the southern end of Seneca Lake in Watkins Glen.

Why did so many female reformers spring up out of western New York in the mid–19th century? There's no simple answer, but it was a time of ferment—of great pressure for social change—abolitionism, temperance, religious revivalism, prison and education reform—and of great economic development.

The opening of the Erie Canal not only transformed New York City, but also made the towns between Lake Erie and Manhattan, including Seneca Falls, Rochester, Waterloo, and Geneva, important centers of commerce and thought.

All of that is available in books. But what is available only by traveling is the sense of history by proximity—seeing how geography led to connections and then ideas. In house after house, the connections came up: Tubman knew Anthony through the abolitionist Frederick Douglass (who knew everyone, including Stanton), who knew Hunt and M'Clintock and Bloomer, who introduced Stanton to Anthony. And it was Anthony who, in 1861, recorded in her diary that she had "fitted out a fugitive slave for Canada with the help of Harriet Tubman."

A Woman's Place: Homes & History Essentials

GETTING THERE

Seneca Falls, New York, is about 270 miles from New York City.

By Car From New York City, take the Thomas E. Dewey Thruway (Interstate 87) to Albany, where it becomes Interstate 90; continue on I-90 west past Syracuse and pick up Rte. 14 south; continue on Rte. 14 south, which leads to Geneva.

By Train Amtrak (☎ 800/872-7245) operates trains from Pennsylvania Station in Manhattan to the Amtrak Passenger Station in Rochester, which is about 35 miles from Geneva. Round-trip fares range from $118 to $182; half price for children 5 to 11.

By Bus Greyhound (☎ 800/231-2222) offers service from Port Authority in Manhattan to Geneva: round-trip fare $99, children $49.50. Greyhound also has service from Rochester to Geneva: round-trip fare $125, $61 for children 2 to 11 years old.

ACCOMMODATIONS & DINING

Belhurst Castle, Rte. 14 South, Geneva (☎ 315/781-0201). May though October, weekend rate $125 to $315; rates based on double occupancy include continental breakfast. November through April, $95 to $245. The company operates the nearby **White Springs Manor,** on White Springs Lane, Geneva; room rates May through October, $125 to $295; November through April, $65 to $265.

Geneva on the Lake, Rte. 14, Geneva (☎ 315/789-7190). Daily room rate based on double occupancy, including breakfast: April through May, $166 to $642; June through October, $189 to $730; November through March, $138 to $533.

Pasta Only's Cobblestone Restaurant, Rte. 5 and Rte. 20, Geneva (☎ 315/789-8498).

HISTORIC SITES

Susan B. Anthony House, 19 Madison St., Rochester (☎ 716/235-6124). Open Wednesday through Sunday 11am to 4pm; last tour at 3pm. Admission $6, $4.50 for seniors, $3 for students, $2 for children 12 and younger, free for members.

Jane Hunt House, 401 E. Main St., Waterloo. Private home; view exterior only from street.

Harriet Tubman Home, 180 South St., Auburn (☎ 315/252-2081). February through October, tours Tuesday through Friday 10am; November through January, by appointment. Suggested donation $3, $2 for seniors, $1 for children under 16.

Women's Rights National Historical Park (includes Elizabeth Cady Stanton House, 32 Washington St., Seneca Falls, and Mary Ann M'Clintock house, William St., Waterloo), Visitors Center, 136 Fall St., Seneca Falls (☎ 315/568-2991, ext. 24). Open daily 9am to 5pm. Self-guided and ranger tours. Admission $2, free for those under 17. Additional $1 admission for Stanton House.

Geneva Historical Society, 543 S. Main St., Geneva (☎ 315/789-5151). Open Tuesday through Friday 9:30am to 4:30pm, Saturday 1:30 to 4:30pm (July and Aug, also Sun 1:30 to 4:30pm); closed Monday. Donations accepted.

OTHER ATTRACTIONS

Watkins Glen State Park, Rte. 14, Watkins Glen (☎ 607/535-4511). Open daily, 8am to sundown; the gorge closes for hiking mid-November, weather permitting. Parking fee Memorial Day through Labor Day, $5 ($6 when pool is open); weekends only after Labor Day.

Wagner Winery, 9322 Rte. 414 South, Lodi (☎ 607/582-6450). Free tours with wine or beer tasting, daily 10am to 5pm.

FURTHER READING

Susan B. Anthony Slept Here: A Guide to American Women's Landmarks, by Lynn Sherr and Jurate Kazickas (Random House, 1997, $20).

Majestic & Brooding, a Fort Holds Its Ground

by Peter Applebome

The most vivid memory I have of my childhood visit to Fort Ticonderoga was not what I witnessed but how I reacted to what I saw.

I remember walking through the arched stone entryway or sally port to the fort, transfixed by an almost palpable sense of history. At its entrance was a bronze plaque listing the historic figures who had walked through the same passageway. I ran through the list of names, paused for a moment, and then marched resolutely along, scuffing my feet on every inch of the ground, hoping to traverse the exact spot—perhaps the very specks of dirt!—where once trod George Washington, Benjamin Franklin, Benedict Arnold, Thaddeus Kosciusko, and the other Revolutionary War heroes Mrs. Thurston had taught us about in third-grade social studies.

I'm not sure exactly what sort of mystical transference I was expecting to experience by my Keds passing more or less over the same ground as Washington's boots; looking for the same specks of dirt was clearly a bit optimistic. But when I brought my own kids, who had spent most of their lives in Atlanta, to Fort Ticonderoga, Fort William Henry, and Lake George, I had no idea whether the history that seemed so dramatic and immediate back then would resonate with them or with me now.

I need not have worried. In the end what struck me most was how vivid and real, yet how forgotten, that history still seemed.

We seldom remember how much of the nation's early history played out in the distant lakes of upstate New York, which is one reason a visit there can seem so memorable for adults and kids. I didn't quite feel the need to scuff my shoes along the ground this time, but when I got to throw in the family-friendly array of activities around Lake George and Bolton Landing, the experience seemed as riveting in my aging boomerdom as it did when I was a kid from Long Island.

"Perhaps no district throughout the wide extent of the intermediate frontiers can furnish a livelier picture of the cruelty and fierceness of the savage warfare of those periods than the country

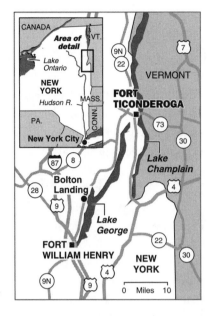

which lies between the headwaters of the Hudson and the adjacent lakes," James Fenimore Cooper wrote in *The Last of the Mohicans*, which we dutifully brought along with us, even if my kids read their Tom Clancy and Calvin and Hobbes instead. Even now, $2^{1}/_{2}$ centuries later, the combination of history, geography, and the structures where the history played out can produce spooky reminders of just how majestic, scary, and lonely military life must have been back then.

The book, the second of Cooper's Leatherstocking Tales, recounts, among other things, the massacre at Fort William Henry, at the southern end of Lake George. But any historic tour of the area has to begin at the north end, at Ticonderoga, the brooding stone fortress the French first built in 1755.

Fort Ticonderoga, Fort William Henry, and the lesser points nearby are all remnants of a time when the British and French were vying for control of the vast, utterly untamed wilderness of North America, and the great waterways of Lake Champlain and Lake George were the keys to the continent. Whoever controlled them controlled transit between the French territory in Canada and the British territory to the south.

The French started building the fort, which they called *Carillon,* on a dramatic rise overlooking Lake Champlain and the portage to Lake George. For more than 20 years it was the subject of contention, held by the French in a great victory in 1758, taken by a British general, Jeffrey Amherst, after a 4-day siege in 1759, taken from the British by colonists led by Ethan Allen and Benedict Arnold in May 1775, retaken by the British in July 1777, and then abandoned and burned by them in October of that year.

Rescued from Oblivion

In 20 years, three nations held the fort, and it was attacked six times. Three times the defenders held it. Three times it fell.

After the British abandoned the fort, it was left a ruin. Settlers in the region looted its stone for building materials, and it became little more than a stone quarry. But in 1820, William Ferris Pell, a businessman and amateur botanist, purchased the site. Nearby, he built a home that was later turned into a hotel. His great-grandson, Stephen H. P. Pell, began the restoration of the fort in 1908. It opened to the public a year later and is now run by the nonprofit Fort Ticonderoga Association.

Fort Ticonderoga is a great place to visit on multiple levels. To begin with, if the fort, at least for boys, is the ur-structure of the imagination, Fort Ticonderoga—with its menacing, intricately decorated cannons; its stone stairways; its grand parade ground, the Place d'Armes; its seemingly impregnable brick walls; its dark caverns for cooking or storing munitions—is a fort extraordinaire. Try visiting it with a troop of Boy Scouts, as I did earlier in the summer, to really get the essence of the experience.

Second, if the best historical experiences often have the blunt logic of geography, Ticonderoga is amazingly graphic. You don't really need to read all that much history to look down toward Lake Champlain and get the idea that whoever held the fort held a remarkably powerful position at a time when the water was the highway.

Third, Ticonderoga has a wonderfully evocative collection of weapons, uniforms, art, and artifacts, all displayed within the carefully restored stone walls of the fort. There are 5,700 pieces in all in the museum collection, plus another 21,500 archaeological specimens ranging from cuff links to cannonballs. The fort also has a library open to researchers year-round. Even the gift shop, and the snack bar with a gorgeous view of the lake, are first-rate.

Finally, there's something compelling in the story of Ticonderoga's rise, fall, and rebirth. On display are a series of paintings of the ruins of Ticonderoga from the 19th century, when it held a particularly vivid hold on the American imagination. In a land where everything was new, Americans made pilgrimages to ponder the ruins of the once-great fort. Women wrote about it in their diaries. Artists brought their sketchbooks and pondered its mysteries. In a more sophisticated way, I guess, they were doing what I did when I walked around scuffing my shoes on the entranceway: trying to commune with the abiding vapors of the past.

A Sitting Duck in the Lake

Fort William Henry, smack-dab in the middle of the village of Lake George overlooking the tour boats plying the lake, isn't nearly as authentic or compelling an experience. After all, when you walk into the museum, the first thing you see is an exhibition of all the movies made of *The Last of the Mohicans,* starting with the four silent versions made in the 1920s and 1930s and leading up to the 1992 version directed by Michael Mann and starring Daniel Day-Lewis. For good measure, a grainy print of the classic 1936 version starring Randolph Scott runs nonstop at the site.

While Ticonderoga is a restoration of the remains of the original and is on the National Registry of Historic Places, Fort William Henry is a privately owned reconstruction of the long-since-destroyed original, which is now part of a hotel complex. And while Ticonderoga is a massive stone fortress, Fort William Henry has a more mundane Lincoln Logs quality.

Still, we were glad we visited it. Fort William Henry's history was brief and violent. It was built overlooking the southern end of Lake George in 1755 by a British major general, William Johnson. Two years later, its 2,500 British and colonial defenders were attacked by 12,500 French and Indian fighters. The invaders pounded the fort with artillery for 6 days and nights until it was all but destroyed. When the defenders surrendered, many were massacred by the Indian allies of the French general Montcalm.

While Ticonderoga seems regal and impregnable, William Henry was anything but, which makes it easier to imagine the sheer terror of being under assault there. The tour guides toss a grenade, fire a cannon, and mold a musket ball in their entertaining half-hour presentation. But the most vivid experience is looking out to the lake, imagining a vast wilderness in all directions and thinking what it would be like to try to defend such a place on a desolate frontier.

There is, of course, more than old forts to Lake George. The town of Lake George may be a little touristy for some tastes. Bolton Landing, just to the north, has a much more leisurely feel. But the 32-mile-long lake is truly gorgeous; it is a famous leaf-season destination; there are great hiking and biking nearby, and accommodations range from modest cabins to high-end resorts like the famous Sagamore. For the theme-park inclined, the Great Escape just south of Lake George is the real thing. We especially liked the Comet, a terrifyingly rickety wooden roller coaster that's considered one of the best of its kind.

It's not as scary as defending a lonely wilderness redoubt, but it is probably as much adventure as most of us care for these days.

ESSENTIALS: SUPPING ON THE PAST

GETTING THERE

By Car Fort Ticonderoga is in Ticonderoga, New York, about 250 miles north of New York City. Take the Taconic State Parkway to Interstate 87. For Fort William Henry, get off at Exit 24 and pick up the Northway to Exit 21. Go right and then left at the light on Rte. 9 for 3 or 4 miles. For Fort Ticonderoga, get off at Exit 28 of the Northway. Take Rte. 74 straight east, about 18 miles, to Ticonderoga.

By Train Amtrak (☎ 800/872-7245) offers daily train service from Penn Station in Manhattan to Fort Ticonderoga. Round-trip fare for the 5-hour ride ranges from

$98 to $116; half price for children 5 to 11.

By Bus   Adirondack Trailways (☎ 212/ 967-2900) has daily service from the Port Authority Bus Terminal in Manhattan to Lake George. The ride is 4½ to 5½ hours, and costs $63.95 round-trip, $32 for children 2 to 11.

ACCOMMODATIONS & DINING

Fort William Henry Resort and Conference Center, 48 Canada St., Lake George (☎ 800/234-0267 or 518/ 668-3081), is on the grounds of the fort, which is opposite the lake and right in town. May 25 through October 7, rooms for two range $89 to $199; October 8 through May 24, $69 to $124.

The Sagamore, 110 Sagamore Rd., Bolton Landing (☎ 518/644-9400). This is the area's best-known high-end resort hotel. A room for two in the fall ranges $190 to $465; in the summer, $240 to $540.

Roaring Brook Ranch & Tennis Resort, Rte. 9N South (Luzerne Rd.), Lake George (☎ 800/882-7665). This hotel, 2 miles from Lake George, has five tennis courts, 30 horses, and wilderness riding. Room rates vary depending on whether riding is included. Basic nonriding rates for two people, with breakfast and dinner, range $142 to $192; during July and August rates rise, $154 to $204.

Leo's Lobster, Rte. 9 South, Lake George (☎ 518/793-2654). Specialties are seafood and beef.

Mario's, 429 Canada St., Lake George (☎ 518/668-2665). Italian cooking with veal specialties.

ATTRACTIONS

Fort Ticonderoga, Rte. 74, Ticonderoga (☎ 518/585-2821). Open daily from early May through October, 9am to 5pm (until 6pm in July and Aug). Admission $10 for adults, $9 for seniors, $6 for children 7 to 12, under 7 free. On October 6 and 7, the fort will celebrate the first of what is planned to be an annual Native American Harvest Moon Festival featuring more than 30 reenactors of tribes, including Abenaki, Iroquois, Delaware, and Mahican.

Fort William Henry, 48 Canada St., Lake George (☎ 518/668-5471). Call for hours.

The Great Escape, Rte. 9N, Lake George (☎ 518/792-3500). Open mid-May through October. Call for hours. Admission $29 for those over 48 inches, $14.50 for those under 48 inches, $20 for seniors, free for those under 2.

New Jersey

A Piece of Portugal: Newark's Ironbound District

by Clifford J. Levy

Scooped from the waters off Lisbon, the sardines landed 36 hours later atop a mound of ice at Ideal Fish, a corner market in one of the more fabled cities in Portuguese lore. Soon the local folk were coming by to size up the catch, a chatty ritual of much poking, smelling, and eyeballing.

"These sardines, they look like life," declared Julio Pereira, who owns the market and is, like many of his Portuguese compatriots, a connoisseur of things from the sea. (The Portuguese know fish the way the Americans know the difference between a Big Mac and a Whopper with cheese.)

Many customers bought sardines, a few did not, but almost everyone lingered amid the tidal odors. They were a nice reminder of home, for though the neighborhood seemed as if it were in Portugal, it was in fact a replica. The Portuguese have been fanning out across the globe since the days of Magellan. In the late 20th century, many have headed straight for Newark.

With nearly 30,000 Portuguese, Newark may be better known in Portugal than it is in the United States. Clustered in a neighborhood called the Ironbound, the immigrants have laid down a latticework of ties between the old country and the new, from the many seafood restaurants and Portuguese bakeries to cultural clubs, each representing an area of Portugal. The Portuguese government even maintains a consulate here.

You can often tell whether an ethnic enclave is thriving by count-ing the number of blank stares you receive when you speak English. In the Ironbound, where the Lisbon newspapers are delivered to the Tucha gift shop even before they reach some parts of Portugal, where the bars are packed on Sunday afternoon with people watching the satellite feed of their beloved Benfica soccer team, it is easy to get by with only Portuguese. Some residents have lived here for 20 years understanding just enough English to navigate the Division of Motor Vehicles.

"This is Portugal," said Isabel Fernandes, who runs Socafe, which caters to the local taste for espresso, selling Portuguese coffees and espresso machines at its shop on Ferry Street, the neighborhood's main thoroughfare. "You can walk into any store and find a little bit of Portugal. Most Americans find themselves in a foreign land down here."

The Ironbound, which is about 20 to 30 minutes by train or car from Manhattan, got its name because it is enclosed by railroad tracks and major roadways. Those barriers have tended to isolate the area from the rest of Newark, which is predominantly black and Hispanic and has struggled to revitalize itself since the riots of the late 1960s. There are few overt tensions between the Ironbound and the rest of the city, yet there is also little amity. Coutinho's bakery, an institution in the Ironbound, sells ornaments for the top of its wedding cakes that have black brides and grooms as well as white ones, but on a typical after-noon there are not many black people on the streets or in the stores.

Autumn is a time of renewal here. The many residents who have gone to Portugal during the summer to see family have returned. The aisles are clogged again at Seabra's, the sprawling Portuguese supermar-ket on Lafayette Street, where the butchers often buff their sausages with cloth, and one of the best-sellers is Luso mineral water from Lisbon. The local councilman, Henry Martinez, begins to receive more complaints about double parking, a chronic problem now in an area that has not experienced such commercial bustle in decades.

On Sunday, after mass at Our Lady of Fatima Church on Congress Street, the sidewalks resound with greetings—"Tudo bem?" ("Everything good?")—and the neighborhood feels like a village. "You must know what it is like, to walk down the street and feel good?" said

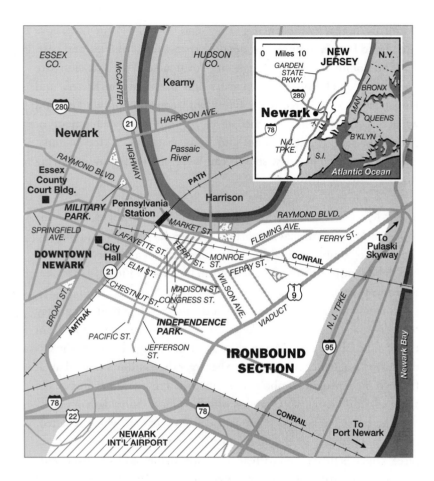

Helen Enes, who organizes exhibitions in the neighborhood of the works of local Portuguese artists.

The most maddening way to explore the Ironbound is on a full stomach, for a walk down Ferry Street provides an enticing survey of the Portuguese culinary landscape, even if the food has at times been doctored for American tastes. There are so many bakeries and cafes that you can buy espresso and *pastel de nata,* the small custard cups that are something of a Portuguese addiction, on practically every other block.

And not only Portuguese specialties: There is a small but venerable Spanish population, represented in the Spanish restaurants. And

Brazilians, drawn by the language they share with the Portuguese, have also settled here in recent years, opening restaurants, bakeries, and bars. The dominant notes, though, are Portuguese. That was clear late one Thursday afternoon, when cafes and bars like the Riviera and La Moda on Ferry Street were filling with construction workers and women were stopping by the stores for the weekly shipment of Portuguese fish. (Fresh sardines and horse mackerel, a kind of tuna, always arrive on Thursday, so fish can be served on Friday, following Roman Catholic custom.)

At Ideal Fish, which is on Pacific Street, a few blocks off Ferry Street, Mr. Pereira said his right-hand man, Bertino Rocha, had gone to Kennedy International Airport on Wednesday afternoon to pick up the fish. To comply with airline rules, the sardines and horse mackerel had to be transported in ice in Styrofoam boxes—393 in all—that were sealed in plastic.

It is easy to spot the immigrants at the market. Upon entering, they typically march right past the American seafood—the red snapper from Florida, the lobster from Maine, the clams from Long Island—to the sardines, which at 6 inches long tend to be larger than sardines canned in oil (though the Portuguese gobble those up, too). Fresh sardines are cooked simply, fried, barbecued, or broiled with little more than a dash of salt.

The other Portuguese staple is cod from Norway, which is salted, dried, and stacked in the stores like plywood. A customer selects a piece, which is then sliced with an apparatus that looks like a paper cutter. The cod must be soaked in water for 2 or 3 days before it can be cooked; it is often broiled with potatoes and garlic.

The sardines are $2.50 a pound and the horse mackerel is $3.25 a pound. That is more than the canned variety, though the customers, who inspect and place the fish in plastic bags with their own hands, don't care. "Every week," Maria da Cruz, who left Portugal in 1972, said of her trips to Ideal Fish. "Some weeks, I spend $100 or more."

The influx to the Ironbound from Portugal is relatively recent. Before the 1970s, the neighborhood was largely populated by Italian, Irish, Polish, and other European immigrants, many of whom referred to the area as "Down Neck." The Portuguese began settling in the 1950s and 1960s when Portugal was one of the poorest countries in

Western Europe, many of them drawn by opportunities at the newly expanded Port of Newark. But unlike the other large Portuguese community in the United States, in New Bedford, Massachusetts, the Portuguese of Newark did not concentrate on fishing or other maritime ventures. They moved into other fields, particularly construction, carpentry, restaurants, and bakeries.

"In Portugal, everybody knows about Newark," said Tony Oliveira, whose family came from Portugal in 1967 when he was 11. Mr. Oliveira is a local officer at the Heavy and General Construction Laborers' Union, whose chapter in northern New Jersey has about 7,000 members, about a third of them Portuguese.

Immigration, both legal and illegal, peaked in the mid-1980s. When Portugal was admitted to the European Union and its economy began to thrive, the number of arrivals dropped. Even so, the largest group of illegal immigrants in New Jersey is Portuguese.

The immigrant success stories here often run through the kitchen. Joao Loureiro and Jorge Fernandes, who left Portugal with little money more than 20 years ago, worked as waiters here before buying the Iberia restaurant (82 Ferry Street) and later opening the Iberia Peninsula (67 Ferry Street).

The food at those two restaurants, as well as at some other stops in the area, including Fornos of Spain (47 Ferry Street), is often more Iberian, a hybrid that appeals to Americans, than distinctly Portuguese or Spanish. Portuguese basics like sardines or salt cod are not prominent on the Iberian menus. Instead there are the familiar seafood stews like *paelha* (*paella* in Spanish), a mix of shellfish and rice that may include chicken or chorizo, a spicy sausage. The prices are cheaper than in Manhattan: The paelha in the Ironbound is often about $19 for portions that can serve two. Salad, thinly sliced fried potatoes, and fluffy Portuguese bread are usually included. There are also plenty of lobster and shrimp dishes.

In restaurants like Iberia, the lunch trade on weekdays is mostly Americans who work in offices in downtown Newark. At other times, there are more Portuguese, and in the early evening construction workers sit at the bar, shoveling down broiled shrimp or pork and clams while sipping Borba wine.

HOW TO VISIT THE IRONBOUND

By Subway PATH (☎ 800/234-7284) has 24-hour service to the Penn Station stop in Newark. Weekend trains leave every 15 minutes from the World Trade Center, Tower 1, for the 22-minute ride. The one-way fare is $1, free for children under 5.

By Train Amtrak (☎ 800/872-7245 for information and reservations) trains to Newark's Penn Station–Raymond Plaza West leave approximately hourly from Penn Station in Manhattan for the 15-minute ride. The one-way fare is $18; 15% discount for seniors, half price for children 2 to 15.

New Jersey Transit (☎ 973/762-5100) trains to Penn Station in Newark leave twice an hour on weekends from Penn Station in Manhattan beginning about 5am. The one-way fare is $2.50 (round-trip, $3.50), free on weekends for children under 12, half price weekdays.

By Bus New Jersey Transit's (☎ 973/762-5100) no. 108 bus to Newark's Penn Station leaves from the Port Authority Bus Terminal, Eighth Avenue and 42nd Street, Monday to Friday every hour beginning at 6am, at 8am weekends. The one-way fare is $1.90, 85¢ for children.

By Car Take the Lincoln Tunnel to the New Jersey Turnpike, to exit 15E; look for Raymond Boulevard sign and follow the boulevard into the Ironbound district.

On some weekend nights, places like Mediterranean Manor (255 Jefferson Street) may feature live fado, the Portuguese blues music.

Brazilian restaurants, many specializing in *churrasco,* or barbecue, have sprung up in recent years. At Brasilia (132 Ferry Street), you can order rodizio de churrasco, an all-you-can-eat barbecue binge of beef, sausage, chicken, and pork, brought to the table on skewers.

After dinner, the bakeries beckon. Three of the largest in the state—Coutinho's, Teixeira's (whose owners are related to the Coutinho family), and Vieira's—were founded by Portuguese immigrants. At the Coutinho's shop at 121 Ferry Street, there are rows of *pastel de coco* (coconut cups) and *bolo de arroz* (rice pudding cakes) for 75¢ each. Portuguese bakeries like Coutinho's also make an array of breads, from *broa,* a dense corn bread ($1.70), to the ubiquitous *papo seco,* the basic dry roll (38¢), and *padinha,* the rye roll (25¢ to 35¢). At Coutinho's headquarters (417 Chestnut Street), many products are still made by hand, though it would be cheaper to use machines.

Mr. Coutinho is part of the second generation, fluent in Portuguese but rooted in America. Freed of the financial pressures that his parents faced, he heads the family charity, the Bernardino Coutinho Foundation, which sponsors the annual Portuguese festival in the Ironbound in June and supports other cultural activities. He is also trying to raise political awareness: Nearly 20,000 Portuguese were counted in Newark in the 1990 Census, but there are only a few thousand registered voters.

Others, too, are grappling with how the community can mature. Ms. Enes, the sponsor of the art exhibitions, said it was sometimes difficult to interest the neighborhood in art. People are so focused on immigrant priorities—making enough money, learning English, supporting relatives—that culture may seem a luxury. But art, she said, can help the Ironbound find its identity.

"You have to understand that once you're uprooted, you come to America and the Americans think of you as a foreigner, but then when you go back to Portugal, the Portuguese think of you as American," she said. "So you are nothing. Where do you belong? Somewhere in the middle of the Atlantic?"

WILDERNESS ADVENTURES
IN STOKES FOREST

by Ralph Blumenthal

"ARE WE OUTSIDE?" WE MOST assuredly were outside, on a trail deep in the piney woods of Stokes State Forest in northwesternmost New Jersey, but my city-bred daughter looked unconvinced. Where was the sky? Why was it so spooky? Where was everybody?

We were alone. Outdoors. That was the point. This, after all, was what we had come for: a weekend of camping while the elements still posed a challenge and the wilds were largely free from interlopers like us.

Well, semi-camping. In a concession to the unpredictabilities of the season and a mom's skepticism ("You're taking her where?"), I had given up the idea of tenting and instead reserved one of the state forest's 15 lean-tos, an enclosed 12- by 14-foot shelter equipped with a wood stove. We would have use of communal rest rooms with flush toilets and sinks. Otherwise, we'd rough it, cooking our meals on an open fire and relying on flashlights and candles for light at night.

It seemed, in particular, a perfect formula for a jaded, animal-loving $5^{1}/_{2}$-year-old, and it was, not counting the maddening swarms of gnats and some anxious moments over a snake.

In fact, as we were to learn, Stokes State Forest, an unlikely wilderness in an easily accessible nook of one of the more industrialized states, abounds in wildlife, noxious and benign. The census of species includes the venomous northern copperhead and timber rattlesnake, snapping turtle, bear, bobcat, coyote, gray and red fox, weasel, porcupine, skunk, otter, mink, and deer, as well as 209 species of birds, from rarely spotted golden and bald eagles to wild turkeys, egrets, herons, hawks, hummingbirds, and woodpeckers.

The preserve, which dates from 1907 and is named for a former governor, covers 15,000 acres of highland forest, land that less than 10,000 years ago lay under several thousand feet of glacial ice. It was an area of thriving American Indian communities with gardens of pumpkins, maize, and tobacco before the first English and Dutch settlers arrived, and the early pioneers built sawmills and dug silver,

zinc, and manganese mines, remains of which are still visible today. The park office displays cases of Indian arrowheads and the bones of a mastodon dug up in the area in 1939.

Our original plan was more adventurous: winter camping. One frigid weekend, we actually scouted potential sites on Ward Pound Ridge Reservation in Westchester County, where three-sided rustic lean-tos are available year-round. But we decided they were too exposed to severe cold, even with a tarpaulin covering the open side. Stokes's enclosed lean-tos, too, are available year-round, but almost every other campground in the region closes for the season, which, I realized after calling around fruitlessly for weeks, might be something of a message. As it was, I had to postpone our spring camping expedition several times because of unseasonable snowstorms and plunging temperatures.

But the winter that would not die finally did, yielding to a tentative spring. Early one Saturday, I loaded the car with sleeping bags, food, and the gadgetry that camping gives guys an excuse to play with—ax and knives, folding saw, kerosene lantern, tarpaulin, grills, stringy light hammock—and set off.

The trip from mid-Manhattan to Stokes State Forest, near Branchville, New Jersey, is an easy one, a straight $1^1/2$-hour shot across the George Washington Bridge, west on Interstate 80, and then north on Routes 15 and 206. From the backseat, Sophie kept up a diverting barrage of conversation.

"Benjamin has an ant farm. Can we have an ant farm?"

"I don't think so."

"Guess how many cough drops I had?"

"I don't know. Twenty?"

"I'm having my second one now. Know what I think eyelashes are made of? Daddy longlegs' legs."

In Sparta, New Jersey, we stopped for last-minute provisions at a market, where Sophie grabbed a *Pocahontas* video. Was she expecting a VCR in the lean-to? We had a tug of war and compromised on a 50¢ container of slime from a vending machine. Back in the car, Sophie said, "I don't want to go camping."

A Welcoming Swarm

Finally, we pulled into the lot outside the rustic park office. As soon as we got out of the car, clouds of gnats and blackflies swarmed around our heads. A bad omen. Sophie started flailing and whimpering.

We made a dash for the office, stopping to read a posted leaflet: "You are in bear country," it began rather ominously. "Black bears are part of the forest environment. People are visitors. Think of yourself as a guest of the forest wildlife." It warned against feeding bears or leaving garbage around and urged that food be locked up in car trunks and never, never left in lean-tos or tents. The details began to sound a little alarming: "If a bear approaches you, blow a whistle, bang pots and pans together, make noise!" At the service window, where I picked up our lean-to key and a park map, a young park worker said she hadn't seen any bears lately, but others in the office said they were around, especially by the garbage dumpsters. As for the flies, the woman said we might try some bug spray, which I had forgotten to bring. But, she added cheerfully, it probably wouldn't help anyway.

"Did she get hurt by the bear?" Sophie asked gravely as we left. "How did she see one?" But then she was on to bug spray. "Would I like the smell? I'm a strange smeller, so maybe I would like it. I like oily smells." Checking the map, I followed a paved and winding road through the forest for about 3 miles to the lean-to, passing substantial-looking comfort stations.

The one-room lean-to, painted chocolate brown, was small and boxy, but, I couldn't help reflecting, still somewhat larger than the 10-by 12-foot Montana shack where Theodore J. Kaczynski, the man who confessed to being the Unabomber, had lived for years. It had a steeply pitched roof and three steps up to the door. It was, strictly speaking, not a cabin—that term was reserved for 10 far more sophisticated, and eagerly sought-after, units with electricity, kitchens, bathrooms, and furniture in another area of the forest.

The inside of the lean-to was bare, with only a wood-burning stove, still stocked with split logs from a previous occupant. The park does not sell or provide wood, but plenty was lying around in the woods for the taking. The interior walls were painted gray. They were clean except for a few marks of graffiti. The floor, also cleanly swept, was a dull red. Outside there were a picnic table and a fire ring with an adjustable cooking grill.

We spread out our sleeping bags and foam pads, laid out the flashlights, candles, and kerosene lantern, and hooked open the two large screened windows. The space accommodated the two of us amply. Four could also have fit, albeit a little snugly.

We collected wood for the fireplace and kindling for the stove and reconnoitered, keeping an eye out for bears and swatting at flies.

"Is it the year of the rat?" Sophie asked.

I said it might be. "Why?"

"Because there's so many bugs out," Sophie said, not bothering to explain.

We walked back to the car and drove out of the park to a nearby fish and game store, the Stokes Forest Sport Shop. While Sophie looked agog at the tubs of live minnows and walls of glittering lures, I bought some insect repellent. We slapped some on and headed back to the forest.

Just past the office, we parked the car and headed down one of the many park trails, Lackner, marked with black circles. The trail paralleled Stony Brook, where some trout fishermen were trying their luck. Sophie stepped to the mushy shore and reached out her hands. "Here fishy, fishy, fishy," she called. "Know why I'm saying that? Because in *Sesame Street* Ernie had a call, and fish jumped in the boat and a shark jumped in the boat. If we don't capture an animal by tomorrow, I'm going to be so angry." She went on, but I had stopped listening. Maybe 10 feet away was something that looked like a gnarled black branch. Or maybe it was a snake. I decided it couldn't be a snake because it was completely motionless. Then I thought: yes, it was a snake. But it was probably dead.

I pointed it out to Sophie and her eyes grew wide. Impulsively, I picked up a long branch and gave it a poke. It was a snake! It shot about a foot in the air and then resettled, once again completely motionless. Sophie was aghast. I was a little shaken myself. "Daddy," she pleaded, "let's go back to the ranger." I was still watching to see if it would move again. "Mommy would say, 'Go back! Don't you dare go so close,'" Sophie said. "Mommy would be terrified."

We walked back to the park office, where parties of other campers were checking in. "We saw a snake! We saw a snake!" Sophie announced, gaining everyone's immediate attention. I described it to the park superintendent sitting behind the window. "Black snake," he said. "A small one. They are harmless," he explained confidently. But he said we should keep an eye out for the timber rattlesnake, with its triangular head, elliptical eyes, hourglass markings, and, of course, telltale rattle. Mostly, he said, they were up on Sunrise Mountain.

Looking for a less stressful diversion, we drove a few miles to a playground and recreation area, Kittle Field, where Sophie cavorted on swings and climbing equipment with other children and then joined one of them in a hunt along the brook for water spiders. We filled our water bottles at a hand pump that gushed deliciously cool well water and drove a little farther, to Stony Lake, where we walked along a wide sandy beach and found another playground.

On the drive back to the lean-to, a car ahead of us abruptly pulled over and I could see why. There was something strange by the side of the road. I pulled over, too, and we ran out to look. It was a large snapping turtle, its green-mottled shell perhaps 18 inches in diameter. It had a sharp, pointy snout, legs swathed in armor-like plate, and vicious-looking claws with long, sharp talons. It sat there unmoving, looking very old. I decided not to poke it.

Sophie wanted me to move it off the road, or at least tell the office, but I figured that it had survived this long without our help and could continue to.

We headed back for dinner. I started a fire, pleased that the smoke seemed to be keeping the gnats at bay. I boiled water in an open pot, which took a long time, and dropped in a bag of frozen mixed vegetables. Then I started grilling franks and hamburgers, some carefully wrapped in aluminum foil; Sophie objects to food with a burn mark. Afterward, we toasted marshmallows, but as each of hers caught fire and blackened, she threw them away.

We cleaned up extra carefully—the prospect of bears will do that— walked down the road to the comfort station to wash up, and prepared to turn in. By 8:30pm, there was still enough fading light as we crawled into our sleeping bags to gaze out at the treetops. There was no need to make a fire in the stove; the evening was even warm enough to keep the windows open. Sophie made sure I latched the door with the eyelet hook. We chatted sleepily and then I heard Sophie's measured breathing.

The foam pad notwithstanding, I found the floor uncomfortably hard. Was it worse on my back or my side? I couldn't decide. But I must have dozed off because the next thing I felt was a finger poking my face. It was pitch black. "I have to go," Sophie whispered.

My watch showed a little past 1am. I flicked on the flashlight, we slipped on our sneakers, unlatched the door, and stepped outside. As we walked down the road, Sophie said she was afraid of seeing bears. "I want to call Mama," she whimpered. Trying to keep my voice level, I said the pay phones at the office were probably shut off for the night and belittled the idea of bears out at that hour. In truth, I was far from confident. To make matters worse, as I played the flashlight along the sides of the road, large rocks threw humped shadows that looked exactly like bears. And I wasn't carrying any pots and pans.

We did what we had to do and nervously retraced our steps to the lean-to. I barred the door and we crawled gratefully back into our sleeping bags. "Dad," Sophie said in the dark, "for some reason I think there are snakes here." I said, no, they didn't get into lean-tos. And then my stomach gave a mighty growl. Sophie flinched. "What was that?" she asked, alarmed. I said I was getting hungry again. "I know how flies protect themselves," she said. "Move fast." I told her to go back to sleep. And she did.

She woke me at 5:45am, as dawn was lightening the lean-to. We made another trip down the road, this time more relaxed, and started the fire for breakfast. There was a tree trunk that someone had started to saw into logs, and with Sophie's help I finished the job, happy that I got to use my folding saw after all. Then—oh happiness!—I got to use my ax to split the logs and gave Sophie a few carefully supervised swings. I boiled water for instant hot cereal and cooked scrambled eggs in a pan. Then we hung the hammock outside and Sophie lazed while I cleaned up. We emptied and padlocked the lean-to, packed up the car, and left to explore other parts of the forest, stopping at the park office to return the key.

A nature trail called Tillman Ravine in the southwest corner of the park looked inviting from a brochure, and we headed there, leaving the car in a parking area and following what the map and signs said was a half-mile trail loop down to Tillman Brook and back. The path was steep and dark, the sky obliterated by a canopy of pine and hemlock. We saw the gushing brook with its crossings of rustic bridges and paralleled it, following what I thought was the trail.

It wasn't. I had lost my bearings. We couldn't get too lost because the road and parking lot were clearly up the hill from the brook, but exactly what was the trail and what wasn't? Then something else occurred to me. I couldn't remember packing up the hammock. Had we left it on the trees at the lean-to? I asked Sophie. She didn't remember taking it down either. "The hammock," she wailed. "The hammock." I promised to go back for the $10 hammock. But first I had to get us out of there. I was looking for the laid logs that were supposed to mark the trail when something by a fallen tree caught my eye.

It was a dark form, partly covered by underbrush. I froze and caught Sophie's hand. She saw it, too. I thought it was a dead black dog, maybe a dog that had drowned in the brook. I could see a bit of tail and what I thought was a muzzle. But what if it was a bear, dead or otherwise?

Sophie wanted a closer look. Maybe the dog was sick, she said. We had to help it. We had to bury it. I pulled her away. What if it—whatever it was—wasn't dead, like the snake? Trail, or no trail, I hightailed it up the hill, pulling a protesting child along. The trail suddenly materialized, and we followed it quickly to the road.

We drove back to the lean-to. There were the two trees that had suspended the hammock. But the hammock was gone! Sadly, we drove to the office to report the loss. The park superintendent listened to the story and unclipped a walkie-talkie from his belt. In minutes he had good news. Maintenance men had recovered it from our spot. We raced to meet them and made the retrieval. We'll need it for our next expedition.

Essentials: Camping in Stokes Forest & Around the Tri-State Area

Reservations are recommended for most campgrounds in the three-state region from Memorial Day through Labor Day. Listings of state and private campgrounds and what they offer are available from the **New York State Travel Information Center** (☎ 800/225-5697 or 800/456-2267); the **New Jersey Department of Environmental Protection,** Division of Parks and Forestry (☎ 800/843-6420); the **Connecticut Vacation Center** (☎ 800/282-6863); and the **Connecticut Campground Owners Association** (☎ 860/521-4704).

Stokes State Forest, the campground mentioned in the accompanying article, is off Rte. 206, Branchville, NJ (☎ 973/948-3820). Open year-round, its daily rates range from $8 for a campsite with latrine to $10 for a campsite with flush toilet within walking distance to $28 for a furnished cabin.

A sampling of other campgrounds in the New York metropolitan area follows. Reservations at state parks can be made up to 11 months in advance by calling ☎ 800/456-2267; www.reserveamerica.com.

LONG ISLAND

Cedar Point County Park, Alewive Brook Rd., East Hampton (☎ 631/852-7620).
Eastern Long Island Campground, 690 Queen St., Greenport (☎ 631/477-0022).
Hither Hills, Rte. 27, Montauk (☎ 800/456-267 or 631/668-2554).

Indian Island County Park, County Rd. 105, Riverhead (☎ 631/852-3232).
Wildwood State Park, Hulse Landing Rd., Wading River (☎ 631/929-4314).

HUDSON VALLEY

Beaver Pond State Park, Beaver Pond, Bear Mountain (☎ **845/947-2792** or 914/786-2701).

Croton Point Park, Croton Point Ave. (off Rte. 9), Croton (☎ **914/271-3293** or 914/271-6858).

Interlake Farm, 45 Lake Dr., Clinton (☎ **914/266-5387**).

Oleana Campground, Rte. 7 (off Rte. 22), West Copake (☎ **518/329-2811**).

UPSTATE NEW YORK

Clarence Fahnestock Memorial State Park, Rte. 301 (off Taconic State Pkwy.). Carmel (☎ **845/225-7207**).

Margaret Lewis Norrie State Park, Rte. 9, Staatsburg (☎ **845/889-4646**).

NEW JERSEY

Allaire State Park, Rte. 524, Wall Township, Farmingdale (☎ **732/938-2371**).

Belleplain State Forest, Rte. 550, Woodbine (☎ **606/861-2404**).

Bull's Island, Rte. 29 (8 miles north of Lambertville; ☎ **609/397-2949**).

Wharton Forest, Atsion Recreation Center, Rte. 206, Shamong Township (☎ **609/268-0444**).

CONNECTICUT

Camp Niantic by the Atlantic, 271 W. Main St., Niantic (☎ **860/739-9308** or 860/649-6121).

Hammonasset Beach, Hammonasset Connector, exit 62 off I-95, Madison (☎ **203/245-2785**).

Lake Waramaug, 30 Lake Waramaug Rd., New Preston (☎ **860/424-3200**).

Looking Glass Hill Campground, Rte. 202, Bantam (☎ **860/567-2050**).

STROLLING BUCOLIC
HUNTERDON COUNTY

by Lisa W. Foderaro

NEW JERSEY IS KNOWN FOR MANY
good things, from beefsteak tomatoes to Bruce Springsteen. But as a
place to head for a quiet country weekend in late fall, the state usually
falls off the radar of urbanites, who drive north to Litchfield County in
Connecticut or to the Hudson Valley in New York.

Well, commit this name to memory: Hunterdon County.

Little known beyond New Jersey, Hunterdon is extraordinary for
its rural beauty and urbane sensibility. In the past 10 to 15 years, it has
sprouted enough restaurants, inns, and interesting boutiques to become
a natural extension of Bucks County, its better-known neighbor across
the Delaware River in Pennsylvania. "What a wonderful place this is,"
wrote an unsuspecting visitor in the guest book of Hunterdon House,
an Italianate Victorian bed-and-breakfast in the borough of
Frenchtown. "With all the bad rap you hear about New Jersey, it's hard
to believe that's where we are." Indeed. With undulating farmland
studded with wineries, and the Delaware flowing past such historic villages as Frenchtown and Stockton, Hunterdon invites comparisons not
to Litchfield but to the Dordogne region in southwest France.

More than half the land is still actively farmed, and although
Hunterdon is the second fastest growing county in the state, it is the
third least densely populated. A government-sponsored farmland
preservation program has kept more than two dozen working farms
going, while gentlemen farmers and horsewomen like Gov. Christine
Todd Whitman have made Hunterdon synonymous with hunt country. Missing from much of the landscape is the background static of

suburban sprawl—strip malls, billboards, and the like. Instead there are long country roads flanked by woods, streams, and, at this time of year, pale fields of withered cornstalks. The only surviving covered bridge in the state is here, too.

Plenty of Charm

The municipalities dotting the banks of the Delaware, from Milford in the north to Lambertville in the south, were once rough-and-tumble mill towns. But over the years most of the factories closed, and so far no new industry has swept through. This leaves the streetscapes—neat but motley rows of Queen Anne, Georgian, Neo-Gothic, and Federal architecture—relatively untouched, like bees preserved in amber. Now tourism is a major industry. But it's an understated sort of tourism that doesn't feel stagy. A better name for it might simply be pleasure.

Fall is an especially pretty time of year to see Hunterdon. The chill in the air inspires walks by day and wood fires by night. And root vegetables, roast meats, and mysteriously rich stocks have taken the front burner at local restaurants, among them two highly praised kitchens.

Staying for a weekend makes it possible to squeeze in all there is to do, from taking a quiet walk on the old canal towpath running along the river, now preserved as the Delaware and Raritan Canal State Park, to stopping by a winery, to visiting tiny villages like Sergeantsville or larger towns like Lambertville, crammed with antiques stores, atmospheric gift shops, and restaurants. A weekend trip will also do justice to the transporting experience that is the Ryland Inn, a white clapboard restaurant in Whitehouse whose chef, Craig C. Shelton, has worked with both Joel Robuchon in Paris and David Bouley in Manhattan.

Arts, Crafts & Pastries

The towns of Hunterdon County beckon to be walked through, their old buildings looked at, their occasionally eccentric shops browsed. Frenchtown made a fine place to start on a recent visit. At the western end of Bridge Street is the Delaware River. Its swirling, mocha-colored waters, churned by a recent rain, moved swiftly south under a steel truss bridge whose heavy stone piers and abutments date back to 1843.

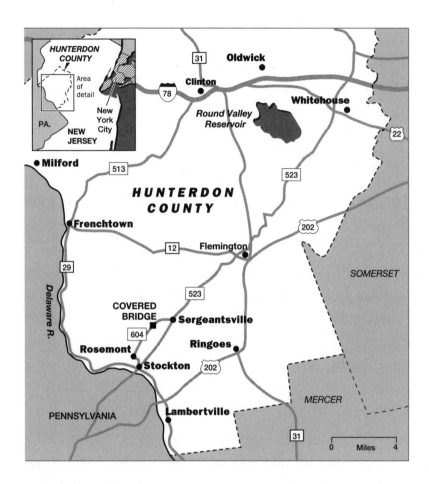

Along Bridge Street are a number of places worth discovering. The Bridge Cafe, housed in a former train station overlooking the river, has excellent baked goods. Across the street stands the Frenchtown Inn, a cozy brick restaurant built in 1805. (Its $22.95 brunch, for the hearty of appetite, includes a basket of warm pastries, a fruit cup, a choice of entrees ranging from eggs Benedict to leg of lamb, and dessert.)

A few storefronts down is the Delaware River Trading Company, a purveyor of rural-chic garden and home furnishings, as well as a few peculiar antiques. Here you'll find everything from silver-plated mint julep cups to hammocks, four-poster cherry beds to antique pitchforks.

There was even a photo album from the 1920s displaying dozens of police mug shots of jewelry thieves.

The next stop is Stockton, reached by driving south on lovely Route 29, or River Road. (The Delaware can be glimpsed through the trees on the right.) Slightly smaller than Frenchtown, Stockton is home to the Stockton Inn, made famous by the Rodgers and Hart song "There's a Small Hotel," from the Broadway musical *On Your Toes.* The inn's fieldstone structure, dating from 1710, has 10 rooms, most with fireplaces and canopy beds, and a restaurant with murals depicting 18th-century farming villages. The stone wishing well of the song is still there, its pool carpeted with coins.

One remarkable store is the half-century–old Phillips' Fine Wines, a veritable museum of the viniculture art and considered by many to be the state's best wine store. There are eight rooms on two floors displaying roughly 5,000 labels, including 200 different Australian wines, 175 California chardonnays, and 150 burgundies. There's even a room devoted just to port.

An example of how Hunterdon's image has recently been polished is the transformation of the low-slung building at the corner of Main and Bridge streets from a gas station to a restaurant, Meil's. At once homey and hip, Meil's has stenciled walls hung with quilts and a menu offering chicken pot pie with buttermilk biscuits, warm sesame duck salad, and a grilled sandwich of brie, tomato, and onion on seven-grain bread.

Lambertville, the southernmost river town in Hunterdon, is also the largest. It could be seen as the rapidly growing kid sister of New Hope, Pennsylvania, right across the Delaware. Eighty percent of Lambertville's handsome brick buildings and row houses were built before 1900. One of the most notable is the James Wilson Marshall House at 60 Bridge Street, an 1816 Federal house with pale green shutters that was the boyhood home of its namesake, the discoverer of gold at Sutter's Mill in California in 1848.

But perhaps more than anything, Lambertville is a shopper's paradise. Whereas Flemington, the county seat, is prized for its outlet shopping, Lambertville does not possess a single chain store. It is known instead for dozens of one-of-a-kind shops reflecting the tastes and personalities of their owners.

Reinboth & Company, at 121 North Union Street, offers things to make life a little more ethereal, from mineral bath salts and German linens to overstuffed leather sofas.

A Diversity of Tables

There is no paucity of fine restaurants in Lambertville. Siam, at 61 North Main Street, features fresh and inexpensive Thai food, while Anton's at the Swan, 43 South Main Street, is the archetypal romantic restaurant. Baroque music fills the dining rooms, where huge gilt-framed mirrors and old engravings surround tables laden with hurricane lamps and china in a pleasing hodgepodge of patterns.

Away from the river, Hunterdon becomes slightly more hilly, and while driving along back roads through the countryside is the main attraction, there is a handful of villages deserving of a quick stop. Sergeantsville in Delaware Township is a mere intersection marked by a blinking light, but on one corner is the Sergeantsville Inn, a beguiling restaurant in a fieldstone house with a wood-burning fireplace. Crossing a swollen creek, a mile west of Sergeantsville on Route 604, is a white covered bridge, the last public one in the state.

Also in Delaware Township is Rosemont, another one-horse town that is perhaps best known for Cane Farm Furniture, a 30-year-old maker of Early American and Shaker reproductions, displayed in a series of renovated chicken coops.

Farther north is the village of Oldwick in Tewksbury Township, its Main Street a seeming New England tableau with two dazzling white churches and an antiquarian bookstore. The Main Street is also home to the deceptively low-key Tewksbury Inn, where in 1994 chef Patrick Robertson (formerly of Le Cirque in Manhattan) catapulted what was essentially a local burger hangout to culinary high ground. The present chef is Kenneth Hoerle, formerly of Aureole.

Dining at an Inn

But the most special dining experience in Hunterdon, possibly in the state, some restaurant critics say, can be found at the Ryland Inn on Route 22 in Whitehouse. The reputation of Mr. Shelton, the chef and owner, clearly reverberates beyond the state's borders, as the helipad on the 50-acre property, where he grows his own herbs and vegetables, attests. His résumé lists several culinary stations of the cross in Manhattan, from Bouley to Le Bernardin to La Côte Basque.

The weighty wine list includes a $3,000 bottle of 1945 Château Latour as well as two pages of bottles at $25 and under. A snifter of cognac—there are 28 to choose from—is best savored in the cigar room on the ground floor, an appropriately masculine sanctum with black walls, formal drapes, and a painting of two golden retrievers. Cigars are available from $5 to $16; thankfully, an effective ventilation system makes a pilgrimage by the nonsmoker bearable.

Postprandial Strolling

After such a rich feast, some low-impact exercise (walking, for example) is in order. The Delaware and Raritan Canal State Park, a 72-mile corridor with 19th-century bridges and stone culverts, runs most of the length of Hunterdon County and continues south to Trenton, where it veers inland toward the Raritan River. The towpath is mostly flat and makes for easy walking and biking. Naturally, it borders the canal, which was one of the country's busiest navigation routes in the 1860s and 1870s, when Pennsylvania coal was brought to New York City to fuel the industrial boom.

Today, the canal is a lazy finger of water that reflects the tall trees overhead, while just beyond is the Delaware River, moving at twice the canal's pace. The section of the path behind Prallsville Mills in Stockton is especially scenic. The mills, a collection of eight historic buildings, are open occasionally for special events, but reservations may be made for a tour. The public is welcome on the grounds, however. Before embarking along the towpath, visitors might walk around the outside of Prallsville Mills. Two of the most striking structures are the grist mill, a four-story building of stone and stucco that dates, in part, from 1711, and the linseed oil mill, a tiny 1790 building made of rich brown stones held together by white mortar.

After a stroll along the canal, a visit to one of the state's most notable wineries, Unionville Vineyards at 9 Rocktown Road in

Ringoes, might be a nice finish for the weekend. When you think of the wine-growing centers of the New York region, the North Fork of Long Island probably comes to mind, or even the Finger Lakes in upstate New York. But New Jersey, which counts 15 wineries in the north and south, has a long history of wine making, and in the past few years has finally gained some recognition. It could be called a renaissance, for London's Royal Society of Arts recognized two New Jersey vintners back in 1767 for their success in making the first decent wine from Colonial grapes. Today, the wineries produce 180,000 gallons a year, placing New Jersey among the top 15 wine-producing states in the country.

Unionville Vineyards was opened in 1993 by Kris Nielsen and Patricia Galloway, although the first vines were planted 5 years earlier. There are now 32 acres of vines, 12 of them in full production. Hunter's White, a refreshing table wine produced from a blend of Vidal Blanc and Cayuga grapes, sells for $8.50 a bottle. The Hunter's White Reserve, made from Vidal Blanc grapes and aged in new oak barrels, sells for $11. Unionville's most popular label is Fields of Fire, a fruity rosé wine at $7 a bottle.

Free tastings are offered Thursday through Sunday 11am to 4pm. The tastings are held on the second floor of a former dairy barn whose 1848 post-and-beam construction was preserved during a recent renovation. The barn is set amid folds of muted green meadows and farms that stretch to the horizon, forming a bucolic idyll.

Suddenly, you realize why they call it the Garden State.

HUNTERDON COUNTY ESSENTIALS

GETTING THERE

To reach New Jersey's Hunterdon County from Manhattan, take the Holland or Lincoln Tunnel to the New Jersey Turnpike to Interstate 78 West; continue on I-78 West to exit 15 (Clinton and Pittstown) and pick up Rte. 513 South; continue on Rte. 513 South into Frenchtown.

ACCOMMODATIONS

Stockton Inn, 1 Main St. Stockton (Rte. 29; ☎ 609/398-1250). Monday through Thursday, $65 to $130; Friday through Sunday and holidays, $90 to $170. Rates are based on double or single occupancy. Rates include continental breakfast; children welcome. Restaurant open Monday through Thursday 11:30am to 2:30pm and 4:30 to 10pm, Friday and Saturday 11:30am to 2:30pm and 5 to 10pm, Sunday 11am to 2:30pm (for brunch) and 3:30 to 9pm. Entrees $6.95 to $15.95 at lunch, $14.95 to $28 at dinner.

DINING

FRENCHTOWN

Bridge Cafe, 8 Bridge St. (☎ 908/996-6040). Open daily 7am to 5pm. Also open for dinner April through October, 6 to 10pm. Lunch entrees $6.50 to $7.50; dinner entrees $10 to $15.

Frenchtown Inn, 7 Bridge St. (☎ 908/996-3300). Open Tuesday through Friday noon to 2pm and 6 to 9pm, Saturday noon to 2pm and 5:30 to 9:30pm, Sunday brunch noon to 2:30pm. Lunch entrees $9.95 to $15.95, $20.95 to $26.95 at dinner; Saturday prix-fixe dinner $48 per person.

STOCKTON

Also see Stockton Inn under "Accommodations," above.

Meil's, Bridge and Main sts. (☎ 609/397-8033). Open Monday through Thursday 9am to 9pm, Friday 9am to 10pm, Saturday 8am to 10pm, Sunday 8am to 9pm. Entrees $4.50 and up at breakfast, $7 to $16 at lunch, $10.50 to $23 at dinner.

LAMBERTVILLE

Anton's at the Swan, 43 S. Main St. (☎ 609/397-1960). Open Tuesday through Saturday 6 to 9pm, Sunday 4:30 to 8pm. Entrees $23 to $29.

Siam, 61 N. Main St. (☎ 609/397-8128). Open Tuesday 6 to 9pm, Wednesday and Thursday 11am to 2pm and 6 to 9pm, Friday and Saturday 11am to 2pm and 6 to 10pm, Sunday 11am to 2pm and 4 to 9pm. Entrees $8 to $13.

OLDWICK

Tewksbury Inn, Main St. (Rte. 517; ☎ 908/439-2641). Open Tuesday through Saturday, 11:30am to 4:30pm and 5:30 to 10pm, Sunday noon to 9pm. Entrees $7 to $15 at lunch, $15 to $28 at dinner.

WHITEHOUSE

Ryland Inn, Rte. 22 West (☎ 908/534-4011). Open Tuesday through Friday 11:30am to 2pm and 5:30 to 11pm, Saturday 5:30 to 11pm, Sunday 5 to 9pm. Entrees $14 to $18 at lunch, $33 to $36 at dinner; daily prix-fixe menu $75 per person. There are also three 8-course tasting menus daily, $88 per person, and a 10-course gourmand menu for $108.

ATTRACTIONS

STOCKTON

Prallsville Mills, Rte. 29 North (☎ 609/ 397-3586). Eight historic buildings maintained by the Delaware River Mills Society. They are open occasionally for special events, but reservations should be made for a tour. Call for hours.

LAMBERTVILLE

James Wilson Marshall House, operated by the Lambertville Historical Society, 60 Bridge St. (☎ 609/397-0770); www. lambertvillehistoricalsociety.org. Call for hours.

DELAWARE RIVER

Delaware and Raritan Canal State Park (☎ 609/397-2949). A corridor along the Delaware River, from north Frenchtown to Trenton to New Brunswick; accessible from Rte. 29. There are parking lots at each crossing of the canal. Open year-round; free admission.

RINGOES

Unionville Vineyards, 9 Rocktown Rd. (☎ 908/788-0440). Free wine tastings Thursday through Sunday 11am to 4pm.

SHOPPING

FRENCHTOWN

Delaware River Trading Company, 47 Bridge St. (☎ 800/732-4791 or 908/ 996-3447). Call for hours.

STOCKTON

Phillips' Fine Wines, 17 Bridge St. (☎ 609/397-0587). Open Monday through Thursday 9am to 9pm, Friday and Saturday 9am to 10pm, Sunday noon to 6pm.

LAMBERTVILLE

People's Store Antiques Center, 28 N. Union St. (☎ 609/397-9808). Open daily 10am to 6pm.

Reinboth & Company, 121 N. Union St. (☎ 609/397-2216). Open Monday through Saturday 10am to 6pm, Sunday noon to 5pm.

ROSEMONT

Cane Farm Furniture, Rte. 519 (☎ 609/ 397-0606). Open Friday and Saturday 10am to 5pm, Sunday 1 to 5pm, or by appointment.

VICTORIANA AT THE SHORE: CAPE MAY

by Jon Pareles

THERE ARE NO PRIMARY COLORS IN Cape May, New Jersey. It's a town of mauves and chartreuses, ochres and pinks, the colors of hundreds of Victorian-era summer cottages that have made Cape May a national landmark. It's a seaside town too, bordered by pale fine sand and green-gray waves.

Situated 160 miles from the Holland Tunnel at the southern tip of New Jersey, dangling into Delaware Bay just below the Mason-Dixon line, Cape May is outside the immediate orbit of New York City. It draws people from New Jersey and Pennsylvania and points south; Lewes, Delaware, is 70 minutes away by ferry. Cape May also stands apart from the rest of the Jersey Shore. It's a cozy, genteel haven. My wife and I visit Cape May whenever we can set aside a few days. This time, as we drove down the Garden State Parkway, we noticed that many of the cars had "firefighter" license plates. The annual New Jersey firefighters' convention was taking place that weekend in Wildwood, just north of Cape May. Historically speaking, those firefighters were arriving more than a century late.

Cape May, once a base for whalers, was a thriving resort by the 1850s. Carriages rolled across the broad beachfront; steamships came up the coast; holiday makers filled big, L-shaped seaside hotels. In 1865, a railroad link to Philadelphia was completed. But arson fires repeatedly devastated the town; the largest, in 1878, destroyed 35 acres. The fires meant rebuilding, and as a result, much of the city dates from the 1860s through the 1890s. Yet by the 1920s, Cape May had been overshadowed by other seaside towns, from Atlantic City to Newport,

Rhode Island. It became a quiet outpost, used for fishing and as a military base.

With little redevelopment, the 19th-century summer cottages remained. Eventually some locals began to see the whimsical old homes as a potential attraction. A preservation movement, begun in the 1960s, put Cape May's 600 Victorian buildings on the National Register of Historic Places in 1970 and secured landmark status for the district in 1976, though not before some beach motels had been established. Part of Washington Street was converted to a pedestrian shopping mall; dozens of cottages were turned into bed-and-breakfasts. Gradually, Cape May won back its tourists.

Now visitors are an unlikely coalition of beachgoers, Victoriana buffs, and bird-watchers, who prize Cape May's location on major coastal migration routes. The town also has some of the best restaurants in New Jersey.

Usually we stay at the Abigail Adams, a small, congenial bed-and-breakfast just one house away from the oceanside Beach Drive, where we're treated more like houseguests than tourists. In the summer season, the owner provides beach tags (required by the town for beach users) and passes for a parking lot a few blocks away; street parking is unmetered during the off-season. The house is one of the Seven Sisters, a semicircle of seven identical houses designed by Stephen Decatur Button, whose imprint is all over Cape May.

This time, however, we spent the weekend at a newly revived landmark: the Southern Mansion, an inn that has restored the George Allen Estate. Allen was a Philadelphia department store magnate who was instrumental in bringing the railroad to Cape May.

Until recently, the Southern Mansion was a haunted-looking three-story house occupying an overgrown city block. But new owners have poured millions of dollars into renovation. Built in 1863 to 1864, the house is an American version of an Italian villa, with a 48-foot-long ballroom and 14 guest rooms. A 10-room annex completed in 1997 imitates the style of the original building. The mansion's exterior has been repainted its original shades of green, beige, and chocolate brown, and a meticulous renovation has put new slate on the roof and fresh gold leaf on the ballroom's giant mirrors.

Even the door hinges and window locks are highly decorated brass. When the new owners took over the estate, they found a trove of original fixtures and furniture in the basement. On the walls are photographs and memorabilia of Allen's daughter, Esther, who was married in the ballroom to one Ulysses Mercur.

Rooms with a View

We could glimpse a sliver of ocean over the rooftops from our third-floor room. It had comfortable Eastlake furniture—a couch, a rocking chair—and a tall, king-size four-poster bed, its mattress raised nearly 3 feet off the floor. For closets, a large armoire had been split in two on one wall of the bedroom, with, oddly, a sink installed between the halves; the toilet and a large shower were in a separate room. Unlike many bed-and-breakfasts, the rooms are equipped with a television (with cable) and telephone.

Cape May is still a fishing town, and we decided to visit one of its institutions, the Lobster House restaurant. Along Fisherman's Wharf, a working fishery has grown into a tourist complex: the restaurant, a raw bar, a souvenir shop, a fish market with a take-out counter, and a bar that serves drinks on a schooner. The Lobster House doesn't take reservations, though, and a few hundred firemen were ahead of us. A hostess said the wait would be 45 to 75 minutes; she was handing out beepers that would vibrate when a table was available.

Unwilling to wait, we called to reserve a table at the Lobster House's upscale rival, Axelsson's Blue Claw. Its own fish market was closed for the evening; it had a less glamorous marina view. There, we settled in for a leisurely dinner, including luxurious pure-crab sautéed crab cakes ($18.25) and a delicately tomato-scented sea bass ($20.95). As she took our orders, the waitress told us the firefighters would parade in Wildwood on Saturday. When we inquired about specifics, she got time and route information from a nearby table of firemen.

We drove back to town, past Jim's Bait and Tackle, where a shark seems to be tearing through the facade of the second floor. There's gratifyingly little nightlife in Cape May: A few bars have cover bands, while some shops stay open until 10pm or later. Columbia Avenue, where gaslights cast flickering shadows on some of the best-preserved Victorians, was quiet except for the clip-clop of a couple taking a carriage tour. Minus the parked cars, it could have been the 19th century.

Along the beach, the better-known Jersey Shore lingers with a small video arcade that closes early and a convention hall where big bands sometimes play. The Beach Theater, a recently subdivided movie house with a classic neon sign, shows first-run movies for $7.75. There were plenty of available seats for the 10pm show of *Tin Cup,* the Kevin Costner golf movie. On the way out, we gave an extra glance to the Ocean Putt, a modest miniature golf course.

Fudge & Architecture

The next morning, we had breakfast in the ballroom: fresh fruit, cereal, and cinnamon French toast with sausages. We looked into the garage-size Firemen's Museum, with its gleaming 1928 fire truck; we passed the Sturdy Savings Bank, a new building with a rare Victorian-style drive-through window. And we walked into town, marveling anew at the eccentric architecture.

In some ways, Cape May's core is like Miami Beach's art deco district, backdated a few decades and moved north: block upon block of daft buildings, all within an easy stroll. Whatever restraint the Victorians may have exercised in their deportment and discourse, their summer cottages repressed nothing. Turrets and gables poke up asymmetrically, windows are scattered across facades, shingles lose their corners, and woodwork trim becomes lace, spider webs, vines, and arabesques.

The Abbey (Columbia and Gurney streets) is a Gothic-revival fancy with a 60-foot tower; a house at 130 Decatur Street has three peaked roofs, an arch like an eyebrow, and porthole-shaped windows on its turret. The Henry L. Hunt House, at 201 Congress Place, sticks out in various directions and styles, including a circular belvedere on the second floor that looks like a miniature merry-go-round. Other places have a reassuring symmetry, like the row of eight formerly identical houses on Stockton Place or the Mainstay (635 Columbia Avenue), another Button building that was once a gambling club. All over town, the colors—some researched, some applied by caprice or intuition—clamor for attention.

Victoriana fills many of Cape May's shops. We looked into Uniquely Yours at the aptly named Pink House (lace dresses, filigreed jewelry, hats) and the Whale's Tale (books, earrings, shells, soaps, toys, even Victorian-design rubber stamps) before things got too cloying. Like other seaside towns, Cape May caters to the sweet tooth. There are four candy makers on the 3-block Washington Mall, and one, Fudge Kitchen, greets all passersby with samples. Purely for research purposes, we decided on a taste test.

We bought chocolate fudge at Laura's, Frahlinger's, Morrow's Nut House, and the Fudge Kitchen on the mall; then we walked to the beach. On a bench by the seaside, we watched long waves roll in while ants and yellow jackets joined us for the test. Fudge Kitchen was the clear winner, velvety and richly cocoa flavored. Laura's, slightly too buttery, was a second choice.

To the Lighthouse

As our blood glucose levels rose, we drove to the lighthouse at Cape May Point, a slim, conical tower 157^1/$_2$ feet high, which was built in 1859. Not long ago, it was repainted from white to a historically accurate tan, with a red top. It is still a working lighthouse, America's oldest, with an automatic beacon. But the town's Mid-Atlantic Center for the Arts now administers it as a museum, and tourists can climb the 199 steps to the top.

The cast-iron staircase is perforated in a diamond pattern that creates magnificent moirés from above and below. With a landing about every 30 steps, the climb wasn't difficult, and there was a cool breeze on the open-air (but securely caged) observation deck. We looked down on the marshy wildlife refuge next to the point's beach and saw a schooner in full sail gliding by a jetty. Offshore was a concrete bunker built under the beach during World War II; 50 years of erosion have raised it well above the waves. In another 40 years, the waves will be at the lighthouse door.

Near the lighthouse, we looked into the Cape May Point State Park office, picking up the found poetry of the *Checklist of the Birds of Cape May County:* "Brown Thrasher, American Pipit, Cedar Waxwing, Loggerhead Shrike." We looked at a display of nests—including one by an Eastern kingbird, which had woven in cigarette filters because nicotine repels insects—and we decided to return on Saturday for the weekly hawk-banding demonstration.

We drove to nearby Sunset Beach, which of course faces west. It has a rougher, pebblier texture than the main beach, and among the pebbles are so-called Cape May diamonds, sea-polished bits of quartz. Offshore is another hunk of concrete: a failed experimental ship built after World War I that became beached while being towed. The concrete boat was inauspiciously called the *Atlantus;* like its namesake, it sank.

We planned dinner at one of our favorites, Frescos, where the Italian cooking makes up for noisy acoustics and slightly rushed service. Like many Cape May restaurants, it has no liquor license, so patrons bring their own wine; Collier's Liquors across the street has a good selection. A rigatoni arrabbiata, with mushrooms and fennel-infused sausage, was gloriously earthy and too generous to finish; grilled tuna arrived with a pesto sauce made of smoked almonds as well as basil. Dinner for two came to $70.

It was time for some exercise. Instead, we signed up for 18 holes at Ocean Putt. I made a few of the par-2 holes by sheer luck, with a hole-in-one on the seventh (the big rabbit). Calculating angles and aiming carefully, I took four and five strokes per hole after that. A 5-year-old boy just behind us was doing better. I wondered if it was possible to be awarded a handicap at miniature golf. But on the way back to the inn, the stars were out, and the waves crashed with serene indifference.

At Saturday's hawk-banding demonstration, we were in the minority without binoculars around our necks. Bill Clark from the Cape May Bird Observatory pulled male and female American kestrels, already banded, from tubes made of juice cans taped together. He pointed out distinctive markings, talked about how the kestrels hunt from the air (using ultraviolet vision to pick out fluorescent mouse droppings), and explained how the banding project has recovered about 1% of the 92,800 birds it has banded. As he spoke, the raptors attacked his hand, drawing blood.

While Mr. Clark displayed a merlin, or pigeon hawk, a buzz went through the crowd, and binoculars were aimed overhead. "A bald eagle," someone whispered, and the man from the observatory raised his own binoculars. "A juvenile bald eagle," he agreed as it swooped by.

A Flashy Parade

We took the 10-minute drive to Wildwood for the parade. Antique and new fire trucks rolled by, all flashing red lights, at least one with a Dalmatian in the cab. We began noting the logos on the doors, like the camel and palm tree from New Egypt, New Jersey, and the skunk from Cologne, New Jersey. And we wondered why all the high-school marching bands were playing "Louie, Louie."

We briefly visited the Wildwood boardwalk, where a young Bruce Springsteen would have felt at home. It has a majestic Ferris wheel and an impressive-looking roller coaster, but we weren't in the mood, and turned back to Cape May. The beach was full, its water still warm enough in September for swimmers and surfers.

Cape May's restaurants are packed on Saturday nights, so we had made advance reservations at the Ebbitt Room of the Virginia Hotel. We still had to wait 20 minutes for a table, retreating to the veranda to avoid an arpeggio-happy lounge pianist. But dinner was gracious and full of innovative dishes.

We considered a moonlight carriage ride for two, but all the drivers were booked. So we rambled through town, with no particular place to go, enjoying the quiet streets.

On Sunday, we made the round of antiques shops, looking into all the nooks of the multidealer Rocking Horse. Back in town, we joined a group carriage tour. Betsy, the driver, offered tidbits of Cape May lore: that the Queen's Hotel (102 Ocean Street) used to be a bordello, how dunes were built to keep the ocean from flooding Beach Drive, and where Norman Rockwell spent summers (at 660 Hughes Street).

On foot, we looked in on the Congress Hall Hotel, a remnant of Cape May's 19th-century heyday that was last rebuilt in 1879; John Philip Sousa used to perform there, and President Benjamin Harrison made it his Summer White House in 1890 to 1891. It's now under renovation, with fancy shops along its tall colonnade and the salvaged anchor of a Spanish warship on the lawn.

We stopped at Rick's Coffee Cafe, which serves seven flavors of coffee along with muffins, croissants, Key lime pie, and tiramisu, and we contemplated the waves one last time. And then, reluctantly, we headed back toward the 20th century.

CAPE MAY ESSENTIALS

Information about Cape May, New Jersey, can be obtained from the **Greater Cape May Chamber of Commerce,** 513 Washington Street Mall, second floor (☎ **609/884-5508**), open weekdays 9am to 5pm, Saturdays 10am to 5pm.

GETTING THERE

By Car From Manhattan, take the Garden State Pkwy. to the end; bear left and take the Cape May Canal Bridge, which leads onto Lafayette St. and into Cape May.

By Bus New Jersey Transit (☎ **973/762-5100**) operates a direct bus to Cape May from Memorial Day through Labor Day; at other times, riders must change buses at Atlantic City. The ride is 5 hours and costs $26.75 one-way, $48.25 round-trip (half price for children 5 to 12 or seniors, free for those under 5). Buses leave daily from the Port Authority Bus Terminal, Eighth Ave. and 42nd St., Manhattan.

ACCOMMODATIONS

Abigail Adams Bed and Breakfast by the Sea, 12 Jackson St. (☎ **609/884-1371**). Open year-round. Room with an ocean view and shared bathroom $125; room with an ocean view and a private bathroom $175 in summer, $95 to $155 in winter. Rates are based on double occupancy and include breakfast. Two-night minimum on weekends, 3-night minimum on holidays. Reservations necessary.

Southern Mansion at the George Allen Estate, 720 Washington St. (☎ 800/381-3888 or 609/884-7171). Open year-round. Rooms (all with private bathrooms) $195 to $295 July and August, with a 3-night minimum; rates discounted in winter. Rates are based on double occupancy and include breakfast and afternoon tea. Reservations suggested.

DINING

Axelsson's Blue Claw, 991 Ocean Dr. (☎ 609/884-5878). Open daily 5 to 10pm from the end of May through Labor Day; schedule changes seasonally; Friday, Saturday, and holiday Sundays only from October through Easter. Dinner entrees $22 to $30.

Ebbit Room of the Virginia Hotel, 25 Jackson St. (☎ 609/884-5700). Open Sunday through Thursday 5:30 to 9:30pm, Friday and Saturday 5:30 to 10pm. Reservations recommended. Dinner entrees $24 to $30.

Frescos, 412 Bank St. (☎ 609/884-0366). Open early May to mid-October, daily 5 to 10pm. Dinner entrees $18 to $26.

Lobster House, Fisherman's Wharf (☎ 609/884-8296). Open daily 11:30am to 3pm and 5 to 10pm (Sun 2 to 9pm). Lunch entrees $9 to $16; dinner entrees $18 to $40.

Rick's Coffee Cafe, 315 Beach Dr. (☎ 609/884-3181). Call for hours.

ATTRACTIONS

Beach Theater, 711 Beach Dr. (☎ 609/884-4403). Call for current schedule and admission.

Cape May Bird Observatory, Cape May Point (☎ 609/884-2736). An information, nature, and workshop center operated by the New Jersey Audubon Society. Open daily 10am to 5pm. Free admission. Also operates an education and research facility in Goshen.

Cape May Firemen's Museum, Washington and Franklin sts. (☎ 609/884-9512). On display is a fire truck and memorabilia. Open daily 8am to 6pm (if you arrive to find it closed, just go into the firehouse and someone will open it up for you). Free admission.

Cape May Lighthouse, Lighthouse Ave. (☎ 800/275-4278 or 609/884-5404). Open January and March, weekends noon to 3pm, weekdays by appointment; April through mid-June and mid-September through December, daily 10am to 4pm; mid-June through mid-September, daily 9am to 8pm. Admission $4, free for one child accompanied by an adult, $1 for additional children.

Cape May Point State Park, Lighthouse Ave. (County Rte. 629), Cape May Point (☎ 609/884-2159). Nature trails, picnics, museum display. Grounds open daily, dawn to dusk; museum open daily 8am to 4:30pm (July and Aug, to 8pm). Free admission.

Emlen Physick Estate, 1048 Washington St. (☎ 609/884-5404); also houses the Mid-Atlantic Center for the Arts (☎ 800/275-4278). A Victorian stick-style house museum offering daily guided tours mid-March through January 2, 10am to 5pm; mid-January and February, Saturday and Sunday 11:30am and 2pm, call for weekday schedule. Admission $8, $4 for children 3 to 12.

Ocean Putt Golf, 401 Beach Dr. (☎ 609/884-7808). Call for hours and prices.

CONFECTIONS

Fralinger's, 324 Washington St. (☎ 609/884-5695).

Fudge Kitchen, 513 Washington Mall and 728 Beach Dr. (☎ 800/233-8343).

Laura's Fudge Shop, 311 Washington Mall (☎ 609/884-1777).

Morrow's Nut House, 722 Boardwalk (☎ 609/884-4966) and 321 Washington Mall (☎ 609/884-3300).

BEACHES

Sunset Beach, Sunset Blvd., Lower Township, No lifeguards are on duty and swimming is not recommended. No passes or beach tags are required.

Town Beaches, along Beach Dr. Beach tags necessary; call for information (☎ 609/884-9525).

CARRIAGE RIDES

Cape May Carriage Company, Washington and Ocean sts. (☎ 609/884-4466). Operates all year, weather permitting. Open May through mid-October, daily 10am to 3pm and 6 to 10pm; mid-October through December and April, weekends only (same hours); January through March, weekends 10am to 3pm. A half-hour group ride accommodating up to eight people costs $8 for adults and $3 for children 2 to 11. A half-hour private ride for six people is $30 for two adults, $40 for four adults, $3 for each child.

ANTIQUING & OTHER SHOPPING

Rocking Horse Antiques, 405 W. Perry St., West Cape May (☎ 609/898-0737). Open daily 11am to 5pm.

Uniquely Yours, 33 Perry St. and Carpenter's Lane (☎ 609/898-0008). Women's apparel and gifts. Open mid-February through New Year's Day, weekdays 11am to 5pm, weekends 10am to 6pm; closed January 2 through mid-February.

Whale's Tale, 312 Washington Mall (☎ 609/884-4808). Jewelry, gifts, and toys. Open April through mid-October, daily 10am to 9pm (July and Aug, until 11pm); mid-October through Christmas, Friday and Saturday, 10am to 9pm; January through March, daily 10am to 5pm.

PRINCETON: NATION'S HISTORY ENTWINED WITH IVY

by Gustav Niebuhr

Historical Riches & Famous People

Is THERE A COLLEGE BUILDING anywhere in the United States that can match the storied past of Nassau Hall at Princeton University, a history that goes well beyond the world of academe? Built of local stone and capped with an impressive bell tower, the building served as the college's centerpiece when it was erected by Presbyterians in 1756.

But in a remarkable 7-year span, it twice served as a seat of government (state and national) and figured in a Revolutionary War battle. New Jersey's first Legislature gathered at Nassau Hall in 1776 and adopted the state seal. In 1783 Congress met there for 4 months with James Madison, a former student, returning as a representative from Virginia.

To walk such historically rich ground is reason enough to visit Princeton. Besides, it is an easy jaunt from New York, thanks to frequent New Jersey Transit trains that run from Pennsylvania Station. About an hour out, the trains stop at Princeton Junction, actually in West Windsor, New Jersey, from which one can catch a one-car shuttle (called the Dinky by locals) for a 5-minute trip into town. The newly arrived will find a pleasant, centrally located hotel called the Nassau Inn, restaurants, a fine bookstore (Micawber Books), and no shortage of shops on and around Nassau Street, the main thoroughfare.

The university lends Princeton an identity that sets it apart from the commercial and suburban mass continually spreading out across central New Jersey. F. Scott Fitzgerald, an undergraduate here when the

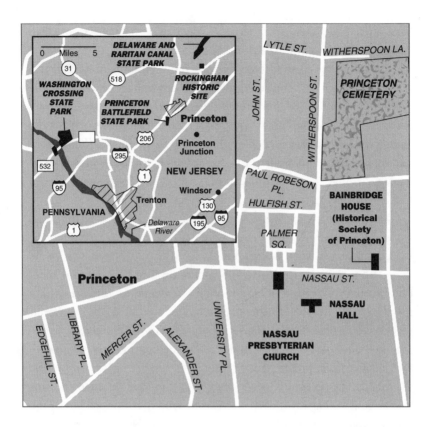

university's 13th president, Woodrow Wilson, was in the White House, snobbishly described Princeton as "rising, a green Phoenix, out of the ugliest country in the world." Fitzgerald evoked Princeton in his first novel, *This Side of Paradise,* which he began during his student days here.

It is a testament to Princeton's cultural depth that Fitzgerald is only a single stone in the diadem of luminaries who have crowned the town with glory, a roster that includes political leaders, scientists, and a breathtaking number of literary figures, from Nobel prize–winning novelist Thomas Mann to the literary critic Edmund Wilson. Albert Einstein lived here. Two centuries earlier, so did Jonathan Edwards, the nation's greatest theologian and the university's third president, who lies buried along with his notorious grandson, Aaron Burr, a Revolutionary

War officer, Jefferson's first vice president and the man who killed Alexander Hamilton in a duel in 1804.

Princeton can claim George Washington not only as visitor but also as victor. The general's embattled colonial troops won an important battle here on January 3, 1777, 9 days after they crossed the Delaware, defeating King George's redcoats and providing a much-needed triumph for the beleaguered revolutionary cause in the early days of the war. The victory was capped by the surrender of British troops holed up in Nassau Hall. They succumbed to Continental artillery fire urged on by Hamilton, who had better luck against the British than he did against Burr.

With so much to absorb, where should one start? I recommend stopping by Bainbridge House, home of the Historical Society of Princeton, a two-story brick house at 158 Nassau Street, two doors down from the intersection with Washington Street. Inside is a small but informative display on local history where one can find everything from pottery created by the Lenape tribe, the area's pre-European dwellers, to a placard with the Fitzgerald quotation. The society sponsors a 2-hour walking tour of centrally located historic sites every Sunday afternoon at 2pm.

On the bright and blustery day I took the tour, an energetic volunteer guide led a crowd of us on a 2-mile loop that stopped before the quietly impressive Greek Revival exterior of Nassau Presbyterian Church, paused at the imposing battle monument a couple of blocks to the south (it was dedicated by President Warren G. Harding), and took in the sight of Morven, the estate built for Richard Stockton, who along with Madison's teacher, the Rev. John Witherspoon, was a signer of the Declaration of Independence. The building served as the executive mansion for New Jersey governors until well into this century.

Our guide pointed out Thomas Mann's former house (now home to Princeton's Catholic campus ministry), then led us to 112 Mercer Street for a look at the modest wood-frame house—still a private home—where Einstein lived while he was at the Institute for Advanced Study nearby. Judging by the neighbors' nonchalance as they went about taking out trash and parking their cars, a crowd along the sidewalk was no cause for remark.

Revolutionary Zeal & a Historic Cemetery

The Princeton Battlefield is about a mile farther down Mercer Street, a distance I chose to drive on my own, rather than walk. The site of Washington's victory is a graceful sweep of land, impressively intact and preserved as an 85-acre state park. On its southern side stands a late Colonial house built by a Quaker farmer, Thomas Clarke, that sheltered the wounded American general Hugh Mercer, who died there several days after he fell in the battle. These days the house is a small interpretive center with written material and exhibits about the battle. In one display case a thick telephone book with a hole blown through it for contemporary demonstration purposes testifies to the destructive power of an 18th-century musket ball.

Anyone ambitious to learn more about Washington's New Jersey campaign ought to consider a detour to nearby Titusville, New Jersey, where the 800-acre Washington Crossing State Park commemorates Washington's crossing of the Delaware on December 25, 1776. His troops marched to Trenton, defeating Hessian soldiers in a surprise attack. The visitor center contains an excellent collection of Revolutionary War military gear.

Closer to Princeton, to its north, lies another state historic site, Rockingham, an 18th-century farmhouse on Route 518 in Rocky Hill, New Jersey, which was Washington's quarters in 1783 while Congress convened in Nassau Hall. Hamilton, Jefferson, Madison, and others met with him there. What it looks like inside I never found out, as I didn't make it past the door, finding the place closed one afternoon, and on another, busy with a tour for a group of children.

Nothing barred my way to the Princeton Cemetery, established in 1757, containing a fascinating record of the town's history. Owned by Nassau Presbyterian Church, but with plots open to a far wider population, it contains the grave of Grover Cleveland, the only Democrat elected president between 1860 and 1912. Born in northern New Jersey, he settled in Princeton after his political career and became a trustee of the university.

The novelist John O'Hara, the parents of the African-American singer and actor Paul Robeson, and Sylvia Beach, founder of the avant-garde Shakespeare & Company bookstore in Paris, a magnet for literary expatriates in the 1920s, also lie here. So, too, do most of the university's presidents, in a plot in the section known as the "Old Graveyard."

Edwards, who became president of what was then called the College of New Jersey shortly before his death in 1758, succeeded his son-in-law, the Rev. Aaron Burr, Sr., president from 1748 to 1757 and the man who supervised the construction of Nassau Hall. Their table-top gravestones bear lengthy Latin inscriptions, as does Witherspoon's nearby. The younger Burr, who studied theology before switching to law, lies at their feet, under an upright stone that briefly notes his military and political service—and discreetly avoids mention of his trial for treason after being charged with plotting to wrest a chunk of the lower Mississippi Valley from the new republic. A pamphlet describing the cemetery's history, with a map showing where to find its famous dead, is available at the historical society.

Parks & Dining

If sightseers find this touring conducive to an appetite, then they will also discover that Princeton has a decent selection of restaurants, with many tending toward the casual and inexpensive—no surprise in a college town. Tiger Noodles offers good, basic Asian fare. Closer to the town's center are the moderately priced Alchemist and Barrister and the newer Mediterra, which is very popular, judging by the crowds on the night I visited with my wife, Margaret Usdansky.

For upscale dining one possibility is the Ryland Inn, a 40-minute drive north on Route 206 and then west on Route 22 to the village of Whitehouse. Breaking from the local sights, we went there one Saturday night for a meal featuring halibut with lobster sauce (Margaret's choice) and salmon with mushrooms and leeks (mine). The bill was, well, impressive at a little more than $200, including wine, but so was the meal.

Princeton also has a good system of public parks. But the most interesting space lies on the town's eastern side, where a state park preserves the old Delaware and Raritan Canal, with a towpath that makes a quiet place for walking, jogging, or bicycling. If you head north along it, toward Kingston, you skirt the shore of Carnegie Lake, with ample chance to watch rowing crews at practice.

In a couple of places you may come across a small sign describing construction of the canal more than 150 years ago by Irish immigrants. Many of those men, who worked in difficult and unhealthy conditions, died of disease. It is a sober reminder of the many anonymous hands that have gone into shaping Princeton and its surroundings.

PRINCETON ESSENTIALS

GETTING THERE

By Car Princeton is about 51 miles south of New York City. From New York City, take Interstate 278 south to the West Shore Expressway. Go west on New Jersey Hwy. 440, then southwest on the New Jersey Turnpike. Take Exit 9 off the turnpike onto New Jersey Hwy. 18 and then go south on U.S. Hwy. 1. This will meet with County Rd. 571, which leads to Princeton.

By Train Amtrak (☎ 800/872-7245) and **New Jersey Transit** (☎ 973/762-5100) operate trains from Pennsylvania Station in Manhattan to Princeton Junction in West Windsor, New Jersey, which is about 2 miles from Princeton. Round-trip fare on Amtrak is $68 to $72, half price for children 5 to 11. Round-trip fare on New Jersey Transit is $14, $7 for children. New Jersey Transit operates the Dinky Shuttle train between Princeton Junction and Princeton with departures every 10 to 15 minutes during the week, and every hour on weekends. Fare is $1.

By Bus **Suburban Transit** (☎ 212/563-3504) offers service from the Port Authority in Manhattan to Princeton; round-trip fare $17, children under 5 ride free.

ACCOMMODATIONS & DINING

The Nassau Inn, 10 Palmer Square (☎ 609/921-7500). Daily room rates, $220 for a double room, $200 for a single; both include breakfast.

Alchemist and Barrister, 28 Witherspoon St. (☎ 609/924-5555). Monday through Thursday 11:30am to 10pm; Friday and Saturday until midnight.

Mediterra, 29 Hulfish St. (☎ 609/252-9680). Daily 11:30am to 4pm and 5:30 to 10pm.

Tiger Noodles, 260 Nassau St. (☎ 609/252-0663). Monday through Thursday, 11:30am to 10pm; Friday and Saturday, 11:30am to 10:30pm; Sunday, 3:30 to 10pm.

Ryland Inn, Rte. 22 West, Whitehouse, NJ (☎ 908/534-4011). Tuesday through Thursday, 11:30am to 2pm and 5:30 to 9pm; Friday, 11:30am to 2pm and 5:30 to 10:30pm; Saturday, 5:30 to 10:30pm; Sunday 5 to 9pm

ATTRACTIONS

Delaware and Raritan Canal State Park, 625 Canal Rd., Somerset, NJ (☎ 732/873-3050). Open dawn to dusk. Free. The park includes the former Delaware and Raritan Canal, now a 34-mile linear trail from New Brunswick south to Trenton.

Historical Society of Princeton, Bainbridge House, 158 Nassau St. (☎ 609/921-6748). Open Tuesday through Sunday, noon to 4pm; weekends only in January and February. Free. A walking tour of the town and campus takes place every Sunday at 2pm; $6 adults, $4 seniors, $3 ages 6 to 12, free under 6.

Nassau Hall, Princeton University. Orange Key Guide Service offers tours of the campus, including Nassau Hall. Meets at Frist Campus Center, Washington St. (☎ 609/258-1766). Tours Monday to Saturday 10am, 11am, 1:30pm, and 3:30pm; Sunday 1:30 and 3:30pm. Closed major holidays and winter recess. Free.

Nassau Presbyterian Church, 61 Nassau St. (☎ 609/924-0103). Sunday services 9:15 and 11am. Office open Monday to Friday, 9am to 12:30pm and 1:30 to 5pm. A member of the congregation is available after each worship service to answer questions and give a brief tour.

Princeton Battlefield State Park, 500 Mercer St. (☎ 609/921-0074). Open daily dawn to dusk. Free. Thomas Clarke House, an 18th-century Quaker farmhouse in the park, is furnished and includes exhibits of weapons and paintings related to the Revolutionary War. Open Wednesday through Saturday 10am to noon and 1 to 4pm, Sunday 1 to 4pm. Free.

Princeton Cemetery, 29 Greenview Ave. (☎ 609/924-1369). Open dawn to dusk. Maps are available at the entrance and at the historical society. Free.

Rockingham Historic Site, 108 County Rd. 518, outside Rocky Hill (☎ 609/921-8835). The site is closed through 2001 for renovations. Thereafter, open Wednesday through Saturday 10am to noon and 1 to 4pm, Sunday 1 to 4pm. Free.

Washington Crossing State Park, 355 Pennington/Washington Crossing Rd., Titusville (☎ 609/737-0623). Open daily 8am to 8pm. The visitor center and nature center are open Wednesday through Sunday 9am to 4pm. Picnic areas, hiking, mountain biking, and horseback riding trails. Parking fee $2 to $3.

FURTHER READING

A Fatal Friendship: Alexander Hamilton and Aaron Burr, by Arnold A. Rogow (Hill & Wang; $14 paperback, $27.50 hardcover).

Pennsylvania

BUCKS COUNTY, HISTORY'S COUNTRY HOME

by Lisa W. Foderaro

Stretched out listlessly along the Delaware River in eastern Pennsylvania, its arcadian landscape dabbed with pre-Revolutionary houses, close (but not too close) to New York City, Bucks County has always held an attraction for those with an artistic bent.

At the turn of the century, a half-dozen landscape artists formed the New Hope Group and began exhibiting their works together nationally. The beauty of Bucks County was thus transported to the Corcoran Gallery in Washington, the Detroit Institute of Arts, and elsewhere. Year-round classes in *plein air* painting further established the reputation of New Hope as a leading art colony.

A few decades later, another infusion of artistic energy came from New York's literati, who made Bucks County their country playground in the 1930s and 1940s. Moss Hart, the playwright, librettist, and director, bought a handyman's special on 87 acres in New Hope, following the lead of his longtime collaborator, George S. Kaufman. Then came Dorothy Parker, queen of the Algonquin Round Table, who plunked down $45,000 for a 14-room fixer-upper on more than 100 acres in Pipersville. And in 1940, Oscar Hammerstein II, the lyricist, settled his family on a 72-acre working farm in Doylestown, where there was surely more wind sweeping down the plain than in his native New York City. Perhaps it was no coincidence that 3 years later he penned the Broadway musical hit *Oklahoma!*

Today, Bucks County is still lovely to behold, its meadows and streams and old stone structures mostly unspoiled, particularly in the

249

northern half. But in other respects, namely its commercial life, Bucks County has the feel of a tourist destination that has over ripened.

Its creative edge has dulled, overtaken by the art galleries and modish shops and restaurants that have recently cropped up across the Delaware in Hunterdon County, New Jersey. New Hope itself, like Provincetown at the tip of Cape Cod, has become a honky-tonk Mecca, with stores devoted entirely to wind chimes or T-shirts. Some of New Hope's finer antiques stores have moved across the river to Lambertville, New Jersey, in recent years. And in spite of some remaining gems, like the frowzy and esoteric Farley's Bookshop and the recently restored Mansion Inn, New Hope's esprit is better captured by a shop that shamelessly calls itself the Tourist Trap.

Fortunately, there's a lot more to Bucks County than New Hope. If you know where to look and what to avoid, you can piece together a weekend that takes advantage of the county's artistic past, enshrined in a handful of outstanding museums as well as in its rich history, which reaches back past the rompings of this century to the cheerless days of the Revolutionary War. One of the most potent images of the war, George Washington's troops crossing the Delaware, originated on these shores in 1776 when General Washington used McConkey's Ferry Inn as his headquarters during the maneuver. The tavern is now the cornerstone of Washington Crossing Historic Park.

A Country Inn

While many shops and restaurants have a worn-out Eisenhower-era feel, there are several inviting inns and bed-and-breakfasts. Few are as tasteful and fresh as Evermay-on-the-Delaware in Erwinna, a village in northern Bucks County. Dating from 1790, the three-story 11-room inn, set on 25 acres, is a study in fastidiousness. On the ground floor, generous sprays of fresh flowers and real classical music (not Muzak) fill the double parlor, appointed with a camelback settee, a grandfather clock, a baby grand piano, and other Victorian antiques. The only disappointment was a gas fireplace that threw off a lukewarm breath on a chilly day.

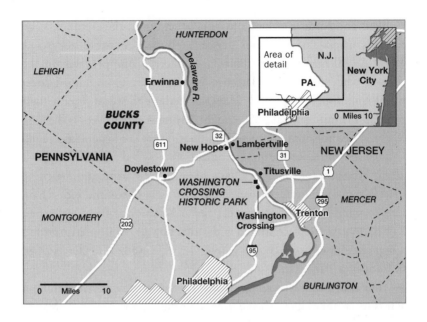

The innkeepers who restored Evermay 19 years ago, Ron Strouse and Fred Cresson, sold it more than 4 years ago. Doubling as chefs, they had drawn national praise for their six-course dinner on weekends. Thankfully, the new owners, William and Danielle Moffly, haven't changed a thing. They even enlisted the former innkeepers in the search for a new chef. He is Jeffrey Lauble, a graduate of the Culinary Institute of America and a former sous-chef at Evermay.

A recent dinner featured gingered butternut squash soup; wild mushrooms with ricotta and rosemary polenta; organic greens with grapefruit, pine nuts, and a mint vinaigrette; loin of venison in a hunter sauce; a cheese course of St. Andre, Montrachet goat cheese, and double Gloucester; and a warm pecan torte. The $68 prix-fixe dinner, which begins with a glass of champagne, is served Friday, Saturday, and Sunday in the pale peach candlelit dining room. Guests staying 2 nights are asked to dine once at the inn. The restaurant is also open to the public.

All the inn's rooms are smartly furnished with antiques and include luxurious little touches, like an extra layer of sheeting on top of the blankets and cordials of hazelnut liqueur set out in the evenings. Each room is named for a famous person in Bucks County history: The James A. Michener Room sports a weathered copy of *Texas* on the dresser, while the Oscar Hammerstein Room features framed sheet music from *South Pacific* and *Oklahoma!* Perhaps the most elegant guest room in the inn—and at $350 a night, the most expensive—is the Col. William Erwin Room on the second floor. There is no memento of old Colonel Erwin, a Revolutionary officer who owned much of the land around the inn, but the room has a baronial headboard and matching marble-topped bureau, as well as a Victorian settee and side chair, uneven wide-planked floorboards, and old-fashioned floral wallpaper. The decorative fireplace stuffed with dried flowers, while pretty, proved a huge frustration to a couple whose idea of nirvana is reading in bed in front of a blazing fire.

The inn, with seven columns and 17 shuttered windows marching across its cream-colored facade, fronts on the Delaware, although a little-trafficked road separates the property from the river. The third-floor guest rooms offer the most dramatic views of the water and the hills of Hunterdon County beyond. There are a few additional suites in a cottage and carriage house next to the main house.

The Michener Museum

A good starting point for exploring Bucks County is the James A. Michener Art Museum in Doylestown, the county seat. The outskirts have succumbed to unrestrained strip development, but downtown has some great architecture, a few inventive restaurants, particularly the Black Walnut at 80 West State Street, and an art cinema.

Bucks County may lack Hunterdon's thriving art galleries, but it can be proud of the Michener Museum, which opened in 1988 in a marvelously moody stone fortress built a century earlier as the county jail. The museum was named for the Pulitzer prize–winning novelist, who died in 1997. A passionate art collector, Mr. Michener grew up in Bucks County and gave a $1 million endowment to the museum when it opened.

While the Michener Museum presents traveling shows of national and international artists, its spiritual core is the collection of 19th- and 20th-century works by such prominent local artists as the primitive painter Edward Hicks, known for his "Peaceable Kingdom" series, and two leading landscape painters from the turn of the century, Edward Redfield and Daniel Garber. The exhibition space of the museum is especially handsome, with high ceilings, skylights, and striking wood finishes. The museum's centerpiece is a serene, sun-filled room devoted to a 22-foot semicircular mural, *A Wooded Watershed,* which Garber painted in 1926 for the sesquicentennial celebration in Philadelphia. The mural, depicting an idealized scene of deer in a wood at the water's edge, had been lost for 60 years. But in 1992 it was discovered behind the stage curtain in an auditorium at Pennsylvania State University in Mont Alto.

In 1996, the museum opened a new wing, which includes a permanent exhibition space honoring nationally recognized artists in all media who have lived in Bucks County. They include Hart, Parker, Hammerstein, the writer Pearl S. Buck, the illustrious painters in the museum's collection, and others, including a long-gone gentleman by the name of Henry Chapman Mercer who defies description in a single word. That's all right, however, because when you get to Bucks County and pick up any tourist brochure, you'll see his name—and the three landmark buildings he left as his legacy—everywhere.

Mercer was by all accounts a brilliant eccentric who was born in Doylestown and lived there at his death in 1930. He was an archaeologist, architect, fiddler, tile maker, and collector who spoke six languages, and apparently perused almost all of the 6,000 books in his library since they bear his notations. After studying history at Harvard and law at the University of Pennsylvania and traveling the world, Mercer got down to business, creating handmade tiles and ceramic reliefs for installation in private and public buildings. He thus became a major figure in the Arts and Crafts movement, a creative rebellion against machine-made goods.

In 1908, with the help of a dozen men and one horse, Mercer began construction on his dream house, a bizarrely beautiful castle he designed himself of hand-mixed, hand-poured reinforced concrete, molding the material the way a sculptor molds clay. The five-story mansion, named Fonthill, has 44 oddly shaped rooms, 32 stairwells, 18 fireplaces, and 200 windows. Just about every square foot of the interior space, whether floor, wall, or ceiling, is covered with his colorful tiles. The effect is that of an inside-out gingerbread house.

The hearth in the library is surrounded by tiles telling the story of the discovery and exploration of the New World. Another fireplace in an upstairs bedroom is framed by tiles depicting Charles Dickens's *The Pickwick Papers*. And in many of the vaulted concrete ceilings are embedded colorful ceramic grape bunches, dragons, acorns, and fleurs-de-lys. Some of the ancient ceramics Mercer collected are also set in his walls, from Babylonian tiles from 2400 B.C., used for invoices and letters, to dozens of Delft tiles, dating from 1600.

As soon as he finished Fonthill in 1910, Mercer began work on a new tile production center on his property. The Moravian Pottery and Tile Works, housed in a Spanish mission–style building also made of reinforced concrete, cranked out tiles that were used in thousands of buildings. The Tile Works, like Fonthill, is open for tours. Visitors can watch as workers create reproductions of Mercer's tiles much as they were made in his time, with local red clay, plaster molds, and large kilns. Hundreds of ceramic reliefs and tiles are sold in the gift shop, from a single decorative tile for $5 to a "fireplace narrative" of the legend of Bluebeard for $1,820.

Mercer's third legacy is the Mercer Museum, another castle in Doylestown, which is even bigger than Fonthill and—you guessed it—made from reinforced concrete. The museum, not far from Fonthill, houses Mercer's collection of more than 50,000 tools, modes of transport, and everyday household items used in America from 1700 to 1850, before the industrial age. Much as they cover every inch of Fonthill, tiles literally coat the museum interior; the larger pieces—from saw frames to animal yokes to stagecoaches—line the walls of a soaring central court and even hang from the ceiling. Dozens of rooms off to the sides focus on specific trades or crafts: gunsmithing, fruit preservation, printing, hat making, animal husbandry, watchmaking, mining, and so on.

A stunning find, and one of the few items not made in America, is a vampire-killing kit from early 19th-century England. The attractive leather case, lined with green felt, displays a pistol with silver bullet, an ivory crucifix, a wooden stake, and garlic powder. A label inside reads: "This box contains the items considered necessary for the protection of persons who travel into little known countries of Eastern Europe, where the population is plagued with a particular manifestation of evil known as vampires."

Back from the Brink

While the Mercer Museum preserves a swath of social history by gathering together things from everyday life, another Bucks County site, Washington Crossing Historic Park, embraces the great-man theory of history, commemorating a momentous event from the nation's earliest days.

By December 1776, General Washington had suffered a string of defeats. The commander of the British forces, Sir William Howe, had driven the Continental Army from Long Island and New Jersey, forcing the American troops to retreat across the Delaware to Pennsylvania. Washington badly needed a victory to muster popular support for the cause of independence. His men were exhausted, freezing, and ill equipped, and his soldiers' tours of duty were to expire at the end of the year. No new volunteers could be expected to join a losing campaign.

So Washington planned a daring assault on the Hessian garrison at Trenton, New Jersey. The garrison was 9 miles south of McConkey's Ferry Inn, the Bucks County tavern on the Delaware that was his headquarters. On Christmas night, 2,400 soldiers crossed to the New Jersey shore in stinging snow and sleet, maneuvering their boats through a gauntlet of ice floes. They successfully attacked the unsuspecting—and most likely hungover—garrison at dawn, winning the Battle of Trenton in 2 hours and reinvigorating the Colonists' commitment to the Revolution.

There are two Washington Crossing parks, the one in Bucks County, south of New Hope, and the other, Washington Crossing State Park, across the river in Titusville, New Jersey. Naturally, the Bucks County park focuses on the activities of 1776 on its side of the river. McConkey's Ferry Inn is the highlight. Washington is believed to have eaten Christmas dinner in the tavern hours before the crossing, and a copy of a letter he wrote, with "McConkey's Ferry" appearing beneath his name, lies on a dining-room table.

Walking through the same shadowy, low-slung rooms that Washington did, you experience the rush that comes from suddenly feeling connected to a piece of history. Time is compressed, and a mythic figure is brought down to human scale.

Also part of the park are two of the original buildings from the Quaker village of Taylorsville, which grew up around the inn in the early 1800s. The Mahlon K. Taylor House, built in 1817, is fully restored with period furnishings, an example of a respectably comfortable household of the day. The Taylorsville Store, which opened in 1828, is now a general store, called the "Patriot," selling mostly souvenirs, such as Colonial costume coloring books and penny candy. (The village's name was changed from Taylorsville to Washington Crossing when the park was founded in 1917.)

Before going on a tour of the properties, however, visitors are asked to sit through a half-hour film about Washington's crossing. The 1967 documentary is narrated by a pipe-smoking Chet Huntley, the former news broadcaster for NBC, who owned a historic house in Bucks County and died in 1974. The film is laughably dated and strangely circular. In between reenacted scenes of fantastic hardship, such as soldiers walking through the snow with only rags wrapped around their feet, are repeated shots of schoolchildren in cat-eye glasses and madras plaid shirts. They are shown pouring into the same auditorium where you are sitting, taking their seats and eagerly gazing toward the front of the room.

Perhaps they are looking at what we get to see when the film finally ends, and the movie screen retracts, revealing a wonderful replica of the famous 1851 Emanuel Gottlieb Leutze painting, *Washington Crossing the Delaware.* The original, which is in the Metropolitan Museum of Art, is 21 feet across and 12 feet high, and so is this copy, skillfully painted in 1970 by Robert Williams. Somehow, the film and this painting seem to say a lot about Bucks County. It is a place respectful of the arts, proud of its history, and sometimes charmingly out of step.

WHERE TO GO & TO STOP: BUCKS COUNTY ESSENTIALS

GETTING THERE

By Car To reach Bucks County from Manhattan, take the New Jersey Turnpike to I-78 West. To reach New Hope, which is central, continue on I-78 West to exit 29 and pick up Rte. 287 South. Continue on Rte. 287 to Rte. 202, which crosses the Lambertville Bridge, and take the New Hope exit, which leads onto Rte. 32 and into New Hope. To reach Erwinna, take Rte. 32 North. To reach Washington Crossing, take Rte. 32 South.

ACCOMMODATIONS & DINING

Black Walnut, 80 W. State St., Doylestown (☎ **215/348-0708**). Open Tuesday through Thursday 5:30 to 9pm, Friday and Saturday 5:30 to 9:30pm, Sunday 5 to 8pm. Dinner entrees $14 to $28.
Evermay-on-the-Delaware, Rte. 32, Erwinna (☎ **610/294-9100**). Rooms (all with private bathrooms) $145 to $350 double. Continental breakfast included. There is a 2-night minimum stay on weekends.

There is one seating for dinner on Friday and Saturday at 7:30pm and Sunday at 6:30pm.
Mansion Inn, 9 S. Main St., New Hope (☎ **215/862-1231**). Rooms (all with private bathroom) $195 to $285. Rates are based on double occupancy and include full breakfast. There is a 2-night minimum stay on weekends and a 3-night minimum on holidays.

SIGHTS & SHOPPING

Farley's Bookshop, 44 S. Main St., New Hope (☎ **215/862-2452**).
James A. Michener Art Museum, 138 S. Pine St., Doylestown (☎ **215/340-9800**). On permanent display are the exhibitions "James A. Michener: A Living Legacy," "A Visual Heritage of Bucks County," and "Creative Bucks County: A Celebration of Art and Artists." Open Tuesday through Friday 10am to 4:30pm (Wed until 9pm),

Saturday and Sunday 10am to 5pm. Admission $5, $4.50 for seniors, $1.50 for students and children 12 to 16, free for children under 12.
Mercer Museum, 84 S. Pine St., Doylestown, and **Fonthill,** E. Court St. and Swamp Rd. (Rte. 313), Doylestown, both run by the Bucks County Historical Society (☎ **215/345-0210**). The museum has an extensive display of items from everyday

life in the 18th and 19th centuries; Fonthill is the "concrete castle" built in the early 1900s by Henry Mercer. Open Monday through Saturday 10am to 5pm (until 9pm on Tues), Sunday noon to 5pm. Admission to museum or Fonthill $6, $5.50 for seniors, $2.50 for children 6 to 17, free for children under 6. A $12 combination ticket is also available.

Moravian Pottery and Tile Works, 130 Swamp Rd. (Rte. 313), Doylestown (☎ **215/345-6722**). Installations and displays of current tile production, as well as workshops in making tile and mosaics. Open daily 10am to 4:45pm; 45-minute tours are offered every half hour. Tour admission $3, $2.50 for seniors, $1.50 for children.

Washington Crossing Historic Park, Rte. 32, Washington Crossing (☎ **215/493-4076**). Tours of three historic houses—Hibbs House, McConkey's Ferry Inn, and the Mahlon K. Taylor House—are offered Tuesday through Saturday 9am to 5pm and Sunday noon to 5pm. The grounds are open Tuesday through Sunday 9am until dark. Admission to the grounds is free. Admission for 45-minute guided tours of the houses $4, $3.50 for seniors, $2 for children 6 to 12, free for children under 6.

Also inside the park is the **Patriot General Store,** on Rte. 532 (☎ **215/493-5411**). Open Monday through Saturday 10am to 5pm and Sunday 12:30 to 5pm.

Washington Crossing State Park, Rte. 29, Titusville, NJ (☎ **609/737-0623**). On the premises are the Johnson Ferry House, with a display of period furniture and an interpretive visitor center. The buildings are open Memorial Day through Labor Day, daily 8am to 8pm; the rest of the year, Wednesday through Sunday 10am to 4pm (the visitor center is open 9am to 4pm). Tours offered Wednesday through Sunday at regular intervals. Free admission; no charge for tours. Parking $2 to $3 Memorial Day through Labor Day.

DOWN ON THE FARM
IN MOUNT JOY

by Ralph Blumenthal

SOMEWHERE A CHILD WAILED, troubling the unfamiliar night. Whose child was it, I wondered groggily from deep inside a soft cocoon of sleep. I stirred awake, heart pounding. Was it mine? Where was I? My watch said 20 minutes to five. There it went again, a piteous cry that suddenly became recognizable. Now I remembered. We were far from Manhattan's comforting lullaby of police sirens. We were on a farm in Pennsylvania. Our little daughter was safe in her bed. And that ghastly din was a rooster's crowing.

We had needed an antidote to civilization, a quick and cheap respite from famous-visitor gridlock and prewinter urban blues. Nothing so venturesome as a Club Med holiday. A weekend out of the city would do. But something different, something that would hold the interest of a fidgety kindergartner who stops to pet every dog she sees and thinks food comes from D'Agostino's. The answer was clear.

As it turns out, there are many farms within reasonable driving distance of the city that accept weekend guests. The list ranges from dude ranches run like resorts to working farms where visitors can pitch in with the chores. We sought the latter and found our barnyard nirvana quite by accident. The first half-dozen places I called, from friends' recommendations and listings in *Farm, Ranch and Country Vacations in America* by Pat Dickerman (Adventure Guides), were filled. Clearly, we were on to something. But one farm in the Amish country of Pennsylvania helpfully recommended another nearby that had only recently begun taking guests and was not yet in the guidebooks.

The place, the Country Log House Farm, about a mile outside Mount Joy, had chickens, sheep, and pigs, said the owner, Jim Brubaker, adding that his brother, Luke, next door, had chickens and dairy cows as well. Our host-to-be—who insisted right off on being called Jim—offered a room that could sleep the three of us (our elder daughter was not along) for $90 a night, including breakfast. It sounded fine, and we booked it. (There is a $10 surcharge for each child.)

Zeroing in on the Amish country was a wise choice, it emerged, because of the wealth of attractions. Family-style restaurants abound, as do farmers' markets, crafts and antiques stores, and shopping outlets. Then, of course, there's the burnished beauty of the Pennsylvania Dutch countryside, where life still moves to the slow clippety-clop of the horse and buggy. Another highlight, certainly from the viewpoint of one pint-size chocoholic, is the proximity of Hershey, with its Chocolate World manufacturing tour, zoo, and amusement park. (The amusement park is closed from late September through mid-May; other Hershey attractions stay open all year.)

The downside is the distance. With heavy traffic, snacks, bathroom stops, and a vicious rainstorm, the trip from mid-Manhattan took us 4 hours. Certainly there are closer farms to be found. But my doubts vanished once we turned into the bucolic farmyard of a red-shuttered, gray vinyl-sided farmhouse opposite animal stalls and four tall grain silos.

Our daughter Sophie didn't wait for us to unload the car. She had spotted some children carrying cats and ran to join them. The farmhouse was a happy surprise. I had pictured rustic, barnlike quarters. This was more *House and Garden* than Ma and Pa Kettle: a modern open kitchen adjoining a skylighted living room with gas fireplace, French doors opening onto a patio, ceiling beams hung with baskets of dried flowers, and an interior wall striped with the exposed logs of the original homestead, believed to date from the 1700s.

Our blue-wallpapered upstairs room was no less fetching. A magnificent blue-and-white Amish quilt covered the bed, and an electric candle with pinpoint bulb flickered cozily in the window. The bedside reading lamps were large and bright, an unexpected boon. The

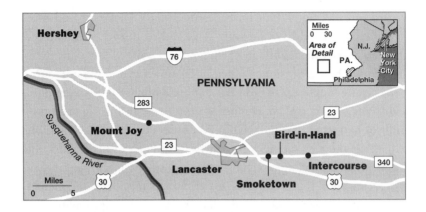

bathroom, equally pristine, was just outside our room; we were assured that although there were two other bedrooms on the floor, we would be the only guests using it that weekend. When we got to look around later, we found that a fourth guest suite in another part of the house was larger and even lovelier, with its own bathroom, but it was booked by a couple celebrating their anniversary.

We got a big welcome from Jim and his wife, Joanne (the gifted decorator, we learned), who introduced us to two visiting families from North Carolina and Maryland with whose children Sophie had instantly bonded. We were summarily waved to the breakfast table and, with the spontaneous intimacy of strangers at an inn, shared a feast of baked oatmeal with fruit topping, egg soufflé, bagels, and cinnamon-raisin bread with jam and honey butter. Jim needs only to work a bit on his coffee, which left us yearning for Starbucks back home.

Jim, who bears a passing resemblance to the craggy Paul Newman of *Nobody's Fool,* told us that he had traced the farm's ownership to 1867, and that his father had bought it in 1945, moving here from another Mount Joy farm. His farm spans 48 acres and his brother has another 242 acres, he said, inviting us on an exploratory tour.

Prying Sophie away from the cats, we went first to the chicken coop, where in the straw-lined chicken nests, Sophie was delighted to find an egg to collect. (Jim confessed later that he had left it there from the day before, his 30 chickens having "gone on strike," as he put it.) Next we moved to an outdoor pen where sheep, rams, and goats trotted toward us expectantly. Our host measured out a bucket of feed mix. "They eat grass and hay," he said. "This is their dessert." He told the children to feed them with an open hand and pointed out a goat with a curious foible: When it got scared, it fell down in a dead faint.

Then he started up an old Farmall tractor hitched to a wagon piled with bales of hay, and we climbed on for a ride to the pig shed over fields of harvested alfalfa. "You'll need deodorant," Jim cautioned. We didn't, but the pigs sure did. Packed flank to flank in pens of 25, the 1,200 swine gave off a powerful stench. And who wouldn't, given their prospects: They come weighing 40 to 50 pounds, are kept there 4 months until they're 250 pounds, and are then sold for slaughter. We rode toward his brother Luke's place, Brubaker Farms, dairy cattle suddenly seeming very alluring. "Look!" Sophie suddenly shouted, jumping off her hay bale. "A chipmunk!"

If I had never given much thought to how chickens were raised for food, a look at the operation in two huge sheds, each 2 city blocks long, showed me more than I wanted to know. The production cycle, in partnership with Tyson Foods, the Arkansas-based chicken empire, begins when Tyson delivers 52,000 day-old broiler hatchlings and the feed supply. The chickens, 26,000 in each shed, are fed and watered by automatic dispensers; farmhands need only walk through daily to remove any chickens that have died. Eight weeks later, Tyson returns to cart the grown chickens off to their fate. Then after the sheds are aired out for a week or two, Tyson delivers 52,000 new chicks. This must have been what Isaac Bashevis Singer had in mind when he became a vegetarian: "Not for my health," he explained, "but the health of the chickens."

The farm's 500 cows have a brighter future, at least as long as they give milk, which they do three times a day, at 4am, noon, and 8pm, when 20 at a time are led into the milking shed and hooked up to milking machines. While farmhands scurried through the shed, swabbing the teats with iodine solution and attaching the suction devices that drain the milk through plastic tubes, Jim hoisted Sophie underneath a waiting cow and showed her how to draw a spray of milk the old-fashioned way. For once, she was speechless.

The udders empty in 5 minutes, after which the suction devices drop off. This being the computer age on the farm as well, each cow wears a numbered electronic necklace that activates measurement of the animal's milk output at each milking. A good cow will give 80 to 100 pounds of milk a day; that's at least 10 gallons, the brothers explained. His cows are fed an appetite stimulant, said Luke Brubaker, who defends the use of federally approved chemical hormones to increase milk production, a practice that continues to split the industry. He and 150 other dairy farmers in his regional cooperative stringently supervise milk quality, he said, knowing that excess antibiotic traces or other impurities are punishable by the loss of the entire tanker load. "You could lose $10,000 by making a mistake," he said.

Jim said he had something special to show us, and led us past a sign reading COW COUNTRY—WATCH YOUR STEP to a pen where a cow in the final stages of pregnancy stood shuddering, about to deliver a calf. Part of the umbilical sac had already emerged, and inside a hoof was visible. "He's having a baby?" Sophie asked, incredulous. It was time for a quick lesson in he and she.

Enthralled, we waited for the birth. And waited and waited and waited. "Could be a few hours yet," Jim guessed. We took a gamble and risked a quick trip back to his farmhouse for a break. We lost. When we returned within the hour, the cow had delivered. The newborn calf, a female still wrapped in its sac, lay unmoving by its mother, which also lay there blitzed. A cowhand climbed into the pen and gave the cow a shove. "Mommy's got to take care of it," she scolded. Roused, the cow began licking her calf clean as it made its first feeble attempts to unfold its legs and stand. The cowhand sprinkled the calf with nutrient-laced feed, which the mother then dutifully licked off. "It's the quickest way to get vitamins into her," the cowhand said.

One of the other visiting families arrived to see the new calf, and Jim showed us around the rest of his brother's farm. The other little girl insisted on seeing the pit where the cow manure was stored for fertilizer. "Well," said our guide, stalling, "it's not real pretty."

It was time for lunch and a drive around the area. Taking a recommendation from Jim, we stopped to eat at the Country Table on Route

283, an immaculately clean family-style restaurant stocked with religious tracts. Platters of roast beef, peppery cabbage slaw, corn, roast turkey, mashed potatoes, quiche, and fruit, along with salad and iced tea, came to $19.95 for all three of us.

On Route 340, we rode to Bird-in-Hand (probably named for a Colonial inn) and spent an hour roaming through the enclosed farmers' market, stocking up on jars of jam and apple and peach butter, sweet and hot pickled peppers, and bags of—what else?—Dutch pretzels. Then it was on to Intercourse, of which *The Intercourse News,* the local shopper, had this to say: "Much speculation exists concerning the name of this little country village." One theory ties it to an old racecourse and an entry road known as "Enter-Course." Another links the name to the joining of two main roads. Today it's the setting of Kitchen Kettle Village, a somewhat cutesy shopping complex with a one-pen petting zoo for children. We shared the parking lot with the delicate and graceful Amish buggies, the horses tied to hitching posts. We had finally gotten Sophie to stop pointing excitedly at the Amish, whom she kept calling "the British."

We skirted Lancaster, which seemed deserving of a more sustained tour on another visit; spot-checked the sprawling Rockvale Square and Tanger discount shopping outlets on Route 30 east of Lancaster; and circled back on Route 23 west of Lancaster, where we passed spectacular mansions and mock châteaus that might have been transplanted from East Hampton, Long Island.

Back at the Country Log House Farm, the cats were waiting. Sophie scooped them up and disappeared.

For dinner on Saturday night (the farm provides only breakfast), we were torn between driving 45 minutes or so back to one of the Lucullan landmarks of Pennsylvania Dutch cuisine—Good 'n' Plenty in Smoketown or Plain and Fancy on Route 340 between Bird-in-Hand and Intercourse (each seating more than 600 people)—and finding something closer. We decided to take a drive through adjacent Mount Joy and almost immediately came upon an extraordinary oasis: a restored antique hotel and brewery carved into three restaurants. The thronged complex on North Market Street, in the center of town, was built around the old Central Hotel and Alois Bube's Brewery, one of the country's last intact pre-Prohibition breweries, registered as a national historic site.

Our timing was perfect. A last-minute cancellation had just opened up a table in the sought-after Catacombs, a dim and vaulted chamber 43 feet below the street. There we dined on vaguely medieval fare: skewered meats and fish, chicken and veal and salad, and a tankard of beer. The setting was extraordinary. But as with many such theatrical dining extravaganzas, the food came in second, and at $84 was hardly a deal.

Tearing Sophie away from the farm for the trip home was a lot easier than it might have been. We uttered a magic word. She said goodbye to a dried worm in the driveway and tumbled into the car. Forty minutes later, we were in Hershey's Chocolate World, a factory exhibition and gift shop, in a chocolate brown cart moving tantalizingly past mock rivers of flowing chocolate and cascades of chocolate bars and kisses. The tantrum came later.

FARM STAYS ESSENTIALS

LANCASTER COUNTY, PA

Country Log House Farm, 1175 Flory Rd., Mount Joy (☎ 717/653-4477). Open year-round (limited weekends Dec through Feb). Rooms (some with private bathrooms) $75 to $90; $10 surcharge per child. Daily rates are based on double occupancy and include breakfast.

Landis Farm, 2048 Gochlan Rd., Manheim (☎ 717/898-7028). Dairy farm that operates year-round. There is a single guest house that accommodates six people. Room $80, $100 for four; $10 surcharge for each additional adult, $5 for each child. Daily rates are based on double occupancy. Breakfast is available for an additional $5 for adults, $2.50 for children.

Old Fogie Farm, Stackstown Rd., Marietta (☎ 717/426-3992). Operates year-round. Rooms (with private bathroom) $685, $10 surcharge per child. There are also family suites with kitchens available for $85 (not including breakfast). Daily rates are based on double occupancy and include breakfast. November through March, winter packages for adults only.

Verdant View Farm, 429 Strasburg Rd., Paradise (☎ 717/687-7353). Rooms for 2 nights with shared bathroom $98, with private bathroom $158 to $178; $10 surcharge for each additional bed, and $4 for each additional breakfast ($3 for a child). A four-room cottage with a kitchen can accommodate up to 14 people. Daily buggy rides and seasonal sleigh and hayrides can be arranged, along with a 2-hour tour of the area and a dinner with an Amish family. Part of a "Winter Getaway" program sponsored by the **Pennsylvania Dutch Convention and Visitors Bureau** (☎ **717/299-8901**).

NEW YORK STATE

Hawthorne Valley Farm Main House, 327 Country Rd. 21C (off Taconic State Pkwy.), Harlemville (☎ 518/672-4790). A working dairy farm open for daily visits only except mid-June to mid-August (when it is open for summer camp for children 9 to 15). Free. **Hull-o-Farms Family Farm Vacations,** Cochrane Rd., Durham (☎ **518/239-6950; www.hull-o.com**). Operates year-round. Three guest houses offer accommodations of two to four bedrooms. Daily rates (including all meals) $95 per adult, $60 for children 10 to 14, $50 for children 5 to 9, $35 for children 2 to 4, free for children under 2. Two-day minimum.

Pinegrove Dude Ranch, Cherrytown Rd. (off Rte. 209), Kerhonkson (☎ **800/ 846-1571**). Open year-round. End of June through Labor Day, 2-night stay, including meals and all activities, from $280 per adult (half price for children 4 to 16, free for children under 4). At other times, $179 to $229 for adults (half price for children). Special packages are available, ranging from $356 per adult for 4 days in winter to $199 per adult for 2 nights during Mother's Day weekend (children are half price for both).

LANCASTER COUNTY ESSENTIALS

GETTING THERE

To reach Lancaster County from Manhattan, take the Lincoln or Holland Tunnel to the New Jersey Turnpike; exit onto the Pennsylvania Turnpike (exit 6) and continue to Rte. 222 South (exit 21); continue on Rte. 222 South to Rte. 30 West and then onto Rte. 283 West.

DINING

Alois's, Bottling Works, Catacombs, all part of Bube's Brewery, 102 N. Market St., Mount Joy (☎ **717/653-2056**). Alois's: open Thursday 5:30 to 9pm, Friday and Saturday 5 to 9pm, Sunday 5 to 8pm. Bottling Works: open daily 11am to 2pm; Monday through Thursday 5:30 to 10pm, Friday and Saturday 5 to 11pm, Sunday 5 to 10pm. Catacombs: open Monday through Thursday 5:30 to 9pm, Friday through Sunday 5 to 10pm. Alois's: six-course meal $32. Bottling Works: entrees $3.95 to $15.95. Catacombs: entrees $17 to $27. Vintage photographs of the brewery are displayed in a museum called Cooper's Shed, open Monday through Friday 6 to 10pm and Saturday and Sunday 5 to 10pm.

Country Table Restaurant, 740 E. Main St., Mount Joy (☎ **717/653-4745**). Open Monday through Thursday 6am to 8pm, Friday and Saturday 6am to 9pm. Entrees $4 to $5 at lunch, $6 to $10 at dinner.

Good 'n' Plenty, Rte. 896, Smoketown (☎ **717/394-7111**). Open Monday through Saturday 11:30am to 8pm. Full lunch or dinner $15.50, $7.50 for children 4 to 12.

Plain and Fancy Farm Restaurant, Rte. 340, Bird-in-Hand (☎ **717/768-4400**). Open Monday through Saturday 11:30am to 8pm, Sunday noon to 8pm. All you can eat $15.95, $7.95 for children 4 to 11, free for children under 4.

AMUSEMENT PARK

Hershey Park, including Chocolate World, Christmas Candylane, Hershey Museum, and Zoo America, Hershey Park Dr., Hershey. Hershey Park is open Memorial Day through Labor Day, and select days and weekends in May, September, and October. Chocolate World, the visitor center of Hershey Foods Corporation, offers a simulated factory tour on how chocolate is made; free admission. Christmas Candylane is open only mid-November to January 2; it offers rides for adults and children, a train ride, and a theater with a Christmas show. Admission for the rides and attractions ranges from 90¢ to $3.60. Admission to Hershey Museum $6, $5.50 for seniors, $3 for children 3 to 15, free for children 2 and under. Admission to Zoo America $6, $5.50 for seniors, $4.75 for children 3 to 12, free for children 2 and under. For hours, show times, and other information call ☎ **800/437-7439.**

SHOPPING OUTLETS

Rockvale Square Outlets, at Rte. 30 and Rte. 896, Lancaster (☎ **717/293-9595**). Open Monday through Saturday 9:30am to 9pm, Sunday noon to 6pm.

Tanger Factory Outlet Center, Rte. 30 East, Lancaster (☎ **800/408-3477**). Open Monday through Saturday 9am to 9pm, Sunday 11am to 6pm.

The Brandywine Valley

by Lisa W. Foderaro

In the brittle light of late winter, the Brandywine Valley, stretching from southeastern Pennsylvania into northern Delaware, emerges in all its muted glory. From either side of narrow country roads, hay-colored fields rise and fall to the horizon. Naked tree branches appear pressed against a mottled gray sky, interrupted by an occasional gristmill or puff of chimney smoke.

This is the time of year when the Brandywine's enchantments don't hit you over the head but rather seep into your soul with their desolate beauty. It is the season most often depicted in a half century of painting by Andrew Wyeth, who is Brandywine born and bred and, at 80, still an active resident and artist. "I prefer winter and fall, when you feel the bone structure in the landscape—the loneliness of it," he said years ago. "Something waits beneath it. The whole story doesn't show."

The giant among three generations of artists, Mr. Wyeth has his work permanently on view at the Brandywine River Museum in Chadds Ford, Pennsylvania, along with that of his father, sisters, and son. His paintings best convey the character of the countryside while also revealing truths in the everyday, whether the slant of light on a windowsill or a dead crow in a field.

If Mr. Wyeth is the Brandywine Valley's favorite son, the Du Ponts are its first family, and it is largely thanks to their generous legacy that the region also offers a rich cultural and educational diet. Longwood Gardens in Kennett Square, Pennsylvania, is internationally known for its 1,050 acres of cultivated plantings. For the winter traveler, there is a

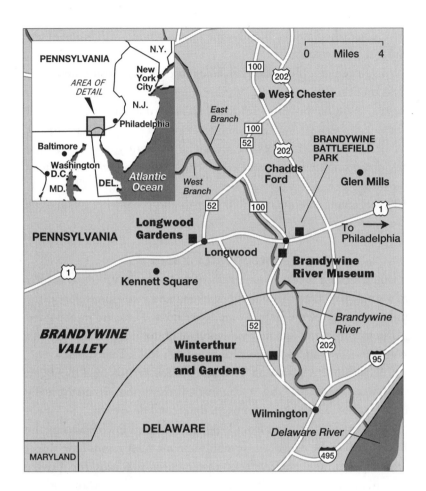

spectacular preview of spring in the dramatic conservatories: 3½ acres under glass that form a museum of international horticulture. Winterthur, a sprawling mansion on the outskirts of Wilmington, Delaware, houses what is arguably the country's finest and largest collection of American decorative arts from 1640 to 1860.

Settled in the early 1600s by the Swedes, who were later joined by English and Welsh Quakers, the Brandywine Valley has a deep sense of its own history. The area, named for the Brandywine River (more creek than river), is dotted with covered bridges and Quaker meetinghouses, gristmills and pre-Revolution stone houses. Brandywine Battlefield

Park, where the Battle of Brandywine was fought in 1777, is one of several historic attractions.

Unfortunately, the valley has, like most places, become somewhat built up over the years. (Mr. Wyeth himself admits that the area never looked quite as vast and uncluttered as it does on his canvases.) Fortunately, though, much of that development is confined to the few major routes that crisscross the area. The moment you turn off onto any of the smaller roads, you are blessedly thrust back in time. One of the most scenic drives through the countryside is along winding Route 100, beginning just outside Wilmington and continuing north for a dozen or so miles.

Sweetwater Farm

It would be hard to take in even a fraction of what the valley has to offer in a single day. Better to stay the weekend and savor the region at the unhurried pace of the Brandywine River itself. There are several good places to lodge (and eat) that are evocative of the area's history, perhaps none more so than Sweetwater Farm in Glen Mills, Pennsylvania.

A fieldstone mansion on 50 acres, Sweetwater has nine fireplaces, dark wood antiques, and a country breakfast that is unabashedly urbane. There are six guest rooms on the second floor of the 1815 main house, part of which dates from 1734 and was used as a hospital by the British during the American Revolution. Four guest rooms have working fireplaces, and all have four-poster queen-size beds and private bathrooms. Three outbuildings housing five suites, three with working fireplaces, are situated on the property, where horses and goats can be seen grazing. A covered swimming pool hints at the pleasures of summer.

What is so refreshing about the inn to the veteran bed-and-breakfast goer is its complete lack of cuteness: You won't find any ruffles or heart-shaped wreaths here. Indeed, there is a certain formality to its antiquated charm, fostered no doubt by 11-foot ceilings and amply proportioned rooms. The inn changed hands in 2000, and the new owners are Victor Cancelmo and Deirdre Conwell.

The dignified demeanor of old wealth is further conjured by hefty moldings painted in Williamsburg colors, Oriental rugs, a few serious antiques, many good reproductions, and, of course, those ubiquitous fireplaces. They draw smoke so well and come with such an unending supply of dry wood that it is tempting to shirk sightseeing duties in favor of a good read by the hiss and crackle.

Ms. Conwell does the cooking. Breakfast might be French toast or eggs Benedict and there is always fresh fruit. The owners appear to be laid-back about rules (which can be enforced with militaristic precision by some innkeepers). Breakfast is served from 9 to 10am, but late sleepers won't go hungry if they slink downstairs at 10:30. And in spite of a noon checkout, it is not uncommon for guests to be encouraged to linger by the fire in the parlor through a cold and blustery Sunday afternoon.

Brandywine River Museum

Since much of the Brandywine Valley's identity is tied up with Andrew Wyeth ("Wyeth Country" is a familiar expression), it is only fitting that its one serious art museum is devoted largely to his and his family's paintings. Set in a renovated 19th-century gristmill on the bank of the Brandywine River in Chadds Ford, the museum is at once classic and modern: classic in its century-old brick facade with weathered herringboned shutters, modern in its curvilinear interior of white stucco and glass.

That duality finds parallels in Mr. Wyeth's work. Many consider him a traditionalist, in the sense that he has pursued realistic landscape and figurative painting in an age of abstraction, keeping alive the spirit of American painters like Winslow Homer and Thomas Eakins. The meticulous detail found in his rendering of fabric, grass, painted clapboard, hair—whatever—is indeed staggering. But to Mr. Wyeth, as well as to some art critics, his work is thoroughly modern, almost surreal in its immediacy. He has even said that he considers his paintings abstract because they transcend the physical elements to capture the spirit of a person or object.

The museum's first- and second-floor galleries contain the works of his father, N. C. Wyeth, a prominent artist and illustrator in his own day who was killed in Chadds Ford when a train struck his car at a railroad crossing. Andrew was 28. His father's tragic death had a profound effect on him and on his approach to landscape painting. Indeed, an all-encompassing melancholy seems to emanate from many of his canvases.

The galleries also display the works of Andrew Wyeth's two sisters, Henriette Wyeth Hurd and Carolyn Wyeth; his son, Jamie; and other artists who painted the Brandywine Valley, including Jasper Cropsey, William Trost Richards, and Howard Pyle.

The gallery on the top floor is reserved for Andrew Wyeth's paintings. They depict the personalities and places in and around Cushing, Maine, where he and his wife, Betsy, spend the summer months, and Chadds Ford, where they spend the winter.

Longwood Gardens

The soaring glass conservatories at Longwood Gardens in nearby Kennett Square are, by contrast, an orgy of color, from lavender orchids and rosy camellias to the feathery yellow flowers covering the weeping branches of the acacia tree.

Entering the conservatories in the midst of winter is like stepping into another world. Outside, the air is cold and clear, but inside rooms like the East Conservatory and Palm House, the atmosphere is as sensuous as a Florida Key: humid, warm, and fragrant. With most of Longwood's 11,000 different plants still hibernating outdoors, the conservatories are an irresistible opportunity to defy the calendar.

In 1906, Pierre S. Du Pont, then the chairman of Du Pont and General Motors, purchased the first 200 acres of what is today Longwood Gardens to save an arboretum from being cut for timber. During his life, he assembled and developed more than a thousand acres into one of the country's foremost gardens, leaving them upon his death in 1954 for the "sole use of the public for purposes of exhibition, instruction, education, and enjoyment."

The conservatories were established in the 1920s by Mr. Du Pont to grow flowers and fruits year-round. Today, they are a stately network of 20 rooms and grand galleries. With tall arched windows, honeycomb glass ceilings, fountains, and winding brick walks, the conservatories are almost as arresting for their design as for the plants they contain, which are arranged thematically. There is, for instance, Fern Passage, with two alcoves of insect-eating plants, including one dear to every fourth-grader's heart: Venus's-flytrap. The Silver Garden is host to plants found in the world's harshest environments, including the organ-pipe cactus, which is two stories high, covered with fine white needles, and as straight and narrow as, well, an organ pipe. The Banana Room instructs that bananas are technically herbs, not trees, despite the presence of a 20-foot plantain whose leaves easily measure 3 feet wide by 9 feet long.

From mid-January through mid-April, the conservatories honor spring, with profusions of tulips, hyacinths, daisies, and daffodils tucked among the permanent collection. The 75-year-old Orangery and the Exhibition Hall, which constitute about a quarter of the conservatory, were reopened in the fall of 1996 following a major renovation.

Winterthur

Visiting this unthinkably large Du Pont mansion is a bit like making a trek to the Metropolitan Museum of Art. You are overwhelmed by the realization that it would take years of return trips to begin to exhaust its contents. There are some 90,000 objects—furniture, textiles, ceramics, glass, paintings—in more than 100 rooms and display areas spread throughout nine floors.

So broad is the collection that, in addition to the 1-hour highlight tour, there are 25 special-interest tours available by request, focusing exclusively on, say, Chinese export porcelain, or Empire furniture. But don't be put off. Even an hourlong tour of a single floor offers a satisfying look at the treasures assembled in this century by Henry Francis Du Pont, a distant cousin of Pierre S. Du Pont. The tour guides deftly weave together strands from the Du Pont family's history with the forces in American and European history that led to the dominance of particular styles of decorative arts during certain periods.

The original 12-room Greek Revival house, built in 1838 and then passed through the hands of a succession of Du Ponts, received its first major addition in the late 1800s. The owners, Henry A. and Pauline Du Pont, also developed Winterthur into an elaborate, self-contained community, adding greenhouses, flower gardens, a dairy farm, a golf course, a sawmill, a post office, even a railroad station. But it was their son, Henry Francis, who, after inheriting the house in 1926, laid the groundwork for Winterthur, the museum. He added a nine-story wing to display his collection of furnishings made or used in America before 1860, transplanting architectural elements from other distinguished houses, like a fantastic free-floating spiral staircase from North Carolina. And he worked with a landscape architect to create natural-istic gardens that are almost as strong a draw today as the house.

Winterthur is set on nearly 1,000 hilly acres, and a shuttle bus pro-vides transportation from the visitor center to the mansion, whose beige stucco facade with burgundy shutters is surrounded by towering tulip poplars. In addition to the period rooms, where antiques are viewed in domestic settings, three galleries in a building adjoining the mansion display still more decorative arts.

Mr. Du Pont opened the house as a museum in 1951 but contin-ued to live on the property in a villa until his death in 1969. Of course, with homes in Manhattan, the Hamptons, and Florida, he wasn't there full-time.

Perhaps it's only natural that feelings of gratitude should mingle with envy, and even some serious reflection about the uses of money, as you wander through the wing that functioned as Mr. Du Pont's life-size dollhouse, or through the conservatories at Longwood Gardens. Both were built with a fortune founded on gunpowder. But the fact is that the residue from that gunpowder has made the Brandywine Valley a remarkably pleasant place to be.

BRANDYWINE VALLEY ESSENTIALS

GETTING THERE

To reach the region from the New York metropolitan area, take the New Jersey Turnpike South to exit 2 (Rte. 322); take Rte. 322 West over the Commodore Barry Bridge into Pennsylvania and continue to Rte. 452; take Rte. 452 North about $4^1/2$ miles to Rte. 1 and continue along Rte. 1 to the various sites.

ACCOMMODATIONS

Sweetwater Farm, 50 Sweetwater Rd., Glen Mills (☎ **800/793-3892** or 610/459-4711). Weekend rates, $175 to $275, depending upon accommodation; $25 less for each room weekdays. Rates are based on double occupancy and include full breakfast and private bathroom. Children are welcome; an additional cot in the room is $35.

DINING

Chadds Ford Inn, at Rte. 1 and Rte. 100, Chadds Ford (☎ **610/388-7361**). Traditional American fare in a charming stone house, which entered the hospitality business in 1736 when John Chad, an English Quaker, turned his father's home into a tavern. Andrew Wyeth prints adorn the walls, and a working fireplace warms the downstairs dining room. Open Monday through Friday 11:30am to 10pm, Saturday 5:30 to 10:30pm, Sunday 11am to 2pm (for brunch) and 4 to 9pm. Entrees $7.25 to $10.50 at lunch, $14.50 to $24.95 at dinner.

Dilworthtown Inn, 1390 Old Wilmington Pike (a quarter mile off Rte. 202), West Chester (☎ **610/399-1390**). New American cuisine is served in a rambling house built in 1758, with 15 intimate dining rooms and authentic gaslight from chandeliers and sconces. Bring your reading glasses: There are more than 825 selections on the wine list. Open Monday through Saturday 5:30 to 10pm, Sunday 3 to 9pm. Entrees $17.95 to $32.

Tavola Toscana, 1412 N. Du Pont St. (off Delaware Ave.), Wilmington (☎ **302/654-8001**). Contemporary Tuscan cooking in a soft, elegant dining room with cream-colored stucco walls and gilt-framed mirrors. The restaurant is in a shopping center, but you'll quickly forget that fact once you're inside. Open Monday through Friday 11:30am to 2pm and 5:30 to 10pm, Saturday 5:30 to 10pm, Sunday 5:30 to 9:30pm. Entrees $8 to $15 at lunch, $12 to $24 at dinner.

ATTRACTIONS

Brandywine Battlefield Park, Rte. 1, Chadds Ford (☎ **610/459-3342**). Open Tuesday through Saturday 9am to 5pm and Sunday noon to 5pm. Admission $3.50, $2.50 for seniors, $1.50 for children 6 to 12, free for children under 6.

Brandywine River Museum, Rte. 1, Chadds Ford (☎ **610/388-2700**). Open daily 9:30am to 4:30pm. Admission $5; $2.50 for students, seniors, and children 6 to 12; free for children under 6.

Longwood Gardens, Rte. 1, Kennett Square (☎ **610/388-1000;** www. longwoodgardens.org).November through March, the conservatories are open daily 10am to 5pm. April through October, the conservatories are open daily 10am to 6pm. Memorial Day through Labor Day, the conservatory and grounds are open for the Festival of Fountain on Tuesday, Thursday, and Saturday until 1 hour after dusk (or about 10:30pm). From Thanksgiving through New Year's Day, the gardens are open daily until 9pm. Admission $12 ($8 on Tues), $6 for ages 16 to 20, $2 for children 6 to 15, free for children under 6.

Winterthur, Rte. 52, Winterthur, 6 miles northwest of Wilmington (☎ **800/ 448-3883;** www.winterthur.org). Museum and garden open Monday through Saturday 9am to 5pm and Sunday noon to 5pm. Admission $8; $6 for groups, students, and seniors; $4 for children 5 to 11; free for children under 5 and members. A guided tour is offered for an additional $5 fee.

APPOINTMENT IN SCHUYLKILL COUNTY

by Doreen Carvajal

For a fleeting moment, you are
Julian English and the road is yours, roaring in a sleek Caddie through
scenic highways of fact and fiction, past coal-patch taverns and slatty
wood houses, gin cocktail parties and country clubs vibrating to the
tunes of Tommy Lake's Royal Collegians. The terrain is Schuylkill
County, the shovel-shaped anthracite coal region of eastern
Pennsylvania, which is barely disguised in the plentiful short stories and
novels of John O'Hara, a hard-drinking and cultivated son of Pottsville.

O'Hara first imagined his "Pennsylvania protectorate," as he called
it, from his retreat at the Pickwick Arms Hotel in Manhattan in 1933.
Typing on a new portable typewriter with an all-black ribbon, he created a parallel world in *Appointment in Samarra*, with its fictional
county of Latenengo populated by the fashionable young married set of
the whirling 1920s and a doomed small-town aristocrat named Julian
English who ended his life in a sealed garage with his Cadillac running.

Known locally as "the Region," Schuylkill County lost its prosperous sheen of wealth with the decline, beginning in the 1940s, of the
coal industry. Yet the territory remains a literary retreat; its melancholy
history and early 19th-century architecture are still fresh characters in
one of America's enduring examples of the "locale a clef."

The term is Matthew J. Bruccoli's whimsical description of vivid
fictional settings with tap roots in reality, like William Faulkner's
Yoknapatawpha (Lafayette County, Mississippi), Thomas Wolfe's
Altamont (Asheville, North Carolina), or Sherwood Anderson's
Winesburg (Clyde, Ohio).

"Driving around Schuylkill County, I had a shock of recognition," said Mr. Bruccoli, O'Hara's biographer and an English professor at the University of South Carolina. "John O'Hara had not just mastered the details, but had managed to get everything right. He had done it in such a way that for people reading about his communities 60 years later, to make it possible for them to have not just an understanding but a feeling for place."

With its grand mansions ascending the hills of Mahantongo Street, Pottsville is the inspiration for O'Hara's fictional community, Gibbsville, Pennsylvania, featured in two other novels and many of the short stories. So were the surrounding Schuylkill towns that he rechristened with names like Swedish Haven, Mountain City, and Taqua. His renderings in fiction were so precise that each mythical town has a geographical twin on a map of Schuylkill County.

"It doesn't matter what fact you want to check out: it's there and he's telling you the truth about something and it wasn't just fiction," said Pamela MacArthur, a Canadian who has been meticulously exploring his descriptions for her doctoral thesis at the University of Sussex in England. Ms. MacArthur said she had checked his references, from a description of the Lenape Indians to the style of a particular fence, and detected no flaws. "When he was being interviewed, he would say it's the novelist's idea," she said. "But when you come down to it, it was fact."

Son of a Surgeon

The oldest son of an affluent local surgeon, O'Hara was born here in 1905. He worked for 2 years as a reporter on *The Pottsville Journal.* In 1928, he left the area for a reporting job in New York. There, he began writing the first of his torrent of short stories that eventually totaled more than 400. *Appointment in Samarra,* his first book, earned him success, notoriety, and 10th place on the Publishers Weekly best-seller list.

O'Hara, who died in 1970, went on to write 13 more novels, most set outside the region. *Butterfield 8, Ten North Frederick, From the Terrace,* and *A Rage to Live* were made into films; *Pal Joey* became a Broadway musical as well as a Hollywood film starring Frank Sinatra.

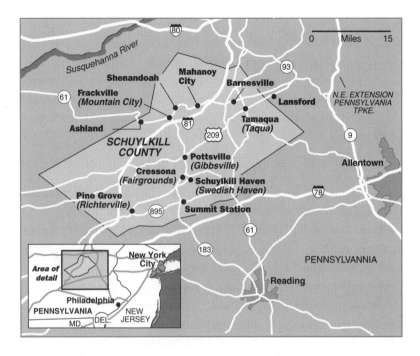

O'Hara's hometown, Pottsville, is the economic hub of Schuylkill County. A city of 16,000 people, it is dominated at its crest by an 18th-century stone courthouse and jail fortress, where six Irish Catholic "Molly Maguire" miners convicted of murdering a constable and a mine boss were hanged on June 21, 1877, a Thursday known as "The Day of the Rope."

Legend has it that Molly Maguire was an Irish widow unjustly evicted from her home, inspiring an anti-landlord movement in the early 19th century in Ireland. Irish miners here, who adopted the name in tribute to those rebels, were caught up in violent struggles that pitted miners against mining bosses, Catholics against Protestants, and Irish against Welsh, English, Scottish, and German immigrant workers. The county historical society at 14 North 3rd Street still houses the original Molly Maguire's trial transcripts, dated newspaper clippings, and even hanks of the ropes that were used to hang the men.

But I confess that my husband and I were drawn to a more unconventional museum, the imposing brick headquarters of Yuengling

Brewery, founded in 1829 by a German immigrant, with its vivid blue-and-white stained-glass ceiling and a dark wooden bar where beer samples are served in plastic cups. Through good times, it has supplied the local citizenry with local ales, and during Prohibition with watered-down 0.05% alcohol brews labeled "near beer." The brewery remains in Yuengling family hands, offering weekday tours and sample tastings of its Porter and Lord Chesterfield ale.

A Fictional Double

Just footsteps from the brewery is the graceful three-story Victorian town house at 606 Mahantongo, where O'Hara spent 12 years of his boyhood and young adult life. A prominent iron plaque marks the home, painted in gray-and-burgundy trim, but there are no tours of the interior because the house has been carved into apartments.

But it doesn't take much to transport a dedicated reader from Mahantongo to its fictional double, Lantenengo Street, a gracious neighborhood of the coal-town upper crust that produced its most eligible brides. Across the street from O'Hara's home are the grand white pillars of the Braun School of Music. And rising up the hill are gingerbread Victorians with spacious porches and the Tudor Jacobean Revival mansion that housed three generations of Yuengling brewers.

Schuylkill County has always been a rather uneasy host to O'Hara's legacy. Today it is more likely to celebrate the memory of the rebellious Irish miners who challenged their bosses rather than O'Hara, who challenged the pretensions of the indulgent country club set. He described that group in *Appointment in Samarra* as "the spenders and drinkers and socially secure, who could thumb their noses and not have to answer to anyone except their families."

O'Hara's literature is rarely used as a teaching tool in the region, said Mark T. Major, a local historian and the executive director of the Schuylkill County Visitors Bureau. "The Molly Maguires just seem more exciting, while John O'Hara isn't as popular," he said.

So excitement here is the Pennsylvania Dutch Folk Festival, or the Molly Maguire weekend. That event will feature a concert, a dramatic reading of the last words of the condemned men hanged in Pottsville, and a walking tour of Mahanoy City, in the footsteps of Irish and native firefighters who rioted in 1834.

"Usually we re-enact the murder of a Tamaqua policeman that led to the hanging of five Irish, but people were getting tired of it," Mr. Major added regretfully.

Of Sweets Past

Still, you don't need a formal festival to celebrate John O'Hara country when you can sample the sweetness of a peanut butter roll just like the ones the author savored in his youth. At Mootz Candies on South Centre Street in Pottsville, the third generation of the Mootz family is still stirring up coconut creams, porcupines, pink meltaways, and black diamond coal candy—licorice that comes with its own coal bin.

We made our own homage to O'Hara by roaming through Schuylkill County in search of abandoned coal breakers and O'Hara-vintage country clubs where perhaps the throbbing urge of Gershwin music could still evoke the sensations of "a tea dance at the club and a girl in a long black satin dress," as he wrote in *Imagine Kissing Pete,* a short story published in the *New Yorker* in the late 1930s.

At the Lakeside Ballroom in Barnesville, a country club where O'Hara's characters did indeed toss down rye cocktails, the orchestra wasn't vibrating with Gershwin tunes. But we did stumble into a "Polka Blast" in full explosion, with members of the Polka Family Band serenading the Coal Crackers Polka Association below a deep blue simulated sky and a whirling mirrored ball.

After a vigorous polka workout, we retreated to the refuge of Mahanoy City, a small town that was once home to an old German brewery that produced Kaier's beer and, of course, the firemen's riot. The brewery has long since closed, but the Victorian mansion built and inhabited by Charles D. Kaier and his heirs is now an opulent bed-and-breakfast with parquet floors, marble fireplaces, chestnut wainscoting, and 12-foot-high ceilings.

Mining & Beer

The beer baron's mansion is within easy touring distance of several museums that dwell on the region's coal-mining past. In Ashland, visitors to Pioneer Tunnel can take an underground tour of a horizontal drift mine that runs 1,800 feet into the side of Mahanoy Mountain. And about a half-hour drive from Mahanoy City, in neighboring Carbon County, is Eckley Miners' Village, a 19th-century coal patch, or company town. Eckley's wooden houses have been preserved by the state and were featured in the 1969 movie *The Molly Maguires,* with Sean Connery and Richard Harris.

During most of our journey, we found ourselves simply touring the map of O'Hara's Pennsylvania protectorate, although at a much more leisurely speed than the author's character, Julian English, who drove as if he really did own the road.

We passed through Cressona and Pine Grove, Tamaqua and Frackville, each with a matching literary double in the pages of O'Hara's literature. We traveled with a library copy of *Gibbsville, Pa.* and *Appointment in Samarra,* the latter a Modern Library edition with yellowing pages and delicate text bookmarked at a literary guarantee from O'Hara: "How much of this novel is all true? It's all true, a rather pompous remark that needs extending."

COVERING THE GROUND OF O'HARA'S PENNSYLVANIA PROTECTORATE: ESSENTIALS

GETTING THERE

To reach Schuylkill County from Manhattan, take the Holland Tunnel to the New Jersey Turnpike Extension (Interstate 78) to Interstate 78 West. Continue on Interstate 78 West to State Rd. 61 (exit 9); continue northwest on State Rd. 61.

ACCOMMODATIONS

Kaier Mansion Bed and Breakfast, 729 E. Center St., Mahanoy City (☎ 570/ 773-3040). In the heart of the anthracite mining region, this Victorian mansion was built by a local brewmaster. It features 12-foot ceilings, a marble fireplace, and the owner's antique dolls. Daily rates, based on double occupancy and incluing breakfast, range $55 to $75.

Stone House Bed and Breakfast, 16 Dock St., Schuylkill Haven (☎ **570/385-2115**). The owners of a local orthopedic shoe factory built this immaculate and imposing stone double house in 1928. Decorated with antiques, it features a small stone teahouse in the garden. Daily rates, based on double occupancy and including full breakfast, range $65 to $75.

DINING

Coal Street Cafe, 22 W. Coal St., Shenandoah (☎ **570/462-9929**). On some nights, a piano player belts out "When Irish Eyes Are Smiling" below lime-green lights twinkling in tribute to the Irish immigrants who settled in the county. The food is fine, but beware of crowds on weekends. Open Monday through Friday 11am to 2pm; Monday and Thursday 5 to 9pm; Sunday noon to 5pm, Friday and Saturday 5 to 10pm.

Dutch Kitchen Restaurant, Rte. 61, Frackville (☎ **570/874-3265**). A comfortable home-style restaurant that offers basic Pennsylvania Dutch recipes: chunky chicken pot pie and coleslaw, as well as steaming pierogi that make you nostalgic for covered-dish church suppers. Open daily 7am to 10pm.

New Garfield Diner, 402 W. Market St., Pottsville (☎ **570/628-2199**). Bing Crosby still croons "Dear Old Donegal" on the jukeboxes of this diner, which is decorated with turquoise booths, pink-speckled tile, and a black-and-white photograph that is a testimony to John F. Kennedy's appearance here in 1960. For less than $5, customers get groaning plates of comfort food: meatloaf, roast chicken, and mashed potatoes. Open daily, 24 hours.

Moot Candies, 220 S. Center St., Pottsville (☎ **570/622-4480**). This specialty chocolate shop is open Monday and Thursday through Saturday 9:30am to 5:30pm.

ATTRACTIONS

Museum of Anthracite Mining, 17th and Pine Sts., Ashland (☎ **570/875-4708**. Open April to November, Wednesday to Sunday 10am to 6pm; closed December to March. Call for admission prices.

No. 9 Mine Museum, Dock and Lansford, off Rte. 209, Lansford (☎ **570/645-7074**). Tours of the mine are scheduled beginning in the summer of 2001. Call for information.

Eckley Miners' Village, Highland Rd., Freeland (☎ **570/636-2070**). Open Monday through Friday 9am to 5pm; Saturday and Sunday 10am to 5pm. Admission $3.50, $3 for seniors, $1.50 for children under 12, $8.50 for a family of four. Guided tours $1.50 for adults and seniors, 50¢ for children under 12.

Lakeside Ballroom, Rte. 54, off Interstate 81 (exit 37), Barnesville (☎ **570/467-2630**). Hours and admission vary with events. Call for more information.

Molly Maguire Weekend. Held mid-June at sites throughout Schuylkill and neighboring counties; includes exhibitions, walking tours, performances, dinners, receptions, and other events. For information call ☎ **800/765-7282,** or check the Schuylkill County Web site www.schuylkill.org.

Pennsylvania Dutch Folk Festival, Schuylkill County Fairgrounds, Summit Station, off Rte. 895 East. An annual celebration with entertainment, education, and pageantry. From mid-June to early July, daily 10am to 8pm. Admission $10, $5 for children 5 to 12, free for children under 5. For more information check their Web site at www.dutchfest.com or call ☎ 800/765-7282.

Pioneer Tunnel Coal Mine, Pioneer Tunnel Coal Mine, 19th and Oak sts., Ashland (☎ 570/875-3850; www. pioneertunnel. com). Open Memorial Day through Labor Day, daily 10am to 6pm; limited hours April through the end of May, mid-September, October, and November; closed December through March. Admission for coal mine tour $7, $4.50 for children 2 to 11, free for children under 2; for the steam train $5, $3.50 for children 2 to 11, free for children under 2.

Yuengling Brewery, 5th and Mahantongo sts., Pottsville (☎ 570/622-4141). Open Monday through Friday 9am to 4pm; tours at 10am and 1:30pm. Free admission.

FURTHER READING

Here is a list of books by John O'Hara set in the area: *Appointment in Samarra* (Random House; $14.50 hardcover, $10 paperback); *Gibbsville, PA* (Carroll & Graf; $27.95 hardcover, $17.95 paperback); *The Lockwood Concern* (originally published by Random House in 1965; reissued by Carroll & Graf in 1986, but out of print; copies at libraries and used bookstores); *Ten North Frederick* (originally published by Random House in 1955; reissued by Caroll & Graf in 1985, but out of print; copies at libraries and used bookstores).

STEAMING THROUGH A WORLD THAT TIME LEFT BEHIND

by William McDonald

THIS IS OLD-TIME PENNSYLVANIA railroad country, but there was nothing of the Rust Belt about it: There was no soot in the air, no grime to speak of, no debris scattered in weeds along the track beds. The landscape was actually scenic, and for a camera-toting tourist at the heart of it, in the historic town of Strasburg, there were plenty of pretty shots to be had—a Georgian brick home serenely overlooking a shady Main Street, a white barn and silo standing crisply by a green pasture, a Victorian station restored to its gabled glory. All with photo-album potential.

But if there's one image from Strasburg that I'll surely keep—one that managed in a single frame to sum up the place, as well as my main reason for being there—it is a picture my camera didn't get. The setting was a coach of an antique train, its iron-horse locomotive billowing steam across a swath of southeastern Pennsylvania farmland on a 9-mile round-trip jaunt between Strasburg and a forlorn-looking junction called, without a trace of irony, "Paradise." The coach, as tall as a lamppost, was rocking and groaning as the train lumbered across fields newly sprouting with corn and rye, signs of late spring in Lancaster County.

A conductor in blue with a handlebar mustache brushed by as he pushed his way up the aisle, and my eyes got pulled along in his wake, drifting from the bobbing heads of passengers to the varnished oak paneling all around to the brass chandeliers swaying overhead.

I think it was the shriek of the locomotive's whistle that summoned me back to the window, or maybe it was just a parent's sixth sense, but I turned to see that my 3-year-old son had poked his head out from under the raised wooden sash and was drinking in sights this New York boy had never seen. I didn't want to lose him, so I grabbed him by the elastic waist of his blue jeans, tugged him inside a bit and didn't let go. Outside, a turkey farm rolled by, then a gang of dull-eyed cows lazing by the tracks, then the Cherry Hill depot, which isn't much of a depot at all but rather a whitewashed wood-frame booth planted by the side of a grade crossing.

It was right about there that the elements of my indelible picture began to arrange themselves. Fifty yards off or so, in a field furrowed as evenly as corduroy, a plow pulled by a team of six horses came into view. Riding on a cross-piece and gripping the reins was a boy of no more than 12. He was wearing a floppy white straw hat, a homespun powder-blue shirt, and a pair of black suspenders holding up his, well, britches. He might have even been barefoot. As the train chugged by, it let out a whoop, and the boy turned and waved.

Freeze frame. Two distinct, even clashing, American traditions had fortuitously and visibly converged: the steam railroad, harbinger of a mechanized age, and the peaceful Plain People, shunners of technological progress, both evoking in their different ways the romance and simplicity of life in the 19th century—or at least our sepia-tinted view of it from the lip of the 21st.

For an instant, the view was a distillation of Strasburg (population 2,600), where the country lanes of the Amish and the railroad tracks of yesteryear intersect. And completing the tableau, at the center of the frame, was a 3-year-old, who had brought us to this point.

Like many a child bolting from toddlerhood, my son has a passion for trains, mostly of the toy variety. (In his case it may be genetic: a great-grandfather was a railroad man on the New Haven line.) And like many parents of children who are both uncontainable and urban—an often incompatible mix—my wife and I needed to get out of the city for a few days and into some unwalled space. The Strasburg area promised to satisfy all parties. It's pastoral, but it's also command central for railroad buffs, being home to one of the oldest operating steam rail lines in America, with a magnificent railroad museum next door, and enough toy trains to occupy even the most fidgety enthusiast, of any age.

A Train Lover's Playground

Our first stop on entering Strasburg was the railroad station, even though we'd come by car, after a 3½-hour drive from New York. Built in 1882 and now fully restored, the station—it's actually the East Strasburg Station—is the centerpiece of a tourist site that's one part living history, one part museum, and one part small-scale theme park. The grounds contain a railroad memorabilia gift shop, a toy train store (a must-see for us), a sweets emporium, a restaurant called the "Dining Car," and a portrait studio in which you can pose stiffly in 19th-century dress advertised as authentic.

You can also tour a restored luxury suite on rails, built for the big shots of the Philadelphia & Reading line in 1916. The coach, with cut-glass ceiling lamps and mahogany paneling inlaid with rosewood, cost a hefty $100,000 to build, the equivalent of $1 million today. It houses separate sitting and dining rooms, three bedrooms, and a full kitchen with bunks for the stewards and chef.

But the real attraction is the Strasburg Rail Road itself, the nation's oldest short-line railroad. Founded in 1832, it became a tourist operation in 1958. Today the line has four fearsomely voracious steam engines, consuming 1,000 gallons of water and a half-ton of hand-shoveled coal per mile, and 14 restored wooden coaches, each with its own 19th-century decor and degree of comfort.

The basic coaches are hardly austere; they come with plush uphol-stered seats, brass-trimmed interiors of polished wood and stained glass, with a working wood stove in one corner. The first-class parlor car, which you can ride for a few dollars more than the usual $8.75 adult fare, is furnished with Gilded Age sofas, tables inlaid with checker-boards, and a bar. One might be tempted to light up a cigar and order a scotch if only the rules permitted it, and if only the bar served alco-holic drinks. Riders can also choose a yellow open-air observation car that was used in the movie *Hello Dolly,* or a dining car that serves both lunch and dinner by reservation.

In the spirit of our journalistic mission, we took two trips of 45 minutes each, riding in a standard coach the first time and the dining car the other. I can report that the basic coach alone would have been fine; my son was amused to be served a hot dog on a train, but his par-ents found the food unappetizing and unbefitting the stately coach in which it was served.

But, then again, you don't come for the food. The feel of history is the thing, and the train provides that in abundance, transporting you back as it trundles through countryside that does its part in stoking the illusion of times gone by.

This area, after all, is home to the Amish; from the train you can see the bearded men in wide-brimmed hats driving horse-drawn bug-gies and hay wagons, the children riding wooden scooters, the bon-neted women hanging hand-washed clothes on the line. The train remains at a respectful remove, but you can hardly observe the Amish from a century-old coach and not imagine you're looking into the past.

The imperatives of the present moment can also be strong, and after a few hours of railroading we were ready for our room at the Historic Strasburg Inn, just outside the center of town. The Railroad Museum of Pennsylvania, directly across the road from the station, would have to wait.

The Historic Strasburg Inn is something of a misnomer. For one thing, it's not really an inn; for another, it's not really historic. Rather, sit-ting imposingly in the middle of a 58-acre spread, it's a 101-room hotel complex done up in colonial style while offering modern amenities:

an outdoor pool, a hot tub, an exercise room, and two restaurants—the casual By George Tavern, which has outdoor dining, and the Washington House, an elegant, white-tablecloth establishment offering plain, over-priced fare.

So one doesn't necessarily go there for the food, either. But in other respects the hotel, among the best in the area, suited us well, providing a comfortable suite and plenty of room for a child to run free as well as swings, a playhouse, and a jungle gym out back. Indeed, the small but true inns in town generally do not allow young children.

History & Local Shoppes

We learned this on a quick walking tour of the Strasburg historic district after unpacking and collecting ourselves. The old town, originally settled about 1733 by Swiss Mennonites, who named it after the cathedral city in Alsace, is clustered around two intersecting streets, Main and Decatur. Main Street has known traffic since at least 1714, when it was part of the Old Conestoga Road, the first westward trail from Philadelphia. Today, dozens of brick, stone, and wood-frame homes, dating from the late 18th century and well into the 19th, line these streets; among them are several 250-year-old log houses that put you in mind of settlers in buckskin shouldering muskets.

The district also has a few stores and businesses, and happily, by all appearances, they're quite local—there's not a Benneton or a Starbucks in sight. There is, for example, Sadie's Rose, which advertises "home-made crafts and canned foods." At Mrs. Penn's Shoppe (gifts and watch repair), a portly Amish man sat on a bench by the door, alternately reading his Bible and dozing. And outside the Yule Shoppe a posted sign pleaded, AMISH FRIENDS PLEASE CLEAN UP AFTER YOUR HORSES!

Which is not to say that Strasburg is just a hitching post, untouched by the wide world. A couple of miles away is Route 30, a deadening strip of outlet malls and fast-food filling stations worthy of Anywhere, U.S.A. And right in town, a coffee shop, Merenda Zug, which doubles as an antiques store, boasts of offering a blend served in restaurants like Le Bernardin and Daniel in New York. On the other hand, there was nothing pretentious about the Strasburg Country Store and Creamery, which dispenses the best ice cream around. And though two of the finer inns in the district, the Strasburg Village Inn and the Limestone Inn, were graciously fitted out, there was nothing stuffy about them. Indeed, the Limestone's proprietor, Denise Waller, exhibited the manner of a solicitous house mother toward her mostly young guests as she took me on a tour of her 213-year-old establishment.

I'd like to say that we wished we had had more time to nose around the historic district, but in truth there wasn't a lot more to see; you can get the flavor of it in an hour. Besides, there was Amish country to explore, and we had a young train aficionado to tend to. So the next day, as planned, we headed back to the railroad museum, about a mile up the road. We were glad we did. The museum is a cool, cavernous 100,000-square-foot barn housing almost 100 pieces of rolling stock along parallel concrete platforms reminiscent of the grand terminals of Europe. One needn't be a railroad buff (I'm not, or at least wasn't) to be impressed and fascinated by this collection. The stock, all either made or used in Pennsylvania, ranges from an 1855 Cumberland Valley baggage and passage car (ONE OF THE OLDEST PIECES OF RAILROAD EQUIPMENT IN EXISTENCE, the sign said) to a modern behemoth, a snub-nosed 1963 diesel freight locomotive. In between are 100 years and untold tons of coaches, cabooses, mail cars, Pullman cars, restaurant cars, private executive coaches, and a big complement of locomotives.

Trains to Go

The museum more than satisfied my and my wife's curiosity about trains; in short, we'd had enough. But my son had other ideas after spotting a store called the "Choo Choo Barn" (which features an animated 1,700-square-foot working display), and next to it a franchise outlet for the Thomas the Tank Engine line of toy trains. So we pulled in off the road, only to emerge an hour later a little wearied but with a new addition to our Thomas set in hand. That, too, might have sufficiently capped our railroad weekend, but as we were leaving Strasburg we decided to go the distance and see the last remaining train attractions in town: the National Toy Train Museum and, next door to it, the oddest motel we'd ever encountered. The museum houses an extensive collection of toy trains and five lavish working layouts that even a 3-year-old can operate. But the Red Caboose Motel and Restaurant is of a more surprising order. It must be the only extant motel consisting entirely of cabooses—more than 30 of them, each refurbished and strung end-to-end in three rows on a lot beside the Strasburg tracks.

The founder, Don Denlinger, a garrulous Mennonite and a native of Lancaster County, can explain how, as a younger man, he came to own the cabooses, which were destined for scrap. He made a $100 bid for them as a lark in 1970, and now, eccentric as it is, the business is altogether right for this patch of railroad country and is thriving, helped in small part by a buggy-ride service on the premises.

It was from the driver's seat of a buggy, in fact, that Mr. Denlinger told us about his motel before turning down a road into Amish country. Then he began unspooling stories about the families in these parts: about the 90-year-old patriarch Gideon Lapp and his seven sons; about an 11-year-old boy who was killed in a horrible farm accident, and whose mother, Mr. Denlinger said, "fainted dead away on the spot." At one point we passed a youth walking by the side of the road. "Enoch, get a horse!" Mr. Denlinger shouted, laughing. New York was still a few hours and another state of mind away. For the time being, we were content just to roll on to the clip-clop of hooves. Every so often, from a distance, from another time, we'd hear a train whistle blow.

From Here to a Place Called Paradise: Essentials

GETTING THERE

By Car From New York, take Interstate 95 to the New Jersey Turnpike, south to Exit 6, then west on the Pennsylvania Turnpike to Exit 21, Rte. 222. South to Lancaster, exiting at U.S. Rte. 30. Follow Rte. 30 for 7 miles east to County Rte. 896, then south to Rte. 741 (Main St. in Strasburg).

By Train Amtrak (☎ 800/872-7245) provides daily service from Penn Station in Manhattan to Lancaster, 8 miles north of Strasburg; round-trip fare ranges $88 to $104; half price for children 5 to 11. A taxi ride (☎ 717/392-2222) from the train station to Strasburg costs $12 to $20 each way.

By Bus Martz Trailways (☎ 800/233-8604) provides bus service from the Port Authority Bus Terminal in Manhattan to Strasburg. Round-trip fare: $39.25; half price for children 2 to 11.

ACCOMMODATIONS

Historic Strasburg Inn, 1 Historic Dr., off Rte. 896, Strasburg, PA 17579 (☎ 800/872-0201; www.historicstrasburginn.com). Room rates, based on double occupancy, range from $99 to $289 and include breakfast.

Limestone Inn, 33 E. Main St., Strasburg (☎ 800/278-8392 or 717/687-8392. Double room rate $75 to $110, includes breakfast.

Red Caboose Motel, 312 Paradise Lane, off Rte. 741, Strasburg (☎ 717/687-5000). July 4 through Labor Day, $69 to $105; otherwise, $39 to $69.

Strasburg Village Inn, 1 W. Main St., Strasburg (☎ 717/687-0900). April 10 through June 11, $79 to $144; June 12 through October, $94 to $159; November through April 9, $69 to $134. Rates based on double occupancy.

DINING

By George Tavern, 1 Historic Dr., Rte. 896, Strasburg (☎ 800/872-0201 or 717/687-9211). Open Sunday through Thursday noon to 10pm; Friday and Saturday noon to 11pm (or later).

Iron Horse Inn, 135 E. Main St., Strasburg (☎ 717/687-6362). Open daily; call for hours.

Washington House, 1 Historic Dr., off Rte. 896, Strasburg (☎ 800/872-0201 or 717/687-9211). Open Monday through Friday 5 to 9pm, Saturday 4 to 10pm, Sunday 4 to 9pm.

ATTRACTIONS

Strasburg Rail Road, Rte. 741 East (P.O. Box 96), Strasburg (☎ 717/687-7522; srrtrain@strasburgrailroad.com). Open daily April through the end of October; November, December, and mid-February through March, weekends only; closed January through mid-February. Call for schedule. Adult fares $8.75, children 3 to 11 $4.50, free under 3.

Railroad Museum of Pennsylvania, Rte. 741 East (P.O. Box 125), Strasburg (☎ 717/687-8628; www.rrhistorical.com/frm). Open Monday through Saturday 9am to 5pm, Sunday noon to 5pm. Closed

Monday from November through March. Admission adults, $6, seniors $5.50, children 6 to 12 $4, free under 5.

National Toy Train Museum, 300 Paradise Lane, off Rte. 741, Strasburg (☎ 717/687-8976; www.traincollectors.org/toytrain.html). Open daily May through October; weekends November, December, and April; closed January through March. Open 10am to 5pm. Admission $3, seniors $2.75, children 5 to 12 $1.50, under 5 free.

Connecticut

THREE PATHS OF HISTORY

by William Grimes

SPRING IS THE SEASON OF NOBLE intentions. The old, shriveled winter creature you behold in the mirror cries out for renewal. So does that gray-tinged complexion. What better way to register the change of season than a self-improvement program that combines outdoor recreation with mental stimulation? Both in moderation, of course.

An ideal spring program is at hand in the dozens of small towns and cities across Connecticut, each with its own historical society that offers walking tours. Some are guided by local historians, on a fixed schedule or as demand arises. Others are self-guided. That is, history-minded flaneurs can pick up a brochure and set forth, beholding the local wonders, free to think their own thoughts and form their own impressions.

A few towns, like Hartford and Litchfield, rent or sell audiocassette guides, allowing visitors to stroll or drive as they like. In a bid for glamour, the Huntington Historical Society offers a cassette guide to Southport narrated by Jason Robards.

Not all tours are created equal. Some focus on architecture, others on local worthies and eminent trees, while still others memorialize the brief, sometimes ephemeral brushes with greatness every town likes to claim.

Wethersfield had its moment. Until the late 18th century, it was known primarily for its red onions and for an infestation of witches in the 1640s that included a husband-and-wife team. In May 1781, however, destiny came knocking at the door of Joseph Webb, a merchant. Into his red clapboard house on Main Street walked George

Washington, accompanied by the Comte de Rochambeau. The two men, sitting at a table in what is now called the Council Room, laid plans for a decisive southward push by American and French forces.

Washington slept not 1 but 4 nights at the stark, rather barnlike clapboard structure, which was built in the 1750s and still stands steady as a rock, flanked by two other mid-18th-century houses. Together with the Buttolph-Williams House, the three make up the Webb-Deane-Stevens Museum, and they are the subject of a 1-hour guided tour that is strong on the details of Colonial domestic life and architecture.

Visitors who note with surprise the rather flashy interior colors of the Webb house, which includes a stunning china cupboard in blue, mustard, and red with a scallop-shell dome, will learn that Early American homes, lacking electricity, relied on bright interior paints to lighten rooms.

Visitors in the fall will take pleasure in the large and quite realistic plastic turkey on the dining room table of the Silas Deane house, and the surrounding pies and vegetable dishes that indicate a Thanksgiving feast. The meal changes seasonally. Because several of the Deanes fell victim to tuberculosis, an upstairs bedroom has been set up as a sickroom, with a handsome mahogany medicine chest on a nightstand. One of the chest's small drawers contains strands of copper wire, and by way of explanation, my guide delivered the kind of eye-opening 30-minute treatise that fully justified the modest cost of the tour. "The copper wires were stirred in vinegar, and the resulting chemical reaction created verdigris," she said. "When you mixed it with a liquid to disguise the taste and then drank it, it alleviated chest pains, although it did nothing for the tuberculosis. So if you ever see a little drawer like that with copper wires in it, that's what they were for."

With my store of knowledge enlarged by one eminently repeatable fact, I felt edified, yet not fatigued. This was as good as anything in *Bill and Ted's Excellent Adventure.*

Wethersfield is the ideal town for a half-day history tour. One of the most perfectly preserved Colonial towns in Connecticut, it has 150 buildings dating before 1850, and the Olde Towne Tourism District—

yes, unfortunately, that's how it's spelled—has a detailed brochure with an annotated map that allows visitors to stroll, look, and absorb at their own pace.

For atmosphere, read *The Witch of Blackbird Pond* by Elizabeth Speare or *Harvest Home* and *The Other* by Thomas Tryon. All are set in Wethersfield. Then walk up and down Main Street, making sure to press as far north as Wethersfield Cove, the town's thriving harbor until a flood in 1692 swept away six warehouses and permanently altered the Connecticut River's course. Overnight, the port became an inlet.

On the way back, take a detour to see the Buttolph-Williams House (1720) on Broad Street. Imposing and stern, it figures prominently in *The Witch of Blackbird Pond*. Finish up with a visit to the Ancient Burying Ground, where, legend has it, the nine victims of the 1637 massacre that touched off the Pequot War are buried. The Wethersfield Historical Society offers tours and a printed guide to the cemetery.

The Industrial Revolution passed Wethersfield by. Instead of machine shops and mills, the 19th century left the gentle, benevolent legacy of Comstock, Ferre (pronounced Ferry), the oldest continually operating seed company in the United States. Stop in and buy a packet of seeds for the famous Wethersfield red onion, which was once shipped from the cove to ports up and down the East Coast, and all the way to the Orient.

The store's manager, Roger Willard, is rather restrained in his sales pitch for the local product. "There's nothing so great about it," he said, "except that it made Wethersfield famous."

A Town Near Hartford

Just a few miles west of Wethersfield is the once-mighty town of Farmington, so famous in the 19th century that when Mark Twain was introduced to Queen Victoria as a citizen of Hartford, he pointed out, helpfully, that Hartford was a town near Farmington.

Farmington is another half-day town with some good history to it and, of course, a local historical society with a can-do attitude. Once the 12th-wealthiest town in the 13 colonies, Farmington has an abundance of 17th-century houses.

Visitors should contact the Farmington Historical Society to reserve a place on the Amistad Sights Walking Tour, a 12-stop proposition that traces Farmington's role in the events surrounding the first civil rights case to reach the Supreme Court.

In 1839, 53 adults and children from the Mende region of Sierra Leone, who had been captured and enslaved, were being transported from Havana to Puerto Rico aboard the ship *Amistad*. After a storm blew the ship out to sea and rations were depleted, the Africans, led by Sengbe Pieh, known as "Joseph Cinque," rose up, killed the captain and the cook, seized control of the ship, and tried to head back to Africa.

Instead, the ship touched land at Montauk Point, Long Island, where the Coast Guard picked up the men and transported them to New Haven, where they were put on trial for mutiny and murder. The court ruled that because the Africans had never been slaves before their abduction, they could not be returned to Cuba or be held liable for their acts. The decision was appealed and went to the Supreme Court, where John Quincy Adams helped argue the case for the defense. The high court upheld the lower court's decision. The incident, long treated as little more than a historical footnote, has captured the attention of scholars in recent years, and Steven Spielberg brought it to a larger public in his 1997 film *Amistad*.

The *Amistad* case galvanized the Abolitionist movement. Farmington, an abolitionist hotbed and a stop on the underground railroad, played host to the Mende natives, who lived and worked in the town while money was raised to send them back to Africa.

Peg Yung, a vice president of the Farmington Historical Society, leads tours of the Amistad Sights trail by request. A second local historian, Ernest R. Shaw, runs a business, Heritage Trails Sightseeing Tours. Most of the time, he's busy taking small bands of tourists around Hartford on daily tours at $15 a pop, but his schedule also includes three Farmington tours.

On the Ancient Evening Cemetery Tour, Mr. Shaw takes visitors through two graveyards, one dating from 1660. Informed sources say that there is sometimes a little surprise in one of the graveyards that elicits shrieks. On the Colonial Dinner Tour, which operates nightly, passengers leave from Hartford's main hotels for a bus tour of Farmington and dinner at an old stagecoach stop, built in 1789.

The Brass Capital

Waterbury, which won and lost in spectacular fashion, is a town that deserves its own Gibbon. Once known as the brass capital of the world, it employed tens of thousands of workers in vast factories that cast, rolled, stamped, and worked brass, the 19th-century equivalent of plastic, into a thousand articles of domestic and industrial use, including pins, buttons, kettles, architectural hardware, lighting devices, photographic equipment, and the famous Ingersoll dollar watches that sold in the millions. By 1890, the city was producing 60% of the nation's brass.

In the city's heyday, from 1850 to the end of World War I, the brass barons and the wealthy of Waterbury built some dazzling houses and mansions in the Hillside District, which has 327 buildings listed with the National Register of Historic Places. The reigning style is Queen Anne; that is, an eclectic (some would say indiscriminate) conglomeration of turrets, towers, wraparound porches, peaks, and gables, with bright colors pointing up the gingerbread details.

New Yorkers will find some familiar names in Waterbury. Fulton Park was created by the firm of Frederick Law Olmsted, who designed Central Park with Calvert Vaux. Waterbury's brick, marble, and granite city hall is one of five buildings designed by Cass Gilbert, the architect who designed the Woolworth Building and the Custom House in Manhattan.

The Mattatuck Museum in downtown Waterbury is a lively little institution with an innovative program of history tours that allows visitors to get a fix on the social and architectural history of Hillside and the Gilbert District and also venture into the newer area of industrial history. It offers a bicycle or trolley tour that retraces Waterbury's manufacturing history. In addition to stopping off at industrial sites, the tour takes pains to provide a kind of illustrated social history. On Wood Street and Oak Street, the Scovill Company built two-story single-family row houses during World War I, each with a different facade to reflect a different national style, for their managers. The workers got barracks.

The tour is also valuable in lending specificity to arid terms like "industrial decline" and "retooling for the future." It is a poignant reminder of how difficult it is for a town to refashion its self-image. The signs of that struggle are evident everywhere in Waterbury, which has sagged badly since the brass industry moved overseas in the 1950s.

"I've been really impressed with the craftsmen here," said Marianne Vandenburgh, a former Ohioan who now owns the House on the Hill, a bed-and-breakfast establishment on Hillside, who carried out an extensive kitchen renovation. "I think it's because this is a town where people made things, and the tradition of working with your hands has been passed along from grandfather to father to grandson. That also may be a reason why it's hard for Waterbury to think of itself in a different way." Despite its troubles, Waterbury has beauty and charm. As a historical text, it makes rich reading, and its most compelling chapters may well be those of sad decline, which, as Gibbon knew, speaks more truthfully about the human condition than triumphant ascent.

ESSENTIALS

WETHERSFIELD

GETTING THERE

By Car From New York City, take I-287 North, then follow I-95 North to exit 48 (I-91 North) at New Haven. Proceed north to exit 26 for Wethersfield.

By Train Amtrak (☎ 800/872-7245) has service to Hartford; from there, you can reach Wethersfield, 5 miles south of Hartford, by taxi.

ACCOMMODATIONS

Butternut Farm, 1654 Main St., Glastonbury (☎ 860/633-7197). Bed-and-breakfast in a Colonial farmhouse with antique furniture and a dynamic goose named Harry. Two rooms with private bathrooms, plus a suite and an apartment with private bathrooms. Rates $79 to $99 double, breakfast included. To reach the inn from New York, take I-91 or Rte. 2 to Glastonbury; from the center of town, drive south on Main St. 1.6 miles to the inn; enter from Whapley Rd. From Wethersfield, take Rte. 3, cross the bridge, and follow Rte. 2 East to exit 8 (Glastonbury Center), which leads to Main St.

Chester Bulkley House, 184 Main St., Wethersfield (☎ 860/563-4236). Bed-and-breakfast in an 1830 Greek Revival house with five rooms, three with private bathroom, and a suite available on request. Rates $85 double with shared bathroom, $95 with private bathroom; $180 suite.

ATTRACTIONS

Webb-Deane-Stevens Museum, 211 Main St., Wethersfield (☎ 860/529-0612). The museum offers tours and programs throughout the year. Open May to October, Wednesday through Monday 10am to 4pm; November to April, Saturday and Sunday 10am to 4pm. Tours depart on the hour from 10am to 3pm. Admission to house and garden tour $8, $7 for seniors and AAA members, $4 for students with ID, free for children 5 and under. Group tours may be arranged on specific themes, such as architecture or decorative arts. A self-guided walking tour, A Tour of the Old Village, is available from the museum.

Wethersfield Historical Society (☎ 860/529-7656). The society manages four sites open to the public: the **Old Academy Library,** 150 Main St. (open year-round Tues through Fri 10am to 4pm, Sat 1 to 4pm.; **Wethersfield Museum Keeney Memorial,** 200 Main St. (open Tues through Sat 10am to 4pm, Sun 1 to 4pm; admission $3, free for children under 16); **Cove Warehouse,** Wethersfield Cove (at the north end of Main St.; mid-May to mid-October open weekends, call for hours; admission $1), with exhibits on the town's maritime history; and the **Hurlbut-Dunham House,** 212 Main St., a brick Georgian house updated during the Victorian period (open mid-Mar through Dec, call for hours; admission $3).

FARMINGTON

GETTING THERE

By Car From New York City, take the Hutchinson River Pkwy. and Merritt Pkwy. to Rte. 8. Proceed north to I-84, exit 39 (Farmington); follow Rte. 4 into the center of town.

By Bus Bonanza Buses (☎ 800/556-3815) run between the Port Authority Bus Terminal and Farmington. The fare is $28.95 for a same-day round-trip, $35.30 traveling on different days.

ACCOMMODATIONS

Barney House, 11 Mountain Spring Rd., Farmington (**☎ 860/674-2796**). Built in 1832, Barney House sits on spacious grounds that were formerly the estate of a founder of the Pony Express and Wells Fargo. Call for rates.

ATTRACTIONS

Information on the Farmington Valley may be obtained from the **Farmington Valley Visitors Association,** 5 E. Main St., P.O. Box 1491, Suite 3, Avon, CT 06001 (**☎ 800/493-5266,** or 860/676-8878 in Connecticut).

Hill-Stead Museum, 35 Mountain Rd., Farmington (**☎ 860/677-4787,** or 860/677-9064 for recorded information). This museum, in a 1901 house designed by Stanford White, has a famous Impressionist art collection that includes four Monets, a Degas, a Manet, and two Cassatts. Open May through October, Tuesday through Sunday 10am to 5pm; November through April, Tuesday through Sunday 11am to 4pm. The last tour begins 1 hour before closing. Admission $7, $6 for students and seniors, $4 for children 6 to 12, free for children under 6 and museum members.

Stanley-Whitman House, 37 High St. (**☎ 860/677-9222**). This restored 1720 saltbox with period furnishings is open May through October, Wednesday through Sunday noon to 4pm; November through April, Saturday and Sunday noon to 4pm, and at other times by appointment. Admission $5, $4 for seniors, $2 for children over 5, free for children 5 to 18; $3 per person for groups of 10 or more. The house can arrange architectural and other walks for groups.

LOCAL TOUR GUIDES

Heritage Trails Sightseeing Tours (**☎ 860/677-8867**) offers a variety of tours guided by Ernest R. Shaw, a historian. The Farmington Canal Tour, which is offered in mid-May, costs $39.95 and includes lunch in a 1795 inn that once catered to the canal traffic. The Graveyards Tour is offered Memorial Day weekend and nightly in October and includes dinner at a Colonial inn ($34.95). The Colonial Dinner Tour of Farmington operates nightly and costs $29.95. There are also daily tours to Amistad sites in Farmington and black-history freedom trails ($15). Reservations are required for all tours. Heritage Trails also sells two 90-minute self-drive audiocassette tours of Farmington and Hartford for $9.95 each plus $2.50 postage.

Peg Yung (☎ 860/677-2754), vice president of the Farmington Historical Society, offers group walking tours, by request, of Amistad-related sites, with groups of 8 to 20 preferred. The cost is $3 per person, $1 for students, with a $25 group minimum. Call her at the number above, or leave a message at the **Farmington Historical Society (☎ 860/678-1645**).

WATERBURY

GETTING THERE

By Car From New York City, take the Hutchinson River Pkwy. and Merritt Pkwy. to Rte. 8 North to I-84 East, exit 21; or take the Hutchinson River Pkwy. to I-684 to I-84 West, exit 21 (Meadow St.).

By Train Waterbury is on the Waterbury branch of **Metro-North's** New Haven Line (☎ 212/532-4900).

ACCOMMODATIONS

House on the Hill, 92 Woodlawn Terrace, Waterbury (☎ 203/757-9901). Bed-and-breakfast at the top of the Hillside District, in an 1888 Queen Anne extravaganza. Four suites, each with private bathroom. Rates $100 to $175 double, including breakfast.

ATTRACTIONS

Mattatuck Museum, 144 W. Main St., Waterbury (☎ 203/753-0381). The museum offers many historical tours as well as permanent exhibitions on the town's history, and art exhibitions. In addition to Brass Beginnings, a 2½-hour tour of the city's industrial past, there are 1-hour walking tours of the Hillside District, the Cass Gilbert Historic District, the Waterbury Green, and Grand and Bank sts. Tickets for Brass Beginnings are $12 (includes museum admission and slide show); the 1-hour tours cost $8.

For a 1-hour self-guided tour of the Hillside District, consult the museum's brochure *Looking Up the Hillside.* The museum also arranges group tours lasting from a half day to 2 days on the region's architecture and history. It also sponsors "Our Towns," a series of lectures and walking tours. A full schedule is available on request.

HISTORICAL WALKS

Many towns and cities across Connecticut offer history tours. The state's 19 regional tourism councils have detailed information on local organizations and events. The councils' addresses and telephone numbers are listed in the booklet *Connecticut Vacation Guide,* which includes a brochure, *Connecticut Freedom Trail,* that maps out an itinerary of 10 sites associated with the abolition of slavery. The vacation guide is available from the **Tourism Division,** Connecticut Department of Economic Development, 865 Brook St., Rocky Hill, CT 06067-3405 (☎ 800/282-6863, or 860/572-5318 for information on the Freedom Trail).

Local historical societies are also good sources of information. They are listed in the *Directory of Historical Societies and Agencies in the United States and Canada.*

The towns and organizations listed below offer unusually interesting or ambitious history tours:

Antiquarian and Landmarks Society, 66 Forest St., Hartford (☎ 860/247-8996), owns and operates 13 historic houses and properties across the state, 9 of which are open to the public from mid-May to mid-October. Call for hours. Admission per house, $4; $1 for children under 17 years; $15 for five houses. The society also has a particularly good self-guided tour of Suffield, prepared with the Suffield Historical Society; it also offers a color brochure of the society's properties and walking tours of Suffield and Wethersfield.

Connecticut Trust for Historic Preservation, 940 Whitney Ave., Hamden (☎ **203/562-6312**). Self-guided bicycle tours with detailed route descriptions are available in past issues of the trust's bimonthly newsletter. One tour is "Cycling to Historic Town Greens: Winsted to Colebrook to Winchester Center." Contact the trust for more information.

Fairfield Historical Society, 636 Old Post Rd., Fairfield (☎ **203/259-1598**). Brochures outlining three self-guided tours are available at the society's headquarters: *Walking Through History: A Walking Tour of Black Rock and Southport Harbor* ($3.50); *Old Post Road and Town Center Walking Tour* ($1); and *Cameron Clark: Colonial Revival* ($3), a driving tour of Colonial Revival homes designed by Clark. Brochures for two self-guided bicycle tours are available as well: *Tree Bike Tours Through Fairfield's Agricultural Past* ($3) and *Fairfield Bicycle Tour: Travel Back in Time* ($5). The society also offers walking tours of the Old Post Road Historic District every other weekend from April to October ($3 for members, $5 for nonmembers). It also offers occasional tours of Southport and Black Rock.

Greater Middletown Preservation Trust publishes two detailed self-guided tours: *A Walking Tour of Early Middletown, 1650 to 1850,* and *A Walking Tour of Main Street, Middletown.* The tours may be obtained by sending a self-addressed, stamped envelope to the trust at 27 Washington St., Middletown, CT 06457.

Litchfield Historical Society (☎ 860/ 567-4501). The society offers a guided group walking tour of historic Litchfield by appointment, as well as a self-guided brochure ($3).

New Haven Preservation Trust (☎ 203/ 562-5919). The trust offers free guided tours of New Haven's 14 national historic districts and two local historic districts, as well as ethnic historic tours.

Norwich Tourism Office (☎ 888/ 4-NORWICH or 860/886-4683). Norwich offers several self-guided tours of Washington and Broad sts., Broadway and Union St., the Olde Burying Grounds, and the town's original settlement area, Norwichtown.

APPLES & ELEGANCE IN LITCHFIELD COUNTY

by Jon Pareles

T HE PLAN WAS IMPECCABLE. IN LATE
October, my wife and I would spend a weekend in tony Litchfield
County in Connecticut, where the country homes of the rich and powerful sit alongside apple orchards on tree-lined country roads. It's a
place where overt ostentation is simply not the thing; the aesthetic calls
for old-money understatement and decorum. Litchfield County offers
a storybook New England countryside of rolling hills and white frame
houses, green-gray brooks and old stone walls, all of it preserved
through assiduous zoning. For a weekend, we would live like the landed
gentry, staying at the Boulders Inn, a country lodge on Lake Waramaug
in New Preston.

According to plan, we'd make the 95-mile trip to the town of
Litchfield. We would revisit its boulevard (Route 63 North) of stately
white New England mansions and its fastidious green. Then we'd settle
in at the Boulders. Perhaps we'd take one of the inn's canoes out for a
paddle on the lake; perhaps we'd stroll the private trail up Pinnacle
Mountain.

But the weather had other plans. On the Saturday we'd chosen, the
skies opened up and flooded every exit route from Manhattan. By the
time we left the interstates for Route 7 in New Milford, most of the afternoon was gone, but the rain persisted. Indoor activities were called for.

Route 7 is the antiques corridor through New England, and we
stopped desultorily at some places on the way; one, the Incurable
Collector, included a cookie-jar museum with more than 2,000 examples, including more cute animals than a Disney retrospective. We

dropped into New Milford's well-advertised weekend flea market, housed in a sprawling industrial shed. Expecting more antiques, we instead found Canal Street north, just the place for obsolete eight-track tapes, hubcaps, Garfield figurines, off-brand pharmaceuticals, used vacuum cleaners, and collector-priced baseball cards and comic books.

As we sloshed up Route 7, mini-malls gradually gave way to New England charm: a white-steepled church, a horse farm, a Colonial graveyard with skinny, listing tombstones. Roadside stands were piled with pumpkins that could fill a passenger seat. On Route 202, the antiques started getting fancier: Earl J. Slack had a set of 12 Hawkes goblets for $1,800, along with African masks, Chinese vases, and a hand-carved portable Buddhist altar from Siam. The elegantly punning Reid and Wright, a used and antiquarian bookseller, had two floors of neatly organized volumes, from century-old Baedekers to a gazetteer of British ghosts; in the parking lot, a Fotomat-size booth sold cappuccino. At Recherche Studio, there was a quintessential New England artifact: a sterling silver miniature oilcan, made by Tiffany. Its function was adding just a few drops of vermouth to that dry martini.

A Mill & Antiques

New Preston (population 1,217) is itself tucked into the Litchfield Hills next to the Aspetuck River, where an old mill house still stands. The center of town, about 4 blocks long, is a clutch of high-end antiques shops and a pharmacy that also sells wine and liquor, presumably to cure different kinds of ailments. We picked up county newspapers there. Doc's, a lakeside restaurant, had been recommended to us, but by the time we looked in we found out that it was booked solid from 6 to 9pm, even on this rainy night. It seemed we'd be cocooning at the Boulders.

We presented ourselves at the inn's reception desk and let the coddling begin. The inn was built in 1895, a wood frame clad in the giant stones that provide its name, on a broad lawn with the lake across the street. At first, it was a summer home; it has housed guests since the 1930s, when outlying cottages were added. More modern bungalows replaced them in the 1960s and 1970s.

We had booked Gem North, half of a cottage up on the hillside with the best view. A table was reserved for us that night for dinner, the woman at the desk said, and would we need an umbrella?

Handel on Cassette

Gem North was uncluttered but carefully equipped. It had a coffeemaker and a refrigerator tucked away in an alcove, a whirlpool tub and a hair dryer in the bathroom, and a clock radio–cassette player by the bed, with CDs of Handel. A window seat, and a deck, looked out on the lake, which was turning

bluish silver in the drizzle, perfectly framed by the trees. Two chairs faced a modern fireplace that was already piled with split logs and crumpled newspapers awaiting a match. I lighted it, and felt my equanimity returning.

Dinner was served in the main house, in a glass-enclosed room facing the lake; during warmer weather, we could have dined outdoors on a patio with the same view. At the next table, a group was avidly discussing the bond market. But we turned our attention to the food, which rewarded it. Boulders follows New American cuisine strategies—seasonal ingredients, Europe-meets-Asia preparations, vertical constructions with a meticulous flair.

Replete, we looked around the main house, which has a homey parlor and a snug television room with an aquarium. A basement game room holds a pool table, a dartboard, and a pinball machine so old it rings bells and only scores in the thousands. We strolled back up to the cottage and rekindled the fire.

By the Fireplace

Nobody comes to Litchfield for nightlife, although we could have taken in a movie in nearby Bantam, where the theater plays the kind of movies seen at the Film Forum and the Angelika in Manhattan. Instead, we eased back and perused the local papers. Stories in *The Litchfield County Times* mentioned residents like Henry Kissinger and Arthur Miller, Sam Waterston and Oscar de la Renta. They also detailed seething community issues: a peculiar gravel-mine deal, a fast-food ban on Route 7, a town manager who smokes despite no-smoking rules in Town Hall, a ladybug infestation. The fire was cozy. "We should have brought marshmallows," my wife said.

While gathering more logs from the woodpile on the front porch, I looked up and saw constellations. The storm had finally cleared.

Morning brought bright sun and riotous colors. Golden and red leaves were reflected in Lake Waramaug and covered the path down to the inn. Breakfast was bounteous: a buffet of cereals, fruit salads (fresh and dried), pastries, and juices, along with a choice of apple-raisin pancakes or omelets with home fries and bacon or sausage (ordinary or Cajun andouille). Sipping tea, we watched two men fishing from a small boat.

Into the Countryside

It was a perfect day to roam the area: clear, not too cool, with the leaves still on the trees thanks to the dry summer. We decided to visit some local attractions on a circuitous route that would take us through plenty of countryside. My rule of thumb was to follow as many roads as possible with "Hill" in their name, promising good vistas. Others had the same idea; sleek Saabs and BMWs shared the country roads with shiny Jeeps and finely preserved old pickup trucks. In the center of New Preston, a couple proudly toted a section of weathered white picket fence out of an antiques store.

The Silo, in New Milford, is a store and cooking school owned by the New York Pops's musical director, Skitch Henderson, and his wife, Ruth. Situated in an old farm up a narrow road, the Silo's store supplies things like trivets and wineglasses, cornichons and sun-dried tomato paste, to local and weekending gourmets. Upstairs in its converted barn is a 25-seat classroom where chefs and cookbook authors give classes on most weekends. A large mirror over the demonstration kitchen's counter provides a better look at the chef's hands. Daniel Leader, author of *Bread Alone* (named after his bakery outside Woodstock, New York), was browning onions for the focaccia he was going to make in a class on Italian breads. The aroma was tempting, but the outdoors beckoned.

Route 67, in Roxbury, was calmly scenic; it led past a bucolic stream, past winding driveways (presumably to opulent estates) and old houses bearing dates in the 1700s and 1800s, past streets with names like Clapboard Road and Sentry Hill Road.

Nearby, in the town of Washington, was the Institute for American Indian Studies, dedicated to prior county inhabitants like the Algonquians. A mother ushered her children through exhibits of arrowheads, baskets, and deerskin leather. Another room held heirlooms from local Indian families, including a pair of elaborately beaded moccasins that had been worn through from dancing. On the grounds, in a forest clearing, stood a reconstructed Indian village: a circle of thatched, hive-shaped homes covered in bark or reeds or twigs, as well as a longhouse and a dugout canoe. It was a ghost town, a silent reminder of a very different New England.

We drove into the center of Washington (chartered 1779, population 3,905), a town out of a Currier and Ives print with white Colonial buildings clinging to leaf-strewn hillsides. The Gunn Memorial Library wasn't exactly the usual small-town hub: It would soon be holding a forum on the United Nations featuring the historian Arthur Schlesinger, Jr. In its own building, the library's historical museum, deserted except for a friendly curator, held a photo exhibition about the town's flood of 1955. Invited to add reminiscences to the guest book, one visitor had written, "My family listened on a battery-powered radio as adventurous souls crossed the flooded center of town in a snorkel-equipped Jeep." Upstairs were rooms with Victorian furnishings, including two spectacular dollhouses, detailed down to miniature cane chairs and playing cards. A photograph with one showed the birthday party at which a little girl, with all her friends in white pinafores, had received the house as a gift.

All Kinds of Apples

We asked the curator for directions to Averill Farm, an apple orchard. "They've got a beautiful old farm," she beamed. "They've been there since 1746." We drove into the farm past rows of apple trees. Ida Red and Red Delicious apples hung down from laden branches, gleaming in the sun like ruby earrings. We could have picked our own, but only a few varieties were available on trees. The farm stand offered more variety: Romes and Empires, Holidays and Galas, Winesaps and Mutsus, Yellow Delicious and Rhode Island Greenings, along with Bosc pears and quinces.

The apples were red and green and yellow, dappled and shaded, spherical and ovoid. We asked the man weighing fruit what his favorite was, and he gave the question serious thought. "I like the Mutsu and the Macintosh," he said. "And the Spartan—go ahead, try one." It was like a crisper, richer Macintosh; we filled another 5-pound bag for $4. On the way out, we passed the old stone farmhouse, beautifully kept after 2 centuries.

We circled back to Lake Waramaug and to the Hopkins Winery. The grapes are processed yards away from their hillside arbors in a converted barn; from a catwalk, we looked down on towering metal vats and big oak barrels while the heady smell of smashed grapes filled the air. The winery offers tastings of its red, white, sparkling, and apple wines.

At the inn across the street, overlooking another lobe of Lake Waramaug from high above, brook trout were swimming in a tank, awaiting their turn as dinner in the inn's Austrian-style restaurant. But the sky was turning pink, so we headed back to the Boulders to watch sunset over the lake from our room.

The inn's Sunday dinner ($18 to $25 entrees) offered slightly more choices than the regular menu. We lingered over cheesecake and cups of tea, and felt all our senses gratified with the day. Back in the room, we gazed out on the blue-black lake and then into the fire, absorbing as much New England comfort as we could before the morning's trip back home.

LITCHFIELD COUNTY ESSENTIALS

A free guide to the county is available through the **Litchfield Hills Visitors Bureau,** P.O. Box 968, Litchfield, CT 06759 (☎ 860/567-4506; www.litchfieldhills.com).

GETTING THERE

To reach the area by car from Manhattan, take the Henry Hudson Pkwy. to the Sawmill River Pkwy.; continue on the parkway to Rte. 684; continue on Rte. 684 to Rte. 84 East; continue on Rte. 84 East to exit 7 to pick up Rte. 7.

ACCOMMODATIONS

Boulders Inn, E. Shore Rd. (Rte. 45), New Preston (☎ **800/552-6853**). Rooms with fireplaces and views of Lake Waramaug. Weekend stays: end of May through end of October, $260 to $380; end of October through the end of May, $210 to $320. All include breakfast. Rates are based on double occupancy and a minimum stay of 2 nights on weekends; children under 12 can be accommodated by special arrangement.

MUSEUMS

Gunn Memorial Museum, 3 Wykeham Rd. (at Rte. 47), Washington (☎ **860/868-7756**). Open Thursday through Sunday noon to 4pm. Donations accepted. May be closed December 2000 to May 2001 for cataloguing.
Institute for American Indian Studies, 38 Curtis Rd. (off Rte. 199), Washington (☎ **860/868-0518**). A reconstructed outdoor Algonquian Indian village, nature trail, and exhibitions. Open Monday through Saturday 10am to 5pm, Sunday noon to 5pm (closed Mon and Tues from Jan through Mar). Admission $4, $3.50 for seniors, $2 for children 6 to 16, free for members and children under 6.

APPLE PICKING

Averill Farm, 250 Calhoun St. (off Baldwin Hill Rd.), Washington (☎ **860/868-2777**). Open daily 9am to 5pm during apple season (Sept and Oct.)

ANTIQUING

Earl J. Slack, Rte. 202, Washington (☎ **860/868-7092**). Open Saturday and Sunday 11am to 4:30pm.
Recherche Studio, Rte. 202 (New Milford Turnpike), New Preston (☎ **860/868-0281**). A collection of formal and

country formal furniture, crystal, silver, and accessories. Open Friday through Sunday 10:30am to 6pm, and by appointment. **Reid and Wright Antiquarian Book Center,** 287 New Milford Turnpike, Rte. 202, New Preston (☎ **860/868-7706**). Open daily, 10am to 5pm.

WINE TASTING

Hopkins Vineyard, Hopkins Rd. (off Rte. 45), New Preston (☎ **860/868-7954;** www.hopkinsvineyards.com). Open Memorial Day through Christmas Day, Monday through Friday 10am to 5pm, Saturday 10am to 6pm, Sunday 11am to 5pm; January and February, Friday and Saturday 10am to 5pm, Sunday 11am to 5pm. March through Memorial Day, Monday through Friday 10am to 5pm, Saturday 10am to 6pm, Sunday 11am to 6pm. Free admission.

FOR GOURMETS

Silo Cooking School, 44 Upland Rd. (off Rte. 202), New Milford (☎ **860/355-0300**). In addition to cooking classes, the store sells kitchen-related items; there is also an art gallery with changing exhibitions. Open daily 10am to 5pm.

UNWINDING IN THE CONNECTICUT RIVER VALLEY

by William Grimes

ABOUT 2 HOURS NORTHEAST OF THE Bronx, New York City begins to loosen its iron grip, and the Middle Atlantic gives way to New England. The transformation is obscured by the numberless suburbs and exurbs that pull southern Connecticut into the city's giant maw. But the influence gradually weakens, and then dies, just about the time that the Connecticut River comes into view.

In days of yore, the stretch of river that runs from Middletown south to Long Island Sound was home to 50 shipyards. Essex, near the mouth of the river, supported nine shipyards, and in 1775 built the first warship of the Revolutionary War, the *Oliver Cromwell*. The neat clapboard houses in towns and villages along the river's banks belonged to sea captains who made their living from the West Indies trade, and took the clipper ships to China. In the 19th century, six tons of elephant tusks found their way every month from Zanzibar to Deep River, where they were turned into piano keys, a local industry that gave its name to Ivoryton, near Essex.

Exhausted by its early labors, the river valley slipped into a dignified repose somewhere toward the end of the 19th century, and, to its credit, has barely stirred since. Dotted with attractive small towns, forests, and parks, it is ripe for browsing, rich in minor attractions that afford maximum pleasure for minimum effort.

The area has history, but not too much. Chester, for example, a picture-postcard town that Frank Capra might have found a little too wholesome looking, gave birth to Samuel Silliman, known to local historians as the father of the modern inkwell. Nathan Hale taught school for a year in East Haddam. That's the kind of history we're talking about.

There are museums, but not too many, and not intellectually taxing ones. The region disdains to strive for a vulgar first. The Cockaponset State Forest is the state's second largest, after Pachaug Forest; likewise, the steam train that runs from Essex to Deep River is the state's second-biggest tourist attraction, after Mystic Seaport. The Connecticut River Valley is the touristic equivalent of the gentleman's C.

Inns and bed-and-breakfast establishments abound, some of them renowned, like the Griswold Inn in Essex, the Ivoryton Inn and the Bee and Thistle in Ivoryton, and the Old Lyme Inn in Old Lyme. One weekend, my wife and I set up base camp farther north, at the Riverwind Inn in Deep River. It was a fortunate choice. The town is less touristed than Essex, which, as luck would have it, was the site of a barbershop-quartet convention the weekend of our getaway, not to mention the town's annual bluefish bake. Any American worried about the country's disintegrating moral fabric should stroll down Main Street in Essex and listen to a spontaneous rendition of "In the Shade of the Old Apple Tree" ringing out in four-part harmony.

New York can do strange, twisted things to the human soul. The owner of the inn greeted me with open hand and cheery countenance. I was immediately suspicious. He began drawing maps to aid me in my quest for leisure during the weekend, offered to telephone a restaurant to make sure I got a last-minute reservation, and, most unsettling, reached to grab one of my bags. I turned a cold eye upon him. What was the game here? Was he a Yankee skinflint seeking some novel gratuity?

By the end of the weekend, the truth emerged. He and his wife are actually good-natured, conscientious innkeepers who try to anticipate the needs of their guests. Oh.

Riverwind is an early 19th-century farmhouse that the owners, Barbara Barlow and Bob Bucknall, restored and packed full of antiques, many of them pig-related, since Ms. Barlow says she cherishes fond memories of the hog farm in Smithfield, Virginia, where she grew up. On the wall of the bathroom of our suite, for example, hung a color print of pigs playing turn-of-the century lawn games. Along with pig-shaped homemade biscuits, the inn's breakfast includes warm slices of Smithfield ham.

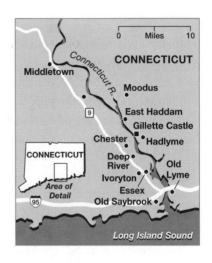

The Goodspeed

The inn's location makes for quick and easy forays north and south. Just across the river in East Haddam sits the Goodspeed Opera House, a Victorian bandbox of a theater built by a local shipbuilder and banker in 1876. The ground floor originally housed retail shops. Restored in the 1960s, the Goodspeed stages three musicals every year. Some, like *Annie, Man of La Mancha,* and *The Most Happy Fella,* have gone on to wider fame and fortune in New York City.

Since my wife and I loathe musicals, it was gratifying to find out that the theater was between shows during our visit and therefore we would not have to wince our way through *Paint Your Wagon.* Its branch theater, in a converted knitting-needle factory in Chester, stages musical works in progress.

Gillette Castle

Those who do not enjoy musicals should cross the river, take in the view, then turn south on Route 151 and follow signs to Gillette Castle State Park. The castle is currently under renovation and will reopen after 2001. In an architectural folly, it was built in 1917 by William Gillette, who amassed millions writing plays like *Secret Service* and appearing onstage in the role of Sherlock Holmes. The house is ugly beyond description, a monstrosity of rough-hewn stone that suggests an ungifted child's papier-mâché classroom project on the Crusades.

It is so repellent that it commands a kind of respect. The interior, a riot of exaggerated textures and unbridled rustication, falls somewhere between a Bavarian hunting lodge and the house in *The Rocky Horror*

Picture Show. Ceramic frog troubadours sit on the massive fireplace mantel. At one time, Gillette amused his guests with a miniature railroad that ran around the grounds. Today, only the stations remain. The view overlooking the river remains intact. This Gillette could not alter.

Timothy Dwight, the president of Yale University, gazed upon the Connecticut River in 1810 and uncorked a purple ode to it, praising "the purity, salubrity, and sweetness of its waters, the frequency and elegance of its meanders, its absolute freedom from aquatic vegetables." The riverbanks did not escape his notice: "there covered with rich verdure, now fringed with bushes, now covered with lofty greens and now formed by the intruding hill, the rude bluff and the shaggy mountain." He liked what he saw and you will, too.

To sustain the mood, head southward on River Road to the water's edge, where a handful of Colonial houses are clustered near the Chester-Hadlyme Ferry, in operation since 1769. Pick up a map of Middlesex County and drive aimlessly through the Cockaponset State Forest, 15,000 acres of woodland with all sorts of intriguing, rutted roads unmarked on standard maps.

At Riverwind, the innkeepers claimed that the best-kept secret in the area was the Canfield–Meadow Woods Nature Preserve, a 300-acre area of ridges, valleys, and wetlands in Deep River and Essex, with marked trails and no bicycles. It takes a keen eye to spot entrances to the preserve, however. My navigational skills, sense of direction, and general ability to function as a competent adult were seriously called into question from the passenger seat as I searched vainly for a promising opening in the forest primeval.

Sundial Herb Garden

Just as idiosyncratic as Gillette Castle, but far more tasteful, is the Sundial Herb Garden in Higganum. There are actually three gardens: a knot garden of interlocking low hedges; a main garden, with a sundial in the center; and a topiary garden with a fountain in the center. Paths in the main garden lead to cleverly designed vantage points that permit the eye to scan the whole as the nose inhales dozens of exotic fragrances. A viewing guide leads visitors through the gardens.

Next to the gardens is an 18th-century barn with an herb shop and tearoom that serves an ambitious afternoon tea on Sunday by appointment from June to mid-October. Ragna Tischler Goddard, who owns the shop with her husband, Thomas, and created the garden over a period of 25 years, is an herbalist whose dedication and enthusiasm make her a saleswoman of almost supernatural powers. Only deep detestation of herbs and all they stand for would be proof against her densely annotated tour around the shop, during which, as if by magic, the merchandise piles up in one's arms. Fortunately, it's not a Jaguar dealership.

Essex Attractions

As the Connecticut River flows to Long Island Sound, it recovers some of its original sense of purpose. Pleasure craft and marinas come into view, and in Essex, something of the old maritime flavor comes back. The town still has a shipyard and a marine-engine works, although its best-known product is the E. E. Dickinson Company's witch hazel, distilled in Essex since 1857. In summer, the waterfront is crowded with yachts.

Essex has succumbed a bit to the culture of the twee curio shop and the monster-cookie outlet. But a walk down Main Street, down to the waterfront park, is still an inspiration, the kind of idealized small-town street that Americans normally experience only in Hollywood films. The street is lined with Federal-style and a few Colonial houses, and most of them blur the line between domestic architecture and domestic bliss. Tourists stop and gaze longingly, and you can almost read the thought bubble: "If only I lived there, I'd be happy."

The Griswold Inn, built in 1776, has an inviting taproom with a potbellied stove. The taproom began life as a schoolhouse, but the citizens of Essex, after weighing their priorities, rolled the thing on logs to its present location and gathered there to drink beer. The base of Main Street opens up on a park that includes the Connecticut River Museum, which has a full-scale working reproduction of the first submarine, David Bushnell's *American Turtle*. A one-man affair, it looks like an elongated brandy cask with propellers. In theory, the operator, cranking the propellers by hand, could direct the turtle and affix a mine to an enemy ship. This was attempted during the Revolution, without success.

The river and its towns read as a chronicle of small triumphs and quirky innovations, unfolding on something less than a heroic scale. It is the region that brought forth three new inkwells and a thousand piano keyboards. Its cranky Yankees built a little opera house, a stone castle, and now a geometric herb garden. All the little pieces fit together in a pleasing pattern. And the river holds it together. Not a great river, but a good, dependable one. Dickens looked up and down the Connecticut, reached into his rich adjectival store, and pronounced it "a fine stream." That seems about right.

CONNECTICUT RIVER VALLEY ESSENTIALS

For information on the Connecticut River Valley, call or write the **Connecticut River Valley and Shoreline Visitors Bureau,** 393 Main St., Middletown, CT 06457 (☎ **800/486-3346** or 869/347-0028). The commission has brochures on the 20 towns within its tourism district.

GETTING THERE

By Car   To reach Deep River and Chester from New York City, take I-95 to Rte. 81 (exit 63); go north to Rte. 148, then east. For Essex and Ivoryton, continue on I-95 to Rte. 9 (exit 70), and go north. Old Lyme is off exit 70, across the river from Old Saybrook.

By Train   Amtrak (☎ **800/872-7245**) has seven trains daily from Penn Station in Manhattan to Old Saybrook. The trip takes 2½ hours. The off-peak one-way fare is $29 (general seating) or $34 (reserved seats); one-way peak tickets $36 (general), $46 (reserved); 15% off for seniors and disabled travelers; half fare for children under 16.

ACCOMMODATIONS & DINING

BED & BREAKFAST

Riverwind Inn, 209 Main St., Deep River (☎ **860/526-2014**). Rates $105 to $185 single or double, full breakfast included.

INNS WITH RESTAURANTS

Bee and Thistle Inn, 100 Lime St., Old Lyme (☎ **800/622-4946** or 860/434-1667). Rates $79 to $159 double or queen-size, all with private bathroom; $5 less for single occupancy (except on weekends or in room no. 7, which is always $79); cottage $210.

The restaurant serves American cuisine. Open Monday and Wednesday through Saturday 8 to 10am, 11:30am to 2pm, and 6pm to closing; Sunday 8 to 9:30am, 11am to 2pm (for brunch), and 6pm to closing; closed Tuesday.

Copper Beach Inn, 46 Main St., Ivoryton (☎ 860/767-0330). Rates in the main house $100 to $160 single or double, including continental breakfast; rooms in the carriage house $130 to $189. Two-night minimum on weekends.

The restaurant serves country French cuisine. Open Tuesday through Thursday 5:30 to 8:30pm, Friday and Saturday 5:30 to 9pm, Sunday 1 to 7pm; closed Monday. Entrees $22 to $29.

Griswold Inn, 36 Main St., Essex (☎ 860/767-1812). Rates $95 to $200 single or double, continental breakfast included.

The dining room serves traditional American cuisine. Open Monday through Saturday 11:45am to 3pm and 5:30 to 9pm (until 10pm Fri and Sat); a $12.95 English buffet breakfast is served Sunday 11am to 2:30pm. Dinner entrees $16.95 to $23.95.

Inn at Chester, 318 W. Main St., Chester (☎ 860/526-9541). Rates $105 with twin bed; $115 with double bed; $125 with queen-size bed; $135 with queen-size bed with canopy; $145 with king-size bed with canopy; $215 suite. Rates include continental breakfast. Rates reduced from January 2 to March 15. Children and pets welcome.

The Post and Beam Room serves New American cuisine. Open Monday through Saturday 5:30 to 9pm, Sunday 11:30am to 2:30pm (for brunch) and 4 to 8:30pm. Entrees $19 to $26.

Old Lyme Inn, 85 Lyme St., Old Lyme (☎ 860/434-2600). Rooms $99 to $158. Restaurant serves classical American cuisine. Open Monday through Saturday noon to 2pm and 6 to 9pm, Sunday 11am to 3pm (for brunch) and 4 to 9pm. Entrees $19.95 to $29.95.

OTHER RESTAURANTS

Du Village, 59 Main St., Chester (☎ 860/526-5301). Country French cuisine. Open Wednesday through Saturday 5:30 to 9pm, Sunday 5 to 8pm. Entrees $23 to $29.

Steve's Centerbrook Cafe, 78 Main St., Centerbrook (☎ 860/767-1277). Eclectic cuisine. Open Tuesday through Sunday 5:30 to 9pm. Entrees $14 to $19.50.

ATTRACTIONS

Connecticut River Museum, Steamboat Dock (at the foot of Main St.), Essex (☎ 860/767-8260). Open Tuesday through Sunday 10am to 5pm; closed Monday and major holidays. Admission $4, $3 seniors and students, $2 children 6 to 12.

Florence Griswold Museum, 96 Lyme St., Old Lyme (☎ 860/434-5542). Open January through March, Wednesday through Sunday 1 to 5pm; April through December, Tuesday through Saturday 10am to 5pm, Sunday 1 to 5pm. Herb garden wraps around the Huntley-Brown House on the museum grounds. Admission $5, $4 for seniors and students, free for children 12 and under and members.

Gillette Castle State Park, East Haddam (☎ 860/526-2336). Restoration through 2001; call for reopening date and hours.

Sundial Herb Garden, Brault Hill Rd. (off Rte. 81), Higganum (☎ 860/345-4290; www.sundialgardens.com). Gardens and shop open Saturday and Sunday (except holidays and the last 2 weekends in Oct) 10am to 5pm. Beginning the day after Thanksgiving and running through December 24, Tuesday through Sunday 10am to 5pm; thereafter, weekends only. Reservations required for afternoon tea, served Sunday only from spring through mid-October. On winter weekends, there are food demonstrations, tea tastings, and horticultural programs. Group tours (including afternoon tea and garden visit) arranged by appointment on selected weekends. Admission $1; program fees vary. **Valley Railroad,** Valley Railroad, Essex (☎ **860/767-0103**). Open mid-June to early September, daily; early September through October, Wednesday through Sunday; late November through late December, Friday through Sunday; early May through mid-June, Wednesday through Sunday; does not run early to mid-November. Call for trip times. One-hour round-trip $10.50, $5.50 for children 3 to 11; 2½-hour train and riverboat ride, $16.50, $8.50 for children 3 to 11. Parlor car $3 extra.

LOCAL THEATER

Goodspeed-at-Chester/Norma Terris Theater, N. Main St., Chester. Season runs May through December. Purchase tickets ($32) through the Goodspeed Opera House box office.

Goodspeed Opera House, Rte. 82, East Haddam (☎ **860/873-8668**). Season runs April through December. Tickets $22 to $44.

DOWN-HOME FOXWOODS CASINO

by Michael T. Kaufman

T HERE I WAS, STUDYING THE SEVEN cards that had been dealt me in Pai Gow poker. No, I was not in some sinister dive in Macao. I was in the cheery, one might even say wholesome, environs of the Foxwoods Resort and Casino in Ledyard, Connecticut, trying to project aplomb and savoir faire as my two $5 chips lay at risk on the green felt table before me.

In fact, I had no idea what I was doing.

This was not particularly unusual. I have over the years spent time in casinos on four continents as a dilettante and a patzer. I would on those occasions imagine myself a cold-blooded James Bond type, betting the ranch without breaking into a sweat. In real life, I turned out to be a chickenhearted dabbler who has never been able to raise the stakes to the point where losing brought significant pain or winning great joy. I would spend my time at blackjack, a game familiar since childhood, or at the slot machines, where I could make a fool of myself in private. In truth, gambling was a long way from my favorite sins.

So what was I doing with the Pai Gow hand?

Well, I was on an educational mission. I was using an expense-account advance to help me investigate and write about some of the other activities offered at casinos. The idea was that with a bankroll of $100, I would wander through the bustling Foxwoods casino trying my luck here and there while looking to find my game.

The resort lies on a reservation in southeastern Connecticut, where, with the help of a nun and Malaysian financiers, the tiny Mashantucket Pequot tribe parlayed a claim of territorial sovereignty into, first, a successful bingo hall, and then the largest moneymaking casino in the Western Hemisphere, raking in profits of $600 million a year. A 600-room hotel seems to be booked every weekend into eternity. More rooms are being added.

There are arcades with shops selling Indian art and doohickeys from all over the United States. Every hour on the hour a light show takes place at a huge crystal statue of a dancing Indian. There are massive sculptures of Indians throughout the 7-acre resort, and a huge Indian museum has recently been built in the complex, which dominates its rural setting, surrounded by thick woods. It crossed my mind that all the Indian motifs might make some customers feel better about losing. After all, losses at Foxwoods are not going to some self-promoting plutocrat like Donald Trump or to a shadowy syndicate, but to Native Americans. So what if there are only a few hundred members of this tribe, or that each one stands to gain a couple of million dollars a year? You can still think of your gambling losses as something like reparation.

A Wary Warm-up

Fortified by the notion, I set off to see what I could do with my employer's $100. My first stop was at the $5 blackjack table, where I thought I would warm up with something familiar. I started with $20 in chips, and after betting cautiously for about half an hour, I was up to $60. Ten minutes later, I was back down to $20. So much for warming up.

I moved over to acey-deucey. This is a game in which the dealer draws a card and places it between two others he has displayed face up. If the third card falls numerically between the two others, the players win; if not, the house wins. I bet $5. The dealer drew a 3 and a 10. The third card, an 8, fell within the spread, meaning that I won $5. Pretty terrific, I thought. I played again and this time the two cards came up as 6 and 8, which meant that if the third card was anything but a 7, my fellow players and I would lose. My fellow players, all of them seemingly retired folk, oohed and aahed and contorted themselves in efforts to assure that a 7 turned up. In fact, a king turned up and we lost. Pretty boring, I thought. I played for about 15 minutes and lost $30.

I proceeded to the roulette wheel. I concentrated at first on betting whether the ball would end up on an odd or even number, virtually an even-money proposition. My intention was to warm up in this way and then attempt any of 10 other possible wagers, like betting on a particular number, where the payoff was 35 to 1; or betting on adjoining pairs (17 to 1), rows of three numbers (11 to 1), blocks of four numbers (8 to 1), or columns of 12 numbers (2 to 1).

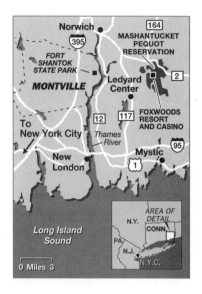

After my timid overture, I felt suddenly inspired. It was March and in March there are three birthdays within my family. My daughter's is the 20th and mine is the 23rd, and amazingly those two numbers lie next to each other. Boldly I placed a $10 chip on the line between the two, which meant that if either came in, I would win $170. The croupier, dressed in a miniskirt with Indian designs, said no more bets and set the wheel spinning. The steel ball stopped on 15, which is the date in March of my wife's birthday.

Enter Reason

Disheartened, I went back to playing odd and even, nursing the dubious pleasure of small gains and small losses. Then a woman joined our glum band with a big stack of chips and the look of confident experience. "What numbers have been running?" she asked me, suggesting that what we were facing was not a matter of random chance or taunting fortune, but a situation in which discerning reason would bring benefit. I shrugged and stupidly told her that I had not noticed.

"No problem," she said pleasantly, and began placing chips all over the board. I counted 15 of the $10 chips. It seemed she knew what she was doing, but it was kind of hard to figure out, with all the hedges.

How to Plan Your Own Foxwoods Weekend

To reach Foxwoods by car, take Interstate 95 to exit 92 and pick up Route 2 West; continue on Route 2 West for about 8 miles. Greyhound offers a daily bus service to Foxwoods from Gate 82 at the Port Authority bus terminal in Manhattan; the round-trip fare is $21. For Greyhound information, call ☎ 800/231-2222.

Great Cedar Hotel at Foxwoods Resort and Casino, Mashantucket Pequot Reservation, is off Route 2 (☎ 800/369-9663). Also on the premises are the **Two Trees Inn,** a New England-style inn, and the **Grand Pequot Tower.**

Daily room rates are based on double occupancy; rooms can accommodate up to four ($10 extra for a rollaway bed). Late November through late March, $125 to $260 (Great Cedar), $90 to $195 (Two Trees), $145 to $295 (Grand Pequot). Late March through late June, $140 to $260 (Great Cedar), $110 to $195 (Two Trees), $155 to $295 (Grand Pequot). Late June through early September, $175 to $260 (Great Cedar), $160 to $195 (Two Trees), $195 to $295 (Grand Pequot). Early September through late November, $140 to $260 (Great Cedar), $110 to $195 (Two Trees), $155 to $295 (Grand Pequot).

I bet on the number 3 because that is how many children I have. My one number lost. One of her bets won, but I could not tell from the size of her chip pile whether she had made a net gain or loss. She went ahead and scattered chips all over for the next spin. After about 10 spins, I was down a total of $60.

I thought it was time for a break, so I found my wife and we went to see if there were any tickets left to see Steve Lawrence and Eydie Gorme, who were singing at the theater adjoining the casino. Here we were lucky. One woman in front of us said the singers had been married for 40 years. Another said she remembered when they started out. The people in the audience seemed mostly older than the singers, who sang dozens of Gershwin songs. It was very pleasant. It cheered me up and I was ready to see what I could do with the $40 remaining from my advance.

I approached the craps table and watched the action. What was going on was even more confusing than what had been going on at roulette. There seemed to be 12 types of bets possible. You can bet with the shooter or against him. You can bet on particular numbers, or on particular combinations of numbers. Like the woman at roulette, many of the players were putting down bets all over the place. I considered joining them, but in the end it seemed like too much responsibility.

Losing, Again

I moved on to chuck-a-luck, a game played with three dice. You can bet on any number from 1 to 6. If one of the dice shows your number, you win the amount you bet. If two dice show the number, you win twice the amount you bet. And if all three dice show the number, you win 10 times the amount wagered. You can also bet on the aggregate amount the dice show. I bet $10 on 4. The three dice came up 3, 2, 2. My nut was down to $30.

That's when I discovered Pai Gow poker.

In this game, the player is dealt seven cards, dividing them into a five-card hand and a two-card hand. To win, both hands must be higher than those held by the house. In the event that a player wins one hand but loses the other, the game is declared a push, in which no money changes hands. This seemed intriguing. I bet $10. In my seven cards were a pair of eights and garbage. What could I do? I offered the pair as my five-card hand and showed a king high for my two-card hand. I lost both to a pair of queens and a pair of twos. I played a second hand, and lost again. I liked this game and felt that if I kept going I was certain to get a push and maybe, who knew, even win. But I was down to my last $10, and since variety was what I was after, I looked for one more diversion.

I found it in pull tabs. This is a game, sold at many Indian reservations, in which for $2 a player can buy a ticket with five tabs. When these are pulled back, they reveal slot-machine symbols, registering either nothing at all or payouts ranging from $2 to $50,000. I bought five. I pulled back the tabs. On the first four, there was zilch. I peeled back the tabs on the fifth card, certain that my dismal luck had to turn, confident that my educational evening was going to end on a high note.

Indeed, it did. I won $2. I bought my wife a cup of tea and we went off to watch the light show at the statue of the dancing Indian one more time.

EXPLORING MYSTIC
SEAPORT & ENVIRONS

by Ralph Blumenthal

WAITING FOR OUR DINNER TO cook the old-fashioned way—in the hearth of a landmark Colonial inn in North Stonington, Connecticut—I leafed through the guest book, my eye caught by this recent entry: "Great, nothing has changed since 1635." *Like,* I wondered, *the writer could know?* Actually, the place, Randall's Ordinary, goes back to only about 1685, but why quibble? For a millennium-era family of Hypercard-carrying Manhattanites, it was plenty old and authentic enough to set the stage for a weekend tour of the historic Mystic area.

In addition to Mystic Seaport, the re-created 19th-century ship-building village, there is the town itself with its quaint drawbridge and, yes, Mystic Pizza, which inspired the movie (although the picture was actually shot in a converted lobster warehouse in Stonington); the Mystic Marinelife Aquarium; Stonington Borough, a sweet town of pastel-hued clapboard homes; Groton, with its naval submarine base; and gritty New London, with its museums and Whale Oil Row.

It was more by chance than by design that we alighted at the inn with the extraordinary name ("ordinary" being an old name for tavern) about 10 miles northeast of Mystic. Since every place I phoned in Mystic was booked for the weekend, I started calling farther afield, not realizing until later my genius in pairing our foray into history with a stay in 300-year-old lodgings now owned, no less, by a Native American tribe, the Mashantucket Pequots, who operate the hugely successful Foxwoods gambling casino on their nearby reservation. (Of course, our daughters would surely have considered it an even more brilliant juxtaposition to have put up at a Days Inn with pool.)

Time did indeed seem frozen at the 27-acre farmstead just off Interstate 95. Two oxen and a donkey grazed in the fields as we hauled our bags into the dim brown Colonial frame structure that a settler named John Randall put up nearly a century before the American Revolution. Since expanded, it now houses the dining rooms and, upstairs, three guest rooms at $115 each on

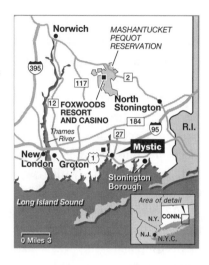

weekends. A dozen other rooms, including a deluxe suite, are in a transplanted 1819 barn, along with the inn's office and a lounge with a squawking African gray parrot. The Randall house is on the National Register of Historic Places, which explains, I figured, why the wrought-iron door latch to one of our rooms hung askew: Even the disrepair had to be landmarked.

Our two facing rooms, off a landing atop a flight of stairs, were alluring: wide-plank floors that listed and creaked authentically, four-poster beds with crocheted canopies, fireplaces, and—surprise!—bathrooms with whirlpool tubs. The old paned windows kept sliding shut: To hold them open for air, I had to prop them up with whatever was at hand. (When one window sprang shut, it fired an ice-bucket lid into the yard below.) There were no televisions (there are in the barn rooms), but there was electricity, along with adequate reading lamps. A lumpy armchair in our room also seemed a candidate for the National Register; when I sat down there was a *sprong!* and a large coiled upholstery spring clonked to the floor.

For our first outing, we headed for downtown Mystic, making a point (as I'd been advised) of parking a few blocks on the near side of the drawbridge to avoid traffic tie-ups. That allowed us the pleasure of walking into town across the Erector set–style span, inhaling the tangy breeze of the Mystic River, where, far below, speedboats churned frothy wakes and sailboats carved the wavelets like curling soap chips.

There was a mandatory (for our family, anyway) stop at the thronged Mystic Drawbridge Ice Cream parlor, dating from the 1800s, and another at the well-stocked Army-Navy store a little farther down West Main Street, where every customer seemed to rate a personal greeting. Just beyond is Mystic Pizza, whose popularity has led to an expansion into the storefront next door. Police officers in shorts patrolled on bikes. I actually saw one driver talk his way out of a parking ticket. Now, that's incredible.

Along the river, we stopped to scout a nice-looking hotel for future reference: the Steamboat Inn, an old ship warehouse. It had some lovely rooms overlooking the water, starting at $120 a night with a 2-night minimum stay on weekends.

Suddenly there were bells and a piercing whistle that made our younger daughter, Sophie, jump. Traffic gates came down, and the roadway split and reared up, counterbalanced by huge descending weights. Everything in town stopped, and we joined the crowd of gawkers. Then through the gap paraded a file of mast tips: the sailboats that line up for the drawbridge openings a quarter past every hour. In 5 minutes, the show was over. The weights rose, the roadway re-leveled, the gates swung up, and life resumed.

Mystic Seaport is a short drive away on Route 27, Greenmanville Avenue. Occupying 17 acres that once bristled with boatyards and marine commerce and then fell into decline in the 1880s, the seaport now bustles again with tall ships and dozens of galleries displaying old trades and crafts. We parked in one of the large lots across the road and entered by one of the two gates, paying $16 each (Sophie entered free) and stepping into an antique world of waving masts and clattering horse-drawn buggies. We clambered aboard one of the old ships, the *Charles W. Morgan*, an 1841 whaling bark that is the last remnant of the nation's wooden whaling fleet, and poked our heads into the old pharmacy, tavern, barrel shop, and general store. For lunch, we joined a lobsterfest near a mock lighthouse. Service was family style on rustic picnic tables under a large tent as a folk singer entertained with sea chanteys.

In the afternoon at the Village Green, children walked on stilts, rolled hoops, and tried out other old-fashioned games with the zest of discovering something new. A daily program offers demonstrations of sail handling, rope making, and fishing by net. There were also role players who invoked characters from 1876, musicians entertaining at the bandstand, and a stargazing show at a building called the planetarium.

Back in our rooms at Randall's Ordinary to rest before dinner, we could hear through the floorboards snatches of the menu being recited downstairs to early arrivals for the 7pm sitting. By the time we came down, I could almost recite it myself: Shaker herb soup, pork loin, duck breast, roast leg of lamb. . . .

With lip-smacking anticipation, we trooped to the hearth to inspect the selections of dark, sizzling meat. It was instructive to watch the cook in knee breeches maneuver the heavy iron skillets and pots over the open fire, which is where all meals at the inn are cooked from largely native ingredients and early American recipes. The ur-cuisine was introduced by the couple who opened the inn in 1987, Bill and Cindy Clark, antiques collectors who became adept at restoring old houses; they sold Randall's Ordinary to the Mashantucket Pequot Tribal Nation for $1.4 million.

But by the time we got back to our seats, the waiter had bad news: The kitchen had run out of all entrees but Nantucket scallops and capon. We had what was left, with peas and corn pudding. The scallops were delicious, the chicken so-so. "Maybe that's why they call it Randall's Ordinary," said my wife, Debbie, her churlish mood only partly mitigated by a dessert of pear and apple crisp. The bill, with a few drinks, came to $155—too much, we thought, authenticity notwithstanding.

The next morning, we headed back toward Mystic to the Mystic Aquarium, drawn by the promise of thousands of sea creatures. Paying $16 each ($11 for Sophie), we emerged in a dim, labyrinthine underworld of fish tanks filled with kaleidoscopic marine life. "Did you ever think how boring their life must be?" asked our teenager, the increasingly skeptical Anna.

A booming announcement summoned us to the indoor marine theater where trained bottlenose dolphins and beluga whales leaped into the air and retrieved objects underwater. A dolphin's natural sonar, or echolocation, is so good that blindfolded it can distinguish between differently shaped toys in the water. Sophie liked it when the trainers tossed them fish so, as she reasoned, "they're not hungry after performing." Before leaving, we trekked the archipelago of small outdoor pools and islands with penguins and seals. The aquarium staff says that the dolphins will soon take a hiatus, leaving the antics to the California sea lions.

Taking a restaurant recommendation from a friendly couple whose dog Sophie had stopped to pet, we headed for Stonington Borough, a few twisting miles east along the coast. This was indeed a gem of a town, with Water Street and adjacent lanes lined with attractive shops, and pristine Colonial clapboards in a palette of luscious hues. Historical markers identified one house as the birthplace of Capt. Edmund Fanning, a late–18th-century trader and explorer; another as the birthplace of Capt. Nathaniel Palmer, a pioneer explorer of the Antarctic archipelago, described somewhat hyperbolically as having "discovered" Antarctica in 1820; a third as the home of Whistler's mother. Anna and I tried to outdo each other naming the colors in the fanciful terms of today's sports clothes catalogues. "Butter cream." "Cornflower." "Mint." "Melon." "Periwinkle." "Mocha." "Bone."

The restaurant we'd come for, the Skipper's Dock, was prettily situated on the water, but a chill wind and the fiercely setting sun drove us off the deck to the inside dining room, where we feasted on steamers and lobster, mussels, fish-and-chips, and corn and salad. With a few drinks and dessert, the bill for four came to a little more than $100.

On the way home, we stopped at the naval submarine base in Groton, where sinister German, Italian, and Japanese submarines flank the entrance to the museum. Inside are World War II battle flags, mementos and trophies of the silent service, and convincingly claustrophobic mock-ups of submarine attack centers with working periscopes.

The unquestioned highlight is the decommissioned nuclear submarine, *Nautilus,* which from its launching in 1955 broke all underwater speed and distance records, became the first vessel to cross the North Pole, and is now a national landmark open to visitors. Holding audiotape tour guides to our ears, we inspected the cramped bunks, well-equipped galley, and ominous torpedo ports.

Our route back took us through New London, where we circled the pier and the historic downtown with its old burial ground, courthouse, and railroad station, and 18th- and 19th-century buildings.

Deciding to indulge in one last lobster blowout, we took a detour back to Noank to find a popular restaurant, Abbott's Lobster in the Rough. After meandering, lost, in Noank, I eased the car over to ask directions when a man said: "Let me guess. You want Abbott's. Left on High. Left on Spring. Left on Pearl." Three juicy lobsters and $60 later, I was trying to translate the directions backward to find our way out when I spotted a large sign. NOW THAT WE'RE HERE, it said, HOW DO WE GET THERE? It told us.

MYSTIC ESSENTIALS

GETTING THERE

By Car To reach Mystic Seaport from Manhattan, take I-95 to exit 90 and pick up Rte. 27; continue to the seaport.

By Train Amtrak (☎ 800/872-7245) runs daily trains to Mystic; one-way fares range $39 to $54; 15% discount for seniors, half price for children 2 to 15 years.

ACCOMMODATIONS

Great Cedar Hotel at Foxwoods Casino and Resort, Mashantucket Pequot Reservation, off Rte. 2 (☎ 800/369-9663). Also on the premises are the **Two Trees Inn,** a New England–style inn, and the **Grand Pequot Hotel.** Daily rates are based on double occupancy. Rooms can accommodate up to four people; additional $10 for rollaway beds. Late November through late March $125 to $260 (Great Cedar), $90 to $195 (Two Trees), $145 to $295 (Grand Pequot). Late March through late June, $140 to $260 (Great Cedar), $110 to $195 (Two Trees), $155 to $295 (Grand Pequot). Late June through early September, $195 to $295 (Great Cedar), $160 to $195 (Two Trees), $195 to $295 (Grand Pequot). Early September through late November, $140 to $260 (Great Cedar), $110 to $195 (Two Trees), $155 to $295 (Grand Pequot).

Randall's Ordinary, Rte. 2, North Stonington (☎ 860/599-4540). Rates, based on double or single occupancy:

Friday and Saturday, $169 to $199 for standard room, $199 to $239 for minisuite, $359 to $399 for silo suite. Sunday through Thursday, $149 to $169 for standard room, $159 to $199 for minisuite, $309 to $359 for suite. Dining hours, Monday through Friday 7 to 11am, noon to 2pm, and 5:30 to 9pm; Saturday and Sunday 7 to 11am, noon to 3pm, and 5:30 to 9pm. Prix-fixe $39 per person. Children welcome; reservations suggested.

Steamboat Inn, 73 Steamboat Wharf, Mystic (☎ **860/536-8300**). Early December to early March, $110 to $119; early March to early May, $140 to $240; early May to early September, $200 to $285; early September to early December, $160 to $275. Daily room rates are based on double occupancy and include breakfast; third guest in room over 16, $35. Children welcome.

DINING

Also see Randall's Ordinary, under "Accommodations," above.

Abbott's Lobster in the Rough, 117 Pearl St., Noank (☎ **860/536-7719**). Open early May to Memorial Day, weekends noon to 7pm; Memorial Day through Labor Day, daily noon to 9pm; Labor Day to Columbus Day, weekends noon to 7pm; closed Columbus Day through April.

Mystic Pizza, 56 W. Main St., Mystic (☎ **860/536-3700** or 860/536-3737). Open daily 11am to 11pm year-round.

Skipper's Dock, 66 Water St., Stonington Borough (☎ **860/535-8544**). Call for hours.

ATTRACTIONS

Mystic Aquarium, 55 Coogan Blvd., Mystic (☎ **860/572-5955**). New displays, completed in 1999, include the beluga whale exhibit, "Alaskan Coast," and an exhibit devoted to deep ocean exploration, "Challenge of the Deep." Open July through Labor Day, daily 9am to 6pm; December and February, hours vary; all other times, daily 9am to 5pm. Admission $16, $15 for seniors, $11 for children 3 to 12.

Mystic Seaport, Rte. 27 (exit 90 off I-95), Mystic (☎ **860/572-5315**). Open November through March, daily 10am to 4pm; April through October, daily 9am to 5pm. Admission $16, $15 for seniors, $8 for children 6 to 12, free for children under 5. In addition to the exhibits, there are trips aboard rowboats, steamboats, and sailboats, mid-May through mid-October; prices range $3.50 for a steamboat ride ($2.50 for children) to $14 for an hour on a self-guided sailboat ($10.50 for Seaport members). Throughout the year, there are special activities included in seaport admission: a Lobsterfest Memorial Day weekend, a Chowderfest Columbus Day weekend, an antique marine engine exposition in late August, and holiday events in November and December. Specialized workshops in boat building, navigation, and open-hearth cooking are offered for an additional fee.

Naval Submarine Base New London, Crystal Lake Rd. (exit 86 off I-95), Groton (☎ **800/343-0079** or 860/694-3174).

Although the base is not open to the public, you can visit the historic ship **Nautilus,** the first nuclear-powered submarine, and the **Submarine Force Museum,** both outside the front gate. You can also see three pre–World War II miniature submarines from Japan, Italy, and Germany. Open Wednesday to Monday 9am to 4pm; closed Tuesday. Free admission.

Whale Oil Row, New London. A row of historic Greek revival houses dating to the mid-1800s that are not open for tours can be viewed from the street. At no. 1 (105 Huntington St.) is the **Chamber of Commerce of Southeastern Connecticut** (☎ 860/443-8332), which offers a selection of tourist brochures and maps, some free; open Monday through Friday 9am to 5pm.

SHOPPING

Mystic Army-Navy Store, 37–39 W. Main St., Mystic (☎ **888/536-1877** or 860/536-1877). Open Sunday through Thursday 10am to 7pm, Friday and Saturday 9am to 9pm.

Mystic Army-Navy Store II (☎ **860/572-5844**) is located in Building 2B, Olde Mistick Village, adjacent to the aquarium.

ICE CREAM

Mystic Drawbridge Ice Cream, 2 W. Main St., Mystic (☎ **860/572-7978**). Open March through December, daily 8am to midnight (closes at 8pm toward end of season); closed the rest of the year.

ADVENTURES ALOFT: HOT-AIR BALLOONING

by Michael T. Kaufman

C ABIN FEVER IS LAPSING. THE season has changed, and what is needed to stir the blood is a new outlook on life, a change of perspective. One could run, ride horses, or fall dangerously in love, but all of this involves energy. Bungee jumping is appealingly passive but probably too drastic. What about hot-air ballooning? From winter quarters on the couch, it sounded like an ideal psychic pick-me-up.

The imagination took over. I could see myself wafting over a picturesque landscape like the great balloonists: the Montgolfier brothers, who first wafted before the French Revolution; Malcolm Forbes; Jules Verne's hero Phineas Fogg; and, of course, Babar, the elephant king. My wife was consulted. Fine, sure, she said, let's go.

As it turns out, there are quite a number of balloonists around New York who will take you up and, what is much more important, bring you down. They charge about $200 per person for rides lasting 1 to 2 hours. Most will take as few as 2 people and as many as 10. Almost all the balloonists offer two departure times: early morning to watch the sunrise and late afternoon, when the winds are generally calmer.

After phone calls to a number of operators, a deal was struck with Matt Fenichel of Airvertising and Airventures of West Simsbury, Connecticut. He was chosen because he has been flying for more than 19 years, because the area in which he operates was relatively unknown to us and mildly intriguing, but mostly because of his low-key but unmistakable take-charge tone.

"You realize that if the weather is at all questionable, we don't go; we reschedule," he explained on the phone. "If it's blowing more than 8 miles an hour at ground level, we stay put, and it won't do you any good to beg." We booked for a Saturday afternoon flight with the following morning as a fallback. We reserved a hotel room in the Farmington Valley area, 90 miles from New York City, and as our scheduled liftoff neared, we anxiously followed the weather reports.

As things turned out, the appointed day was snowy, rainy, and windy. I wondered if things were balmy in Simsbury. My wife wondered if I was balmy in the British sense. At about that point, Mr. Fenichel called to say the weather was awful up there, too, and that we should come up the following week. I did not beg.

A week later, all systems proved to be go. The 2-hour drive from Manhattan was pleasant. We checked into the Avon Old Farms Hotel, a neo–olden-times establishment nearby. We called Mr. Fenichel, who told us to meet him in the parking lot behind the Gemini restaurant in the area. There he and the six members of his crew unpacked and unfurled a blue balloon they had towed in a trailer. Since we were the only passengers, a relatively small balloon was being readied, but it still measured 87 feet from top to bottom. We joined the crew members in pulling it open as Mr. Fenichel blew air into the bag with a gas-generated fan. The basket was attached. We climbed in. Mr. Fenichel turned up the gas on the propane burner just above our heads, and we had liftoff.

The sensation is not at all like flying. Nor is it like taking an elevator ride. Rising in a slow, steady ascent above rooftops and then treetops, being driven forward by a weak breeze, we felt more a part of nature than its conquerors. All of us who have been on planes know that what keeps us up there is Bernoulli's principle, which holds that air currents across curved surfaces, like those of the wings, produce a drop in pressure. But how many of us really believe that?

By contrast, the technology that takes and keeps a balloon aloft is homey, basic, and much more immediately credible. You don't need to be a rocket scientist to know that hot air rises. It is something that can be fully grasped by anyone who has ever heard a teapot whistle or seen a legislature in session.

Hot-Air Ballooning Essentials

Here is information about two balloon trips in the New York metropolitan region. Schedules and rates are subject to change, so confirm times and prices when you call to reserve.

Airvertising and Airventures, West Simsbury (☎ 860/651-4441). Different packages and charter rides available year-round. Rates start at $200 per person for a 1- to 1½-hour group ride to $245 for a private ride. The company also offers weekend excursions ($600 to $1,500) and weeklong trips ($1,000 to $28,000).

Berkshire Balloons, P.O. Box 706, Southington (☎ 203/250-8441). Dawn and dusk flights east of Waterbury, followed by a champagne toast, are offered year-round at $225 per person for a 1-hour flight. Overnight packages, including a bed-and-breakfast stay, are $545 for two people.

"It's really very simple," Mr. Fenichel explained. "I turn up the flame, and we go up a bit. I turn the flame down, and we hover a while. When the air in the balloon cools a bit, we start to descend and I turn up the gas again." As he spoke, his hand on the gas valve, we had risen to about 800 feet, heading slowly over the Farmington River.

It was a comfortable height offering distant views of Hartford to the west and Springfield, Massachusetts, to the north. Immediately below us, new suburban developments gave way to old tobacco farms and a wilderness of forest, ponds, and marshes near the fast-moving river. At one point, six deer could be seen, and Mr. Fenichel allowed the balloon to settle down a bit for a closer view. The deer were unaware of our presence until the pilot turned up the burner so that we could rise above looming trees. They heard the rather loud noise and bolted.

It was not scary, not even when our basket brushed the uppermost branches of tall trees. "Don't worry about that," Mr. Fenichel said. "Sometimes we do that to slow down." In this case we were doing it to take a look at buds and birds. During the ride, I grew very attached to the basket and thought how wonderful and comforting that it was made of wicker, not plastic or aluminum, but the stuff of rocking chairs and baby carriages. "It's a funny thing, but nobody has ever found anything that's as light and strong and flexible," our pilot explained.

The wind, not very strong, shifted direction, and we did the same. "Up here Mother Nature is in full command," our pilot said. "I can control our altitude, but she controls our direction." As we passed over roads, cars would stop, and people would get out to look and wave and shout to us. Mostly they shouted, "Where are you coming down?" We shouted back truthfully, "We don't know." As

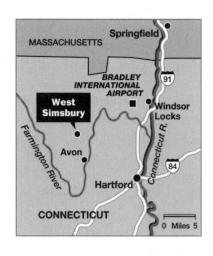

we drifted in this manner, it occurred to me that ballooning, while pleasant enough for anyone, could be therapeutic for control freaks and anxiety sufferers. First you don't know if you are going to rise, and when you do, you have no idea where you are going to end up.

We saw more deer, more houses, more cars, and more people happily waving to us. We saw planes heading to and from Bradley International Airport in Windsor Locks, somewhere over the ridge ahead of us. We could only hope they saw us. I kept looking for the van in which Mr. Fenichel's crew was presumably tracking us, to meet us on landing. Mr. Fenichel tried to reach them by radio but failed. *Aha,* I thought, *things are getting interesting.* Neither my wife nor Mr. Fenichel seemed much concerned. *Aha,* I thought, *perhaps I am more of a control freak than I knew.*

Not wishing to alarm anyone, I just asked how long we had been aloft.

"About an hour and a half," the pilot said, and then, clearly reading my mind, added, "We have enough gas here for about 2 hours more, but we'll come down when we find the next suitable spot." On our trajectory all I could see were trees, but then a sudden gust shifted our flight. "Oh, look," I said hopefully, "a nice snow-covered field." "I'm afraid that's a pond with thin ice," the pilot said. Once again I thought how good it was to have him along.

Within minutes, a real field not far from a road loomed into view, and Mr. Fenichel, after guiding the balloon over a stand of trees, brought it down in a landing that was no more jarring than a jump of 2 feet.

And as we climbed out of the basket, we were welcomed by the cheers of the chasers, who had successfully tracked us to the spot. They were joined by five farm youngsters who very happily joined in deflating the balloon, rolling it up, and stowing it and the basket in the trailer behind the van. Twenty minutes later, we were headed back to the parking lot behind the restaurant for the last part of the flight, the champagne ritual.

Mr. Fenichel explained that this in fact dated back to the 18th-century balloonists, who landed in farmers' fields as we had just done. Often they would be met, not by happy youngsters, but by farmers who attacked the balloons with pitchforks, thinking they were infernal devices of diabolical design. The balloonists took to carrying wine with them to soothe and placate farmers, and a tradition was born.

We drank the wine and had some fine cranberry cake provided by our tracking team. We toasted them and our adventure and said goodbye. We had a fine meal at the hotel restaurant and a good night's rest, and the next morning we drove back toward the city through a landscape over which we had hovered. It had been a good weekend, and we were content, not unlike Babar and his wife, Celeste.

Other Destinations Within Easy Reach of New York City

NEWPORT, OLD MONEY'S OCEANSIDE RETREAT

by Robin Pogregin

Needless to say, the hotel neglected to mention the foghorn.

What foghorn is that? you may ask.

Oh, just the tone resembling a test of the emergency broadcasting system that pierced the otherwise peaceful sea air every 10 seconds during my first attempt to sleep through the night on Narragansett Bay. (I seriously contemplated setting out in my pajamas to find the fog patrol and destroy the horn, but it occurred to me that I might then have a shipwreck on my conscience.)

Aside from that minor hitch, my husband and I had a truly idyllic weekend in Newport, Rhode Island. While the downtown harbor bustled with tourists filling up on fried clams at restaurants along the water and dodging in and out of shops along Thames Street, the City-by-the-Sea on the tip of Aquidneck Island also offered quaint narrow side streets, mansions of old-money grandeur, and seaside silence.

Newport, founded in 1639, became a thriving seaport, with captains bringing pineapples—now the island's symbol of hospitality—home from trips to the West Indies as well as sugar and molasses to make Newport rum. These days, Newport is perhaps best known as the country's yachting capital, although the city lost the America's Cup to Australia in 1983. White sails whip across the bay in regattas throughout the summer.

Having arrived on a Saturday after an easy 3½-hour drive from New York City, we had hoped to spend both nights at the Castle Hill Inn and Resort. Unfortunately, the hotel had only Sunday night available. As a result, our first home base was Oceancliff I and II, a two-building condominium resort on Ridge Road that did not come close to approximating Castle Hill's old-world charm. Nevertheless, after upgrading from what felt like a basement room on the ground level to an airy second-floor duplex, we were very comfortable and, in fact, would recommend the place to those traveling as a family.

The first floor of our room had a living room, a bedroom, a bathroom, a kitchen area, and an outdoor deck overlooking the water. On the second floor, reached by a spiral staircase, was a large master bedroom and a bathroom with a Jacuzzi-style tub.

Oceancliff shares its site with the Oceancliff Historic Inn, a former villa, built in 1896.

After checking in, my husband and I headed back to the harbor to find a restaurant for lunch and decided on Christie's of Newport. While the food was unremarkable, Christie's had just the feeling we were looking for: outdoor tables overlooking the water, hearty lobster rolls served with french fries, and an upbeat crowd.

Later, I felt compelled to sample the requisite "you're in a New England town, how could you not have some fudge" fudge. Every afternoon at four except on Monday and Tuesday, the big wooden paddles come out at Country Kettle Fudge on Thames Street, where the staff beats fudge by hand in copper kettles. The shop features fudge in about 20 different flavors, including such unusual varieties as pistachio, chocolate chip, and cheesecake. (My preference was the triple chocolate, and I went back for more the next day.)

A Restful Afternoon

We spent the rest of Saturday afternoon relaxing at the hotel (I napped; it was possible to do so at that hour) and then made the 10-minute drive back into town for dinner. With stores open late and restaurants in full swing, the harbor was abuzz with sidewalk traffic, including people trolling for antiques in stores along Franklin and Spring streets or stopping in for beer and chowder at pubs along Bowen's Wharf or Bannister's Wharf.

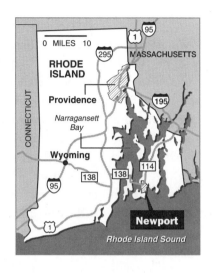

For dinner, we chose a place called "Scales and Shells," and I can hardly imagine that Newport offers better. Conveniently situated on Thames Street, the restaurant beckons with a crisp, teal blue–trimmed exterior, wide windows, and black-and-cream–checked tablecloths. Inside, crowds cluster at the raw bar to suck on Neddicks oysters, Cherrystone clams, or lobster claws and sip cold glasses of white wine while they wait for their tables.

The wait can be considerable; the main restaurant does not take reservations. Having learned this in advance, we had secured a table in the restaurant's upstairs area, called "UpScales," which accepts reservations and offers a somewhat more limited menu.

Among the specialties of the husband-and-wife chef team, Debra and Andy Ackerman, are sizzling servings of lobster *fra diavolo* over linguine in huge sauté pans, and marinated toro tuna (she cooks upstairs, he downstairs). My husband started with clams (Sicilian littlenecks steamed in white wine, garlic, and thyme) and finished with clams (linguine *alle vongole*). I had the fried artichokes as an appetizer, followed by butterflied shrimp from the restaurant's mesquite grill, accompanied by an ear of corn that was blackened from the grill, with the kernels as sweet as candy.

Then we returned—stuffed—to our hotel, to bed, and to . . . the foghorn. It sounded throughout the night, which, from what I could tell, was hardly even cloudy.

Strolling & Shopping

The next morning, we started with breakfast at the Coffee Corner, a place on Broadway and Friendship streets, a short distance from the harbor, that had been recommended for its French toast. We had the pancakes, which were only so-so. I suspect it is better to try one of the more central breakfast spots recommended by Richard Saul Wurman in his *Newport Guide,* among them Annie's, Muriel's, and Poor Richard's.

Driving back into town (where parking is hard to find on weekends), we walked around a bit. The shopping inclined can stop in at everything from the Gap and Rockport to the Nutcracker Suite Christmas Shop, which sells strikingly original ornaments year-round and an impressive variety of painted nutcrackers, displayed on the staircase.

For lack of time, we never made it to the historic district known as the Point.

After our stroll, my husband went to play squash at the Newport Squash Club while I toured the Elms mansion, built in 1901 as a summer residence for the Pennsylvania coal magnate Edward J. Berwind. Modeled after the Château d'Asineres near Paris, it evoked another world, rich with pillars of purple breccia marble, doors of Santo Domingo mahogany, and chandeliers of Baccarat crystal.

The Elms's sprawling grounds, especially the meticulously maintained formal gardens, offer tranquil strolling away from the bustle of the city. This is the elegance that inspired drawing-room chroniclers like Edith Wharton and Henry James, and seeing Newport's opulence firsthand, it is easy to see why.

The Newport Preservation Society owns eight remarkable mansions (once incongruously called "cottages") in Newport, which was long a destination of robber barons, yachtsmen, and society figures who made it one of the world's most elite summer resorts. Rosecliff, for example, built in 1902, was the filming site for *The Great Gatsby.* The Vanderbilts summered in Newport, as did John F. and Jacqueline Kennedy, who were married at the Auchincloss family's Hammersmith Farm, known for a time as the "Summer White House." It is now privately owned and not open for tours.

After picking up my husband, we drove over to Ocean Drive for the much-touted brunch at Castle Hill, which lasts from 11:30am to 3pm and offers everything from baked oysters to eggs Benedict. Seating for the brunch is first come, first served, although guests of the hotel are given priority. As we were not yet guests (check-in time is 2pm), we had to take what was available, which was a table indoors rather than on the deck.

The room we ate in—the Sunset Room—was lovely, with wraparound windows overlooking the water and tablecloths and upholstered high-backed chairs. But the wooden tables outside, topped with Bass and Guinness beer umbrellas, were clearly the place to be, with direct views of the expansive green lawn sloping down to the water and live music from a bass and piano duo.

In the late afternoon, we got in line with the rest of the world to tour the mansion to beat all mansions: the Breakers. Built in 1895 as the summer home of Cornelius Vanderbilt, it has 70 rooms, 27 fireplaces, and a breathtaking view of the Atlantic Ocean. We marveled at the music room, which was built in France, disassembled, shipped to Newport, and reassembled at the Breakers by French artisans; the billiard room, with its ceiling and floor mosaics; and the formal dining room, with 12 rose alabaster columns with gilded capitals.

The tour even took us through the kitchen and pantry to admire such details as the mortar in which herbs were crushed, the pantry where fresh flowers were cut every morning, and the 200 place settings of Vanderbilt china trimmed in 22-karat gold. Walking through the 114,000-square-foot mansion under 40-foot ceilings, one cannot help wondering what it would be like to repose at this palace every summer.

Entering Castle Hill

Time to check in at Castle Hill, truly a gem of a hotel, perched on the site of a former watch house on a secluded peninsula. Thornton Wilder was one of the inn's frequent visitors.. The hotel proper has only nine guest rooms, but it has other accommodations: six cliffside guest rooms in what it calls the Harbor House, 18 private beachfront cottages with kitchens, and a chalet with two bedrooms. Our room was cozy and inviting, with windows overlooking the lawn and bay, yellow wallpaper, a small, drop-leaf desk stocked with bound volumes of *Reader's Digest* condensed books, and a spacious bathroom with powder blue bath rugs.

As we pulled into the parking lot on Sunday evening, however, the scene was far from placid. Rather, we found ourselves in the thick of what is evidently a tradition in Newport: Sunday sunset cocktails at Castle Hill. The porch, bar, and lawn were overflowing with people in their 20s and 30s holding plastic cups of icy daiquiris: men, showered after a day at the beach, in crisp collar shirts; women beginning to shiver in short dresses and sandals as the setting sun took the day's warmth with it.

Although Sunday cocktails at Castle Hill is clearly not about eating, there was a casual barbecue set out on the lawn, and my husband and I enjoyed a picnic of burgers and grilled chicken sandwiches while the social constellations shifted and whirled behind us, and sailboats went gliding by on the bay.

With just about an hour of light left in the sky, we set out to walk as much of the famous Cliff Walk as we could before nightfall. According to the map, the path, with mansions on one side and sea on the other, starts in town at Memorial Boulevard and concludes 4 miles away, at the beginning of Bellevue Avenue. We began at the Bellevue Avenue end and completed the walk just after dark.

On the Cliffs at Dusk

The path, which is rocky at first and later becomes paved, was beautiful at that hour: The fading light gave the jagged coastline a gentle blue-gray hue as the waves crashed 60 feet below.

As lights came on in the majestic homes along the water, we could get a better glimpse of the life going on within the elegant bay windows: Land's End, a house built in 1870 with a yellow exterior and black trim, which had belonged to Edith Wharton; Rough Point (1891), the secluded hideaway of Doris Duke; the Chinese Teahouse (1914), and Alva Belmont's Oriental pavilion, where she held several of her "Votes for Women" rallies.

Upon finishing the walk, we took a cab back to our car, and—unwilling to call it a weekend just yet—drove into town for dessert: warm crème brûlée, apple tart, and a glass of port at Pronto on Thames Street.

Back at Castle Hill, we snuggled into bed looking forward to the morning's free corn johnnycakes, a Newport tradition, to be eaten with butter, not syrup. Too tired to read, we turned out the light and would have fallen asleep quickly had it not been for . . . the foghorn, back for a repeat performance.

Faced with the second fitful night of sleep in a row, I might have entertained ever more violent fantasies of ferreting out the fog patrol and hurling the offending horn into the sea once and for all. But after another full day of falling in love with the place, I found that the honks were beginning to sound almost soothing, like Newport's own nautical lullaby.

NEWPORT ESSENTIALS

Further information about lodgings, attractions, sailing expeditions, and Newport's annual jazz and folk festivals is available from the **Newport County** **Convention and Visitor's Bureau,** 23 America's Cup Ave., Newport (☎ **800/ 326-6030**).

GETTING THERE

By Car From Manhattan, take I-95 North to the exit for Rte. 138 East, near Wyoming, RI, then follow the signs to the Jamestown and Newport bridges.

By Bus Bonanza Bus Lines (☎ **800/ 556-3815**) runs four buses daily from the Port Authority, at Eighth Ave. and 42nd St., Manhattan, to Newport; the 6-hour ride costs $39.50 one-way or $71.75 round-trip; half price for children 2 to 11.

By Train Amtrak (☎ **800/872-7245**) has daily train service from Penn Station, at Seventh Ave. and 34th St. in Manhattan, to West Kingston, RI, which is about a half-hour drive from Newport (a cab from the train station costs about $40). One-way fares range from $45 to $64; 15% discount for seniors, half price for children 2 to 15. Amtrak also offers daily service from Penn Station to Providence, RI, where public buses run regularly to Newport.

ACCOMMODATIONS

Castle Hill Inn and Resort, Ocean Dr. (☎ **888/466-1355** or 401/849-3800). Rooms range $395 to $600 in high season (May through Oct), and from $145 to $395 in low season (Nov through Apr); $25 for each additional person. Rates are based on double occupancy with full breakfast and afternoon tea; 2- or 3- night minimums may apply on weekends.

Oceancliff I and II, Ridge Rd. (☎ **401/846-6667**). June through September (high season), Monday through Thursday $220 to $230; Friday and Saturday $320 to $340; off-season, $95 to $195. Rates based on double occupancy.

DINING

Annie's, 176 Bellevue Ave. (☎ **401/849-6731**). Open daily 7am to 4:30pm. Entrees $8 to $12.

Christie's of Newport, 351 Thames St. (☎ **401/847-5400**). Open Monday through Thursday and Sunday 11:30am to 9:30pm, Friday and Saturday 11:30am to 10pm. Entrees $18 to $24.

Coffee Corner, 283 Broadway (☎ **401/849-2902**). Open Monday through Friday 7am to 2pm, Saturday and Sunday 7am to 1:30pm. Entrees $4 to $6.

Poor Richard's, 254 Thames St. (☎ **401/846-8768**). Open daily 7am to 4:30pm. Entrees $2.65 to $9.95.

Pronto, 464 Thames St. (☎ **401/847-5251**). Open daily 5 to 10pm (until 11pm during summer). Entrees $11 to $24.

Scales and Shells, 527 Thames St. (☎ **401/846-3474;** 401/847-2000 for Upscales, the upstairs dining room). Open Sunday through Thursday 5 to 10pm, Friday and Saturday 5 to 11pm. Entrees $10.95 to $22.50.

ESTATE VISITS

The Breakers, Ochre Point Ave., at Ruggles Ave. (☎ **401/847-1000**). Open late March through October, daily 10am to 5pm; closed mid-January through March.

Elms, Bellevue Ave. (☎ **401/847-1000**). Open late March through October, daily 10am to 5pm; January through late March, weekends 10am to 4pm. Closed November and December.

Land's End, Ledge Rd. (☎ **401/847-4883**). Private.

Marble House, Chinese Teahouse, Bellevue Ave. (☎ **401/847-1000**). Closed early 2000 for construction; from early

April, open daily 10am to 6pm.

Newport Preservation Society, 424 Bellevue Ave. (☎ **401/847-1000;** www.newportmansions.org), manages 11 estates, 8 of which can be visited. Visitors can see all the estates for $35.50, any two for $21, three for $25, or five for $29. Prices for individual estates range from $10 to $15; $4 for children 6 to 17.

Newport Squash Club, 8 Freebody St. (☎ **401/846-1011**). Open October through April, Monday through Friday 9am to 8pm; May through September, Monday through Friday 9am to 6pm;

weekends, 9am to 2pm. Fee $10 per person for 45 minutes.

Rosecliff, Bellevue Ave. (☎ 401/847-1000). Open April through October,

daily 10am to 5pm; closed November through March.

Rough Point, Bellevue Ave. Not open to the public.

SHOPPING

Country Kettle Fudge, 359 Thames St. (☎ 401/849-2228). Open daily 11am to 7pm (until 11pm or midnight during summer).

Nutcracker Suite Christmas Shop, 22 Mill St. (☎ 401/846-7385). Open

summer, daily 10am to 10pm; rest of year, Sunday through Thursday 10am to 6pm, Friday and Saturday 10am to 9pm.

EVENTS

Annual Classic Yacht Regatta, Labor Day weekend. Race on Saturday 10am to 4:30pm at the Museum of Yachting, Fort Adams State Park, on Ocean Dr. (☎ 401/847-1018). In addition to the sailing races, there is a parade on Sunday at 2pm, exhibitions, and a slide show. Museum open mid-May through October, daily 10am to 5pm; November through mid-May, by appointment only. Admission $4, $3 for seniors and children 3 to 12, free for children 2 and younger.

Annual Newport International Boat Show (☎ 800/582-7846). Held over 4 days in September (Sept 13 to 16 in 2001), 10am to 6pm, along the water by the Newport Yachting Center, Old Port Marine and Bannister's Wharf, on America's Cup Ave, and Waites Wharf on Thames St. Daily admission $12 on weekdays, $15 on weekends; 2-day pass, $22; 3-day pass $30, free for children under 12.

Learning to Snowboard at Vermont's Stratton Mountain

by Neil Strauss

T HE FIRST TECHNICAL TERM ADDED to a beginner's vocabulary when learning to snowboard is "face plant." These words describe what happens when the downhill edge of a moving snowboard touches the mountain, sending the rider flying with a violent jerk face-first into the snow. From the chairlift at Stratton Mountain in Vermont, snowboarders and skiers have a bird's-eye view of faces being planted all over the slopes. For beginners, face plants are a common occurrence; for the intermediate snowboarder, face plants are a constant fear; and for anyone who has spent a long day on the mountain, face plants are what happen over dinner in a hot bowl of soup.

On a wintry Friday, some friends and I drove to Stratton with the purpose of learning how to snowboard. Although this is not the closest mountain to Manhattan (it's more than a 4-hour drive), Stratton, which calls itself the birthplace of snowboarding, has distinct advantages over closer mountains. Hunter, just 2½ hours from New York City, tends to get overcrowded, with toddlers on leashes and large groups of teenagers and families knocking each other over. Mount Snow, just south of Stratton in Vermont, offers more of a singles scene. As saturated with trails as it is with expensive ski wear, the medium-size mountain is a better place to ride once you have passed the face-plant phase of snowboarding. And though Killington, also in Vermont, is the biggest resort in the area, with the self-given nickname the Beast of the East, most of the trails are not snowboard-friendly.

Stratton is a well-groomed, picturesque mountain, almost entirely devoid of the ultrasteep, mogul-filled, or bone-breaking slopes that attract hotshots. Even a tyro can ride to the top of the mountain and find a variety of long, gentle, winding trails to take. The mountain's specialty is intermediate trails: nice declines, long and wide, that evenly fluctuate from steep to not so steep. It's perfect for the beginning snowboarder. There is also an area of the mountain set aside for snowboarders only, full of snow mounds that serve as jumps and a hollowed-out half-pipe dug lengthwise into the surface of the snow for those who are good enough for flips, spins, and other stunts.

Though skiers and snowboarders often complain of pricey lift tickets and equipment rentals, the real robbery takes place before the trip even starts. It happens when shopping for ski apparel. If you talk to the commission-oriented sales staff at most sports stores and gravitate toward the products labeled as specially made for snowboarders, it can easily cost $1,000 to buy the clothing you need to be warm, dry, and safe: a Burton Duo-Lite parka with advanced snow-sealing enclosures ($220); Smith Classic goggles with Fog-X ($60); direct-grip Gore-Tex gloves ($100); snow pants with removable kneepads ($180); a wool sweater ($100 to $200); long underwear with moisture-wicking fabric and other clothes for layering ($100 to $200); forward-lean socks and silk-blend sock liners ($25), and a Mossimo hat ($25). A waterproof outfit put together by scavenging department stores, vintage shops, and friends' closets can look just as good and function just as well on the slopes, minus only the brand names.

Though there are some quaint old inns and hotels 20 minutes from Stratton in the town of Manchester, we chose to stay closer to the slopes, at the mountain's own condos. For those who reserve early and are willing to pay a little extra, a condo can be rented so close to the mountain that you can literally ski to the chairlifts. Ours was a comfortable but generic-looking affair with two bedrooms, a nice-size kitchen, a living room, and a stone fireplace. Though $396 a night was steep, it included lift tickets for the four of us (normally $60 a weekend per person) and discounted admission to the Stratton Sports Club, where those who haven't had enough exercise can swim and play tennis and those who are exhausted can relax in the sauna or get a massage.

Having become something of an expert in beginner hills, I can say that Stratton's was among the best. It was long and evenly sloped, which is an advantage over, say, Mount Snow's, which is so small that you hardly have time to learn anything on the way down. Stratton's is also shielded by trees from the rest of the trail so that beginners aren't knocked over by experts.

Though snowboarding magazines offer hundreds of photographs of riders flying through the air as if jet-propelled, they never capture one of snowboarding's equally striking images: the tangle of bodies on the ground invariably found at the exit of the beginner hill chairlift. Exiting a chairlift on a snowboard can be harder than traversing a mountain because only one of your feet is strapped into the board when you're not heading downhill, making maneuvering on the tiny exit ramp a difficult balancing act.

The Ski and Snowboard School is at the base of the bunny hill, which is where my friends and I signed up for $25 group lessons after renting boots and an all-purpose snowboard called a freestyle board for $31 a person. Though snowboarding has been around since 1969 when a Utah surfer named Dimitrije Milovich tried to find a way to entertain himself in the winter, it began entering the popular consciousness in the mid-1980s. Now, at Stratton, almost every teenager and about one-third of everybody else had snowboards strapped to their feet.

More so than in skiing, owning your own equipment for snowboarding can make a big difference. At the rental counter, none of us was given boots snug enough to prevent our feet from lifting out of the heel of the boot (a no-no in snowboarding); the Burton-brand boards, though new, were already worn away on the base and edge, and the bindings could not be set for our particular riding stances, as we didn't know what they were yet.

As we split off into different lesson groups, some of us found the experience frustrating, others rewarding. It all depended on the size of the group and whether the instructor was someone who really wanted to teach or a vacationing college student just working at the mountain so he could spend the winter skiing and partying. In my 12-member group, with two instructors who were members of the party category, most of the time was spent sitting in the snow waiting for each member of the group to tumble, one by one, down 25-yard sections of the hill. I did, however, receive a few essential tips on how to scrape down the hill on the heel and toe edges of the board and how to execute a

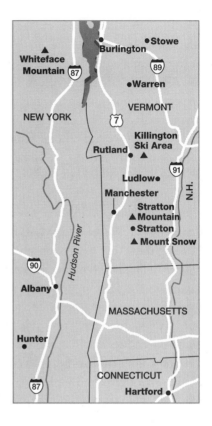

falling-leaf pattern (gliding down the hill alternating from the front to the back of the board without ever completing a more difficult full turn).

Most of the staff spoke the language of surfers—"dude," "rad," "wipe out"—so incessantly that the students began picking it up. Though some beginners take lessons all weekend, we decided not to sign up for the next course and to learn from our mistakes instead.

As anyone who has switched from skiing to boarding will tell you, learning to snowboard is not all that difficult. It's easy to adjust to the fact that you can slide down the mountain facing any direction, and that your feet are strapped fast to the board and won't come out even after a severe fall. The challenge is in learning a new type of balance and coordination, different from skiing, surfing, and skateboarding, in which your legs and feet are in constant communication with the slope of the mountain.

After a few frustrating, bruising runs down the bunny trail, we decided to throw caution to the wind and take the poetically named American Express lift midway up the mountain. It proved to be the brightest idea we had all day. From the beginning to the end of each run down the mountain, we all became better snowboarders. Just having more time to fall, to get frustrated, to navigate through forking trails made all the difference. And snowboarders sharing the chairlift with us were happy to offer advice, suggest trails, and even help us down the hill. We were always quick to apologize to our new friends for bowling them over when clumsily exiting the chairlift.

By the end of the day, we were taking the lifts to the top of the mountain and learning to turn from the heel edge of the board to the toe edge. As in skiing, you don't just point your feet down the mountain and go. You carve from side to side (or from the toe side of the board to the heel side) for control and speed-reducing friction.

For a nourishment break, it's best to avoid the main base lodge, home to an overpriced junk-food cafeteria and a lost-and-found desk where people can be seen filling out stolen-property forms for snowboards that disappeared during their meal. (Tip: Invest $2 in the ski and snowboard checking hut.) Instead, snatch some free orange juice from one of the tents offering ski-equipment demonstrations at the base of the hill and head to the resort's entrance, where there sits, well groomed as artificial snow, an artificial town square with ski-wear shops, restaurants, and cafes. The best of these was Mulligans, a pub and restaurant no less overpriced, but with a light pecan-crusted salmon for those in need of a protein boost and smoky, sumptuous baby-back ribs for meat eaters who don't mind a few stains on their expensive ski clothes.

In the late afternoon and evening, Manchester is the destination of choice. In its own promotional brochures, the town sometimes calls itself "Historic Manchester Center." The first impression we had in driving through Historic Manchester Center was, "Wow, there are a lot of outlet stores!" Ralph Lauren, Calvin Klein, Giorgio Armani, Tommy Hilfiger, Movado, and dozens more promise bargains at their company outlets, though the prices don't seem to be any cheaper than at Bloomingdale's. Instead, we spent our time at the Museum of Fly-Fishing, which is not just an eye-opening initiation into a very active subculture but also a way to see the tackle of Presidents Jimmy Carter and Ronald Reagan.

For dinner, we made reservations at the Black Swan, a 15-year-old restaurant operated by the Whisenhunt husband-and-wife team: Richard, the chef, and Kathy, the hostess. The restaurant is in a 160-year-old farmhouse that has been divided into several tiny dining rooms. The main courses we sampled—the filet mignon with béarnaise sauce, the rack of lamb with garlic mashed potatoes—were delicious, and the array of choices on the dessert tray were as beautiful to look at as they were to eat.

We ended the night early at the Equinox Hotel, a tastefully garish Colonial-era hotel with a sprawling lobby that took an hour to explore and a cozy tavern where a band, though ailing from the flu, was playing high-spirited folk and pop standards. The hotel also had a school of falconry and, for those intrigued by their visit to the Museum of Fly-Fishing, a pond for practicing the sport.

On Sunday morning, muscles ached that we didn't even know we had used—from the ankle to the neck—and bruises had begun to emerge on our shins and backsides. Some of us refueled with eggs and pancakes, others with Advil.

We began the morning as voyeurs, gliding down to the mountain's snowboard park. The area is basically an intermediate slope with four snowy ramps for snowboarders to jump from and, at the bottom, an icy half-pipe with riders cruising up the rounded edges and launching themselves into the air. Punk songs by NOFX and Bad Religion blared from a nearby boom box, giving the area the feeling of a skateboard park. Watching the riders fly over the snow, clutching the edges of their boards five or six times in a single run down the half-pipe, answered the question that had long been burning in our minds: Just why is it that snowboards seem cooler than skis?

We spent the day all over the mountain, finding favorite trails (Upper Drifter, Old Smoothie, Suntanner) and taking chairlifts like Snow Bowl and North American, which started in the middle of the mountain and had shorter lines than the lifts at the bottom. The gondolas, the only lift that goes directly to the top of the mountain, were closed while workers chipped away at the ice on the support poles.

Though the trails are generally well marked, about 60% of the runs from the top of the mountain are marked with black diamonds, for experts only. Though not as difficult as the black diamonds on other mountains, we ran into a bit of a predicament when we followed some skiers through a clearing and found ourselves on a double black-diamond trail called Upper Spruce. As I was doing my best to keep from losing control on the steep slope, I suddenly saw one of my friends whiz past at lightning speed. It would have been impressive if he wasn't heading down headfirst on his back. He slid a good 50 yards before he was able to stop himself, and in the process just may have invented a new sport. We also learned a thing or two about moguls on the run. Lesson No. 1 was not to lean back, or the moguls become something akin to the jumps in the snowboard park.

Perhaps the greatest feeling of the day was catching the last lift up the mountain at 4:30pm, and winding down the trails all alone, actually, after 2 days, able to snowboard with some coordination and a minimum of face plants. We decided to celebrate by eating at the one restaurant that every guidebook and ski instructor had recommended: the Birkenhaus, an Austrian-style inn and restaurant near the mountain.

Because it was Sunday night, and weekend warriors were already beginning their long drive home, it was almost empty. The best thing about the meal was the bread: We left our Wiener schnitzel, our salads, our potato pancakes, and our chicken half-eaten. Perhaps resorts do come to life only on holidays and Friday and Saturday. On Sunday, they probably give their chefs the night off.

STRATTON & MANCHESTER ESSENTIALS

Stratton, on Stratton Mountain Rd. in Stratton Mountain (☎ **802/297-2200;** www.stratton.com), has 90 trails, 12 lifts, and six snowboard parks open to skiers and snowboarders November to April, daily 8:30am to 4pm. Daily lift tickets are $55 on weekdays, $60 on weekends and holidays. Daily snowboard and boot rental is $42, $37 for children. Introductory lesson with equipment and lift ticket $79 ($25 per person for a group lesson).

GETTING THERE

By Car From New York City, take I-95 North to I-91 North in New Haven, CT; stay on I-91 from New Haven to Vermont, Exit 2 at Brattleboro, VT. Follow the signs to Rte. 30. Drive approximately 40 miles north on Rte. 30 to the Village of Bondville, and turn left at the Stratton Access Rd., located in the center of Bondville; it is 4 miles to the resort.

An Alternate Route: Take I-87 North to I-787 North at Albany, NY; from there, take I-787 to the exit for Rte. 7 East (the sign will say TO BENNINGTON, VT). Follow Rte. 7 East, which turns into Rte. 9 at the Vermont border, to Bennington. In Bennington, follow U.S. Rte. 7 North to exit 4 at Manchester, VT; turn right at the bottom of the exit ramp on Rte. 11 East/30 South. After approximately 5 miles, the routes will divide; stay right following Rte. 30 South approximately 7 miles into the Village of Bondville; continue following the directions above.

By Bus Greyhound (☎ **800/231-2222)** offers service to Manchester, VT, daily from the Port Authority Bus Terminal in Manhattan; the trip takes approximately 5 hours. Call for schedule and fares.

By Train Amtrak (☎ **800/872-7245)** travels to Brattleboro, VT, daily from Penn Station in Manhattan. Call for schedule and fares. From Brattleboro, Stratton can be reached by either car or bus.

ACCOMMODATIONS

For mountainside accommodations on Stratton Mountain, call ☎ **800/787-2886.**
Equinox, Main St. (Historic Rte. 7A), Manchester Village (☎ **800/362-4747).** Open year-round. 183 rooms and suites (some wheelchair accessible). Rates $189 to $339 double; $499 to $899 suite.

DINING

Black Swan, Main St. (Historic Rte. 7A), Manchester Village (☎ **802/362-3807).** Open year-round, Thursday through Monday 5:30 to 9pm; closed first 3 weeks in November. Dinner entrees $14.75 to $26.

Mulligans, in the Village Square, Stratton (☎ **802/297-9293).** In winter, open Monday through Thursday 11am to 10pm, Friday 11am to midnight, Saturday 11am to 11pm; closed mid-April through May. Dinner entrees $13 to $21.

ATTRACTIONS BEYOND THE SLOPES

American Museum of Fly-Fishing, Main St. (Historic Rte. 7A) and Seminary Ave., Manchester Village, VT (☎ **802/362-3300).** Year-round, daily 10am to 4pm; closed holidays. Admission $3, free for children 14 and under and museum members.

MORE SNOWBOARDING ESSENTIALS: OTHER AREA RESORTS

It is now possible to snowboard, rent snowboard equipment, and take snowboarding lessons at most major American ski resorts. Aside from having to wear leashes connecting their boards to their boots, snowboarders are usually free to do anything that skiers do. Like Stratton, many resorts have snowboard parks, which are runs for snowboarders only. These usually include snow structures designed for performing by snowboarders. Common structures include half-pipes (giant tubes cut in half), tabletops (flat areas of snow), and rails (logs).

IN NEW YORK STATE

Hunter Mountain, Hunter, NY (☎ **518/ 263-4223;** 800/775-4641 for mountainside accommodations). 53 trails and 14 lifts, plus snowboard park with half-pipe. Open November to April, daily 9am to 4pm. Daily lift tickets $38 weekdays and $46 weekends, $23 weekdays and $29 weekends for children and seniors. Daily snowboard and boot rental $25, $18 for children and seniors. Introductory lesson with equipment and lift ticket is $45, $22 per person for group lesson.

Whiteface Mountain Ski Area, Rte. 86, Wilmington, NY (☎ **800/462-6236;** 800/447-5224 for accommodations). 70 trails and 11 lifts, plus one-half–mile terrain park with lift; half-pipe. Open November to April, daily 8:30am to 4pm. Daily lift tickets $46 weekdays and weekends, $35 for those 13 to 19 and 65 to 69, $19 for those

7 to 12, free for children 6 and younger. Daily snowboard and boot rental $31 for those 13 and older, $27 for those 12 and younger. Introductory lesson with equipment and lift ticket is $55, $20 per person for group lesson.

IN VERMONT

Killington Resort, Killington Rd., Killington, VT (☎ **802/422-6200;** 800/ 621-6867 for mountainside accommodations). Call for hours and prices.

Mount Snow, Rte. 100, West Dover, VT (☎ **802/464-3333;** 800/245-7669 for mountainside accommodations). 130 trails and 23 lifts; two alpine parks, open to both snowboarders and skiers; and two half-pipes. Open November through April, weekdays 9am to 4pm, weekends 8am to 4pm. Daily lift tickets are $49 weekdays and holidays, $55 weekends; $45 weekdays and $49 weekends for those 13 to 18; $31 weekdays and $35 weekends and holidays for those 6 to 12 and 65 and older; children 5 and under free. Daily snowboard and boot rental $32, $22 for children. Introductory lesson with equipment and lift ticket is $70, $33 per person for group lesson.

Okemo Mountain Resort, 77 Okemo Ridge Rd., Ludlow, VT (☎ **802/228-4041;** 800/786-5366 for mountainside accommodations). 98 trails and 14 lifts, plus two terrain parks, one half-pipe, and one super pipe. Open November to April, weekdays 9am to 4pm, weekends 8am to 4pm. Daily lift tickets $51 weekdays and $56 weekends and holidays; $46 weekdays and $48 weekends for those 13 to 18 and 65 to 69; $34 weekdays and $36 weekends for those 7 to 12 and 70 and older; free for those 6 and under with lift ticket. Daily snowboard and boot rental $30. Introductory lesson with equipment and lift ticket is $55, $50 for children and seniors, $30 per person for group lesson. Also a 2-day package with equipment, lift, and lesson for $99, $89 for juniors and seniors.

Stowe Mountain Resort, 5781 Mountain Rd., Stowe, VT (☎ **802/253-3500;** 800/253-4754 for mountainside accommodations). 48 trails and 11 lifts, plus two terrain parks, one half-pipe, and one super pipe; also, a yurt for snowboarders, featuring a sound and video system. Open November to April, weekdays 8am to 4pm, weekends 7:30am to 4pm; skiing early January through mid-March, Thursday through Saturday to 9pm. Daily lift tickets $54 ($56 holidays) weekdays and weekends, $34 for children and seniors ($35 holidays). Daily snowboard and boot rental $26, $16 for children. Introductory lesson with equipment and lift ticket $94, $30 per person for group lesson.

Sugarbush Resort, Sugarbush Access Rd., Warren, VT (☎ **802/583-2381;** 800/537-8427 for mountainside and area accommodations). 115 trails and 18 lifts, plus two snowboard parks and one half-pipe. Open November through late April, weekdays 9am to 4pm, weekends 8:30am to 4pm. Daily lift tickets $55 weekdays and weekends, $35 for children 12 and younger and 65 and older. Daily snowboard and boot rental $30. Introductory lesson with equipment and lift ticket is $65, $30 per person for group lesson.

A LITERARY TOUR
OF THE BERKSHIRES

by Elisabeth Bumiller

In THE FALL OF 1899, A YOUNG
woman of old New York society and fledgling literary notice grew disgusted with what she considered the vapid wasteland of Newport, Rhode Island, the family resort that both defined and imprisoned her. On an impulse, she packed up her dogs, her servants, and her husband and headed for Lenox, Massachusetts, and the fashionable Berkshire mountain retreat where there were plenty of millionaire "cottagers," too, but where Nathaniel Hawthorne had completed *The House of Seven Gables* and Herman Melville had written *Moby-Dick.*

Within 3 years, the young woman, Edith Wharton, had built the Mount, a classical American home of painted white stucco and green shutters, modeled on a grand 17th-century English country house. There, she wrote *The House of Mirth,* entertained Henry James, and lived through the ugly end of her marriage. Today the Mount is as much a reflection of the Wharton psyche as her tragic heroine, Lily Bart.

My family and I spent a recent weekend touring the Mount and wandering around other literary landmarks of the Berkshires. We went to Melville's Arrowhead farm in Pittsfield, then to Hawthorne's reconstructed "little red house" behind Tanglewood, and finally to William Cullen Bryant's family homestead in Cummington. The tour guides ranged from superb to dotty to nonexistent, but every house except Hawthorne's was worth the trip. The weekend turned out to be a journey into a past when writers sought inspiration from the quiet hills for their turbulent ideas.

On the way, we also soaked up Shakespeare, modern dance, and Mozart, small samplings of the local offerings that weekend. In summer, the Berkshires are such a banquet of culture that when I jogged through Tanglewood on Saturday morning, I was serenaded by violins playing at breakfast on the outrageously green lawn. As Wharton herself once wrote, "The truth is, I am in love with the place—climate, scenery, life & all."

Wharton's Legacy

Lenox is an easy 3-hour drive up the Taconic Parkway from New York City, with meandering country roads to perk up the last leg. Early on Friday evening, my husband and I and our two children, ages 8 and 4, checked into the Apple Tree Inn, a big white frame house with a friendly staff and a rose-bordered pool overlooking the hills. Then we picked up picnic supplies and headed to the Mount, 5 minutes away.

There, in the dusk on Wharton's front lawn, near the remains of her French flower garden, we spread out a tablecloth, ate cold barbecued chicken, and slapped at mosquitoes. Picnics are very much allowed—the grounds are open from May through October—but there was not a soul around and the silence made me feel sacrilegious. I imagined the author of *The Age of Innocence* and *Ethan Frome* coming out on her terrace and ordering a servant to remove us. Wharton was always a terrific snob.

Afterward we walked to Wharton's old stable for a likable production of *All's Well That Ends Well* put on by Shakespeare and Company, the theater group that performs at the Mount.

We returned the next morning for an hourlong group tour of the house, led by a well-informed and sardonic Kathleen Forrest, a history major at the University of Massachusetts at Amherst. When Ms. Forrest took us into the Mount's Italian-inspired gallery, she pointed out the terrazzo floor that Wharton had installed, then remarked: "She said it would keep the room cool and easier to clean. I'm not quite sure how she knew that because she never cleaned a floor in her life."

The Mount naturally had abundant staff and was largely run by Teddy Wharton, Edith's husband, freeing her to write in the mornings.

Ms. Forrest told us that Wharton awakened at 6am, wrote in longhand while still in bed, and then let her pages fall to the floor to be collected later by the maid.

Biographers describe a woman who largely hid the arduous work of her writing, a profession unsuitable for a woman of her class and time, from her constant houseguests. The Wharton biographer Percy Lubbock describes how "a gay little note, thrown off as it were between chapters, would appear for the guest on his breakfast tray, with a greeting and plan for the day."

By 11am, Wharton surfaced to play hostess, overseeing walks, carriage rides, motor trips into the countryside, and amusing dinners. Henry James wrote to Wharton's sister-in-law from the Mount, "I need scarcely tell you that I am very happy here, surrounded by every loveliness of nature and every luxury of art and treated with a benevolence that brings tears to my eyes." Like Wharton, James reveled in a country house that rejected the Victorian clutter of the era for light, simplicity, and common sense.

In fact, Wharton, who is considered to have had nearly professional competence in architectural design, had strong opinions on interior decoration and was co-author, with the architect Ogden Codman, Jr., of an arch and witty book on how to outfit an upper-class home. Published in 1897, the book, *The Decoration of Houses,* mounts a full-scale attack on the heavy swags and gewgaws of the homes of Wharton's childhood.

"House decoration has come to be regarded as a black art by those who have seen their rooms subjected to the manipulations of the modern upholsterer," it says, adding that the average American drawing room was so uncomfortable that "no one will ever sit in it except the luckless visitor who has no other refuge."

The book says a visitor should at least be entitled to the solace of a few books in the room, "but as all the tables in the room are littered with knickknacks, it is difficult for the most philanthropic hostess to provide even this slight alleviation."

In contrast, the rooms of the Mount are large but still comfortable and intimate, with much air and natural light. French doors open onto a sunny Italianate terrace from four rooms on the main floor. The most

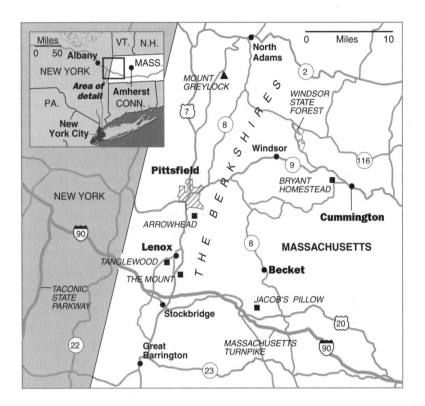

interesting is Wharton's oak-paneled library—women of the era were not supposed to have libraries—which looks like an elegant men's club. Unfortunately, neither Wharton's books nor her library desk, a large table called a *bureau-ministre,* much recommended in *The Decoration of Houses,* is in the house.

Unhappy Love Affair

Teddy Wharton's smaller study adjoins the library, and as Ms. Forrest took us through, she described Edith's love affair with the bisexual Morton Fullerton—"It didn't end all that well"—as well as Teddy's apparent manic-depression, followed by his embezzlement of Edith's trust fund to buy a house for his mistress. The couple parted ways, and in 1911 Edith sold the Mount and moved to France. She never lived in the United States again.

For a long time the house was in disrepair, the result of a court fight between Edith Wharton Restoration, the nonprofit group that owns the house and grounds, and Shakespeare and Company, the acting group that performs plays on the property. The court case was settled in the late 1990s. The troupe's lease will expire in 2003, but Shakespeare and Company may move to their new quarters down the road before then. When we visited, I liked the decrepit state of the house. It seemed honest, like a real house abandoned by its owner. At the least we were allowed complete freedom to wander the grounds, something unthinkable should the Mount become an exquisite museum.

Today the house is in process of restoration, which would no doubt please Wharton. Throughout her life she kept her homes as artfully as she structured her sentences. The exterior restoration was completed in 2000, and the restoration of the interior is ongoing. Edith Wharton Restoration is now trying to raise $35 million to complete restoration of the entire property.

Next stop was 10 minutes away, at Arrowhead, the claustrophobic farmhouse where Melville wrote *Moby-Dick*.

Three guides took us through two rooms each. The first guide was confused and the second rude. ("Sir, I don't like to be bossy, but we ask people not to touch anything," she snapped when a hapless soul in our group got too close to a bookcase.) But the third, Janet Cook, age 74, was a great enthusiast. Melville, she told us, was such a literary star when he married that he had to change the location of his wedding to escape the groupies.

"How do you like them apples?" she asked us, thrilled. "He was the first literary sex symbol!"

The highlight of the tour was the small upstairs study where Melville wrote *Moby-Dick*. Looking out the window, we could see his view of the two humps of Mount Greylock that even in summer suggest a huge whale.

Ms. Cook told us that Melville often locked himself in to write, that his was not a happy family, and that he had an intense friendship with Hawthorne. "When they met, something unusual happened," she said.

She did not go so far as to say that Melville was in love with Hawthorne, as some scholars believe. Nor did she introduce any debate about whether Melville beat his wife, as an Ohio State University Melvillean announced in 1994. Ms. Cook's tone was respectful, even awed. I think Melville would have liked her tour.

We stopped briefly at a replica of the house where Hawthorne lived from the spring of 1850 to the fall of 1851, now a fund-raising headquarters for the Boston Symphony Orchestra. Inside is a modern office, nothing more, and no sense at all of the writer.

Dance & Music

After dinner, we drove to the Jacob's Pillow Dance Festival in Becket for a spectacular performance by Ballet Hispanico, an Upper West Side–based company that fuses Hispanic culture and contemporary American dance.

We spent Sunday afternoon listening to the Boston Symphony Chamber Players at Tanglewood, where the grounds are a Garden of Eden. Even the forest-green garbage bins are tasteful, with sides so high that nothing as unpleasant as an ice-cream wrapper mars the aesthetic. People up close listened intently to Wagner's *Siegfried Idyll* and *Mozart's Serenade in G* for strings. Farther back they read the newspaper and napped. Everyone was well behaved.

Last stop was Cummington, 40 minutes away, for a look at the home of Bryant, the poet and influential abolitionist editor of the *New York Evening Post*. We were too late for the 1 to 5pm tour, and the pretty, cream-colored farmhouse with light brown trim was closed. But the trip was well worth it for the peaceful views from the front porch overlooking the hills, and the two rows of graceful old sugar maples, planted by Bryant and his brothers a century and a half ago, lining the drive.

We had a picnic dinner at a swimming hole in Windsor State Forest just down the road, then took a fast look at Windsor Jambs, a waterfall that was a big hit with the children.

For me the biggest hit of the weekend was the Mount. On the way back home, I pored over the 1985 Pulitzer prize–winning biography of

Wharton by R. W. B. Lewis to find descriptions of the home and what it meant to its mistress. The best thing I found was an excerpt from *The Fullness of Life,* a short story Wharton wrote in 1891 alluding to the emotional and sexual limitations of her marriage:

"I have sometimes thought that a woman's nature is like a great house full of rooms: there is the hall, through which everyone passes in going in and out; the drawing room, where one receives formal visits; the sitting room, where the members of the family come and go as they list; but beyond that, far beyond, are other rooms, the handles of whose doors perhaps are never turned; no one knows the way to them, no one knows whither they lead; and in the innermost room, the holy of holies, the soul sits alone and waits for a footstep that never comes."

Though I'm sure Wharton wouldn't like all the tourists tramping through the Mount, looking for clues to her nature, I think I found some. The house was, after all, a creation of her imagination, just like her writing. And it reveals an outwardly conservative woman of money, discernment, and social position whose Berkshire escape gave her room to pour her rebellion into her writing.

BERKSHIRES ESSENTIALS

GETTING THERE

By Car To reach Lenox from Manhattan, take the Henry Hudson Pkwy. to the Saw Mill Pkwy. to the Taconic Pkwy. Continue on the Taconic Pkwy. to the Massachusetts Tpk. Take the Massachusetts Tpk. East to exit 2, U.S. Rte. 20 West; follow Rte. 20 West into Lenox.

By Bus **Bonanza Bus Lines** (☎ 800/556-3815) offers daily service to Lenox from the Port Authority Bus Terminal, Eighth Ave. and 42nd St.; round-trip fare $62.50, half-price for children 2 to 11.

ACCOMMODATIONS

Apple Tree Inn, 10 Richmond Mountain Rd., Lenox (☎ 413/637-1477). Rates during the season, weekends or weekdays, based on double occupancy, range from $170 for a room with private bathroom to $330 for a suite; off-season, the daily rate ranges from $55 to $165. Children are welcome.

DINING

Church Street Cafe, 65 Church St., Lenox (☎ **413/637-2745**). Late June through August, open daily 11:30am to 2pm and 5:30 to 9pm; rest of year, open Tuesday through Saturday, same hours; closed Sunday and Monday.

Loeb's Food Town, Main and Housatonic sts., Lenox (☎ **413/637-0270**). Open Monday through Thursday and Saturday 7am to 6pm, Friday 7am to 7pm, Sunday 7am to 4pm.

ATTRACTIONS

Arrowhead, 780 Holmes Rd., Pittsfield (☎ **413/442-1793**). Melville's farm is open Memorial Day through October, hourly tours 10am to 4pm. Admission $5, $4.50 for seniors, $3 for those 16 to 25, $1 for children 6 to 15, free for children under 6.

Jacob's Pillow Dance Festival, off Rte. 20, Becket (☎ **413/243-0745**). Call for schedule and ticket information.

The Mount, at the junction of Rte. 7 and Rte. 7A and Plunkett St., Lenox (☎ **413/ 637-1899**). Open Memorial Day through October, hourly tours 9am to 2pm. Admission $6, $5.50 for seniors, $4.50 for children 13 to 18, free for children 12 and under.

Shakespeare and Company, at the Mount (☎ **413/637-3353** or 413/ 637-1199). Call for schedule and ticket information.

Tanglewood, Rte. 183 (West St.), Lenox (☎ **800/274-8499** or 413/637-5165). Call for schedule and ticket information.

William Cullen Bryant Homestead, Cummington (☎ **413/634-2244**). Open late June through Labor Day, Friday through Sunday and Monday holidays 1 to 5pm; Labor Day through Columbus Day, weekends and Monday holidays 1 to 5pm. Admission $5, $2.50 for children 6 to 12, free for children under 6.

Windsor State Forest, River Rd., Windsor (☎ **413/684-0948**). Open May through October, dawn to dusk. Parking $3.

WHERE HISTORY & BEACHES MEET

by Charles Strum

LOOK AT A MAP AND YOU'LL SEE THE problem instantly: The pint-size right triangle of land called Delaware looks like a cartographic afterthought.

Its northern tip is embedded in Pennsylvania. The rest seems to be a province of eastern Maryland, which itself resembles a Rorschach blot between Chesapeake Bay and the Atlantic Ocean. What's more, the southernmost sliver of the Eastern Shore turns out to be part of Virginia.

The whole peninsula is called Delmarva, a coinage as cluttered as the acreage it was meant to unify. Why can't Delaware have the rectangular boldness of, say, Kansas?

All right, this is a quibble over a small place with multiple personalities. Once you get 100 miles south of industrial Wilmington, the name Du Pont vanishes from consciousness, and Delaware, indeed, begins to look very much like Kansas, unrelentingly rural and as flat as barn siding. But go east, and the sameness of southern Delaware's farm country gives way to bay and ocean beach with some of the most curvaceous sand dunes on the Atlantic.

From Lewes (pronounced *Loo*-iss), a 360-year-old village of boat builders and fishermen tucked into the crook of Cape Henlopen at the mouth of Delaware Bay, to Rehoboth Beach and its sisters, Bethany Beach, Dewey Beach, and Fenwick Island, the compact 25-mile ocean coastline makes a weekend excursion feel like a visit to someone's rambling summer compound. Your host has left no one unprovided for:

368

shopping and sightseeing in historic Lewes, boardwalk amuse-
ments in Rehoboth Beach, and,
in a state with no sales tax, three
sprawling outlet malls with 140
high-end retailers on Route 1,
the main north-south highway.

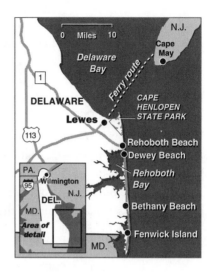

Once the ancient preserve of
American Indian beachcombers,
the coast's harbors and inlets
eventually lured pirates and
other plunderers (the Dutch and
the British). The pirates, among
them Captain Kidd, were
rumored to have buried their
treasure onshore; the Dutch and the British occasionally fired cannonballs at the populace from the safety of the bay. And through it all, the
shore has always offered four-star avian hospitality during the spring
migration, when millions of horseshoe-crab eggs make Delaware the
prime layover for red knots and other birds commuting between South
American winter homes and Arctic breeding grounds.

But no invasion has been as enduring or as lucrative as the invasion
of the summer people, a tradition that dates to the 1870s, when
Rehoboth Beach, the hub of the Delaware shore, became a Methodist
campground. You can still find Methodists and campgrounds, but
mostly you will find families from the Mid-Atlantic states, the Capitol
Hill crowd (Rehoboth, 125 miles from Washington, has long billed
itself as "the nation's summer capital"), and a share of the 20-some-
things. They fill the low-rise boardwalk hotels and the dignified
Colonial and Cape Cod homes for rent deep in the city's cool pine
groves, a feature that distinguishes Rehoboth Beach from the nearby
New Jersey shore, where shade usually comes from a beach umbrella.

In Delaware, the beaches are free (no tags, no fees) and summer
feels like a religious rite, with the beach as altar and the parking meter
a kind of collection plate.

Up and down Rehoboth Avenue, the wide four-lane main street in Rehoboth Beach, where earlier in the century vacationers arrived at the mile-long boardwalk by steam locomotive, parking meters are the most visible sign that summer is in session. The city implants the meter heads about a week before Memorial Day and extracts them the second Sunday after Labor Day.

Gorged from continual daily feedings (10am to midnight), the meters are a gold mine—4.4 million quarters last season, or $1.1 million in revenue. Much of it pays for a workforce that grows from 64 to 200 full-time employees—from beach patrol to police force to sanitation crew—to serve a community that bulges to as many as 50,000 in July and August. Year-round, the city has fewer than 1,500 inhabitants.

By Ferry Across the Bay

My 12-year-old son, Alec, and I decided to preview the season on a recent weekend. We knew we'd have a 170-mile drive down the Garden State Parkway to Cape May, but we were looking forward to a leisurely ferry ride at the end of it.

After a 3-hour trip from northern New Jersey, we easily spotted the blue and yellow signs for the Cape May–Lewes Ferry, a five-boat fleet that began service in 1964 and now carries 1.5 million passengers annually. Each vessel can carry 1,000 passengers and 100 vehicles. In peak season, a family of four in a car or van would pay $39.50 one-way. The 17-mile voyage across Delaware Bay to Lewes takes about 70 minutes.

Alec and I crossed on the *Cape Henlopen,* grazing in the snack bar and picking over trinkets in the gift shop. The bay was calm—we picked up a three-dolphin escort midway—and the boat eventually reached its cruising speed of about 16 knots. As we drew near Lewes, we caught sight of some of the cylindrical watchtowers at the former Fort Miles, a warren of concrete gun emplacements built by the Army in 1940 to guard the bay against submarines preying on Allied oil tankers from Wilmington and Philadelphia. German subs were sighted (one surrendered in 1945), but ordnance from Fort Miles never engaged one. Climb the 110 steps to the top of a tower, and you'll have a panoramic view.

The guns themselves are gone now, and the fort is part of Cape Henlopen State Park, a pristine preserve of dunes, marshes, meadows, and woods threaded by nature trails and bike paths, just outside Lewes, which is only a mile or so from the pier.

We made our way to the Bay Moon Bed and Breakfast, which I had picked out of a book called *Recommended Bed and Breakfasts, Mid-Atlantic States,* by Suzi Forbes Gates (Globe Pequot Press, 1995). The Bay Moon, an 1887 Victorian home, had changed hands only months before, but the transition must have been smooth. Our host, Pam Rizzo, cooked up magnificent breakfasts; served wine, soda, and cheese at cocktail time; and even provided a bored preteenager with a selection of popular videos for viewing in our room. Alec chose *Dante's Peak,* a volcanic romance.

On our first full day, we toured Lewes, which calls itself the first town in the first state (Delaware having been the first colony to ratify the Constitution, in 1791). It was settled by Dutchmen from the town of Hoorn who had come looking for whales in the bay in 1631 but found that swans were more plentiful. Three hundred years later, in 1931, the town dedicated a scaled-down copy of Hoorn's city hall. It stands today near the center of town as the Zwaanendael Museum, which means "valley of the swans."

A two-story exhibit center of local artifacts, history, and lore, the museum is a good way to get started. The story of a British warship, HMS *deBraak,* is one of the highlights. Known to have preyed on Spanish ships in the New World, the *deBraak* sank in a squall off Cape Henlopen in 1787; treasure hunters speculated for years about the wealth that might have been aboard. When the ship was finally found and raised in the mid-1980s, there was no loot, but there were thousands of artifacts from the period.

More slapstick than drama is the brief story of another British ship, the *Poictiers* (pronounced *Pahs*-tee-ay), that unfolds in a delightful example of English epistolary understatement—a framed copy of a handwritten letter from a British naval commander to the chief magistrate of Lewes during the War of 1812.

Dated March 16, 1813, the officer's letter says:

> *Sir,*
>
> *As soon as you receive this, I request you will send 20 live bullocks with a proportionate quantity of vegetables and hay to the Poictiers for the use of Britannic Majesty's squadron now at this anchorage, which will be immediately paid for at the Philadelphia prices.*
>
> *If you refuse to comply with this request I shall be under necessity of destroying your town.*
>
> *I have the honor to be, sir, your very obedient servant,*
>
> *J. P. Beresford Commodore*
>
> *and commander of the British Squadron in the*
>
> *Mouth of the Delaware.*

On April 6 and 7, having heard nothing from Lewes, the commodore shelled the town, killing a chicken and wounding a pig.

Alec and I found a cannonball from the Poictiers lodged in a stone foundation of the Marine Museum on Front Street. But as Alec pointed out, Beresford's gunners would have had no shot at the old house now; their sights would be blocked by Cinnamon Falls Gourmet Coffee and the House of Candles.

The ineffectual cannonball is just a block north of the graveyard at St. Peter's Episcopal Church, where such notables as the *deBraak's* captain, James Drew, and four Delaware governors are buried. There's also the inexplicably odd stone of Elizabeth H. Cullen, born "February 30th, 1760."

A Little Night Music

Before tourism, Lewes made its money turning huge catches of menhaden into fertilizer. Now, shopping, dining, and sportfishing are its mainstay. And while there's a large beach at Lewes, the more popular ones start about 7 miles down the road at Rehoboth Beach.

After a day at the arcades or the rides at Funland on the boardwalk, there is almost always an open-air concert. On our last night on the shore, a kind of *Ah, Wilderness!* mood enveloped the bandstand as this essentially old-fashioned summer town and some young out-of-towners prepared to get to know each other.

It was nearly 7:30, and Bill Berresford, director of the Mansfield, Pennsylvania, High School Band (and no relation to the old commodore), was fixing a sticky saxophone valve for a nervous teenage musician while 80 of her colleagues, warming up, shifted in metal folding chairs on the bandstand and tootled chaotically.

Above them, stars were already popping into view. Facing them, about 200 yards away, was the churning Atlantic. Directly in front of them, wandering among the white wooden benches, random strollers gradually took the form of an audience.

Joan Berresford, the director's wife and also a music teacher, explained that the band takes a 2-day trip at the close of the school year, sometimes venturing to Pittsburgh or Philadelphia to play the national anthem for the Pirates or the Phillies. Every 4 years, the band goes to Rehoboth Beach and Bethany Beach for concerts and some well-earned relaxation.

"Most of these kids are from farm country," Mrs. Berresford said. "It took us 7 hours to get here, and many of them have never seen the ocean."

When the concert ended at 9 o'clock, the band got a standing ovation. The next morning, squinting into the hazy sun after a late night of beach food, 80 young people from north-central Pennsylvania put their blankets on the sand and walked toward the surf.

GETTING AROUND ON THE DELAWARE SHORE: ESSENTIALS

For information, contact: **Lewes Chamber of Commerce and Visitors Bureau,** P.O. Box 1, Lewes, DE 19958 (☎ **302/645-8073**), will send useful guides with maps and walking tours. The bureau is in the 18th-century Fisher-Martin house near the center of town.

Rehoboth-Dewey Beach Chamber of Commerce, P.O. Box 216. Rehoboth Beach, DE 19971 (☎ **800/441-1329** or 302/227-2233). Write or call for a complete packet with information on lodging and restaurants.

GETTING THERE

By Car   From the New York area, take the Garden State Pkwy. to the end (about 170 miles) and watch for the signs to the Cape May–Lewes Ferry. At the height of the summer, the ferry makes 15 crossings each way, every day. A car or minivan and driver cost $20 ($18 off-peak), with $6.50 ($4.50 off-peak) for each additional passenger over age 5. Larger vehicles cost more. Motorcycles, bikes, and passengers on foot cost less. You can reserve a spot for a $5 fee, or take your chances at the pier. Crossing takes 70 minutes. For information, call ☎ **609/886-1725** in New Jersey; for reservations, 800/643-3779; in Delaware, ☎ **302/426-1155.**

By Bus   **Peter Pan Trailways (☎ 800/ 343-9999)** has daily bus service from the Port Authority Bus Terminal in midtown Manhattan to Rehoboth Beach. One-way fare is $56.50, round-trip $112.50; half price for children 2 to 11 years old.

ACCOMMODATIONS

Atlantic Sands Hotel, on the boardwalk at Baltimore and Maryland avenues, Rehoboth Beach (☎ **800/422-0600**). Only outdoor pool on the boardwalk. 114 rooms. Rates $145 to $213 weekdays and $198 to $280 weekends in peak season, $75 to $185 weekdays and weekends off-peak. Daily room rates are based on double occupancy. Children welcome.

Bay Moon Bed and Breakfast, 128 Kings Hwy., Lewes (☎ **302/644-1802**). Six rooms in restored Victorian house. Rates based on double occupancy $135 to $150 in peak season, $95 to $135 off-peak. Open year-round. Children welcome.

Inn at Canal Square, 122 Market St., Lewes (☎ **302/644-3377**). At the edge of the Lewes-Rehoboth Canal. 19 rooms. Rates based on double occupancy, $155 to $185 weekends in peak season, weekdays $125 to $160; $85 to $145 weekends off-peak, weekdays $70 to $119. Open year-round. Children welcome.

DINING

Kupchick's, 3 E. Bay Ave., Lewes (☎ **302/ 645-0420**). A beach landmark for steak and seafood. Open daily 4:30 to 10pm. Entrees from $14.95.

La La Land, 22 Wilmington Ave., Rehoboth Beach (☎ **302/227-3887**). Monday through Friday 6 to 10pm, Saturday and Sunday 6 to 11pm. Entrees $19 to $29. Closed mid-November through mid-April.

La Rosa Negra, 128 Second St., Lewes (☎ **302/645-1980**). On Lewes's main shopping street, a mixture of Italian dishes and seafood, with a varied wine list. Open daily 11am to 2pm and 4:30 to 9pm (until 10pm Fri and Sat). Entrees $7.95 to $21.95.

Obie's by the Sea, Boardwalk and Olive Ave., Rehoboth Beach (☎ **302/227-6261**). Open-air bar beside the sea. Sandwiches, burgers, french fries, and a full bar. Open in season from 11am.

ATTRACTIONS

Cape Henlopen State Park, a mile east of Lewes (☎ **302/645-8983**). The park has more than 4,000 acres of dunes, marsh, and piney woods, with beaches and trails for hiking and biking. It's a great place for bird watching. The nature center runs programs for adults and children. There is also the observation tower of Fort Miles, used by Army gunners and coast watchers during World War II. The park is open all year, 8am to sunset; admission $5 a carload, $2.50 for Delaware residents.

St. Peter's Episcopal Church, Second and Market sts., Lewes. The original congregation here dates to 1707; the current structure was built in 1858. The churchyard contains interesting gravestones, including those of four Delaware governors.

Zwaanendael Museum, Savannah Rd. and Kings Hwy., Lewes (☎ **302/645-1148**). The museum has exhibitions on local history and lore; the building is an adaptation of the city hall in Hoorn, the Netherlands, where the first Dutch settlers came from. Open Tuesday through Saturday 10am to 4:30pm, Sunday 1:30 to 4:30pm. Free admission.

EMERALD ISLES, BOSTON'S OWN

by Carey Goldberg

BOSTON, JULY 13

It feels like a dream.

You alight on an island, not knowing what awaits you, not quite sure what you are supposed to do there. An overgrown concrete path pulls you past riotous sea roses to mysterious ruins, pillars reaching for the open sky like a small Temple of Luxor, only smothered in tangled trees.

Or a freshly mown trail of sweet grass leads you up and over a wooded hill to a deserted beach strewn with mussel shells and driftwood and Dadaist detritus: a glove, another glove from a different pair, a shoe, a soda bottle, a fish skeleton the size of an oven mitt.

Or you wander into an imposing granite fort, walls 4 feet thick, that is riddled with winding staircases that take you from the light into the dark, some leading up to old cannon emplacements and sea air, some leading to black dead ends.

And here is the strangest part of all: You haven't even left Boston. You have simply left the overtrodden path of the Freedom Trail and the other usual sights for one of the city's oldest and newest attractions: the islands of Boston Harbor.

The islands are so little known that most guidebooks barely mention them, and it never occurs to most Bostonians to visit them, unless they are sixth graders on a class trip to the historic fort on George's Island.

But heroic, if still slightly confused, efforts are under way to transform the 30 islands, which became part of the national park system in

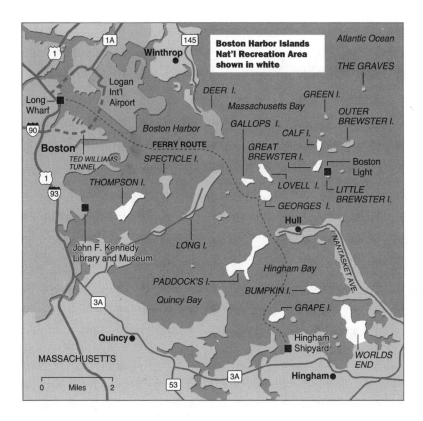

1996, into recreation spots the public will actually use, now that the harbor has changed from one of the country's dirtiest to one of its cleanest. There is talk of a "poor man's Nantucket," and of plans to increase the annual flow of visitors to the islands to 500,000 from 100,000.

And though much is still a work in progress, the Boston Harbor Islands National Recreation Area already offers a fine weekend's worth of exploration, from the ruins on Bumpkin Island to the well-trafficked fort on George's, even to overnight camping on the well-mown sites of Grape Island.

The rate of progress can be a bit frustrating: There were some loud complaints in Boston in July 2000 that more islands were not open for public viewing of the Tall Ships, which paraded in July of that year.

And descriptions of which islands are open and what programs they offer, as printed in brochures and posted on the islands' Web site, www.bostonislands.com, need careful checking by telephone before serious planning begins.

On the other hand, who knows? Perhaps the islands, which range in size from less than an acre to more than 250, will be overrun with visitors when the park finally gets its act together. And considering the complex partnerships that run the islands, with players ranging from the city to the state to the federal government to environmentalists to island advocates, it is rather amazing that anything has been done at all.

Here, then, is an up-to-the-minute description of two ways to do the islands as they are. The tame way: Take the ferry to George's Island and go by water taxi to the others. The wilder way: Kayak to Grape Island, where you can camp overnight and explore the surrounding waters.

An Easy Ferry Ride

The tame way does not seem quite so tame if you are 7 years old, like Nathan Robinson, whose parents kindly volunteered him as a child trip-tester, or 5, like his sister, Nellie. As the ferry that leaves Long Wharf in downtown Boston every hour on the hour steamed out into the harbor, Nathan wore a smile as broad as the horizon. "I can't believe I'm really going to an island!" he exclaimed as his elders hummed the theme to *Gilligan's Island.*

The bellies of planes zooming in to land at Logan Airport, just across the harbor, seemed to loom just a few feet above the ferry. We passed the hotels and the exhibition center of the Seaport District and, a few minutes later, the twin mounds of Spectacle Island, a former giant dump that has been capped with dirt from Boston's Big Dig highway project and landscaped into a park. It is not yet open to the public.

In 45 minutes, we had arrived at George's Island, a 28-acre chunk of land that holds Fort Warren, a 19th-century bastion built around a great pentagonal swath of lawn and offering sweeping harbor views from its ramparts. Its house-size powder magazine is empty now, a dark hall of echoes, but on the ramparts there are still the remains of the emplacements that once held guns so big that they had a range of

8 miles. The fort never saw actual battle, but during the Civil War it was used as a prison for Confederate soldiers and was long seen as pivotal in the sea defense of Boston.

These days it is a place for picnics and baseball and knit-browed contemplation of the quirky course of history. For an hour or so, we wandered up and down the staircases, looked out from a viewing tower over nearby islands and the elongated stretch of skyscrapers that is the Boston cityscape, and poked our heads into thick-walled rooms with nothing in them.

Then Nathan and Nellie decided it was time to head for the snack bar, which, late on a weekend afternoon, had nothing to offer but corn bread and candy bars. When going to any of the islands, visitors are well advised to bring their own food and particularly their own drinks: Most of the islands lack water.

Theoretically, there are supposed to be water taxis—free shuttle boats—from George's Island to five others. In fact, in late June, the park was offering shuttles to only two, Grape and Bumpkin. Since those islands were on our schedule for the wilder harbor trip, we contented ourselves with corn bread and a crowded ride back to Long Wharf, where the charge for parking two cars at $24 each in the garage at the wharf far outdid the price of the ferry tickets: $8 round-trip for adults and $6 for children.

Asked to rate the trip from 1 to 10, Nathan and Nellie gave it a solid 8; both said the best thing about it was the ferry ride.

A Hard but Happy Way

On the wilder tour of the harbor, it was the ride, too, that was the most fun. But because it was a water road less traveled by, its logistics were more complex.

Stephen Lines, my dauntless photographer friend, and I decided to camp on Grape Island—not because that was the island we really wanted to camp on, but because, whatever the brochures might have said about the availability of camping on three harbor islands, this was the only one actually open for camping in June. (Less law-abiding folks just forgo the required permits and camp on various islands.)

Asked what the problem was with the other islands, park officials plunged into tales of pier damage and political complexity. Whatever. There were no reservations left for campsites on Grape Island, but we were told that people often failed to show up, and, in fact, when we decided to risk it anyway, we found about half of the dozen or so campsites empty.

Grape Island can be reached by ferry, but oh-h-h, no, that would be much too easy, so we decided to kayak there, a small jump of a paddle out of the town of Hingham, southeast of Boston. Eastern Mountain Sports in Hingham, just a mile or so from the ferry terminal, rents kayaks by the hour, day, or weekend.

After a pleasant stroll into World's End, a peaceful, marshy peninsula that is officially part of the national park, we drove to the gigantic parking lot for the commuter ferries that link Hingham to Boston and found a good ramp into the water for our boats next to the South Shore Lobster building. From there, as night was falling, it was less than a mile's paddle in protected, though heavily trafficked, waters to Grape. For some reason, although Eastern Mountain Sports rents boats, paddles, and life preservers, it refused to rent us spray skirts, so the ride was wet. I improvised by covering my knees with my jacket.

The truth is, if you came upon the 50 acres of Grape Island in some suburb, you would be underwhelmed. It would seem like just a small stretch of charming, hilly farmland. But because it is surrounded by water, its bayberry smells are all the sweeter, its hills afford the most astonishing of views, and the small grape arbor that stands near the ferry dock seems to be welcoming visitors into a world with a touch of magic, one that feels very "away." An entry in the guest book hanging at the arbor read, "Hidden treasure so near the city."

The outhouse near the campsites was locked, but the sites themselves were grassy and private, each with a picnic table and enough woods around them to make the lack of an outhouse not too big a problem. Note: Mosquitoes can apparently take the ferry free.

The next day, the 10am ferry disgorged just three people: a couple with lawn chairs and a man who must have been a birder because he kept standing around, sharp-eyed.

On a Path to Surprises

After wandering the beach a bit, we set out for Bumpkin Island. (Well, all right, I thought it was Peddock's Island, but that's what comes of having no sense of direction and consulting a harbor map that says right on it that it should not be used for navigational purposes.) It was a bit of a rough paddle, in wind and waves, which made the shores of Bumpkin look all the more inviting.

Bumpkin Island has a fancy-looking pier, but the park managers had said it was not open yet, and there was no one else on the island but a motorboating family. From the pier, a concrete path lined by salt-spray rose bushes (who, you wonder, lugged all that concrete here?) leads off around the island and up to the ruins of a children's hospital that burned down in 1945, its roofless pillars now swamped in a jungle of trees. It seems a pity to tell you that, though—so much of the fun comes from following a path without knowing where it leads. So I've purposely left out another interesting ruin that you will come upon if you ever take that Bumpkin Island path.

Like the other islands, Bumpkin offers a strong sense of history—physical reminders that though it seems like nowhere now, it used to be a much busier place that seemed closer to the city. Many of the islands were popular spots from Indian days and well into the Colonial era. On Bumpkin, there is the hospital ruin; Gallop's Island used to have a resort and an immigration station. Spectacle Island used to have houses of ill repute and a horse-rendering factory. Lovell's has the remains of a fort used during the Spanish-American war, and Peddock's has the remains of a fort, too.

Where History Shines

These summer days, the islands offer a plethora of programs as well, from guided walks to narrated boat rides, with plenty of chances to practice the Bostonian habit of learning history until it is coming out of your ears.

But the historic spot of all historic spots in the harbor is Little Brewster Island, site of Boston Light, billed as the oldest continuously staffed lighthouse in the country. No regular ferries go to Little Brewster, but there are weekend tours leaving from Fan Pier, and Friday tours from the John F. Kennedy Library in the Dorchester section of Boston.

It was only a little jaunt, this trip of maybe 5 nautical miles from Hingham to Grape Island to Bumpkin and back to Hingham, but the wonder of it was that it did feel like a full-fledged outdoor adventure, one undertaken without ever leaving metropolitan Boston. No other major city, island boosters here say, has such an array of islands so very close to its shores. It is, to steal their phrase, a veritable urban archipelago.

But an urban archipelago without batter-dipped shellfish. Leaving Hingham, we stopped at the Hingham Lobster Pound, where the paper buckets of fried clams served as happy reminders that there will always be certain inimitable advantages to life on the mainland.

BOSTON HARBOR ISLANDS ESSENTIALS

TOURING THE ISLANDS

The **Boston Harbor Islands** are 215 miles northeast of New York City. Currently, six islands are open to the public daily in summer: George's, Gallop's, Grape, Bumpkin, Lovell's, and Peddock's. Open 9am to sunset.

Ferries to George's Island, operated by Boston Harbor Cruises, leave hourly from 10am to 5pm from Long Wharf in downtown Boston, adjacent to the New England Aquarium. Ferries leave George's Island at 10 minutes before the hour, from 10:50am to 5:50pm. For information, call ☎ **617/227-4321.** Round-trip fare $8, $7 for seniors, $6 for children 4 to 12, free for under age 3. Parking available at nearby lots.

The company also runs ferries from Hingham daily at 10am, 12:45pm, and 3:30pm. Ferries from both locations drop passengers at George's Island, where a free water shuttle can take them to other islands. For information call ☎ **617/ 223-8666.**

Boston Light Tours. A ranger-guided tour of Boston Light on Little Brewster Island departs late May through mid-October, Saturday and Sunday from Fan Pier in South Boston. Tickets (including boat transportation, parking, and guided tour): $25 adults, $20 seniors, $15 for children 6 to 12, free for ages 5 and under. Friday tours, which depart from the John F. Kennedy Library, also include the library and its museum. Tickets: $29 adults, $22 seniors, $15 for children 6 to 12, free for ages 5 and under. Group rates are available. For information and schedule, call ☎ **617/223-8666.**

Camping on the islands is available by permit, daily mid-June through Labor Day; weekends in spring and fall. For permit information call ☎ **617/223-8666.**

GETTING THERE

By Plane Continental (☎ 800/525-0280) has 16 nonstop flights daily from Newark to Logan International Airport. At press time, the lowest round-trip fare required a 21-day advance purchase and a Saturday stayover, with travel taking place from Monday through Thursday. A 14-day advance fare required a Saturday stayover and travel on Monday through Thursday. US Airways (☎ 800/428-4322) operates a shuttle every hour on the hour from La Guardia, 5am to 9pm. A 14-day advance fare was offered at press time, with a Saturday or Sunday departure, or travel from 10am to 2pm or 7pm to 10pm Monday through Friday, with a Saturday stayover. Delta (☎ 800/221-1212) flies every half hour from La Guardia, from 6am to 9:30pm. The lowest round-trip fare required a 3-day advance purchase and travel on Saturday or Sunday, and a 14-day advance purchase required a Saturday stayover. Fares at press time ranged from $116 to $229, and may change; special deals may also be offered.

By Car Boston is about a 4-hour drive from New York City. Take Interstate 95 to Interstate 90 (the Massachusetts Pike), then Interstate 90 east to downtown Boston.

By Train Amtrak (☎ 212/630-6400) leaves daily from Pennsylvania Station to Boston South Station, beginning at 1am. The trip takes about 5 hours. Round-trip fares $102 to $144, half price for children 5 to 11.

By Bus Greyhound (☎ 800/231-2222 or 212/971-6300). Buses leave from Port Authority every hour on the hour, noon to 11:30pm. Fares are $40 one-way or $75 round-trip; children 2 to 11 years old $20 one-way, $37.50 round-trip. The ride is about 4 hours each way.

DINING

Hingham Lobster Pound, 4 Broad Cove Rd. (☎ 781/749-1984). Tuesday through Thursday 11am to 7:30pm, Friday and Saturday 11am to 8pm, Sunday noon to 8pm.

BOAT RENTALS

Eastern Mountain Sports, 211 Lincoln St., Anchor Plaza, Hingham (☎ 781/741-8808). Kayak rental, from mid-May through early October, $40 or $50 a day, depending on the boat; weekend rates, 5pm Friday to 5pm Monday $80 or $100. The rate includes life jackets, a tie-down kit, and a paddle.

AN ISLAND LOVED FOR
WHAT IT DOESN'T HAVE

by Barbara Strauch

To be frank, my first thought as the ferry pulled into the dock at Block Island was: *Uh-oh.*

It was only 11am, already 86°, and ferry passengers, impatient and hot, pushed into the boat stairwell. On the deck below, cars revved engines. A middle-aged man in a black Mercedes station wagon laden with three small children, two red kayaks, and four bicycles drummed his fingers on his steering wheel and frowned.

My own little group was no better. Although Block Island, off the Rhode Island coast, blossomed in the Victorian era because of its cool sea breezes, there were none to be felt today. Richard, my normally semi-articulate husband, was walking in circles and saying, "Huh?" My normally semi-adventurous children were cranky. Meryl, 11, reminded me that she had been "born in a blizzard" and couldn't "take this heat." Hayley, 13, said flatly that the island looked "really long" and that she was "not biking the whole thing."

Off the boat, things got even worse. Swarms of fanny-packed tourists jammed the tiny sidewalks of Old Harbor, the larger of two villages on the island. With its too-quaint-for-me-in-this-heat Victorian storefronts, it looked like a theme park on a bad day. The streets churned with rented bicycles. Couples too old for this sort of thing wobbled on blue mopeds. Hotel porches were crammed with beer-drinking, tank-topped teenagers.

The idea had been to celebrate the end of a long year by making a trip to an island, staying at an inn and taking a bike ride. We had neither the time nor the money for the Caribbean. I didn't want a long

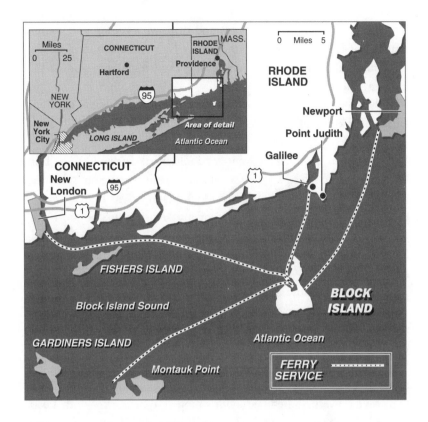

drive, so Martha's Vineyard and Nantucket were out. And I didn't want glitz, so there went the Hamptons.

Long ago, someone mentioned Block Island to me as a nice, quiet place, and, once I discovered there was a ferry from New London, Connecticut—only 2 hours from our house in Rye, New York, where we could leave the car and just take our bikes—that was it. Obviously, on the first hot weekend of June, we were not alone in entertaining this bright idea. But what could we do? Swinging backpacks over shoulders, we pedaled into the roiling humanity.

And here's where one of those happy travel mistakes came in. We found our way to the Blue Dory Inn, where I thought we were staying. It had awards as "Best Bed and Breakfast," and cottages on the beach. But when we got there, again I thought: *Uh-oh.*

The inn was cute and flowery, and there were cottages on a small beach. But it was just around the corner from the main drag in Old Harbor, good for those who wanted shops and restaurants and, at this moment, all wrong for me.

Then a pleasant woman looked carefully at the confirmation I had failed to look carefully at and said sweetly, "Ahh, you're in the Adrianna, up the hill."

So back on the bikes we went. The Adrianna, sister inn to the Blue Dory, turned out to be a 100-year-old sea captain's house on a rise near Calico Hill. (Like all good islands, Block Island has its share of ghost, pirate, and shipwreck stories. One of my favorites was about a ship loaded with calico cloth that went aground, with local residents rescuing its cargo and letting it dry on the hill, which now carries its name.) An equally pleasant woman led us to our little cottage at the back of the inn, which had a little gold plate on the door that said BEACH PLUM. Inside we encountered purple wallpaper, antiques, and, most important, a small loft upstairs for the girls. Within half an hour, Meryl was upstairs finishing her Harry Potter book; Hayley, our Huckleberry Finn, had found a fine climbing tree out front; Richard was sitting in a big white wicker chair, happily fiddling with a camera lens, and I was lying on a flowery quilted bed—not a moped to be heard—with a cool breeze blowing in over window boxes. I thought: *"Hmmm . . . Maybe this will be okay."*

What's Not There

Among the panoply of the world's islands, Block Island is not among the exotic or even the semi-chic. The Clintons do not vacation here. Steven Spielberg does not own a big house here. This is the place Donna Karan is not. On the map, Block Island looks like a smallish duck, its beak pointed northward toward the Rhode Island shore, 12 miles away. The map shows a tiny airport, a northern area labeled "Sandy Point," two areas in the south called "Southeast" and "Southwest Point," one squiggly road—and otherwise, not much.

"People come here for what it doesn't have, rather than what it does—there is no golf course, for instance," said Scott Comings of the

Nature Conservancy, a private, nonprofit environmental group that is gobbling up space all over the world, including Block Island. Geologically, Block Island was born about 12,000 years ago when a glacier subsided and left the sandy moraine that now includes Long Island, Block Island, Martha's Vineyard, and Nantucket. A native tribe, the Manisses, lived here for hundreds of years as hunters and gatherers. After being discovered (European-wise) in 1614 by a Dutch trader and explorer, Adrian Block, who gave the island its name, the island was first owned by the Massachusetts Bay Colony, then purchased by a small group of colony men. In 1661, 16 settlers, their wives and children, and their cows arrived to set up a farming and fishing community. (The cows were pushed overboard to swim ashore, according to local lore.)

Two centuries later, the residents built a pair of harbors, the tourists arrived, and Block Island, washed by the Gulf Stream, became known as the Bermuda of the North, with dozens of magnificent Victorian hotels. But as the automobile replaced the steamship, interest in Block Island dwindled. By the middle of the 20th century, the population had fallen below 500, and the grand hotels were vacant.

The real-estate boom in the 1980s changed that. The tiny island was rediscovered to such a degree that the residents were horrified. Plans for a housing development in one of the wildest parts of the island, Rodman's Hollow, appalled them enough that they formed a land trust to buy up threatened property.

Today, the local conservancy group and the Nature Conservancy own about 30% of the island and hope to purchase more. The Nature Conservancy named Block Island one of 12 "Last Great Places" in the Western Hemisphere. This designation put it alongside the Texas hill country, the Florida Keys, and the Condor Reserve in Ecuador, and was aimed, Mr. Comings said, at "highlighting it as a beautiful place that was both endangered and ecologically significant."

Block Island is a crucial stopping point for more than 100 species of birds, in particular young migratory songbirds that get blown away from shore and use the island as a pit stop.

Mr. Comings said there were 1,500 houses on the island today, twice as many as there were 30 years ago. And there are still 1,000 building lots available, making "development the biggest threat," he said. While clearly not as luxurious as Nantucket or Martha's Vineyard, Block Island, Mr. Comings said, is being rediscovered. "It's equidistant between New York and Boston, and it's beautiful," he said. "You do the math."

Touring by Bike

The point of our trip, of course, was to bicycle around the island and take short hikes along the system of trails called the Greenway. Since the whole route was only 13 miles, we felt confident enough on Sunday morning to wait until after a wonderful breakfast, served on the third floor of the house by one of the innkeepers, who made strawberry pancakes, scones, and tea.

At 9:15am we set off, down through Old Harbor, past couples walking hand-in-hand to churches whose ringing bells were the only sound in the village. We rode up Spring Street, past the Hotel Manisses, with its companion 1661 inn nearby overlooking the ocean, with its own vegetable garden and an animal farm that welcomes visitors. The hotel has a garden restaurant where we had had a lovely $150 lobster dinner (for four) the night before.

We biked up a short hill, by the Spring House, a huge white Victorian hotel booked for a wedding, with guests chatting on the porch. We rode onward silently, passing, on one side, miles of stone walls covered with pink wild roses, purple beach plums, and yellow honeysuckle; and on the other side, tall beach grass and dark blue-green ocean. It was glorious.

It was also, at about the third steep hill, where one's true personality emerged. I had spent the morning assuring the rest of the family that this was a very short ride, only 13 miles, a piece of cake. But I had forgotten about hills, and about halfway up the third big one, I stopped. It was hot. I was out of breath, boiling, and wondering again what I had gotten us into. I was quickly put to proper shame. Hayley whizzed by, yelling, "Mom, don't you think you should stop at the top of the hill?" Meryl pedaled calmly by and said, "I assume this hill has to end sometime." And never-exercise Richard rode steadily past with only a slightly sarcastic "You coming?"

So on we went. Block Island does not have bike paths, but it does have paved roads that snake along the island's coastline. It also has miles of dirt roads and paths. While the girls have versions of mountain bikes, I rode a sort of hybrid bicycle, and Richard had only a skinny-tire Sears $100 special. (Mopeds are mercifully not allowed on the dirt paths; if you're going on a lot of dirt paths, I would recommend renting a mountain bike with gears for about $20 a day.)

Our first stop was Mohegan Bluffs, where a new wooden stairway leads down past rows of raspberry bushes to a beach with pounding waves. This was where bands of Mohegans came in bark canoes to fight the local Indians. The vista was beautiful, moving Richard to call it the Big Sur of the East and remark that it was "worth the whole trip."

Encouraged, we pushed on. We went around the southern tip of the island, down dirt and grassy roads and past a few cedar-shingled houses sitting on remote cliffs. At the edge of one bluff we found a small wooden sign that signaled our destination: a short sandy path down to Black Rock Beach.

There would be, in the next day or so, plenty of nice times on this placid island. We spent two delightful afternoons swimming off clean beaches a 5-minute bike ride from our inn; we had a perfect 6-mile bike ride in the morning fog up Corn Neck Road to the northern tip of the island at Settlers Rock, which commemorates the original settlers, who had names like "Trustram Dodge" and "Tormot Rose."

There were a couple of inevitable bad moments, too. On the first day, before we decided to cut our 13-mile bike ride in half, we got hopelessly lost in the heat, winding from one unmarked road to another with a bad map and worse tempers. We spent an hour at a marina that had too many mopeds and motorboats.

But at that moment at Black Rock Beach, life was as it should be. Hayley and Meryl stood on a flat rock playing a game of who could get the wettest the fastest. Richard and I sat on another rock, our feet in the foam, listening to the clattering of pebbles as they washed back with the waves. The sound of the smashing surf erased a year's worth of worry. I looked up and down the white beach and saw no one.

A SEASIDE SOJOURN: ESSENTIALS

Block Island, off the Rhode Island coast, is 185 miles northeast of New York City.

GETTING THERE

FERRY SERVICE

There is year-round ferry service from Point Judith, RI, and summer service from Providence and Newport, RI; New London, CT, and Montauk, NY. If you are taking a car on the ferry, you have to book months in advance. If you go without a car, you'll find plenty of taxis at the other end.

Montauk   To reach the Montauk Ferry from New York City, take the Long Island Expressway east to Exit 70. Go south on Rte. 11 to Rte. 27, east to Montauk. Turn left at the traffic circle and down Edgemere Rd. to Montauk Harbor. Fares are $40 round-trip, $20 for children 5 to 12, free for those under 5. This is a passenger ferry only; no cars. For information call ☎ **631/668-5700.**

The **Long Island Rail Road (☎ 718/217-5477)** connects to the Montauk ferry.

Point Judith   From New York City, take I-95 North to Exit 92 and bear right on

Rte. 2 to Rte. 78 (Westerly bypass). At Rte. 1, turn left to Rte. 108 (signs to Galilee and Point Judith). Go south 3 miles on Rte. 108 to the Block Island Boat sign and turn right, then left. For information and fares call ☎ **401/783-4613.**

New London   From New York City, take I-95 North to Exit 83W for downtown New London. At the third light, turn left onto Governor Winthrop Boulevard, go straight over the railroad tracks, and bear right to the ferry entrance. For information and fares call ☎ **401/783-4613.**

Amtrak (☎ 800/872-7245) has a connection at New London to the ferry.

BY PLANE

New England Airlines (☎ 800/243-2460) offers daily 12-minute rides from Westerly, RI; round-trip fare $69, $46 for children 2 to 11. There is no plane connection from New York to Westerly except by charter.

ACCOMMODATIONS & DINING

Adrianna Inn (☎ 800/992-7290 or 401/466-5891; www.blockislandinns.com). One of a group of Victorian inns, including the **Blue Dory Inn.**. Rates in high season for two people range from $135 to $145 for a room with a shared bath, $165 to $225 for a room with a private bath. Cottages accommodating two to eight people range from $175 to $495.

Hotel Manisses and the 1661 Inn, Spring St. (☎ **800/626-4773** or 401/466-2836;

www.blockisland.com/birestors). A 19th-century Victorian hotel with a nearby inn and guest cottages set on a high hill about a quarter mile from town. Rates, including breakfast, for two people range from $50 to $375 and for a family of four from $130 to $300 a night. Open all year. The Hotel Manisses Dining Room is open mid-April through mid-May on weekends; Mid-May through October 5:30 to 9pm (10pm weekends). Entrees range from $18 to $35.

Spring House Hotel, Spring St. (☎ 800/ 234-9263), is an old Victorian hotel. Rates, including breakfast, for two people in high season from June 12 to Labor Day, $175 to $375. Families in two-room suites, $345 a night. The Spring House Restaurant has entrees starting at $16.

BIKING & HIKING

There are no bike trails on Block Island but there are 30 miles of paved roads, in particular one that snakes around the coastline and one that runs up to the north of the island. Island Moped and Bike is at 53 Water St. (☎ 401/466-2700). Call for rates. Maps are available. A moped requires a driver's license.

A copy of the Greenway trail map, showing 20 miles of trails all over the island, is available by sending a stamped, self-addressed envelope and $1 to the **Nature Conservancy,** Box 1287, Block Island, RI 02807.

INDEX

Notes

Notes

Notes

Notes

Notes

Notes

Notes

Notes

FROMMER'S® COMPLETE TRAVEL GUIDES

Alaska
Amsterdam
Argentina & Chile
Arizona
Atlanta
Australia
Austria
Bahamas
Barcelona, Madrid & Seville
Beijing
Belgium, Holland &
    Luxembourg
Bermuda
Boston
British Columbia & the
    Canadian Rockies
Budapest & the Best of Hungary
California
Canada
Cancún, Cozumel & the
    Yucatán
Cape Cod, Nantucket &
    Martha's Vineyard
Caribbean
Caribbean Cruises & Ports
    of Call
Caribbean Ports of Call
Carolinas & Georgia
Chicago
China
Colorado
Costa Rica
Denmark
Denver, Boulder & Colorado
    Springs
England
Europe

European Cruises & Ports of Call
Florida
France
Germany
Greece
Greek Islands
Hawaii
Hong Kong
Honolulu, Waikiki & Oahu
Ireland
Israel
Italy
Jamaica
Japan
Las Vegas
London
Los Angeles
Maryland & Delaware
Maui
Mexico
Montana & Wyoming
Montréal & Québec City
Munich & the Bavarian Alps
Nashville & Memphis
Nepal
New England
New Mexico
New Orleans
New York City
New Zealand
Nova Scotia, New Brunswick &
    Prince Edward Island
Oregon
Paris
Philadelphia & the Amish
    Country
Portugal

Prague & the Best of the Czech
    Republic
Provence & the Riviera
Puerto Rico
Rome
San Antonio & Austin
San Diego
San Francisco
Santa Fe, Taos & Albuquerque
Scandinavia
Scotland
Seattle & Portland
Shanghai
Singapore & Malaysia
South Africa
Southeast Asia
South Florida
South Pacific
Spain
Sweden
Switzerland
Texas
Thailand
Tokyo
Toronto
Tuscany & Umbria
USA
Utah
Vancouver & Victoria
Vermont, New Hampshire
    & Maine
Vienna & the Danube Valley
Virgin Islands
Virginia
Walt Disney World & Orlando
Washington, D.C.
Washington State

FROMMER'S® DOLLAR-A-DAY GUIDES

Australia from $50 a Day
California from $70 a Day
Caribbean from $70 a Day
England from $70 a Day
Europe from $70 a Day

Florida from $70 a Day
Hawaii from $70 a Day
Ireland from $60 a Day
Italy from $70 a Day
London from $85 a Day

New York from $80 a Day
Paris from $80 a Day
San Francisco from $60 a Day
Washington, D.C.,
    from $70 a Day

FROMMER'S® PORTABLE GUIDES

Acapulco, Ixtapa &
    Zihuatanejo
Alaska Cruises & Ports
    of Call
Amsterdam
Australia's Great Barrier Reef
Bahamas
Baja & Los Cabos
Berlin
Boston
California Wine Country
Charleston & Savannah
Chicago

Dublin
Hawaii: The Big Island
Hong Kong
Houston
Las Vegas
London
Los Angeles
Maine Coast
Maui
Miami
New Orleans
New York City
Paris

Phoenix & Scottsdale
Portland
Puerto Rico
Puerto Vallarta, Manzanillo &
    Guadalajara
San Diego
San Francisco
Seattle
Sydney
Tampa & St. Petersburg
Vancouver
Venice
Washington, D.C.

FROMMER'S® NATIONAL PARK GUIDES

Family Vacations in the
    National Parks
Grand Canyon

National Parks of the American
    West
Rocky Mountain
Yellowstone & Grand Teton

Yosemite & Sequoia/
    Kings Canyon
Zion & Bryce Canyon

FROMMER'S® MEMORABLE WALKS

Chicago
London

New York
Paris

San Francisco
Washington, D.C.

FROMMER'S® GREAT OUTDOOR GUIDES

Arizona & New Mexico
New England

Northern California
Southern California & Baja

Southern New England
Vermont & New Hampshire

FROMMER'S® BORN TO SHOP GUIDES

Born to Shop: France
Born to Shop: Hong Kong,
  Shanghai & Beijing

Born to Shop: Italy
Born to Shop: London

Born to Shop: New York
Born to Shop: Paris

FROMMER'S® IRREVERENT GUIDES

Amsterdam
Boston
Chicago
Las Vegas
London

Los Angeles
Manhattan
New Orleans
Paris
San Francisco

Seattle & Portland
Vancouver
Walt Disney World
Washington, D.C.

FROMMER'S® BEST-LOVED DRIVING TOURS

America
Britain
California
Florida

France
Germany
Ireland
Italy

New England
Scotland
Spain
Western Europe

THE UNOFFICIAL GUIDES®

Bed & Breakfasts in California
Bed & Breakfasts in
  New England
Bed & Breakfasts in the
  Northwest
Bed & Breakfasts in Southeast
Beyond Disney
Branson, Missouri
California with Kids
Chicago
Cruises
Disneyland
Florida with Kids

Golf Vacations in the
  Eastern U.S.
The Great Smoky &
  Blue Ridge Mountains
Inside Disney
Hawaii
Las Vegas
London
Mid-Atlantic with Kids
Mini Las Vegas
Mini-Mickey
New England with Kids

New Orleans
New York City
Paris
San Francisco
Skiing in the West
Southeast with Kids
Walt Disney World
Walt Disney World for
  Grown-ups
Walt Disney World for Kids
Washington, D.C.
World's Best Diving Vacations

SPECIAL-INTEREST TITLES

Frommer's Britain's Best Bed & Breakfasts and
  Country Inns
Frommer's France's Best Bed & Breakfasts and
  Country Inns
Frommer's Italy's Best Bed & Breakfasts and
  Country Inns
Frommer's Caribbean Hideaways
Frommer's Adventure Guide to Australia &
  New Zealand
Frommer's Adventure Guide to Central America
Frommer's Adventure Guide to India & Pakistan
Frommer's Adventure Guide to South America
Frommer's Adventure Guide to Southeast Asia
Frommer's Adventure Guide to Southern Africa
Frommer's Gay & Lesbian Europe
Frommer's Exploring America by RV
Hanging Out in England

Hanging Out in Europe
Hanging Out in France
Hanging Out in Ireland
Hanging Out in Italy
Hanging Out in Spain
Israel Past & Present
Frommer's The Moon
Frommer's New York City with Kids
The New York Times' Guide to Unforgettable
  Weekends
Places Rated Almanac
Retirement Places Rated
Frommer's Road Atlas Britain
Frommer's Road Atlas Europe
Frommer's Washington, D.C., with Kids
Frommer's What the Airlines Never Tell You